Digital Existence

Digital Existence: Ontology, Ethics and Transcendence in Digital Culture advances debates on digital culture and digital religion in two complementary ways. First, by focalizing the themes 'ontology,' 'ethics' and 'transcendence,' it builds on insights from research on digital religion in order to reframe the field and pursue an existential media analysis that further pushes beyond the mandatory focus in mainstream media studies on the social, cultural, political and economic dimensions of digitalization. Second, the collection also implies a broadening of the scope of the debate in the field of media, religion and culture – and digital religion in particular – beyond 'religion,' to include the wider existential dimensions of digital media. It is the first volume on our digital existence in the budding field of existential media studies.

Amanda Lagerkvist is Associate Professor of Media and Communication Studies at Stockholm University, Sweden, and was appointed Wallenberg Academy Fellow in 2013. She is head of the research program "Existential Terrains: Memory and Meaning in Cultures of Connectivity" (http://et.ims.su.se) in the Department of Media Studies at Stockholm University, funded by the Knut and Alice Wallenberg Foundation, the Marcus and Amalia Wallenberg Foundation, and Stockholm University (2014–2018). She has worked in the fields of media philosophy and media memory studies, and is now developing existential media studies, by focusing on memories of the dead online, after death communication, online mourning and shared vulnerability, the digital afterlife and the transcendence industry. She is the author of *Media and Memory in New Shanghai: Western Performances of Futures Past* (Palgrave Macmillan, 2013) and the co-editor of *Strange Spaces: Explorations Into Mediated Obscurity* (Ashgate, 2009). She is currently writing a monograph entitled *Existential Media*, contracted by Oxford University Press.

Routledge Studies in Religion and Digital Culture
Edited by Heidi Campbell, Mia Lövheim, and Gregory Price Grieve

Buddhism, the Internet, and Digital Media
The Pixel in the Lotus
Edited by Gregory Price Grieve and Daniel Veidlinger

Digital Judaism
Jewish Negotiations with Digital Media and Culture
Edited by Heidi A. Campbell

Methods for Studying Video Games and Religion
Edited by Vít Šisler, Kerstin Radde-Antweiler and Xenia Zeiler

Online Catholic Communities
Community, Authority, and Religious Individualisation
Marta Kołodziejska

Digital Existence
Ontology, Ethics and Transcendence in Digital Culture
Edited by Amanda Lagerkvist

For more information about this series, please visit: www.routledge.com/religion/series/RDC

Digital Existence
Ontology, Ethics and Transcendence
in Digital Culture

Edited by Amanda Lagerkvist

LONDON AND NEW YORK

First published 2019
by Routledge
2 Park Square, Milton Park, Abingdon, Oxon OX14 4RN

and by Routledge
711 Third Avenue, New York, NY 10017

Routledge is an imprint of the Taylor & Francis Group, an informa business

© 2019 selection and editorial matter, Amanda Lagerkvist; individual chapters, the contributors

The right of Amanda Lagerkvist to be identified as the author of the editorial material, and of the authors for their individual chapters, has been asserted in accordance with sections 77 and 78 of the Copyright, Designs and Patents Act 1988.

All rights reserved. No part of this book may be reprinted or reproduced or utilized in any form or by any electronic, mechanical, or other means, now known or hereafter invented, including photocopying and recording, or in any information storage or retrieval system, without permission in writing from the publishers.

Trademark notice: Product or corporate names may be trademarks or registered trademarks, and are used only for identification and explanation without intent to infringe.

British Library Cataloguing-in-Publication Data
A catalogue record for this book is available from the British Library

Library of Congress Cataloging-in-Publication Data
Names: Lagerkvist, Amanda, 1970– editor.
Title: Digital existence : ontology, ethics, and transcendence in digital culture / edited by Amanda Lagerkvist.
Description: New York : Routledge, 2018. | Series: Routledge studies in religion and digital culture | Includes bibliographical references and index.
Identifiers: LCCN 2018019032 | ISBN 9781138092433 (hardback : alk. paper) | ISBN a9781315107479 (ebook)
Subjects: LCSH: Self-presentation. | Online identities—Philosophy. | Social media—Philosophy. | Existentialism.
Classification: LCC HM1066 .D54 2018 | DDC 302.23/1—dc23
LC record available at https://lccn.loc.gov/2018019032

ISBN: 978-1-138-09243-3 (hbk)
ISBN: 978-1-315-10747-9 (ebk)

Typeset in Sabon
by Apex CoVantage, LLC

Contents

Notes on contributors	vii
Acknowledgements	xi
Foreword by John Durham Peters	xiv

Digital existence: an introduction   1
AMANDA LAGERKVIST

PART I
Media ontologies   27

1 Irremediability: on the very concept of digital ontology   29
JUSTIN CLEMENS AND ADAM NASH

2 Umwelt and individuation: digital signals and technical
being   61
JONAS ANDERSSON SCHWARZ

3 Thrownness, vulnerability, care: a feminist ontology
for the digital age   81
MARGARET SCHWARTZ

4 Digital unworld(s): the Bielefeld Conspiracy   100
YVETTE GRANATA

PART II
Being human: extension, exposure and ethics   115

5 You have been tagged: magical incantations, digital
incarnations and extended selves   117
PAUL FROSH

vi *Contents*

6 Surveillance, sensors, and knowledge through the machine   137
SUN-HA HONG

7 Social media and the care of the self   156
GANAELE LANGLOIS

8 The ethics of digital being: vulnerability, invulnerability, and 'dangerous surprises'   171
VINCENT MILLER

PART III
Transcendence: beyond life, death and the human   187

9 The internet is always awake: sensations, sounds and silences of the digital grave   189
AMANDA LAGERKVIST

10 Digital rituals and the quest for existential security   210
JOHANNA SUMIALA

11 Cybernetic animism: non-human personhood and the internet   227
DEVIN PROCTOR

12 Death in life and life in death: forms and fates of the human   242
CONNOR GRAHAM AND ALFRED MONTOYA

Afterword   264
CHARLES M. ESS

Index   278

Contributors

Jonas Andersson Schwarz (PhD) is Associate Professor at Södertörn University (Stockholm, Sweden), specializing in structural analysis of the digital media ecology. After several years of research on digital piracy and file sharing, he has recently shifted focus towards digital platforms, primarily addressing these as economic and epistemological mediators. He has always taken a keen interest in the philosophical dimensions of media theory, sociology and cultural studies, primarily with a focus on the embedding of everyday life in technological structures.

Justin Clemens is a poet, scholar and translator. He has published essays, edited collections and monographs on a range of poetical, psychoanalytic and philosophical thinkers, including François Villon, John Milton, Jacques Lacan, Alain Badiou, Giorgio Agamben, Jacqueline Rose and others. With Thomas Apperley and John Frow, he was the recipient of an Australian Research Council Grant investigating 'Avatars and Identities,' which has supported his contribution to the current volume; he is currently an Australian Research Council Future Fellow researching 'Australian Poetry Today.' He is an Associate of the Melbourne School of Continental Philosophy and teaches at the University of Melbourne.

Charles M. Ess is Professor in Media Studies, Department of Media and Communication, University of Oslo, Norway, and previously the Director of the Centre for Research in Media Innovation (CeRMI), University of Oslo. His research and publications emphasize cross-cultural and ethical perspectives in Internet Studies, and Information and Computing Ethics. Recent books include *Digital Media Ethics* (Polity Press, 3rd edition, forthcoming), and (with Mia Consalvo) *The Handbook of Internet Studies* (Wiley-Blackwell, 2011). Ess is a founding member of the International Association for Computing and Philosophy (IACAP); he has served as Vice-President and then President of the Association of Internet Researchers (AoIR) and as President (2012–2016) of the International Society for Ethics in Information Technology (INSEIT).

Paul Frosh teaches in the Department of Communication and Journalism at the Hebrew University of Jerusalem, Israel. His research spans visual viii *Contributors*

culture, media aesthetics, consumer culture and media witnessing. His books include *The Poetics of Digital Media* (Polity, forthcoming), *The Image Factory: Consumer Culture, Photography and the Visual Content Industry*; *Meeting the Enemy in the Living Room: Terrorism and Communication in the Contemporary Era* (edited with Tamar Liebes); and *Media Witnessing: Testimony in the Age of Mass Communication* (edited with Amit Pinchevski). He is currently engaged in a research project on iconic photographs and Israeli collective memory, as well as writing about digital image genres such as selfies and screenshots.

Connor Graham is Senior Lecturer at Tembusu College, Singapore, and a Research Fellow at the Asia Research Institute at the National University of Singapore. His research centres on living and dying in the times of the internet, with a particular focus on new information and communication technologies. Recently he has been situating his research in Asia.

Yvette Granata is a PhD candidate at SUNY Buffalo, USA, in the Department of Media Study's theory and practice program. Her work explores media, technology, philosophy and non-philosophy. She also writes about the tactics of socio-political and techno-material art practice. She has published in *Ctrl-Z: New Media Philosophy Journal, TRACE Journal, NECSUS: European Journal of Media Studies*, and the *International Journal of Cultural Studies*. Her media artwork has been exhibited at the Harvard Carpenter Centre for the Arts, the Eye Film Institute in Amsterdam, Film Anthology Archives in New York, the Kunsthalle of Light and Media Art in Detroit, Papy Gyro Nights Festival in Bergen, Norway and Hong Kong, Videoarte Festival in Camaguey, Cuba, and Hallwalls Contemporary Arts Centre in Buffalo, New York, among others. Her film design work has appeared on screens at the Sundance Film Festival, Tribeca Film Festival, Rotterdam, Cannes, Berlinale, the Rome International Film Fest, SXSW and CPH:PIX.

Sun-ha Hong is a Mellon Postdoctoral Fellow in the Humanities at MIT, USA, in Comparative Media Studies/Writing. His research examines the ideals and fantasies surrounding new media technologies. His current book in progress, *Fabrications: Knowledge and Uncertainty in the Data-Driven Society*, explores changing boundaries of what counts as known, probable, and certain, in two major scenes of the datafication of contemporary America: (1) the Snowden Affair and electronic state surveillance; (2) the rise of self-tracking technologies over the past decade. His work has been published in journals such as *First Monday, Surveillance & Society* and the *European Journal of Cultural Studies*.

Amanda Lagerkvist, PhD, is Associate Professor of Media and Communication Studies at Stockholm University, Sweden, and was appointed Wallenberg Academy Fellow in 2013. She is head of the research program "Existential Terrains: Memory and Meaning in Cultures of Connectivity" (http://et.ims.su.se) in the Department of Media Studies at Stockholm University, funded by the Knut and Alice Wallenberg Foundation, the Marcus and Amalia Wallenberg Foundation, and Stockholm University (2014–2018). She has worked in the fields of media philosophy and media memory studies, and is now developing existential media studies, by focusing on memories of the dead online, after death communication, online mourning and shared vulnerability, the digital afterlife and the transcendence industry. She is the author of *Media and Memory in New Shanghai: Western Performances of Futures Past* (Palgrave Macmillan, 2013) and the co-editor of *Strange Spaces: Explorations Into Mediated Obscurity* (Ashgate, 2009). She is currently writing a monograph entitled *Existential Media*, contracted by Oxford University Press.

Ganaele Langlois is Associate Professor in the Department of Communication Studies at York University, Toronto, Canada. She is Associate Director of the Infoscape Lab (www.infoscapelab.ca). She is the author of *Meaning in the Age of Social Media* (Palgrave, 2014), and co-editor of *Compromised Data: From Social Media to Big Data* (Bloomsbury, 2015).

Vincent Miller is Reader in Sociology and Cultural Studies at the University of Kent, UK. He has authored several publications in the theme of digital culture, including two books: *The Crisis of Presence in Contemporary Culture* (Sage, 2016) and *Understanding Digital Culture* (Sage, 2011). He has also authored various articles in the field on topics including the rise of 'phatic' media culture, social media activism, memes, contagion and ethics.

Alfred Montoya is Associate Professor of Anthropology in the Department of Sociology & Anthropology at Trinity University in San Antonio, Texas, USA. His work concerns modes of governance around HIV/AIDS prevention and control in Vietnam, global health humanitarianism and science, technology and society studies.

Adam Nash is a Melbourne-based artist, composer, programmer, performer and writer. Nash is internationally recognized as one of the most innovative and influential artists working in virtual environments, game engines, real-time 3D and mixed-reality technology. His work explores virtual environments as audiovisual performance spaces, data/motion capture sites and generative platforms. His work has been presented in galleries, festivals and online in Australia, Europe, Asia and the Americas, including peak festivals SIGGRAPH, ISEA, ZERO1SJ and the Venice Biennale. He is Director of the Playable Media Lab in the Centre for Game Design Research and Program Manager of the Bachelor of Design (Digital Media), both at RMIT University, Australia.

John Durham Peters is María Rosa Menocal Professor of English and of Film & Media Studies, Yale University, USA. He has published widely x *Contributors*

on media history and theory, and in fields adjoining media studies such as anthropology, music, philosophy and religious studies, and social theory. He is the author of many articles and essays, and of *Speaking Into the Air: A History of the Idea of Communication* (1999), *Courting the Abyss: Free Speech and the Liberal Tradition* (2005), and *The Marvelous Clouds: Toward a Philosophy of Elemental Media* (2015) with the University of Chicago Press.

Devin Proctor is an anthropologist. He is a PhD candidate at The George Washington University, USA, focusing on media, identity, religion, STS and most things with "cyber" in front of them. For the past five years, he has engaged in ethnographic fieldwork with the Otherkin community – a group of people who identify as other-than-human. His work uncovers how digital mediating technologies can facilitate new subjectivities, changing what it means to be a human being. In corporeal form, he resides in the Washington, DC, metro area with his wife and two kids. In virtual form, he is in front of you right now.

Margaret Schwartz is a feminist media theorist working primarily with questions of embodiment and materiality in the context of archival and containment media. Her book *Dead Matter: The Meaning of Iconic Corpses* was published in 2015 by the University of Minnesota Press. She is currently working on a project that theorizes an ethics of care in the context of gestational surrogacy and other gendered forms of social reproduction. She is Associate Professor of Communication and Media Studies at Fordham University, USA.

Johanna Sumiala is Associate Professor of Media and Communication Studies at the Faculty of Social Sciences, University of Helsinki, Finland. She is an expert in the fields of media sociology and media anthropology, digital ethnography and visual culture. She has recently published articles on mediatized violence and ritualized (online) communication and she is the author of the book *Media and Ritual: Death, Community and Everyday Life* (Routledge, 2013).

Acknowledgements

Digital media span our entire existence. This book is the outcome of a recently initiated conversation about this condition. International in scope and global/universal in significance, its focal point has been the research program *Existential Terrains: Memory and Meaning in Cultures of Connectivity*, which I have headed during the past four years in the Department of Media Studies at Stockholm University. The program is funded by the Knut and Alice Wallenberg Foundation (KAW), the Marcus and Amalia Wallenberg Foundation, and Stockholm University. As part of the collaborative effort of KAW and the five Swedish Academies, I was appointed Wallenberg Academy Fellow 2013, with the mandate to develop an existential approach to digitalisation by placing a particular but not exclusive focus on death online, and to conduct basic research in this field.

The project hosts an international network called DIGMEX, which organises workshops, seminars, open lectures and international conferences every other year at the Sigtuna Foundation in Sweden. The first conference took place in October 2015, "Digital Existence: Memory, Meaning, Vulnerability," and it successfully introduced the field of existential media studies. It was followed by "Digital Existence II: Precarious Media Life" in October 2017, which saw the convening of representatives from Singapore to the United States, from Australia to Canada, from the United Kingdom to Israel and from the Nordic countries as well as continental Europe. This volume represents some of the papers presented at these two events, yet expands beyond them to include other voices that are also an important part of this dialogue.

This book argues that an existential approach is needed to grasp the complexity of the technological developments of our time. Approaching the internet as existential terrain *par excellence* provides avenues for exploring the fundamental human condition of being faced with the contingency, absurdity and simultaneous quest for profundity and meaning in our lives. Eyebrows were raised, however, when I suggested eight years ago that we should study digital media *existentially*, and that, for instance, Kierkegaard could be helpful in this pursuit. Can a Christian thinker be good for *anything*, and especially for studying the frontiers of digital life in a culture that

xii *Acknowledgements*

is, and should be, secular, some asked? But if in our time we are encountering and exploring the larger issues of life and death, meaning and meaninglessness, loneliness and sociality, the finite and the infinite on the internet, where else should we begin? If we wish to understand our mediated 'present age,' to discuss the fates of human responsibility and ethics, and to explore the prospects for living a passionate and authentic life, who else should we consult? If digital media is about existence, about *being*, the first thing we need to do is to ask what we can learn about our age by drawing on existential philosophy, and its classic concepts and perspectives, to then develop these further for our contemporary technologised culture.

Equally untimely, for some in the new posthumanist vanguard, was the call for revisiting the humanoid existential question, and the question of human finitude. Was that not just an anthropocentric obsession and a thing of the past? Empirically though, death was all around. With 'Web 2.0,' it seemed to have returned to everyday life: in the support groups for the bereaved online, on online memorials, in blogging about terminal illness, in suicide groups and prevention on the internet, and within the digital inheritance area. With a focus on these phenomena, *Existential Terrains* has set out to explore and conduct basic research on, as well as offer a theorisation of, how fundamental existential issues are pursued, when people's lives and memories are increasingly shaped in, by and through digital media forms. But equally important in the project is to probe those existential issues and challenges we are facing due to digitalisation. Our aim in both cases has been to do this in awareness of differentiation across cultures and religious contexts, as well as how such issues are affected by the embodied situatedness and power asymmetries that pertain to gender, race, class, sexual orientation and disabilities, etc. The objective has thus been to pursue how these dimensions relate to both the affordances and stakes as well as to the predicaments of the digital human condition.

This volume has come into being in the hope of offering a different mapping: one that may enable a different type of journey. In order to 'boldly go where no one has gone before,' one needs – besides maps – brave companions. I wish to extend my thanks to the team of researchers that have been engaged in various parts of the project and conference organisation during this enterprise: Michael Westerlund, Katerina Linden, Evelina Lundmark, Yvonne Andersson, Kristina Stenström, Anna Haverinen and Tim Hutchings. My sincere thanks go to the eminent scholars who have supported this project by serving on its advisory board: Anna Reading, Mia Lövheim, Tony Walter, Amit Pinchevski and Charles M. Ess. Charles is also our scientific advisor on digital ethics and was our visiting professor in the program in 2017. I have also been greatly privileged by the invaluable support of distinguished scholars José van Dijck and John Durham Peters. It would have been even more daunting to set out on this type of expedition without your esteemed and generous company.

Acknowledgements   xiii

Any existential pursuit is necessarily more than an intellectual exercise. It is lived and embodied, and entails all the struggles of life, including feeling the weight of the undertaking, and the loneliness that comes with major tasks being assigned. Stumbling and losing one's way – in order to find new ways ahead – is part of the human condition, and hence is crucial also for scholarship. But when lost at sea, I looked at the stars for guidance! Johanna Sumiala, Margaret Schwartz, Birgitta Svensson, Knut Lundby, Dorthe Refslund Christensen, Kristina Fjelkestam, Paul Frosh, Ylva Habel, Steffen Krüger, Andrew Hoskins, Mona Abdel-Fadil, Kristina Riegert and Karin Becker: Thank you for your essential support during different parts of this new voyage.

Amanda Lagerkvist

Foreword

To be or not to be

Around 1600 Shakespeare's Hamlet posed the question of existence in exquisitely precise digital form: "to be or not to be." There were two options only. Hamlet wavered, dilly-dallied and postponed an answer. Perhaps his aim was to live in the in-between. But by not answering the question, he of course did answer it: suspension of the question meant continuation of being. Hamlet's harshly discrete option was followed around 240 years later by Søren Kierkegaard, whose book *Either/Or* both pondered and provoked the choice between existential options: you couldn't have it both ways. You could live aesthetically or ethically: not both. These melancholy Danes are here joined almost 180 years later by a Swede, Amanda Lagerkvist, who continues with the same questions in the same spirit and has done the tireless and valuable work of convening this conversation.

Only now the on-off either-or circuit lies in the networked transistors that work behind our back. Every second on earth today sextillions of devices are answering Hamlet's question at the speed of light (much faster than he did!) More transistors have been manufactured than there are stars in the Milky Way, but the stars are much easier to see, even in our light-polluted cities. Our digital devices hide away below the threshold of our perception and knowledge. Infrastructures like to lurk in the background. Digital media have become so pervasive in our lives and worlds that it takes special work to make them strange again. (And plenty of corporate effort is put into making them invisible; it doesn't happen naturally!) Defamiliarisation is one of the foremost missions of digital media studies. There are many ways and means to do so: historical, economic, political, cultural, literary, cinematic, artistic. The critical fields are white already to harvest.

This volume gambles on another approach: that digital media can be studied in their most basic lineaments, as forms of being. This angle proves to be enormously fertile. The book spreads a delicious feast. Its readers will learn about eukaryotes, Edward Snowden, tagging, pee-proof underwear, blackmail and disappearing German cities (to name a few.) But it is perhaps not so much in the suggestive details and rich case studies that the principal

Foreword   xv

contribution of this volume lies but rather in the reframing of the larger intellectual stakes. To study media, this volume pleads, means to ask what existence is, what right action is, and how we might transcend the whole thing. The true, the good and the beautiful (or the sublime) return in new form. If research on digital culture as a whole took the lead from this volume, the field would be grander, more serious, more searching, and a bit more strange. That would be a very good thing!

Digital existence – is that an oxymoron? It is well-known that *digits* can mean our fingers – the means by which the human environment has been made – and also the integers, 1, 2, 3, 4, 5 ad infinitum. Digits are both profoundly concrete (when they are fingers) and ethereally abstract (when they are numbers). Numbers have the curious property of being the ultimate philosophical objects: you can see four apples or three rocks, but you have never seen a pure "four" or "three." (The numerals "4" and "3" are obviously not such things – they are arbitrary symbols for the mysterious qualities, quantities, concepts, classes, or whatever it is that numbers are). Because of their abstraction, numbers can be both violent and useful. Their existence hovers forever between being and nonbeing. In that way, they are a bit like us.

The difference between 1 and 0, said Leibniz, was that between Creation and the Abyss. Digital reckoning switches between Unity and Nothing. Leibniz also wrote that music is the exercise of the soul that is doing arithmetic without knowing it. He understood both that digital media often do their work in the background and that secret conclaves of calculation can often produce beautiful things that carry us away in time. He and others dreamed of a world composed of numbers. We live in the bushy outgrowth of such dreams. Pascal, Leibniz, Babbage, Boole, Turing, Wiener, von Neumann – did they have the slightest inkling of the vast shallow warmish oceans of social media, the escapades of blockchain, or the surveillance by state and market that their genius would bring about? Part of the drama, even chutzpah, of studying existential media in the digital context is the vast distance between the grandeur and the banality – new media, old humanity, cosmic vision, petty squabbles. We desperately need both the grandeur and the critical analysis of this volume. There is a long history of thinking big about digital phenomena, and this volume takes its worthy place in the tradition.

John Durham Peters
Groundhog Day 2018, New Haven

Digital existence
An introduction

Amanda Lagerkvist

Ecologies and epiphanies of the digital

What does it mean to be a human being in the digital age? The digitalisation of society, everyday life and our entire lifeworld raises a number of existential issues that relate both to what is mundane and to what is extraordinary. As interfaces are designed to captivate our attention and imagination, we have become glued to our screens and devices for pleasure, by need or convenience. They have simultaneously become part of our *existence*, with all its inevitable quests for meaning and value, and of our struggle with what seems evacuated thereof. And looming in the deep space of media technology – hidden back-stage within what for most of us are impenetrable algorithmic procedures to which we have rapidly become habituated to accede – we are at once tracked and traded by the workings of these profoundly affective and capitalistic yet irreducibly *existential media* (Lagerkvist 2016).

These circumstances evoke a number of pressing questions: How do our environmental and wearable, all-encompassing and increasingly automated technologies co-shape, bring about and transform the human condition? And what are the burdens as well as benefits of the digital instantiation of deep-felt human and existential necessities and needs? What of ethics and our relation to what is known about the world itself and about us (through data) and what lies beyond, to the transcendent?

In an article in *The Guardian* based on interviews with a group of 'refuse-niks' at the heart of the tech industry, James Williams (an ex-Google strate-gist who built the metrics system for the company's global search advertising business) describes these media as the "largest, most standardised and most centralised form of attentional control in human history." Williams was for-merly in the front row of creating the technology that he is now, as a PhD student at Oxford, studying, critiquing and even fearing. He does not believe talk of dystopia is far-fetched and worries about the fate of democracy. But, for him personally, in addition, the issues and questions that began to irk him were also deeply *existential*:

> He says his epiphany came a few years ago, when he noticed he was surrounded by technology that was inhibiting him from concentrating

2   Amanda Lagerkvist

on the things he wanted to focus on. "It was that kind of individual, existential realization: what's going on?" he says. "Isn't technology supposed to be doing the complete opposite of this?"[1]

The question that pestered Williams – *what is going on?* – he defined as an individual existential realisation, prompting him to act ethically. Such moments of self-disclosure or critical reflection are, however, not exclusive experiences for those who built these systems and probably understand them the best. In fact, similar concerns as well as epiphanies in relation to dominant technologies are as old as our relationship with them itself.[2]

Worries about automation, or of being engulfed or controlled by technologies, thus have a long history in media theory, the philosophy of technology, and in critiques of modernity overall. To problematise the role of media in society and its powers within everyday life is very old news for anyone in the field of media studies, whose legitimacy and birthright were precisely the concerns raised by the thrust of propaganda during the World Wars, and the ostensible effects of electronic media on the public. According to the philosopher of technology Don Ihde, much of mid-twentieth-century concerns with technology had to do with their autonomous runaway character, their Frankenstein-like shape. These anxieties were captured by Martin Heidegger in the early 1950s:

> No-one can see the radical changes to come. But technological advance will move faster and faster and can never be stopped. In all areas of his existence (*Dasein*) man will be encircled ever more tightly by the forces of technical apparatuses and automatic devices. These forces, which everywhere and every minute claim, enchain, drag along, press and impose upon man under the *Gestalt* of technological installations and arrangements – these forces, since man has not made them, have moved along since beyond his will and have outgrown his capacity for decision.
> (Heidegger, in Ihde 2010, p. 19)

We may disagree with Heidegger on many things. But perhaps we can agree with him that technologies are not neutral, and that they are forceful. We might also find something prophetic in his words about the complete saturation of technologies in our lifeworld. In what we now call the 'data-driven life' and the attention economy of, for example, social media, it is ever more true that "every minute [they] claim, enchain, drag along" and impose themselves upon us. These words eerily forebode our contemporary "capture culture" in which we are both involved in capturing our everyday lives through practices of digital archiving, and are at once inescapably captured by digital media (Smolicki 2017). Media mine us while having become increasingly "sticky," having been designed to affectively attach themselves to us, to our very sense of meaning and being (Pybus 2015; Langlois 2014). Heidegger's utterance seems to echo, before the fact, the sense that we have indeed moved from a situation where media machines and humans seemed more like discrete entities, to a situation in which we are "wired into existence" (Turkle 2011, p. liv) through them.

Digital media are indeed highly influential in moulding and shaping the lifeworld. For John Durham Peters they are even "the deep background for life on earth" (2015b, np.). In *The Marvelous Clouds: Towards a Philosophy of Elemental Media*, Peters draws inspiration from Martin Heidegger, but also from Marshall McLuhan and André Leroi-Gourhan, to propose in a realist and new materialist vein, that digital media are elemental, which implies that they are ecological, environmental and logistical. Instead of being alien or external forces (cf. Clark 2000, p. 238), they are therefore "our infrastructures of being," and carry both ethical and existential weight (2015a, p. 15). Conceding Heidegger's stress on technologies as always and already part of our being, elemental media philosophy thus sees humans and technologies as mutually co-constituting each other. Media are nothing less than "our situation" (Kittler 1999).[3] But even more profoundly, as existential media studies will add, they also *reveal something cardinal to us about us* (Scannell 2014). In this way they are deeply *existential*, since they involve and effect "humanity in its essence" (Ihde 2010, p. 54). This applies both to the digital ecologies we inhabit, and are ordained to navigate, and to the epiphanies such navigations may engender.

The point of departure for this volume is the assumption that the question of *being human* is for networked populations today highly entangled with digital media. It aims to illustrate how digital and human vulnerabilities intersect, as we inevitably steer and stagger through our digital existence with the help of those tools that also brought this world into being. The book seeks to investigate our digital culture in light of both the existential predicaments and possibilities it offers. Beyond thinking about technology as either neutral (and instrumental) or as determining (and threatening), the existential approach suggested here pursues media through *an ethics of ambiguity* (de Beauvoir 1947), which allows us to describe digital technologies as both beneficiary and burdensome – and at once. This resonates with Bernard Stiegler's *pharmacological approach* (Stiegler 2010, 2012, 2013, see also Derrida 1981), which posits technologies as always being both poison and cure. For Mark Coeckelbergh, similarly, technologies are profoundly intermeshed with our existential vulnerability; even as they are essentially invented to overcome human vulnerabilities, they always induce new ones. This situation also prompts us to take responsibility for what types of vulnerabilities we can live with, and for how we wilfully craft our technological world (Coeckelbergh 2013).

Reflecting upon the technologies we use – that deeply inform our worldviews, lives, embodied sense ratios, affective responses, structures of incentive and leeway for action – is an important aspect of our relationship with them. Beyond potential reflex responses to the contrary, *nota bene*, it is possible to reflect on and even critically scrutinise dominant technologies,

4   Amanda Lagerkvist

without belonging to a 'Luddite camp,' or without providing a lopsided or apocalyptic account of the maleficent effects of strong 'powerful media' on an audience defined as the prey of modernity. And although digital culture is undoubtedly another phase of our continuous long human history in, with and through (media) technologies, it is also fair to argue that the latest developments seem to encompass unique changes at the same time. These provoke new questions. Hence, without denying continuity in both human existence and in media technologies, it seems valid to maintain that something *is* in fact shifting. Cautiously stressing novelty, in turn, does not mean to say that we are in a brave new digital world, entirely distinct and cut off from everything that came before, and that the internet is the greatest invention since the printing press.[4] This also means, I propose, that we need to move beyond thinking about technologies as either *new* and exciting or *habitual* and banal (Chun 2016). Instead, one may purport that some of the medium specificities of the internet and the platform society, and not least their all-pervasive ecological qualities, entail challenges as well as possibilities that need a critical and creative intervention. Hence, as much as they may be full of promise and/or boringly mundane, media are also life-defining and *momentous* (Lagerkvist 2016). Such an intervention is what this volume promises to offer, through the emergent field of existential media studies.

Existential media studies and digital religion

To begin to address these developments, this book argues that we need an existential optics that will allow us to see other contours of these contemporary phenomena, and thereby raise different questions in relation to the culture of connectivity (van Dijck 2013). It aims to demonstrate that existential approaches can bring important issues to the table in the debates surrounding both digital media and digital religion. The purpose of this volume is therefore to introduce the field of existential media studies, and to present core ideas and trajectories for researching our digital existence. This calls for an important disclaimer: While drawing inspiration from existentialist thinkers (such as Søren Kierkegaard, Karl Jaspers, Hannah Arendt, Martin Heidegger, Simone de Beauvoir, Maurice Merleau-Ponty and others), the intention is neither to read the philosophers within this school 'by the letter,' nor to do comprehensive justice to them or to the wealth of discourse and critique their works have inspired. Instead, and much more modestly, the collection aims to substantiate what the 'existential' can mean *today* by returning to some of these authors' key concepts. As will be demonstrated throughout, moreover, the existential also needs to be brought into conjunction with our contemporary digital times, in part by enabling exchanges between perspectives from existential philosophy and the new materialism. In addition, all contributions undertake existential probings from various disciplinary backgrounds, and with the aid of a diverse range of theoretical sources of inspiration and methodological approaches. Their common ground is their intention to contribute to existential media studies.

The volume is structured into three parts reflecting three central themes within the philosophy of existence: *ontology, ethics* and *transcendence*. This broad scope allows for addressing questions such as: How do media relate to Being itself? What existential and ethical challenges are involved when our selves are quantified, extended and distributed? How do big data, tracking and mass surveillance affect or threaten our sense of existential security? What is the role of the digital for mediating the spiritual, transcendent and existential dimensions in life, within and beyond groups of self-identified religious believers? And will digital memorials, communities of grief online, and digital rituals reshape the realms of death and grief?

This book brings fresh questions and approaches to the study of digital media culture and reframes some of the important debates in the field of digital religion. In relation to the latter more specifically, it offers a timely re-articulation of research on digital media and digital religion in three complementary ways. First, it draws upon the work of scholars who challenge mainstream media studies by providing a reframing of media in light of the importance of 'the religious' for understanding media culture – specifically, how religious institutions, practices, beliefs and so on transform and are transformed by media – and of media and mediation for understanding religion. Here, contributing to this work, which has already made headway in media studies through the flourishing field of *media, religion and culture* (see, for instance, Hoover and Lundby [eds.] 1997; de Vries and Weber [eds.] 2001; Stolow 2005; Morgan [ed.] 2008; Campbell 2010; Lövheim 2011; Cheong et al. [eds.] 2012; Lynch et al. [eds.] 2012; Sumiala 2013), the digital is *further reframed* by pursuing an existential media analysis that pushes beyond the mandatory focus in media studies into the social, cultural, political and economic.

Second, the collection also broadens the scope of the debate in the field of media, religion and culture itself – and digital religion, in particular – beyond 'religion,' to include the wider existential dimensions of digital media. The starting point is thus to explore what it means to be a human being, to exist, in the digital age. One aim is to highlight this variety of aspects of our technologised existence and how technology itself potentially (re)shapes the existential. This echoes the possibility envisioned by Stewart Hoover for the study of digital religion to be an endeavour in which we may explore the "actual contribution 'the digital' is making to 'the religious'" (2012, p. ix). But furthermore, and in line with Heidi Campbell's work on digital religion, we might also ask, in turn, how existential meaning making practices potentially reshape the digital (what Campbell (2010) refers to as *the religious social shaping of technology*).

Hence, while drawing on debates on digital religion, the ambition is also to push the envelope and to offer a new vantage point, through which we

6 Amanda Lagerkvist

can envision an existential approach that is not primarily or exclusively concerned with 'religion.' Rather than beginning with religion and its fate or transformations in the digital age, the edict that encapsulates this project is that 'existence precedes religion' (Lagerkvist 2016). This means that if 'religion' is bracketed in a phenomenological manner (meaning here basically setting aside one's preconceptions, assumptions and definitions of it, in order to *re-centre religion* as an object of study, cf. Hoover and Echabibi 2014) – and is instead subsumed under the heading of 'the existential' – then we may consider all human beings as existential creatures. This implies that the scope widens to include the ways in which people broadly (with or without confessional beliefs) engage with digital media with existential implications, both in everyday life and in life-defining moments. These engagements, importantly, may involve experiences that could be described as 'spiritual,' for instance in various forms of techno-spirituality or in after death communication on the internet (see Lagerkvist, Chapter 9, this volume).

Third, the volume seeks to open up a conversation between the field of digital religion and media philosophy, in particular existential philosophy and the philosophy of technology. Crucially, as already discussed above, this will be achieved by acknowledging the ecological, environmental and possibly all-encompassing role of digital media in the latest phase of what has been termed Web 2.0, or the culture of connectivity (van Dijck 2013; Floridi [ed.] 2014; Peters 2015a), or what I prefer to call the *existential terrains of connectivity*. With the purpose of encapsulating the scope of the existential media analysis, I will in the next section suggest how such a terrain can be mapped, while also outlining three entryways through which it can be approached and critically engaged with.

Existential terrains of connectivity: three entryways

I have elsewhere proposed an existential approach to digital culture, by suggesting that classic themes in the philosophy of existence – such as death, time, *being there* (absence and presence) and *being-in-and-with* (the self and community) – could be harnessed and reworked, 'upgraded' and mobilised, in order to unpack our digital existence (Lagerkvist 2016). Placing particular emphasis on the '*throwness*' – understood as the uncertainty, precarity and vulnerability – of the digital human condition, the existential refers both to the mundane quest for meaning and to extraordinary, transformative and traumatic events that transcend the everyday. I also emphasise that these involve experiences that may border on, or outright express, a sense of the 'numinous' or the 'sacred.' Importantly, the approach also retains and reinvents a perspective on the self/the subject/the human, beyond both the liberal humanist subject and the affective forces replacing him/her of the new materialism, by creatively positing Kierkegaard's *den Enkelte* (the singular individual), that is, the *exister* – a stumbling, hurting, relational, ambivalent, embodied, striving, self-aware and clueless, yet responsible, human being – as the primary subject in media studies.

As the case of the refuseniks illustrates, the potential to realise one's unique responsibility, for oneself and others, as existing in the world, is here key. But as this collection displays, this is an exclusive concern neither of belatedly morally roused designers, engineers and product managers, nor of the long-term debates of philosophers or scholars. Instead this is a major issue for all: *we are all existers*. And even though the exister may experience profound existential loneliness, s/he is in fact always simultaneously – and always already – a *co-exister*, since s/he is born by and defined by others, dependent on and related to them. This also makes him/her profoundly vulnerable (Arendt 1946/1994; Butler 2004). Keywords for the approach – vulnerability, ambivalence, limits and transcendence – will be retained in the following, as I further delineate the existential terrain through three vantage points, or points of access: *existential conditions, existential experiences* and *existential strivings*. These are intended, in turn, to expound and substantiate the volume's three sections: ontology, ethics and transcendence.

Existential conditions

The first vantage point consists of basic *existential conditions*. These correspond to what Heidegger (1927/1962) called our existential givens (*existentialia*) of, for instance, care, being-toward-death, time, understanding, sociality, the task to create meaning, and our human thrownness. But included in those fundamental structures of human existence are also technologies themselves. This is what Tim Clark (2000) calls the tradition of "originary technicity," or what Stiegler in his philosophy of technology termed the "originary prostheticity" of the human (1998). In this perspective, which Stiegler traces to Martin Heidegger and Jacques Derrida, the long Western tradition of thinking about technologies as instrumental and extrinsic to being human is refuted. Instead, humans emerge through tool use. In the following section, I will foremost focus on this feature of the givenness of being, but I will return to some of the other existentialia listed by Heidegger in later sections.

In recent debates in media philosophy scholars frequently refer to, or even adopt, a Heideggerian perspective on technology (cf. Kim 2001; Berry 2011; Kember and Zylinska 2012; Scannell 2014; Gunkel and Taylor 2014; Mitchell 2014; Miller 2015; Hong 2015; Peters 2015a; Chun 2016; Lagerkvist 2016). This scholarship underlines what has also been discussed from the outset of this introduction: that technologies and humans are mutually co-constituted. These contributions stress the materiality and mundaneness of media, and the debate has centred around the *tools* we use to craft and manage our existence. This has engendered a media ontology that emphasises that media *ground us in Being* (cf. in particular Peters 2015a). In this perspective, digital media disclose us to ourselves, and our world to us, as they equip us with tools to navigate it.

Furthermore, taking as its point of departure John Durham Peters' proposition that media studies may have the grandiose ambition to "be a successor

8   *Amanda Lagerkvist*

discipline to metaphysics, as the field which accounts for the constitution of all that is" (2015a, p. 320), the first section of the volume will consequently attend to "Media Ontologies," and how we may address the role of digital media in bringing our contemporary world and its subjects into being (cf. Kittler 2009). In Part I, authors engage in the daunting and admittedly difficult, if not irresolvable, task of trying to identify the defining characteristics of 'the digital' (see Clemens and Nash, Chapter 1, this volume) – and thence of digital being, as well as of its discontents and limits (see Schwartz, Chapter 3, and Granata, Chapter 4, this volume).

Noteworthy debates on technology crystallise into two seemingly discrete positions on the very relationship between technology and being. In order to pedagogically offer a synopsis of their main traits, I will simplify them somewhat here. The first, as already discussed from the outset, offers an all-encompassing perspective on technology, providing a media ontology that describes the co-evolution and 'onto-genetical' relation between the human and technics. In moving beyond the subject-object distinction in Western philosophy, in line with the philosophy of existence, this camp also conceives of humans as the result of a co-constitution and imbrication of biology, culture and technology. We are essentially *technical beings*. From this view there is seemingly nothing outside (digital) mediation. Everything is mediated or pervaded by human crafting (cf. Verbeek 2005, 2011; Peters 2015a). This means that there are no non-mediated ('pure,' 'authentic' and 'natural') phenomena.[5] And by consequence, there are certainly no 'pristine' existential, religious or ethical states, or experiences. In other words, there is no other beside mediation and technology. This is a position on technology that has sometimes been taken up in the field of media, religion and culture in both historical and aesthetic approaches (see Stolow 2005, 2013; Morgan 2008) and in media centric sociological approaches, such as mediatisation theory (see Hjarvard and Lövheim 2012).

On the other side of the fence, a different existential position on technology might instead maintain, no doubt provocatively, that there could in fact be non-mediated human activities, phenomena and experiences. In this view, there may exist particular absolute and irreplaceable experiences that can't be subsumed by the digital and that require a break away from certain *types* of mediation – perhaps as in Albert Borgmann's notion of embodied "focal activities" (Borgmann in Ess 2002). A hug, a meal or the wind cannot be completely digitalised, for instance. Such a stance could highlight the radical role of touch and argue that it in effect exemplifies an 'other' of digital mediation (see Schwartz 2018). It would maintain a differentiated scale of dependency upon, or influence from, whatever medium is dominating at a particular historical time. Hence, in this perspective, there is some room for diversity within a regime of over-arching mediation. There may then be centres and peripheries of the reach of the digital. So even if on some level everything is mediated, not every aspect of human experience and life may be subject to, and indeed fitting for, a digital instantiation. From this vantage point one would also be able to challenge an all-inclusive view of digital mediation, and account for the reality and perhaps also value of non-mediation. We could also draw on Kierkegaard, who stressed the role of non-mediation as a fact of life and a trait of death: in his *oeuvre*, mortality itself and "the mortal individual obstructs the system's attempt to totalise the world as image" (Peters 1997, p. 13). From the standpoint of existential philosophy, one could thus argue that there are particular experiential and existential fields that may transcend the mediated, or where digital mediations fail to deliver. From this perspective, which echoes some current uses of the term "post-digital" (Lindgren 2017), there may be something outside the digital in a digital ecology, because there are limits to any medium.

This relates to questions about *authenticity*. The human task to achieve an authentic sense of being (what Kierkegaard calls the existential or ethical stage, what Heidegger calls *Dasein*, and what Jaspers refers to as a realised *Existenz*), versus inauthentic forms of life, runs through the entire history of existentialism, and among philosophers of technology, modern technologies have often been held responsible for obstructing us in that endeavour (see an overview in Verbeek 2005, Chapters 1–2). This also touches on contemporary debates on authenticity in the field of digital religion that have sought to ascertain, for instance, whether online rituals can ever be as authentic or real as physical ones or whether the virtual domain can offer what face-to-face interaction affords (cf. Radde-Antweiler 2008, 2012). The purpose of such an approach, as already suggested, is thus to restore the central place of embodiment as not fully reducible to the digital.

Apart from being limited, the workings of digital media are for many of us so difficult to comprehend that they are, in fact, inscrutable (Chun 2011). They are also *irreducible*. This means that an iPhone is *both* a *tool* in my hand that I need for managing my everyday life *and* an epitomisation of connective capitalism, linking me and my movements to a large global economic *system* of instantaneous connections, minings, trackings and exploitations. This relates to the important distinction within the philosophy of technology between traditional technologies: artefacts, crafts, tools and equipment (*ars, technē*), and modern technologies: large-scale technologies and wide-ranging sociotechnical systems (*technology, technics*) (Dreyfus 1984). Referring to the latter, Heidegger argued that the essence of technology is "by no means anything technological" (1977, p. 3); instead, it is an *enframing* – that is, the turning of the world itself, nature and our fellow human beings into a standing reserve for exploitation.[6]

To retain a sceptical acknowledgement of such attributes of technological world-making will be critical for existential media studies. But apart from thinking about the essence of technology, however, in terms of what 'the digital' effects, or what the 'digital object' fundamentally *is* (cf. Kim 2001; Hui 2016), it is important to acknowledge in a more concrete, contextually specific and post-phenomenological manner what things do, as well as what we do with our tools (Ihde 1979, 1990; Verbeek 2005). Aiming to

10 *Amanda Lagerkvist*

bring in this dimension, the volume defies and seeks to bridge the typically binary scholarly preoccupation with either *Technology* (as a philosophical and ontological problem) or *technologies* (as an anthropological and phenomenological dominion of human experience and agency). This brings us into the experiential realm.

Existential experiences

The existential terrains of connectivity imply particular possibilities and predicaments that also give rise to particular *experiences* of embodied vulnerability. This is the focus of the second section of this book: "Being Human: Extension, Exposure and Ethics." Being vulnerable is, however, a given fact of life – in pre-digital, digital, as well as post-digital settings – and, hence, is the most basic of existential experiences (Coeckelbergh 2013). This relates to what Søren Kierkegaard described as the *groundlessness* or indeterminacy of our existence (Arendt 1946/1994). Kierkegaard refuted any Hegelian totalizing and absolute claim to knowledge, and regarded as futile any conclusive synthesis in human life or history (Kierkegaard 1846/1960). Drawing inspiration from Kierkegaard, the existential approach stresses innate uncertainties and aporias in (digital) human existence. This relates to what Heidegger calls the 'thrownness' of the human condition. Being thrown into a pre-given world means finding ourselves in a particular place, at a historical point in time, and among a particular group of people in utter uncertainty, and with the inevitable task of making meaning. To be thrown means both openness and constraints at once; we are *there*, thrown into the world, with the possibility of realizing our potential within the limits of our given situation. In complementing the media ontology discussed above, which stresses that media ground us in being, I suggest we pay equal attention to our thrownness in light of our innate and *originary human exposure*, and hence our *groundlessness*. Therefore, today, as we are digitally thrown, we are also becoming in and with the rapidly changing technological world, in displacement. Hence, our culture of connectivity is an ambivalent existential terrain (Lagerkvist 2016, 2017). As existential philosophers such as Karl Jaspers (1932/1970) or Emmanuel Levinas (1961/1991) would argue, however, this very vulnerability is in fact a source of fecundity: It enables the opening of a space for productive *action, ethical choice* and *meaning making* in relation to the situation into which we are thrown.

Hence, existential experiences also involve the search for meaning. Meaning and meaning making are important keywords in the field of media, religion and culture. Approaching digital cultures existentially may therefore draw on the field's emphasis on the need for a broader understanding of the meaning making and mediated qualities of religion, and the religious and ritual qualities of the media (Sumiala-Seppänen et al. 2006; Lynch et al. [eds.] 2012). And focusing on digital humans as (co-)existers, struggling and striving precisely through digital everyday navigations to make meaning communally, connects with the attention paid to rituals and community in the field of media and religion (Helland 2012; Sumiala 2013). When death or loss strikes, existential experiences typically include the 'meaningless' – that is, suffering, the void, anxiety, exile, loneliness, and interruption (cf. Taylor 2007). But in turn, social media environments sometimes offer crucial ritual means for restoring the world. In support groups online, for instance, co-existers turn to the internet as a literal lifeline, in *shared vulnerability* (Lagerkvist and Andersson 2017). These groups provide patterns of predictability and a sense of existential security in the face of bottomless grief and loss of meaning (cf. Lagerkvist 2013, see Sumiala, Chapter 10, in this volume).

As this illustrates, the given yet emergent connective world thus entails possibilities for meaning making and consolation. But our technologically enforced lifeworld also consists of excruciating phenomena, such as far-reaching automation, trolling, panopticism and the eeriness and obscurity of big data. Since these emergent phenomena challenge many extant ethical models, they require new frameworks and guidelines to be carefully developed, in order to address this situation. This section of the book will contribute to such discussions in the field of *digital media ethics*, which is, according to Charles M. Ess, an "ethics for the rest of us." The approach pays attention to the manifold ethical challenges evoked for all whose lives are informed by the use of digital media, and aims to offer possible resolutions to these challenges (Ess 2013, 2015, 2017, see Langlois, Chapter 7, this volume).

In an important contribution to existential media studies and digital media ethics, Vince Miller (2015) pursues the investments of digital media in the political economy of neoliberalism. Inspired by Heidegger's techno-criticism and the concept of enframing, he scrutinises what the essential features of digital technologies imply, enforce or set off. Miller discusses how the *digital enframing* of social media networks objectifies human beings, thereby ushering in ethical havoc (for instance, in the shape of trolling and cyberbullying) in digital culture. In his reading, this is due to the crisis of embodied and emotional presence, and ethical accountability, in networked life (Miller 2015, see also Chapter 8, this volume). Other examples abound. Not least, the phenomenon of virality is important to problematise since it is an example of what the philosopher Byung-Chul Han (2014) deems the lack of *existential duration in digital culture*, due to its inherent temporal instantaneity. Important questions need to be raised: Will the speed of viral reality foster ethical and political judgment, that is, *phronesis*? Is it conducive to the needs and necessities of human beings as existential beings?[7]

Yet other pressing concerns relate to and complicate the classic questions of *being there* in a world, and of knowing ourselves. Where exactly *are* we in the world, as our selves are distributed and extended? And what can we ultimately know about ourselves through data? Issues of loss of control and of 'existential security' in relation to the data-driven life also concern questions about where our traces can be located and whether they can be saved. On

12 Amanda Lagerkvist

the other hand, in a post-scarcity memory culture, many of our existential challenges revolve around those memories that outlive both our needs and intentions as search engines remember every step we have taken (Lagerkvist 2014; Hong 2015, see also Andersson Schwarz, Chapter 2; Hong, Chapter 6; and Frosh, Chapter 5, this volume). Again, this brings us to the question of limits and 'non-mediation,' to debates about the right to be forgotten, the necessity of forgetting and need for disconnection (cf. Mayer-Schönberger 2008; Hoskins 2014; Lagerkvist 2017). As these phenomena reveal, existential experiences relate to limits in several ways (Jackson 2011, 2013). Of existential import is therefore also the question of interruption, disconnection and silence (Pinchevski 2005). It is through an emphasis on limits and a potential value of the void that we may unlock the third gateway for entering into the existential terrain: *existential strivings*.

Existential strivings

As existential beings, we are thrown into a world of and within limits against something else. One may propose that media technologies offer a channelling of searchings of the beyond and of the transcendent dimensions in life. This is the theme of the third section of the book: "Transcendence: Beyond Life, Death and the Human." It focuses on how our digital existence is related to those existential experiences that involve the extraordinary and the transcendent (Aydin and Verbeek 2015). According to Karl Jaspers, these relate to those particular *limit-situations* in life (of death, loss, crisis and guilt) (1932/1970), which require something of us since we are expected to act in response to them, in order to "become ourselves." These imply what I will term *existential strivings* at the limits of the known. Such strivings conjure what lies in the shadows, beyond our sense of control and, importantly, beyond words. The existential is therefore also defined in light of those existential strivings toward what Jaspers calls 'existential elucidation' (1932/1970) that can only take place beyond scientific methods and truth claims, as a human being seeks a relation to another human being in communication: in transcendence.

As already mentioned above, this connects to the strong interest in rituals and ritual theory in the field of digital religion, and yet by reclaiming these within an understanding of what Johanna Sumiala calls our 'ritual existence,' the book endeavours to open the field to broader frameworks of interpretation beyond the ones offered through the keyword 'religion' (cf. Chapter 10, this volume). Such strivings also encompass the experience of endings. The focus on finitude is key in classic existential philosophy for the deliberation on what makes us human (cf. Graham and Montoya, Chapter 12, this volume). In Kierkegaard (1849/1989), it is through the acknowledgement of our subjective mortality that we may come to lead an authentic life; this is further echoed in Heidegger's concept of *being-toward-death*. These experiences thus relate to limits, to the beyond, as well as to ghostly, mediated returns.

Digital existence 13

Perhaps because of the clout of all-pervasive digital media, existential strivings could also be conceived of as a retort, activating the previously discussed dimensions of non-mediation. This approach thus recognises that there are fields of experience that reach beyond (particular modes of) mediation. Here existential strivings also include the need for what I call "techno-existential closure." This can be exemplified, for instance, with the need some mourners feel to shut down and erase the memorial profiles and accounts of their deceased loved ones, or the need more broadly to step back and reflect (as in the case of the tardy unease among the refuseniks of Silicon Valley who were discussed previously) in response to increasingly compulsive forms of connectivity (Lagerkvist 2017).

Hence, when media users are reconceived as striving existers, many of their movements and practices online may also be reconceived, which may alter how we appreciate the digital. From this point of departure, we are able to acknowledge that their activities online – including and beyond those we would earmark as religious – are in fact *existential* activities and strivings. Here a new understanding of the digital as well as of digital religiosity may emerge. This relates to debates in the sociology of religion calling for new understandings of people's changing relationship to transcendent and existential dimensions in life in an ostensibly secularised society, or, perhaps, a "post-secular" Western society (Woodhead and Heelas 2000; Habermas 2008). Sharing this point of departure, this volume suggests that the exploration of existential themes occurs vividly and ubiquitously within the realm of digital media. One of its objectives is to provide new analytical focus on the uncharted forms of existential meaning making in the realm of the digital (cf. Aupers and Houtman 2010; Campbell and Lövheim 2013). Hence, the existential dimensions of digitalisation may also be discussed by turning attention to different forms of non-confessional and *vernacular religiosity* that are also at play in digital contexts (Bowman and Valk [eds.] 2015; Walter 2016; see, for instance, Frosh, Chapter 5; Lagerkvist, Chapter 9; and Proctor, Chapter 11, this volume). In this way, the current volume also contributes to the discussion on digital religion, which is now in a 'fourth wave' that followed from the previous descriptive, categorical and theoretical waves (see Campbell 2012; Campbell and Lövheim 2013) or what Gregory Price Grieve calls the waves of awe, routinisation and theorisation (Grieve 2012, pp. 110–113). But whereas this fourth wave has primarily provided for methodological refinement, this volume seeks to offer a novel existential instalment to expand the horizon of the digital, and possibly of digital religion.

This point can also be linked to the latest debates in this field, which have moved on from focusing on the internet's medium specificity (e.g., distinguishing between 'religion online' or 'online religion,' cf. Helland 2000) to a perspective that sees digital religion as integrated in everyday religious life and material practice, where offline and online are always co-implied (Lövheim and Campbell 2017; Campbell 2016). This may help us investigate

14 *Amanda Lagerkvist*

the ways in which existential meaning or non-meaning is not always a question of what we can cognitively grasp, or semantically convey, but what can be wrought through other modes such as the visual, embodied, tacit, affective and material (Morgan [ed.] 2010). And this also relates to the ambition of existential media studies to forge new understandings of media beyond representationalism. This is linked to the appreciation of media as elemental, ecological and environmental. By stressing media technologies as part of the natural-cultural, or techno-existential, mystery that is our common world, we ultimately tap into what Peters dubs 'media theology' (Peters 2015a).

This volume

The volume addresses a broad range of concerns in our time of deep techno-cultural saturation. As the above hopefully illustrates, it offers a fresh perspective, inspired by existential philosophy, for an exploration of several pressing themes and features of our digital existence. Having identified three interrelated and overlapping, yet distinct, ways of conceiving of the existential, and specifically in relation to the digital, these trajectories will now be further highlighted. In order to capture the dimensions of existentiality discussed through the vantage points of *conditions* (relating to givens and ontology), *experiences* (relating to human vulnerability and ethics) and *strivings* (relating to limits and to the transcendent), the book is divided into three corresponding sections: Part I: "Media Ontologies"; Part II: "Being Human: Extension, Exposure and Ethics"; and Part III: "Transcendence: Beyond Life, Death and the Human."

Part I: Media Ontologies addresses the big and basic questions in our contemporary digital lives: our being in and becoming with the digital world. Here, contributions offer a theorisation of our contemporary digital existence, through a focus on the ontogenesis of data, technics and being, while also pointing to the inherent antinomies in digital culture, and to the need for alternate digital ontologies in the face of the technocratic and masculinist connective world we inhabit.

In Chapter 1, "Irremediability: On the Very Concept of Digital Ontology," Justin Clemens and Adam Nash set out by questioning whether there is such a thing as digital ontology at all, and if so, how it is different from 'traditional ontology,' or, at least, from 'non-digital' or 'pre-digital' ontology. They also probe what the adjective 'digital' actually signifies, including how it differs from 'data' or 'information.' The authors argue that the digital may in fact overturn the concept of 'ontology' itself, and that digital ontology is a paradoxical, nonsensical or contradictory phenomenon that resists its own consistent formalisation. Clemens and Nash begin with a preliminary analysis of some influential recent approaches in digital ontology (Floridi, Boellstoerff, Fredkin), showing that they prioritise epistemology over ontology. Next, they re-examine some of the most important twentieth-century ontologies (Heidegger, Simondon, Stiegler, Badiou), arguing that digital technologies expose new phenomena that have no precedent in any metaphysical or logical tradition. These comprise not only the extraordinary advances in 'positive' knowledge thereby gained (as are studied and manipulated under such rubrics as 'big data'), but also new kinds of cognitive deadlocks and dilemmas that have emerged. The authors conclude that digital technologies therefore present aporias, or impasses of knowledge, to any attempt to think the ontology of the digital and that it is only on the basis of these aporias that the new lineaments of a properly digital ontology can be discerned.

In this section, contributors further raise important questions about the prospects for individuation through the personalisation of media environments. In Chapter 2, "Umwelt and Individuation: Digital Signals and Technical Being," Jonas Andersson Schwarz fuses Gilbert Simondon's theory of technological being with Jakob von Uexküll's biosemiotic concept of Umwelt, in order to seek out a more integrative, dynamic, vitalistic theory of media technology. His aim is primarily to facilitate a critique of the speculative, idealistic hyperbole around data and information that we see today. Andersson Schwarz argues that it is no coincidence that Simondon's techno-philosophy has been re-appropriated in recent years, mainly since his relational, evolutionary ontology is radically different from standard linear models of digital information. He argues that it allows us to understand embedded technological agency and the conceptual gap between that which is captured by surveillant data infrastructures and lived phenomenological existence. Likewise, as digital media platforms increasingly rely on algorithmically customised (i.e., personalised) modes of media dissemination, Umwelt theory offers a way to theorise these highly artificial "user experiences" fed back to users by digital platform providers. Even as Andersson Schwarz offers a much-needed critique, his approach ultimately also affirms technology as a symbiotic process, which points towards a utopian potential for human co-habitation with digital infrastructure. This contrasts with much of the current, actual technocratic governance familiar to us (apps, platforms, interfaces), where the user is offered, at best, modes of co-creativity that are constrained and highly conditional and, at worst, only mere illusions of participation.

Other chapters in this part similarly offer a media philosophy of being that seeks to problematise the constraining features of these media, highlighting the limits of what these technologies afford, while envisioning alternative ontologies for our media age. In an effort to propose a critical feminist ontology of care, Margaret Schwartz juxtaposes in Chapter 3, "Thrownness, Vulnerability, Care: A Feminist Ontology for the Digital Age," two mediations of female embodiment. The first is a consumer product called Icon underwear, which is marketed exclusively via online platforms such as Instagram and Facebook and is designed to help women manage light incontinence. The second is a group of self-described hackers called the GynePunk collective that repurposes computer technologies as feminist-, queer- and

16 *Amanda Lagerkvist*

trans-friendly gynaecological tools and sex toys. Both Icon underwear and the GynePunk collective materialise female embodiment via technologies of representation, surveillance and containment. Both frame the female body in its vulnerability, as incontinence and reproduction are sites of sexual difference as well as bodily and emotional fragility. Yet they have very different responses to how to *care* for that vulnerability: one through a neoliberal ethos of self-reliance through consumerism, and the other through collective technological poaching and revisionist history. Schwartz shows that the ways different media situate and frame this vulnerability produce different ontologies and argues that a truly feminist ontology for the digital age proceeds from an ethics of care.

This section also brings into view the perhaps counterintuitive sense in which digital media may in fact *undo* worlds rather than bring them about. In Chapter 4, "Digital Unworld(s): The Bielefeld Conspiracy," Yvette Granata examines production and erasure practices enabled by software via the lens of 'The Bielefeld Conspiracy,' an internet phenomenon from the 1990s that claimed that the real German city of Bielefeld did not exist. Ubiquitous software is often understood as producing urban space itself. But Granata looks to the opposite phenomena of ubiquitous deletion practices and the manner in which digital erasure is now equally a part of our digital existence. Through an analysis of various erasure effects, data and digital practices of deletion, she thinks through the Bielefeld Conspiracy as a contemporary phenomenon in conjunction with philosophies of New Realism, such as Markus Gabriel's meta-metaphysical nihilism, which claims that 'the World does not Exist.' Granata ultimately charts the ontology of digital erasure as the production of what she calls the 'digital unworld' – the structurally supported digital ontology of ubiquitous erasure.

In **Part II: Being Human: Extension, Exposure and Ethics,** the volume seeks to highlight the particular features of our digital and human vulnerability and the ways of being human that emerge in digital existence. It concerns those existential and ethical challenges and potentials involved when our selves are networked, quantified and distributed. One key issue that the field is struggling with concerns the question: Does hyper-connectivity imply a heightened sense of embodied connective presence – through social media, tagging and sharing selfies – and/or is anxiety, shock and loneliness saturating our mundane being-in-the-digital-world? In Chapter 5, "You Have Been Tagged: Magical Incantations, Digital Incarnations and Extended Selves," Paul Frosh offers some preliminary theoretical propositions on the existential condition of *being tagged* in photographs uploaded to social media platforms. He argues that social tagging is a contemporary intensification of long-standing procedures for maintaining our being in the world: the naming of persons and the figural incarnation of bodies, hence of human practices that instantiate, replicate and disseminate the embodied subject discursively and visually. However, tagging is also an operative and generative procedure: when you tag someone, your contacts and theirs are notified,

Digital existence   17

and the tagged photograph is frequently replicated in contacts' various feeds. Tagging is therefore a computationally realised magical incantation, where uttering the name instantly multiplies body-images of the named. By alerting our contacts about our being tagged, tagging becomes a recurrent rite of naming and incarnation that invites confirmation and assent (likes, comments). It is thus a way of performing phatic sociability through the 'selving' of others – by virtue of their named body-images – usually without their prior permission. Frosh argues that tagging finally puts visual 'flesh' onto the informational and computational 'bones' underpinning the network apparatus. It materialises and animates the social network platform as a connective social body that is populated through the continual proliferation, identification and confirmation of the named body-images of its constituent members. Frosh concludes that it thus produces a powerful poetic-ideological effect: the palpability of the apparatus as a sensuously inhabited world.

How is our being-in-the-world crafted today by big data? What does it mean to 'know' that we are being surveilled? And how do big data affect the prospects for achieving meaningful phenomenal human knowledge? In Chapter 6, "Surveillance, Sensors, and Knowledge Through the Machine," Sun-ha Hong argues that to know the world and ourselves through data and its machinic custodians is an exercise in stretching our phenomenological horizons. On one hand, big data promises unprecedented knowledge of the world 'out there' – a world which technology itself renders more complex than ever, a world which we are nevertheless exhorted to know for ourselves in order to function as rational and informed subjects. Meanwhile, the same technologies for exhaustive measurement and correlative prediction turn 'in here' to the privacy and domesticity of the individual body, promising 'to know us better than we know ourselves.' Hong discusses how these technologies seek to pre-empt human sense experience, bringing forth previously amorphous aspects of each individual life into that harsh and discrete field of objective knowledge. Charting these two related ways – 'recession' and 'protrusion' – in which new technologies reconfigure the phenomenological relationship between sense experience and knowledge, Hong examines two scenes of datafication in contemporary America: the Snowden Affair, and the emerging generation of self-tracking technologies.

What is the purchase of software and algorithms on our sense of meaning, affect and being, and how can we account for the contemporary prospects for transindividuation and caring for the self? In Chapter 7, "Social Media and the Care of the Self," Ganaele Langlois stresses how in the past few years, a new critique of corporate social media has emerged broadly. Focused on software, networks and algorithms, this critique examines how specific articulations of the technical, the economic, and the psycho-social radically redefine and ultimately short-circuit processes of self-production and self-exploration. These span Stiegler's exploration of technical deindividuation through the mining of the psyche within informational and semio-capitalist contexts, to software studies' investigations of the non-human,

18 *Amanda Lagerkvist*

automated shaping of conditions of existence. Langlois argues that we are currently seeing the emergence of a new political economy of the psycho-social which makes visible that corporate social media radically intervenes in the processes through which we make sense of ourselves and others, and through which we develop both intra-psychic and inter-psychic bonds. Langlois examines how Foucault's exploration of the care of the self can open the door to a reconceptualisation of social platforms. She argues that while much has been done in terms of envisioning and designing alternative social networks that answer to important political questions such as freedom from surveillance and guarantee of anonymity, the question of sociality and the building of reflective spaces where we can engage in an ethics of coming to being, in the world and to others has been somewhat under-explored. In turn, the chapter asks how we can envision software-based practices for the care of the self.

A related pressing ethical issue regards social robots now entering into our lives. Another concerns the role of technological affordances for producing a culture of trolling and hate. What are the ethical predicaments of anonymity online, or the moral costs involved in the loss of anonymity in social media? In Chapter 8, "The Ethics of Digital Being: Vulnerability, Invulnerability, and 'Dangerous Surprises,'" Vincent Miller tackles these questions, arguing that the key defining features of digital being, at least in terms of ethical engagement with others via technological interfaces and networks, is a heightened state of both invulnerability and vulnerability. Departing from Merleau-Ponty, who suggested that embodied existence in the world is defined by a stance of vulnerability and the anticipation of 'dangerous surprises,' Miller shows that in digital existence, our continuous, archived, digital presence, distributed in a multitude of networks, archives, databases and servers, opens us up to increased vulnerabilities of which we are only partially aware. These vulnerabilities become more present to us when we hear of or are the victims of trolling, a data breach, hacking scandal or other forms of 'dangerous surprises.' Miller looks at two incidents in detail: the five-year-long trolling campaign against Nicola Brookes, and the 'Ashley Madison hack' of 2015. In line with recent perspectives launched in the field of existential media studies, Miller uses these examples to investigate the notion of *vulnerability* as one key way of being in the digital age. Concluding that digital being consists of a contradictory stance to the world: of heightened invulnerability in our social encounters with others, alongside a heightened vulnerability to a host of unknown 'dangerous surprises,' he suggests that the negotiation of this stance is fundamental to any development of an ethics for the digital age.

The third section of the volume, **Part III: Transcendence: Beyond Life, Death and the Human,** represents four techno-anthropological approaches that all deal with the extra-mundane and extra-human: the dead, death rituals, animism and the fate of "the human." In Chapter 9, "The Internet is Always Awake: Sensations, Sounds and Silences of the Digital Grave,"

Digital existence 19

I explore after death communication online, and read the technology off the dead, and the dead off the technology, to probe the peculiarities of the digital dead. I relate their presence to the history of electronic presence, and argue that as *ghost effects* of the medium, they are like the net itself, awake and seemingly attentive. Among networked populations, importantly, the dead are both online, and they are getting the message, but they are at once mute: a bunch of 'lurkers' loitering about. This suggests that the dead impersonate the leading social media platform of our age. Hence, I argue that digital media embody the transcendent by enabling connective presence per se and one-way communication with the dead. There is no expectation (as, for example, in the case of the spiritual telegraph) of receiving an answer from the grave. But at the same time, the dead can be fully *connected to*. This turns the network as a ritualistic 'totem' – a universally presenced, numinous and all-enveloping force that is always there, awake and watching – offering techno-spiritual sensations of the digital dead. Arguing that physical graves are media of absence as they mediate a particular form of silence, and as such are *existential media*, I conclude that the jury is still out on whether the over-abundance of digital traces and buzzings of the dead will ever afford such existential virtues.

This discussion touches upon the shape that mourning and memory work take in our contemporary media environment, which leads to the question of the key features of digital rituals. In Chapter 10, "Digital Rituals and the Quest for Existential Security," Johanna Sumiala tackles such issues and contributes to the field of existential media studies by applying a media anthropological approach to the analysis of death and related ritualisation in digital media. She argues that death rituals are considered to be motivated by a fear of annihilation and that rituals have significant transformative and imaginal potential to help individuals and communities cope with that fear and to create new life. The existential dimensions of the inner workings of death rituals are further discussed by empirically investigating the ritual practices of mourning and by paying tribute to the victims, as identified in digital media, of the Charlie Hebdo attack that took place in Paris in January 2015. In conclusion, the chapter seeks to rethink the dilemma of existential security and the ritual search for order and predictability, in the context of liquid digital media.

Can the religious and anthropological connotations of animism illuminate what we do online? This is the argument put forward by Devin Proctor in Chapter 11, "Cybernetic Animism: Non-Human Personhood and the Internet." Proctor defines digital existence by stating that when people use the internet, they are in fact engaging in animist practice. Animism, broadly defined, is an ascription of spiritual essence to non-human entities. Similarly, internet use involves occupying space with both human and non-human others: 'bots' and self-replicating codes, exerting agency and acting in supposedly human ways. Proctor calls this experience *cybernetic animism* – a process that draws from theories of animism, computer science,

20 *Amanda Lagerkvist*

cybernetics, cellular biology and iconicity. Arguing that the experience is not new, but rather ancient and quite common in many areas of the world, Proctor proposes that we can uncover truths about our own technologically hyper-mediated selves by looking to the belief systems of small indigenous societies in Brazilian jungles and Siberian tundra. In the contemporary West, a scientific context that seems diametrically opposed to animist foundations, acknowledging an animist world view is very difficult. Proctor has studied a group that nevertheless does this: the Otherkin community – a group primarily based on the internet, who identify as other-than-human. They recognise their bodies' biological humanity but argue that they also contain non-human aspects, manifesting in non-material forms such as bodily urges, dreams and memories. With their pagan/animist belief structure and reliance on technological mediation, the Otherkin epitomise cybernetic animism. Proctor concludes with a provocation: just as Otherkin must figure out ways to reconcile the animist denial of Western epistemological constructs, so must all internet users recognise that they already live, work and play in animist practice.

By similarly budging other monolithic conceptions prevalent in Western contexts, in Chapter 12, "Death in Life and Life in Death: Forms and Fates of the Human," Connor Graham and Alfred Montoya offer an anthropological and Foucauldian approach to pursue "the human" as a question, a historical, contingent figure, and one of quite recent invention, rather than as a given. They also offer a distinction between the concept of "human-as-is," the being, concrete, existing, mortal instance of a human being, from the concept of "human-as-category," the enframing, abstract, general, human being in discourse as an object. They thereby map the characteristics of "the human" through time; drawing on Foucault's 1970s work examining forms of subjectivity, they also briefly trace its development from the sixteenth-century European adoption of the idea of "Man," through the more contemporary figures of "The Human" in human rights discourse, to Virilio's "terminal citizen." Their tracing shows how evolving notions of "the human" are inseparable from history, politics, media and technology. But critical treatment of this figure also includes an interesting examination of its deployment in scholarship that centres on digital media, design and mortality, including work from existential media studies on the mortal and hurting "exister." Extrapolating further the forms and fates of 'the human' in digital existence, Graham and Montoya thereby offer an analysis of how, in light of the design of new digital technologies that reshape the practices and discourses of death and dying, the incessant malleability of the human form and evolving nature of human existence are assured.

Notes

1 Interview and article by Paul Lewis, in *The Guardian*, 6 October 2017.
2 See, for instance, John Durham Peters, *Speaking into the Air: A History of the Idea of Communication* (1999, p. 33ff).

Digital existence 21

3 This position also finds its proponents across a wide array of different intellectual currents within posthumanism and the new materialism. For instance, this take on technology features in the feminist posthumanism of Donna Haraway, Karen Barad, Susan Hekman and Rosi Braidotti. It is axiomatic in the media theory of W.J.T. Mitchell and Mark B. Hansen, drawing on the work of Bernard Stiegler; and in the media archeology of Jussi Parikka, drawing on Wolfgang Ernst. This approach is also prevalent in the media phenomenology and object oriented ontology of N. Katherine Hayles, drawing on, for instance, Graham Harman and Levy Bryant, and in the actor network theory and speculative realism of authors such as Bruno Latour, Quentin Meillassoux and Alain Badiou. In postphenomenology, it is also manifest in the mediation theory of Peter-Paul Verbeek. Despite their differences, these scholars share a stress on the materiality of mediation, on the agency of matter and on the downplaying *or* re-envisioning of subjectivity. See Bradley (2011) for an overview of some of these approaches.
4 As utopian visionaries argued in the 1990s, see, for example, John Perry Barlow's "A Declaration of the Independence of Cyberspace" (1996).
5 Beyond the opposition between virtual and real, however, scholars who stress originary technicity also budge what they conceive to be untenable modern conventions of distinguishing the natural from the cultural. Within the 'flat ontology' of ANT, scholars will typically hold that an artifice is as real as the natural environment (cf. Latour 2013), and the natural environment is thus always mediated.
6 This very distinction mirrors two alleged positions, one often associated with the early Heidegger (1927/1962) and one with the later Heidegger (1977). According to Don Ihde, one may legitimately speak about Heidegger's *technologies* in the plural, since he actually employed different conceptualisations in different parts of his philosophical work (2010). Ihde argues that there are three conceptions and propositions of technology in Heidegger's *oeuvre*: (1) Technologies are not neutral; (2) Technologies are distinguishable as either traditional tools or modern large-scale systems; (3) Technology is a metaphysical perspective and force. While it may seem as if he was romantically celebrating small-scale tools and equipment as a natural state of affairs, and critiquing large-scale technology as a dangerous 'destining', leading to objectification, this latter danger was in fact deeply ingrained within Western cultural history all along, which would mean that this systemic menace was also built-in in the earlier modes of technological practice. See a discussion in Clemens and Nash, Chapter 1, this volume.
7 Amanda Lagerkvist, "On Virality: Valuing Existential Voids in Digital Media", *Religion Going Public*: http://religiongoingpublic.com/archive/2017/on-virality-valuing-existential-voids-in-digital-media. Accessed: May 20, 2018.

Bibliography

Arendt, H., 1946/1994. What is Existential Philosophy? *In*: H. Arendt. *Essays in Understanding, 1930–1954: Formation, Exile and Totalitarianism*. New York: Schocken Books, 163–187.

Aupers, S. and Houtman, D. (eds.), 2010. *Religions of Modernity: Relocating the Sacred to the Self and the Digital*. Leiden: Brill.

Aydin, C. and Verbeek, P. P., 2015. Transcendence in Technology. *Techné: Research in Philosophy and Technology*, 19 (3), 291–313.

Barlow, J. P., 1996. A Declaration of the Independence of Cyberspace, https://www.eff.org/cyberspace-independence

Berry, D. M., 2011. *The Philosophy of Software: Code and Mediation in the Digital Age*. Basingstoke: Palgrave Macmillan.

22   Amanda Lagerkvist

Bowman, M. and Valk, U. (eds.), 2015. *Vernacular Religion in Everyday Life: Expressions of Belief*. London: Routledge.

Bradley, A., 2011. *Originary Technicity: The Theory of Technology from Marx to Derrida*. Basingstoke: Palgrave Macmillan.

Butler, J., 2004. *Precarious Life: The Powers of Mourning and Violence*. London: Verso.

Campbell, H., 2010. *When Religion Meets New Media*. London: Routledge.

Campbell, H. (ed.), 2012. *Digital Religion: Understanding Religious Practice in New Media Worlds*. London: Routledge.

Campbell, H., 2016. Surveying Theoretical Approaches within Digital Religion Studies. *New Media & Society*, Online first May 27.

Campbell, H. and Lövheim, M., 2013. Introduction: Rethinking the Online–Offline Connection in the Study of Religion Online. *Information, Communication & Society*, 14 (8), 1083–1096.

Cheong, P., Fischer-Nielsen, P., Gelfgren, S. and Ess, C. (eds.), 2012. *Digital Religion, Social Media and Culture: Perspectives, Practices and Futures*. New York: Peter Lang.

Chun, W. H. K., 2011. *Programmed Visions: Software and Memory*. Cambridge, MA: MIT Press.

Chun, W. H. K., 2016. *Updating to Remain the Same: Habitual New Media*. Cambridge, MA: MIT Press.

Clark, T., 2000. Deconstruction and Technology. *In*: N. Royle, ed. *Deconstructions: A User's Guide*. Basingstoke: Palgrave Macmillan, 238–257.

Coeckelbergh, M., 2013. *Human Being @ Risk: Enhancement, Technology, and the Evaluation of Vulnerability Transformations*. Berlin: Springer.

de Beauvoir, S., 1947. *The Ethics of Ambiguity*. Paris: Gallimard.

Derrida, J., 1968/1981. Plato's Pharmacy. *In*: B. Johnson, trans. *Dissemination*. Chicago, IL: University of Chicago Press, 63–171.

de Vries, H. and Weber, S. (eds.), 2001. *Religion & Media*. Stanford, CA: Stanford University Press.

Dreyfus, H., 1984. Between Technē and Technology. *Tulane Studies in Philosophy*, 32 (1984), 23–35.

Ess, C., 2002. Borgmann and the Borg: Consumerism vs. Holding on to Reality. *Techné*, 6 (1).

Ess, C., 2013. *Digital Media Ethics*. New York: Polity.

Ess, C., 2015. New Selves, New Research Ethics? *In*: H. Ingierd and H. Fossheim, eds. *Internet Research Ethics*. Oslo: Cappelen Damm, 48–76.

Ess, C., 2017. Digital Media Ethics. *Oxford Research Encyclopedia of Communication*. Online Publication Date September 2017. doi:10.1093/acrefore/9780190228613.013.508

Floridi, L. (ed.), 2014. *The Onlife Manifesto: Being Human in a Hyperconnected Era*. Berlin: Springer Open.

Grieve, G. P., 2012. Religion. *In*: H. Campbell, ed. *Digital Religion: Understanding Religious Practice in New Media Worlds*. London: Routledge.

Gunkel, D. J. and Taylor, P. A., 2014. *Heidegger and the Media*. New York: Polity.

Habermas, J., 2008. Secularism's Crisis of Faith: Notes on Post-Secular Society. *New Perspectives Quarterly*, 25 (2008), 17–29.

Han, B.-C., 2014. *I svärmen: Tankar om det digitala*. Stockholm: Ersatz.

Heidegger, M., 1927/1962. *Being and Time*. New York: Harper & Row.

Digital existence 23

Heidegger, M., 1977. *The Question Concerning Technology and Other Essays*. New York: Garland Publishing.

Helland, C., 2000. Online-Religion/Religion-Online and Virtual Communities. *In*: D. E. Cowan and J. K. Hadden, eds. *Religion on the Internet: Research Prospects and Promises*. New York: JAI Press.

Helland, C., 2012. Ritual. *In*: H. Campbell, ed. *Digital Religion: Understanding Religious Practice in New Media Worlds*. London: Routledge.

Hjarvard, S. and Lövheim M. (eds.), 2012. *Mediatization and Religion: Nordic Perspectives*. Göteborg: Nordicom.

Hong, S.-H., 2015. Presence, or the Sense of Being-There and Being-with in the New Media Society. *First Monday*, 20 (10). Available at: http://journals.uic.edu/ojs/index.php/fm/article/view/5932 (accessed: 5 October 2015).

Hoover, S., 2012. Foreword: Practice, Autonomy and Authority in the Digitally Religious and Digitally Spiritual. *In*: P. H. Cheong et al., eds. *Digital Religion, Social Media and Culture, Perspectives, Practices and Futures*. New York: Peter Lang, vii–xi.

Hoover, S. and Echabibi, N., 2014. Media Theory and the 'Third Spaces of Digital Religion.' Essay. Available at: https://thirdspacesblog.files.wordpress.com/2014/05/third-spaces-and-media-theory-essay-2-0.pdf (accessed: 20 August 2014).

Hoover, S. and Lundby, K. (eds.), 1997. *Rethinking Media, Religion and Culture*. London: Sage.

Hoskins, A., 2014. The Right to be Forgotten in Post-Scarcity Culture. *In*: A. Ghezzi, Â. Pereira and L. Vesnić-Alujević, eds. *The Ethics of Memory in a Digital Age: Interrogating the Right to be Forgotten*. Basingstoke: Palgrave Macmillan, 50–64.

Hui, Y., 2016. *On the Existence of Digital Objects*. Minneapolis: University of Minnesota Press.

Ihde, D., 1979. *Technics and Praxis*. Dordrecht: D. Reidel Publishing Company.

Ihde, D., 1990. *Technology and the Lifeworld: From Garden to Earth*. Bloomington: Indiana University Press.

Ihde, D., 2010. *Heidegger's Technologies: Postphenomenological Perspectives*. New York: Fordham University Press.

Jackson, M., 2011. *Life within Limits: Well-Being in a World of Want*. Durham, NC: Duke University Press.

Jackson. M., 2013. Lecture at 'Studying Religion in the Post-9/11 World: The Importance of Taking Religion Seriously from a Humanities Perspective in Troubled Times.' Harvard Divinity School, The Center for the Study of World Religions. Available at: www.youtube.com/watch?v=623Eovasu-U (accessed: 10 August 2015).

Jaspers, K., 1932/1970. *Philosophy* (Vol. 2). Chicago, IL and London: University of Chicago Press.

Kember, S. and Zylinska, J., 2012. *Life after New Media: Mediation as Vital Process*. Boston, MA: MIT Press.

Kierkegaard, S., 1846/1960. *Concluding Unscientific Postscript*. Princeton, NJ: Princeton University Press.

Kierkegaard, S., 1849/1989. *Sickness Unto Death by Anti-Climacus*. Harmondsworth: Penguin.

Kim, J., 2001. Phenomenology of Digital-Being. *Human Studies*, 24, 87–111.

Kittler, F., 1999. *Gramophone, Film, Typewriter*. Stanford, CA: Stanford University Press.

24 Amanda Lagerkvist

Kittler, F., 2009. Towards an Ontology of Media. *Theory Culture Society*, 26 (2–3), 23–31.

Lagerkvist, A., 2013. New Memory Cultures and Death: Existential Security in the Digital Memory Ecology. *Thanatos*, 2 (2). Available at: https://thanatosjournal.files.wordpress.com/2012/12/lagerkvist_newmemorycultures_than2220131.pdf (accessed: 21 August 2014).

Lagerkvist, A., 2014. A Quest for *Communitas*: Rethinking Mediated Memory Existentially. *Nordicom Information*, 36 (2), 205–218.

Lagerkvist, A., 2015. The Netlore of the Infinite: Death (and beyond) in the Digital Memory Ecology. *The New Review of Hypermedia and Multimedia*, 21 (1–2), 185–195.

Lagerkvist, A., 2016. Existential Media: Toward a Theorization of Digital Thrownness. *New Media & Society*, Online first 13 June 2016.

Lagerkvist, A., 2017. The Media End: Digital Afterlife Agencies and Techno-Existential Closure. *In*: A. Hoskins, ed. *Digital Memory Studies: Media Pasts in Transition*, New York: Routledge, 48–84.

Lagerkvist, A. and Andersson, Y., 2017. The Grand Interruption: Death Online and Mediated Lifelines of Shared Vulnerability. *Feminist Media Studies*, Online first June 7, 2017.

Langlois, G., 2014. *Meaning in the Age of Social Media*. Basingstoke: Palgrave Macmillan.

Latour, B., 2013. *An Inquiry into Modes of Existence: An Anthropology of the Moderns*. Cambridge, MA: Harvard University Press.

Levinas, E., 1961/1991. *Totality and Infinity: An Essay on Exteriority*. Dordrecht: Kluwer Academic Publishers.

Lindgren, S., 2017. *Digital Media and Society*. London: Sage.

Lövheim, M., 2011. Mediatisation of Religion: A Critical Appraisal. *Culture and Religion*, 12 (2): 153–166.

Lövheim, M. and Campbell, H., 2017. Considering Critical Methods and Theoretical Lenses in Digital Religion Studies. *New Media & Society*, Special Issue: Critical methods and theoretical lenses in Digital Religion studies, 19 (1), pp. 5–14.

Lynch, G., Mitchell, J. and Strhan, A. (eds.), 2012. *Religion, Media and Culture: A Reader*. London: Routledge.

Mayer-Schönberger, V., 2008. *Delete: The Virtue of Forgetting in the Digital Age*. Princeton, NJ: Princeton University Press.

Miller, V., 2015. *The Crisis of Presence in Contemporary Culture: Ethics, Privacy and Disclosure in Mediated Social Life*. London: Sage.

Mitchell, L., 2014. Life on Automatic: Facebook's Archival Subject. *First Monday*, 19 (2). Available at: http://firstmonday.org/article/view/4825/3823 (accessed: 15 August 2015).

Morgan, D. (ed.), 2008. *Keywords in Media, Religion and Culture*. London: Routledge.

Morgan, D. (ed.), 2010. *Religion and Material Culture: The Matter of Belief*. London: Routledge.

Peters, J. D., 1997. Beauty's Veils: The Ambivalent Iconoclasm of Kierkegaard and Benjamin. *In*: A. Dudley, ed. *The Image in Dispute*. Austin: University of Texas Press, 9–32.

Peters, J. D., 1999. *Speaking into the Air: A History of the Idea of Communication*. Chicago, IL: University of Chicago Press.

Peters, J. D., 2015a. *The Marvelous Clouds: Towards a Philosophy of Elemental Media*. Chicago, IL: University of Chicago Press.

Peters, J. D., 2015b. Life, Death and Time on the Digital Ship. Keynote lecture at *Digital Existence: Memory, Meaning, Vulnerability*, Conference organized by DIGMEX and The Sigtuna Foundation, 26–28 October 2015.

Pinchevski, A., 2005. *By Way of Interruption: Levinas and the Ethics of Communication*. Pittsburgh, PA: Duquesne University Press.

Pybus, J., 2015. Accumulating Affect: Social Networks and Their Archives of Feelings. *In*: K. Hillis, S. Paasonen and M. Petit, eds. *Networked Affect*. Boston, MA: MIT Press, 235–250.

Radde-Antweiler, K., 2008. Virtual Religion: A Religious and Ritual Topography of Second Life. *Online–Heidelberg Journal of Religions on the Internet*, 3.

Radde-Antweiler, K., 2012. Authenticity. *In*: H. Campbell, ed. *Digital Religion: Understanding Religious Practice in New Media Worlds*. London: Routledge.

Scannell, P., 2014. *Television and the Meaning of 'Live.'* New York: Polity.

Schwartz, M., 2018. On Love and Touch: The Radical Haptics of Gestational Surrogacy. *In*: Z. Papacharissi, ed. *A Networked Self and Love*. New York: Routledge, 213–229.

Smolicki, J., 2017. *Para-Archives: Rethinking Personal Archiving Practices in the Times of Capture Culture*. Doctoral Dissertation, Malmö University.

Stiegler, B., 1998. *Technics and Time, 1: The Fault of Epimetheus*. Stanford, CA: Stanford University Press.

Stiegler, B., 2010. Memory. *In*: W. J. T. Mitchell and M. B. Hansen, eds. *Critical Terms for Media Studies*. Chicago, IL: University of Chicago Press, 64–87.

Stiegler, B., 2012. Relational Ecology and the Digital Pharmakon. *Culture Machine*, 13, 1–19.

Stiegler, B., 2013. *What Makes Life Worth Living: On Pharmacology*. Cambridge: Polity Press.

Stolow, J., 2005. Media and/as Religion. *Theory, Culture & Society*, 22 (4), 119–145.

Stolow, J. (ed.), 2013. *Deus in Machina: Religion, Technology and the Things in-Between*. New York: Fordham University Press.

Sumiala, J., 2013. *Media and Ritual: Death, Community and Everyday Life*. London: Routledge.

Sumiala-Seppänen, J., Lundby, K., & Salokangas, R. (eds.), 2006. *Implications of the Sacred in (Post)Modern Media*. Gothenburg: Nordicom.

Taylor, C., 2007. *A Secular Age*. Boston, MA: Harvard University Press.

Turkle, S., 2011. *Alone Together: Why We Expect More from Technology and Less from Each Other*. New York: Basic Books.

van Dijck, J., 2013. *The Culture of Connectivity: A Critical History of Social Media*. Oxford: Oxford University Press.

Verbeek, P.-P., 2005. *What Things Do: Philosophical Reflections on Technology, Agency and Design*. University Park: Pennsylvania State University Press.

Verbeek, P.-P., 2011. *Moralizing Technology: Understanding and Designing the Morality of Things*. Chicago: University of Chicago Press.

Walter, T., 2016. The Dead Who Become Angels: Bereavement and Vernacular Religion. *OMEGA: Journal of Death & Dying*, 73 (1), 3–28.

Woodhead, L. and Heelas, P., 2000. *Religion in Modern Times: An Interpretive Anthology*. London: Wiley-Blackwell.

Part I
Media ontologies

1 Irremediability
On the very concept of digital ontology

Justin Clemens and Adam Nash

The implications of the digital for ontology

This essay discusses what we and many others have termed 'digital ontology' (hereafter DO). We begin by posing the following linked questions: What is DO? Does DO 'exist' at all? If so, how does DO differ from 'traditional ontology,' or, at least, from 'non-digital' or 'pre-digital' ontology? What does the adjective 'digital' signify here? How does it differ from adjectives that may seem quasi-synonymous with it, such as 'data' or 'information'? Why should we speak about *ontology* or perhaps even *ontologies* (plural) at all, let alone *digital* ontologies? Should we not rather speak – as many have and do – of something like 'digital physics'? And how would we go about answering these questions if we did not avail ourselves of what seems to be a fundamental feature of ontological questioning, that is, a search for a method? Yet what if it is precisely the search for a method that the 'digital' undermines or overturns? Indeed, does the digital also overturn the concept of 'ontology' itself? Could it be that DO is a paradoxical, nonsensical or contradictory phenomenon that resists its own consistent formalisation?

We reuptake these difficult questions here in order to offer some background, arguments and provisional answers, and do so in a sequence of regulated steps. First, we stage some of the new issues raised by digital technologies, precisely by bringing out the problems that digital technology itself poses for research into digital technology. This staging is done by way of what has only very recently become – in the last two decades – one of the most commonplace of everyday acts: a browser search on the internet for a phrase. Although the very many complexities of such searching are by now well-studied and well-known, we briefly rehearse some of these here in order to draw out a few of their consequences for research.

Second, in doing so, we identify, situate and explicate several major strands of thinking regarding DO today, with respect to three modalities in particular: the anthropological, the analytic and the physical, represented here respectively by the recent work of Tom Boellstoerff, Luciano Floridi and Edward Fredkin/Stephen Wolfram and others. We will show that each of these modalities comes to be caught in something like a contradiction, which derives from their uncertain self-positioning between epistemological

30 Justin Clemens and Adam Nash

and ontological concerns. Precisely because they begin with the new *propositions* concerning *knowledge* that seem to be generated by digital technologies, they end attempting to *know* by constructing doctrines of *being* out of their own contingent epistemological closures. Here, the conceptual restrictions derive from a commitment to a covert dialectic of the limited/unlimited/delimited, whereby what we know becomes either a limit to our knowledge of the being of the other (e.g., being as the other of knowledge), thereby alternatively refusing *or* projecting an empty vision of being onto the other side of this knowledge *or* they project this knowledge in an unlimited fashion *directly* onto 'being itself' (e.g., the universe is itself a digital computer). This apparent divergence derives from their systematic solidarity with each other regarding the priority of *epistemic* questions.

Third, following this summary, analysis and critique of these key contemporary positions regarding DO, we return to some of the most influential twentieth-century thinkers of the relation between technology and ontology, including Martin Heidegger, Gilbert Simondon, Bernard Stiegler and Alain Badiou. This return enables us to establish certain requisites for *any* ontology that avoid the difficulties that beset Boellstoerff et al., even if, in turn, we will disagree with these thinkers regarding the proper method and sense of a *contemporary* ontology. Our disagreement will hinge on certain new pragmatic and conceptual phenomena exposed by digital technologies that have no real precedent in any metaphysical or logical tradition, whether mathematical or naturalist, materialist or idealist.

Here, the evidence is provided by three essentially contemporary problems, simultaneously conceptual and technical. The first of these is the so-called 'P v. NP problem,' formalised in 1972, an as-yet unsolved dilemma which poses whether certain computational problems whose solution can be rapidly checked in polynomial time can also be solved in polynomial time. The second concerns the claims made by non-classical ('paraconsistent') logics developed in the wake of operational difficulties that emerged first in post–World War II computing, which don't uphold an absolute exclusion of contradiction, in contrast to classical logic which depends upon the law of non-contradiction. Third is the operational necessity that all data be simultaneously modular and modulated, that is, at once created as elemental 'bits,' yet bits that are essentially mutable. We will treat these aporias as opening onto ontological questions.

So, fourth, taking up the challenge of these aporias – that is, *impasses* of *knowledge* that do not thereby necessarily designate immutable *limits* to our thinking of *being* – we suggest that it is in this epistemological rift opened by digital technology that the new lineaments of a properly DO can be discerned. In conclusion, then and on this basis, we briefly present a new theory of DO, which doesn't treat contradictions as explosive or entailing only trivialities. Rather, we maintain that: ontology is always onto-technology, that is, digital; onto-technology is always a-temporal, im-personal, and inconsistent; its contemporary character is discerned through the *new impasses* that have been revealed to us by binary computation; these impasses deliver a new sense of being that also immediately and irremediably affects the grounds of knowing and action too. For reasons that will hopefully become apparent in the course of this chapter, we will name this paraconsistent DO *ir-re-mediable*.

Too much, too little, too fast, too diverse, too repetitive

On 7 January 2017, an online search from Melbourne, Australia, for the syntagm 'digital ontology' turned up 'About 1,040,000 results' in '(0.59 seconds).' Almost nothing in this sentence would have made any sense that was not science-fictional until very recently – perhaps not even until the beginning of the twenty-first century. Yet, through a version of a paradox well-known to media scholars, the unprecedented speed, reach, size and accessibility of such an information search seems, through its very power, to have been almost-immediately 'naturalised.' This paradox – that what is most novel and most shocking about contemporary information technology is also its most banal, everyday feature – should induce us to think again about the status of this 'banal estrangement.' For the rapid transformation of irreality to banality hasn't necessarily served media scholars well. Part of the problem with such 'an approach to an approach' is that it may have already been irremediably falsified by the new technologies themselves. The very self-evidence and extremity of the information revolution may, by another, associated paradox, seriously inhibit, if not render impossible, any viable account (e.g., well-founded, evidence-based, plausible, or persuasive) of its status. Perhaps it is the case that these technologies make it impossible to know the very knowledge that they alone make possible to know. Modern media may be, precisely, *ir-re-mediable*.

Even trying to face this truly gigantic set of results, available to us practically immediately, should suggest some serious, perhaps constitutively disabling practical difficulties (see Andrejevic 2013). No one person – nor two people, nor even a dedicated team of people – would be able to sift through this vast array of results in any acceptable fashion in any acceptable time. Given the global extension, sheer number, speed and instability of the information, the evidence itself beggars any possibility of a synoptic account, let alone the viable reproduction or review of the results by a third party. To refer to a Hegelian concept: the paradox of absolute knowledge is that its instantiation entails its evacuation. This is a theme foundational to our argument, to which we will return throughout this essay.

Let us simply take the first page of our search, on which there are 11 results: 'Against Digital Ontology – Luciano Floridi'; 'Digital Ontology – Cultural Anthropology'; 'Is There an Ontology to the Digital – Cultural Anthropology'; 'Digital Ontologies | Material World'; 'What Is Digital Ontology | IGI Global'; 'Against Digital Ontology – PhilSci Archive'; 'Digital Physics – Wikipedia'; 'Against Digital Ontology | SpringerLink'; 'Against Digital

32 Justin Clemens and Adam Nash

Ontology – Oxford Scholarship'; '[PDF] Against Digital Ontology – Luciano Floridi'; 'For Whom the Ontology Turns: Theorizing the Digital Real.'

There are a number of relevant features about this shortlist. First, the repetitions: Luciano Floridi's paper *Against Digital Ontology* appears five times, in at least three different versions (the author's prepublication manuscript, a paper in the journal *Synthese*, and a chapter in the book *The Philosophy of Information*), linked to four different sites, two of these academic sharing sites (Philsci-Archive and Philosophy of Information), two of them proprietary publishing sites (Oxford Scholarship Online and Springer). Two of the links are to '*Cultural Anthropology* (print ISSN 0886–7356; online ISSN 1548–1360), the peer-reviewed journal of the Society for Cultural Anthropology, a section of the American Anthropological Association'; another to the blog 'Material World,' based at University College London, which hosted workshops which led to the *Cultural Anthropology* publications already noted; one link is to an article by Tom Boellstorff, who is also a contributor to the aforementioned *Cultural Anthropology* issue; another is to a Wikipedia article on 'Digital physics'; yet another is to the proprietary site IGI Global, which provides the definition 'The view that reality is essentially digital in nature,' and linking to 'Learn more in: A Scientist-Poet's Account of Ontology in Information Science.' All the sites are English language, linked to powerful institutions based mainly in the United Kingdom or the United States.

The well-known issue of algorithmic closure – that Google searches operate according to proprietary algorithms that select results on the basis of prior searches, among other factors – is alarmingly patent from the outset. Searches in French for '*ontologie numérique*' turned up 'About 163,000 results (0.34 seconds); in German, for *digitale Ontologie*, 'About 223,000 results (0.69 seconds).' Despite the literalism of such translations of 'digital ontology,' it is clear that, even in closely related modern European languages, there is a notable divergence of terms and results. Presumably it is also of some significance that the comparable Wikipedia pages for '*Physique numérique (théorique)*' and '*Digitale Physik*' also turn up on the first page of search results, offering very similar accounts to the English version. The problems of filter bubbles, repetitions-too-numerous-to-handle, uncategorised or miscategorised links, indefinite linkages, and incommensurable multiple languages, can thus be added to the difficulties regarding any initial basic efforts to delimit the field.

One might initially think that these difficulties could be overlooked or treated as if they were simply a matter of size and speed, such that so-called big data methodologies, software and hardware would be able to handle. Indeed, these new methods might seem to be the only ways to handle such vast unstable quantities of information. Unfortunately, we need to specify right away that, for structural reasons, this cannot be the case. On the contrary, big data simply exacerbates the problems, rather than resolves them – and in a number of important ways. We have already mentioned the fluctuating semantics of philosophical keywords, as well as their variable translation both intra- and inter-lingually. We could also immediately invoke the gap (discussed below in more detail) between terminology and concepts. We could also point to the difficulty of deciding the status of a model of the logic of a system which takes place within the system that it is itself nominally modelling. Certainly, some of these problems are ancient, even foundational philosophical *topoi*, and therefore not dependent upon digital technology. Yet they are by no means circumvented or resolved by the new technologies: on the contrary, they are radicalised.

Even if we were to act as if these difficulties had not insuperably altered the very status of knowledge itself, and were to turn to the content of the first page articles in English, we would still encounter severe, perhaps irreconcilable differences regarding the sense and reference of the syntagm 'digital ontology.' Let's take only three of these, that is, three quite different projects which turned up, albeit in different guises, on our first page of English language results, Luciano Floridi, Tom Boellstoerff, and the so-called digital physicists. As we shall see, these are quite different projects; yet, despite these differences, we will also suggest some unexpected continuities. Whether our demonstration holds at all, even constrained to the very first page, is something that, as we have said, is today *absolutely indeterminable*, given the affordances of digital technology itself.

An informational ontology?

Floridi's much-circulated and much-cited attack on the very notion of 'digital ontology' takes the phrase in a highly technical sense: the doctrine that "the ultimate nature of reality is digital, and the universe is a computational system equivalent to a Turing machine."[1] Floridi wishes to criticise this account in favour of his own sceptical proposal for an *informational ontology*, that is, that "the ultimate nature of reality is structural."

Drawing on Immanuel Kant's famous account of the antinomies of pure reason in the first *Critique*, he seeks to show how the difference between considering nature as discrete (digital) as opposed to continuous (analogue) is itself a consequence of "features of the level of abstraction modelling the system, not of the modelled system in itself" (Floridi 2009, p. 160). In reconstructing the alleged claims of DO, Floridi considers its fundamental thesis to be that the physical universe is founded on discrete entities, that all "reality can be decomposed into ultimate, discrete *indivisibilia*" (Floridi 2009, p. 153). Floridi gives an extended thought experiment in which four agents, which he angelically names Michael (an ontological agent, "capable of showing that reality in itself is either digital or analogue"), Gabriel (a translation agent), Rafael (an epistemic agent) and Uriel (who shows the irreducibility in observations of reality), all resembling Turing machines, interact in such a way as to render it moot whether reality in itself is either digital or analogue. If there is not the space here to examine Floridi's impressive neo-Kantian

34 Justin Clemens and Adam Nash

argument in the requisite detail, it is worth underlining that it depends upon an intricate faculty structure which relies on there being a gap between the *noumenal* ('reality in itself') and any possible knowledge we might have of it. For Floridi, again, "digital and analogue are features of the level of abstraction," and not at all of reality itself. (One might suggest that this judgment is itself a consequence of the theory's initial separation of knowledge and the real, which, in giving priority to epistemology, already happily determines the outcome of the case.)

Floridi is therefore concerned to separate the 'informational' from the 'digital,' precisely because, depending on the level of abstraction, the former can present *either* as analogue or digital, continuous or discrete. Moreover, as Janice Richardson specifies, Floridi elsewhere

> distinguishes between the infosphere, as the environment in which our information is transferred, and the Infosphere (with a capital I). The reference to the 'Infosphere' involves a bolder ontological claim. The Infosphere refers to everything that exists; the whole of Being.
> (Richardson 2016, p. 139)

Such Being is constituted by "structural objects that are neither substantial nor material . . . but cohering clusters of data" (Richardson 2016, p. 139). It seems that Floridi is proposing an ontology that gives us transmaterialist organisations of data as its basic, well, *data*.

In his more recent work on the conceptual logic of systems modelling, in which Floridi offers criticisms of the resources of both Kantian (conditions of possibility as feasibility requirements) and Hegelian options (conditions of systemic instability) while calling for a third way, he continues to insist on the priority of the epistemological over the ontological. Here Floridi's own imagery is (unconsciously) revealing: "compare the conceptual logic of a watch with the conceptual logic of the design of a watch," he says (Floridi 2017, p. 496). But a watch is exemplarily an eighteenth-century mechanical time-piece, whereas the logic of contemporary design, no matter its level of abstraction or, indeed, whatever its alleged materiality, is that it is a construction of *information about the information from which it is made*. This suggests that the opposition Floridi offers, between the (allegedly more) modest claim to simply model a system ('epistemological') and the alternate claim that "the logic of a model of a system is the logic of the system" ('ontological') is false or, at least, insufficient. His own third option is to propose one that attends to "a design logic of future conditions of feasibility of a system" (Floridi 2017, p. 516). But another third (or fourth) option – which doesn't, *contra* Floridi, presume that *knowledge* is paramount for such a program – is precisely that 'the logic of a model of a system is included in the system which it models.' We will see how this latter option functions below in our discussion of Heidegger and others.

A digital ontology?

Boellstorff relies on a different, far less technical sense of 'digital ontology' than Floridi, taking off from what he sees as a deleterious general opposition between 'the digital' (or 'the virtual,' which he understands, relatively plausibly, as essentially synonymous in most of the articles he surveys) and 'the real' (see Boellstorff 2016). Noting that influential scholars from a variety of disciplinary backgrounds make the same reduction of physical to real, and digital to unreal, Boellstorff presents rather a 'quadrant,' in which we find the more complex set of oppositions 'A physical and real,' 'B digital and real,' 'C physical and unreal,' 'D digital and unreal,' before proceeding to a potted account of the imbrication of ontology in anthropology along the lines of a 'turn,' i.e., a trope with many 'entailments,' some good ('helpful'), other bad ('unhelpful'). As Boellstorff continues:

> Metaphors are not all-determining, but their entailments matter, shaping and revealing pathways of thought and practice. With regard to ontology, the most damaging entailment of the turn metaphor is that turning takes place around an axis, a still centre held constant.

Boellstorff's method requires him to be at once anthropologically/sociologically self-locating (he speaks of his personal and institutional background) and linguistically saturated (he self-reflexively interrogates the work done by the dominant metaphors in the field), as he surveys a slew of contemporary academic material dedicated to the theme of 'ontology.' By doing so, he comes to an axial decision regarding this material:

> If the ontological turn pivots around a bolt of difference shared with its epistemological foil, the danger is a form of closure, rather than an extension that opens to new conceptualizations of the human and parahuman. One reason I do not cast my intervention in the language of critique is that such language has largely served to further rotate analysis around the bolt of difference.
>
> (Boellstorff 2016)

Boellstroff's proposal is to shift to an 'archipelagic' account of ontology, which, instead of privileging difference *per se*, draws on the work of Gabriel Tarde to consider imitation as "a relation of similitude that preserves difference." Here, then, we have an open and relational ontology in which diverse materials which are themselves already bundles of mimetic relations constantly enter into new relations that create, as they preserve, existing differences.

In these two presentations we have too-rapidly summarised, the disciplinary methods, sets of references, conceptions of 'digital ontology,' and

36 Justin Clemens and Adam Nash

conclusions are so wildly different that it is difficult to see how they are even speaking about the 'same' 'thing.' Floridi, drawing on a broadly analytical philosophical framework deriving from Kant, discusses the abstract structuring of information by new technologies according to the conceptual projections made by their adherents onto the structure of physical being itself; he argues that such a projection falls prey to the Kantian account of the antinomies that necessarily arise when forms of presentation are taken for things themselves, and counters accordingly that the proper response is to recognise the primacy of the operations of the multiple structures that produce information (representation) as such. The universe is not, therefore, a computer (discrete, computational, deterministic), but rather a totality of structures of information. Boellstroff, by contrast, relies integrally upon varied phenomenological-linguistic experiences to make his points, which for the most part circumvent the technical aspects of the new media – such as Second Life – of which he gives some 'thick' descriptions. Neither Floridi nor Boellstroff are working with the same sense of the terms, the same evidence, the same references, the same arguments, nor perhaps even with the same object.

A digital philosophy?

Defining an ontology by and through epistemological claims is especially evident in the work of the so-called *Digital Physicists*, as exemplified chiefly by the scientists Stephen Wolfram and Edward Fredkin. Positing the universe as a digital computer, the very assertion that Floridi attempts to do away with, in a manner that is eminently susceptible to Floridi's Kantian argument of the antimonies as discussed above, the assertion nonetheless bears more than a passing resemblance to Floridi's own informational epistemology-as-ontology. The basics of the theory are properly characterised as *it from bit*, a concept first proposed by the quantum physicist John Wheeler in 1989, where "every physical quantity, every it, derives its ultimate significance from bits, binary yes-or-no indication" (Wheeler 1995; see also Floridi 2009 for a concise summation). Digital physics attempts to show that all of everything – not just matter, but also movement, thought, evolution, literally *everything* – is the result of ongoing, elaborate processes of computations built of fundamental binary operations. Yet it ultimately offers a description of a process-based philosophy that is not so dissimilar to other such philosophies prominent in the twentieth century, including those of Bergson, Whitehead, Simondon and Deleuze.

Stephen Wolfram's *Principle of Computational Equivalence*, for example, states that "any process whatsoever can be viewed as a computation" (Wolfram 2002, p. 716). Based on Turing machine-like finite-state computations, as expressed in *cellular automata*, Wolfram has done an impressive amount of experimental work investigating rules to apply to cellular automata in order to show that enormous complexity, including such that can imitate physical processes, can emerge from relatively simple starting states. He goes further to assert that not only can universality (i.e., that any complex process of computations can imitate, or actually become, any other complex process of computations) be achieved by these processes, and not only that any sufficiently complex process is in fact universal, but that there is an upper limit to computational sophistication and that "almost all processes except those that are obviously simple actually achieve this limit" (Wolfram 2002, p. 721).

Wolfram goes on to assert that this kind of computation therefore subtends all phenomena in the universe, without actually doing any philosophical, or even logical, work to show that this assertion can be true, rather than simply a representation of observable phenomena. For his part, Edward Fredkin makes this same assertion and goes so far as to call his ideas *Digital Philosophy* (Fredkin nd). Underlying this philosophy are several key assumptions, most notably that discrete entities ultimately constitute all qualities and therefore can be represented in binary form. This assumption certainly allows the systematic experimentation of Fredkin's digital philosophy to produce results, such as with Wolfram's cellular automata, and as such it bears a resemblance to other attempts at ontology that rely on certain axioms in order to be useful, most notably Alain Badiou's set-theoretical ontology as discussed below. And of course, such an assumption subtends the idea and practice of digital computing generally. These scientific investigations of process do not self-evidently prove or demonstrate any legitimate ontological claims, which remain simply as descriptions, observations or unsubstantiated claims. This conflation of demonstrable representation of observable phenomena with rigorous philosophical claims is not uncommon in contemporary scientific literature, which sometimes claims, as does Stephen Hawking in the tellingly named *The Grand Design*, that "philosophy is dead" (Hawking and Mlodinow 2010, p. 5), whilst pursuing such baldly philosophical goals as a *theory of everything* without so much as an attempt at showing how this epistemology has managed to, or can, replace ontology.

Nonetheless, scientific experiment and observation continues to yield the, ostensibly foundational, two elements (or, more accurately, *principles*) of quantisation and relation. In quantum physics, as implied in its name, the most basic processes of the universe rely on quantised units (or perhaps, rather, values), with no continuous 'in-between.' Some quantum physicists and philosophers are trying to conceive of this as an ontological condition, by asserting that these units or values only have meaning in relation to other units or values. In other words, there are no individuals at the quantum level, only quantised relations (see Barad 2007).[2] The rationale for such an ontological assertion is an assumption that empirical observation has peeled back enough layers that it now reveals the very workings of reality. In the Kantian terms of two such philosophers, the logicians Newton da Costa and Décio Krause, *Empirical Reality* has coincided with *Reality*, inconsistency is in Reality (Hegel was right!), and a reconsideration of

38 *Justin Clemens and Adam Nash*

inconsistency is required (Costa and Krause 2014). The theoretical physicist Carlo Rovelli has developed a theory called relational quantum mechanics (RQM) to countenance this. In RQM, any absolute value or property (such as state, time, quantity, event, etc), is replaced only with informational relations. The ontological move comes in the assertion that "quantum mechanics is a theory about the physical description of physical systems relative to other systems, and this is a complete description of the world" (Rovelli 1996, p. 1637), and that there is no need to distinguish between systems (for example, observer/observed) because all that exists is information, which is shared between systems in relation.

As David Bohm says, "all that is clear about the quantum theory is that it contains an algorithm for computing the probabilities of experimental results. But it gives no physical account of individual quantum processes" (Bohm and Hiley 1993, p. 2). For Rovelli, in a move that perfectly aligns with Simondon's transductive process as described below, this is because it is ontologically true that there are no individual processes, but only relations of information.[3] Recently, Newton da Costa and Olimpia Lombardi have attempted to formulate a paraconsistent logical modal ontology that is adequate to this assertion of non-individuality (Costa and Lombardi 2014). Of paraconsistent logics, we will speak more later. For now we note the reliance, proposed in RQM, on an informational model that echoes Floridi's notion of information structures and exchange, even if in RQM it is a more strictly Shannonist definition of information, i.e., as the number of alternatives, or choices, available to any interaction when one alternative "is chosen from the set, all choices being equally likely" (Shannon 1949, p. 1). At the same time, it reinforces certain assumptions that motivate the experiments of the digital physicists.

No ontology?

'Digital ontology,' then? It seems that there is now simultaneously too much to know, too little to know, too many ways to know, and that things are too fast to know. This perhaps suggests the need for a radical scepticism about the very possibility of DO. We therefore underline that the theories of information and their operations we have quickly examined above still take the problematic of epistemology as the entry point to any possible ontology, where 'ontology' comes to be the term deployed as a supplement to the epistemological issues, whether as a uncircumventable cognitive metastructure or as a shifting embodied topology. Yet if ontology is still often seen as an addendum to epistemology, the global impact of the new technologies has evidently been so intense that ontology – the question or problem of being, of existential possibilities – cannot be entirely avoided. In other words, it seems we can't circumvent the problem of the ontology of our new technological real – which undoubtedly fuels the contemporary enthusiasm for ontologies of all kinds. But what is, if anything, specifically new – or, if you like, 'emergent' – about the contemporary enthusiasm for 'digital ontology'?

This might seem a familiar issue in any scholarly field, 'the experts disagree.' But this would be to miss, in addition to the features we have already listed – scale, number, speed, redundancy, proprietary, automation, etc. – the peculiar centrality of the term 'ontology' in the realm of the 'digital.' For perhaps the current situation constitutes the beginnings of ontology, rather than its ruin. We might even be tempted to assert that the contemporary enthusiasm for ontology is a direct consequence of the new technologies. 'Ontology,' which was traditionally an extremely technical component of the metaphysics of being (the word was only coined in the seventeenth century as an orientation and support for early modern taxonomies of ancient metaphysics), has become a crucial signifier across an enormous range of disciplines that previously would have subordinated, ignored, or even rejected its claims, not least for working computer scientists themselves.

This suggests that ontology has become central to the lived lives (e.g., the phenomenology, the experiences, the practices, the thoughts, etc.) of people globally as something that affects them – us! – integrally, as a direct consequence of digital networks and devices that now constitute a new dispensation of action and knowledge. In fact, as our too-short shortlist already indicates, we find an astonishing range of ontological questioning everywhere, and it is clear that this ontological questioning is explicitly integrated with the questions concerning technology. Moreover, it is attempting this along extra-epistemological lines. Having already suggested the difficulties of ontological questioning that begins from the epistemological issues, we now turn to several peak moments in the theorisation of this integral bond between ontology and technology which try to circumvent the priority of epistemology. If it is impossible to do justice to the thought of the pertinent figures examined here, we will nonetheless attempt to extract certain key innovations in the thinking of onto-technology without undue reduction. From there, we briefly sketch an ontology that, while seeking to integrate these strong modellings, also seeks to go past them to establish the elements of a contemporary DO of inconsistency.

Being, time, technology: Martin Heidegger

Martin Heidegger remains one of the crucial touchstones for any contemporary thinking of the relation between ontology and technology today. The central figures of so-called 'Object Oriented Ontology' (OOO), Graham Harman, Ian Bogost and Timothy Morton, for example, explicitly take off from and constantly return to Heidegger's thinking, while media theorists such as Friedrich Kittler and Rafael Capurro also point to Heidegger as key to the thinking of technology per se (see Kittler 2006; Capurro and Holgate 2011). Even those thinkers who are highly critical of Heidegger's

40   Justin Clemens and Adam Nash

contribution, mark him as indispensable for the return of ontology in twentieth-century philosophy.

It is therefore crucial to underline that one of Heidegger's decisive interventions was to return 'ontology' *per se* to the centre of all thinking, metaphysical, philosophical, or otherwise. Indeed, the declaration of such a return constitutes the famous *incipit* of *Being and Time* (1996 (1927)), in which Heidegger analyses the history of philosophy not only as a 'forgetting of the question of the meaning of Being,' but, given the forgetting has itself been so thoroughly accomplished nobody is any longer aware of it, 'a forgetting of the forgetting of the question of the meaning of Being.' Yet this state of affairs has in some profound way itself been *destined* by the very thinkers who first broached the question of Being, the ancient Greeks. The opening of the question was therefore already in a certain sense the closure of the question; the re-opening of the question requires an attempt to construct another way of opening-in-the-double-closure-of-the-original-opening. Let us note: Heidegger fundamentally questions the very division between epistemology and ontology we noted above in our discussion of some of the contemporary opinions regarding digital and informational ontology; or, rather, he confronts the fact that epistemology is, at least in modernity, *de facto* presumed as the way into any such ontology.

What is so striking in the current context regarding Heidegger's return to ontology is that from the very first he links the question of Being to the question of technology as absolutely co-dependent phenomena, even if the question of technology comes to be considered in a number of not-altogether-familiar-senses. In *Being and Time*, for instance, institutions of transmission – that is, pedagogical and philosophical institutions – are already considered as themselves particular temporal technologies which, in and by their very success, serve to conceal and betray what they would reveal and faithfully pass down, 'simultaneously' stupefying and staggering the thought-experience of time. Hence, for example, Immanuel Kant 'dogmatically' takes over Descartes' position regarding the priority of the subject, thereby obscuring "the decisive connection between time and the 'I think'" (Heidegger 1996, p. 24). Yet this obscurantism is not a feature that could simply be broken with as if a matter of will or intention, having been constitutively inscribed within the metaphysical enterprise as such; moreover, even the obscurantism itself offers something 'new,' not only in the forms of the express modes of philosophical conceptuality and technique developed by each thinker, but in the unthoughts that such modes also uncannily project.

At once within and against this tradition of the transmission of the forgetting of the forgetting of the meaning of Being, Heidegger proposes a certain destruction, deconstruction or 'abuilding' [*Abbau*] of this tradition. One of the most famous early moments of the analysis engages the 'damaged tool,' which, for Heidegger characterises our very 'first' apprehension of a world-qua-world. Since our naïve ways of going about the world necessarily involve a constant deployment of equipment, which, in our very habituated

Irremediability 41

inculcation into its use, simultaneously entails a kind of becoming-invisible of both means and ends, it is only when our intentions and actions are unexpectedly interrupted by a 'disturbance of reference' that we might come to a reflection upon our own situation.

It is only through such a disturbance, through the sudden becoming-unhandy (broken, missing, displaced) of equipment (i.e., *das Zeug*, the familiar technologies of our everyday use), that the already-yet-only-now character of our own 'world' is revealed. We must be careful not to reduce the subtlety of the paradoxes which Heidegger's phenomenological descriptions always seek to expose to us, as this already-yet-only-now character of constitutive belatedness has a number of extraordinary consequences. First, the tool materially obtrudes in becoming-unusable, alerting us to the fact of its materiality-beyond-us-with-us. Unreflective familiarity becomes estranging availability becomes unusable materiality. Second, in this material event of the advent of material that de-tools the tool, the *in-order-to* structuring of our own world simultaneously becomes available. The punctual, accidental un-handiness of the tool alerts us to the limits of our world, as it evinces a certain instability and contingency of that world. A world, *our* world, always has an aspect of handiness to it in the web of practiced familiarity, and it is to these 'facts' we have the chance of attending when such basic familiarity is thwarted.

This early account of the absolute centrality of technology qua equipment as crucial in *establishing* any world *as* world for us also, as we have seen, means that it is through damaged technology that we are apprised of the necessary *handiness* of any world. There is no world that is not in some ways pragmatically 'to-hand.' Yet every world is also contingent, the outcome of a vast history of vanished events. So the very revelation of the limits of our world can turn us towards the realisation that there must be an other, not just of 'our' 'world,' but of all possible worlds. If this other cannot be a world (by definition), it is also nothing *but* this world, given being is not a thing that subsists outside of its appearings: hence, those anxious encounters with the nothing, with nothingness. This 'nothing' is a kind of abyssal other-of-world-in-which-worlds-world. There, the claims of technology are themselves momentarily abolished in the affect of anxiety, As Giorgio Agamben phrases it:

> It is not simply a matter . . . of an occasional unutilizability. The specific power of anxiety is rather that of annihilating handiness, of producing a "nothing of handiness" (*Nichts von Zuhandenheit*). In annihilating handiness, anxiety does not withdraw from the world but unveils a relation with the world more originary than any familiarity.
>
> (Agamben 2015, p. 43)

This is also where the famous analysis of the 'ontological structure of *Dasein* as care' (*Sorge*) comes in: we must be beings who are constitutionally

42   Justin Clemens and Adam Nash

concerned with (our own) being; this ontological care is essentially temporal (see also Schwartz, Chapter 3, this volume, for a more detailed account of those aspects of care as it relates to our contingent 'thrownness,' its irremediable situatedness in a place and time, and, especially, its feminist implications).

If Heidegger thereafter ceaselessly revises this position, it is still on the basis of this triplet of *establishing-apprising-vanishing* that his later thought of technology develops (and which, by the way, shows that the problematic of what we could call 'ontological obsolescence' is a feature of his thinking from the start). If there is no space here to examine properly the further development and motivations of Heidegger's thought in this regard subsequent to *Being and Time*, we underline that it remains centred on the problem of technology. As Hubert Dreyfus usefully summarises, there are at least three different stages in Heidegger's thinking of equipment, which are comprised of: (1) craftsmanship (*techné*); (2) industrialisation (pragmatism); and (3) cybernetic control (systems theory) (see Dreyfus 1992, pp. 173–185; Dreyfus 2004; Dreyfus and Spinosa 2003).

In his thinking through of these stages, all sorts of concomitant shifts occur in Heidegger's thinking regarding the priority of *Dasein* as well as its orientation to and imbrication with affect, which is displaced after *Being and Time* towards a thinking of the 'mirror-play' of mortals, gods, earth and sky (or, to again simplify: death, force, ground and transcendence as mutually-indissociable aspects of medium-disclosure); the relation of *physis to poiesis* to *techné* to *aletheia* is further complicated along these lines; and his long-standing analyses of the pre-Socratics and various poets are constantly nuanced and deepened. Because Heidegger is committed to the disclosure of Being by language ('Language is the house of Being,' and so forth), his attentiveness to the ancient establishment of certain philosophical concepts by the Greeks involves a radical philological tracking of their subsequent vicissitudes: *physis*, for example, emerges as a term for the presencing of nature-as-being, before 'nature' itself is fixed into a particular zone of beings; *poiesis* as making is linked originally to *techné*, artisanal knowledge, which at first discloses, then closes over, the un-forgetting of truth that is *a-letheia*, etc. (for an exceptionally detailed and persuasive account of Heidegger's work in this regard, see Schürmann 1987).

So the early analysis of 'care' as ontological structuring of the non-relation between equipment and anxiety as dis-jointed temporalising not only renders technology irrevocably entwined with ontology, but provides the decisive impetus for Heidegger's own life-long rethinking of ontology on the basis of technology, which, as it places the question of presencing through events at its centre, concomitantly comes to think of the essence of technology as an event of *Ge-stell* ['Enframing'] (see Heidegger 1977b). This entails a shift from attending to *this* or *that* kind of equipment or technique – whether handy or not, available or not, reliable or not – to a world-historical modality of revealing of the *essence of technology* in the modern age, basically

Irremediability   43

since Descartes and Galileo. Heidegger's account is absolutely magnificent. If, chronologically speaking, modern technology (roughly dating from the late eighteenth-century industrial revolution) relies upon modern physics (early seventeenth century) for its construction and theorisation, modern physics must *already* have been an expression of the *essence* of technology in order to get started at all. If this sequence had therefore already encrypted what would only become evident later, in a complex form of jet-lag – the emergence of modern physics, the development of modern technology, the revelation of the essence of technology as already-there in the physics – this intrication itself has a history.

We shouldn't underestimate the complexity of Heidegger's position: the essence of technology becomes graspable in our time after a century or so of radical technological development, itself predicated on an earlier revolution in mathematical physics, which itself was already indiscernibly governed by the aforementioned essence, and that essence could never have installed itself without a prior history that goes back, in disjoint and contingent modalities, to the ancient Greeks. The history of Being is a history of finite, disjoint revelations utterly dependent upon forms of technicity. This history also reveals that the contemporary essence of technology is a form of enframing, which concatenated the totality of what appears into a 'standing-reserve,' that is, entirely unautonomous networks of dependent matter, technologies and creatures whose energies are unlocked, transformed, stored, distributed and rerouted (this sequence of inseparable operations, we might say, constitute Heidegger's extension of Aristotle's four causes).[4] Where the Heidegger of *Being and Time* would have stressed the *availability* of tools as integral to the world-making of individuals and societies, and the Heidegger of the 1930s the *reliability of* equipment as exposed in and by the work of art, the later Heidegger stresses the regulating and securing, the *enframing*, of the totality of existence under global conditions that a priori constrain the apparition of anything as always already formalisable and quantifiable. There is no simple way out of such a situating, which entails that nothing can appear that is not available as a resource. For the later Heidegger, the breaking of a hammer offers no new possibilities either for knowledge or action in a world of near-total de-autonomisation – which is tantamount to a world of near-total technological autonomisation.

Yet, as is also well-known, Heidegger leans heavily on great German poetry, especially that of Friedrich Hölderlin (but also George Trakl and Rainer Maria Rilke), for his theses regarding the destitution of our times, the danger of modern technology, and the constitutive too-lateness of our thinking. "Where the danger is," Heidegger quotes, "There the saving power grows" (Heidegger 1977b, p. 34). And if he will also later notoriously add "Only a god can save us" (Heidegger 1977a), his point is that poetry, as a form of *techné* that survives into the epoch of modern technology, still retains, if in a seriously attenuated form, a resistance to the present, a power of truth that, in its anachronistic otherness to the present, perhaps will aid

44   Justin Clemens and Adam Nash

in a questioning that leads beyond our current enclosure. Moreover – and this is a crucial 'moreover'! – what is at stake in poetry is precisely a use of language that, made from language itself, breaks with the very language from which it is made. As such, a poem is an 'event,' in which the distinctions between 'empirical' and 'transcendental,' 'ontic' and 'ontological,' etc., are no longer operative nor viable. Yet, since it is only through language that there is any opening of being in the first place, it is only poetry, in its constant reopenings of language that the thinking of being can survive in our time of cybernetic command and control.

From technology to time to transduction: Gilbert Simondon

At the same time as Heidegger is rethinking onto-technology, Gilbert Simondon is elaborating a quite different, if perhaps equally profound, thought of technology and individuation – the process by which beings or objects become differentiated. For Simondon, technology is a genetic proposition, an evolving structuration that mediates humans and the world, as both a theory and a praxis. Yet theory and praxis had been rendered asunder in human culture, opposing representation to activity. In this vein, it is a mistake to think that technology has replaced humans, rather that because of the forced dichotomy between theory and praxis, it was humans "who in fact provisionally replaced the machine before truly technical individuals could emerge" (Simondon 2016, p. 81). Technical reality is human reality, where humans and technology are correlated, constantly involved in a mutually-informing process of co-individuation. This is only possible because the ongoing process of individuation (for Simondon, there is no principle, only the process) occurs within and through the 'pre-individual,' an oversaturated or metastable environment that is both occupied by, and carried within, the individuating process. For Simondon, everything is only ontogenetic individuation through transduction, where two or more disparate entities procedurally combine to create a new entity that carries the previously disparate entities within it. Therefore we must think of 'technology' and 'technical beings' in the same sense with which we think of 'humanity' and 'human beings,' i.e., not as some given that exists only as present for something else, rather as an ongoing transductive process of individuation within an oversaturated, or *metastable*, environment that informs such individuation in an ongoing, reticulated system of structuration through information. Broadly speaking, this is Simondon's concept of *transindividuation*. Here we identify a similarity with Heidegger's concept of technology as revealed to have been *already-there*, as well as with the recent efforts towards a relational quantum mechanics. See also Jonas Andersson Schwarz' chapter (Chapter 2) in this volume for a discussion of the transductive relationship between individual subjects and the wider contemporary digital environment.

In this sense, any technical object should not be understood as a material entity, but rather as the ongoing outcome of an ongoing process of transduction. Similarly, humans and technology are engaged in an ongoing ontogenetic process of transduction, and cannot properly be spoken of as separate individuals, except in a misguided sense that leads to a false dichotomy. Simondon speaks of 'technical being,' and sees machines as technical objects only in this ontogenetic sense. Philosophically, he desires that technical being be integrated into human culture, by allowing no opposition between humans and machines: rather each is a part of each other. As Simondon says, "the machine is that through which [humanity] fights against the death of the universe; it slows down the degradation of energy, as life does, and becomes a stabilizer of the world" (Simondon 2016, p. 21). In this, he is relying on a concept of regulative information, saying that although culture adopts a regulative stance towards humanity, it requires the integration of technical being in order to transcend its "specialised and impoverished" (Simondon 2016, p. 20) state to become general. This is in keeping with Simondon's observation of a tendency from the abstract to the concrete, by which he means a process of convergence and adaptation according to a certain inner resonance that ensures a generative coming-into-being.

Some commentators, including Bernard Stiegler, feel that, in this, Simondon becomes trapped in a Bergsonian metaphysics of vitalism, but this inner resonance that Simondon describes is not a vital spirit, and he is careful to point out that between the concepts of adaptation and vital spirit, there is no possible mediation. So he proposes rethinking this in terms of the "individuation of oversaturated systems" (Simondon 2016, p. 168) in an ongoing resolution of tensions through structuration:

> Tensions and tendencies can be conceived as really existing in a system: the potential is one of the forms of the real, as completely as the actual. The potentials of a system constitute its power of coming-into-being without degradation; they are not the simple virtuality of future states, but a reality that pushes them into being. Coming-into-being is not the actualisation of a virtuality or the result of a conflict between actual realities, but the operation of a system with potentials in its reality: coming-into-being is a series of spurts of stucturations of a system, or successive individuations of a system.
>
> (Simondon 2016, p. 168)

This is where we may find a way of understanding digital computing, for the computer is not so much itself a machine as it is all machines, or a universal machine, a machine that can be any other machine. But these machines cannot really be said to exist in the world, and yet equally can it not be said that they do not. We discuss this *dialetheia*, or true contradiction, in more detail below. Further, it allows us to identify the processes and products of digital computing in terms of transduction and ontogenesis, or coming-into-being, for anything that we perceive via computing is never really an 'object,' except in the most procedural sense. For example, our search results, with which

46 *Justin Clemens and Adam Nash*

we opened this article, are an ongoing process of transduction, not only in respect of the continually changing search algorithm and its dynamically modulated results in response to the changing world, but literally, in that to perceive those results is to participate in an ongoing transductive process of amplifying reticulations and resolutions of tensions between electricity, magnetism, wireless signals, light emitting diodes, retinas, hands, memory, language and culture (see also Andersson Schwarz, Chapter 2, this volume).

The challenge therefore is to understand the digital in these terms, as a "culture of technics" (Simondon 2016, p. 81) and, given Simondon's insistence on the tendency to concretisation, explore the implications of the advent of the binary computing universal machine for the history and future of humanity and its world in digital terms. And yet, for Simondon the theory/praxis dichotomy is false. Indeed all binary distinctions are false, despite his insistence on the maintenance of the law of contradiction. And we agree, but only in as far as we understand such a position to positively require the law of the excluded middle, in order to discern whether an absolutely minimal difference subtends the ontogenetic process to allow the possibility that something be and not be at the same time. We discuss this distinction between, and utility of, the laws of excluded middle and contradiction in detail below. For now it suffices to say that Simondon's study of technical process affords useful ground from which to examine the apparent logical inconsistencies that arise in the digital era.

From transduction to technics: Bernard Stiegler

In the wake of Heidegger and Simondon, Bernard Stiegler takes up certain key topics from each. From Heidegger, Stiegler takes the always *already-there* of technics to develop a theory of anamnesis and hypomnesis – roughly, internal and external memory – that shows that technology actually constitutes time for humans. This is because Stiegler takes seriously the Heideggerian notion of being as forgetting. Stiegler reads this as meaning that the history of (our) being is inscribed in technology, and therefore that time must be thought within the "horizon of an originary technicity *qua* an originary forgetting of the origin" (Stiegler 1998). This, therefore, is how the already-thereness of technology works, as an interaction between anamnesis and hypomnesis.

Stiegler relies on Simondon's transductive processes to both think this through and demonstrate its historical, and future, nature. Indeed, Stiegler draws a direct correlation between anamnesis/hypomnesis and Simondon's psychic/collective individuation, with both pairs mapping to internal (within a being, or the being as environment for internal individuation) and external (between a being and its environment for individuation and transindividuation) encounters. Stiegler also shares Simondon's concern with the historical, cultural, rendering asunder of theory and praxis or, for Stiegler, *episteme* and *tekhne*. Again, Stiegler sees this as the cause of the Heideggerian forgetting, thinkable in terms of anamnesis and hypomnesis.

Stiegler sees a parallel between Heidegger's already-there and Simondon's pre-individual, from which individuation proceeds. Further, Stiegler also sees a parallel between Heidegger's being-in-the-world and Simondon's notion of the reticulated relationship between individuation and its environment, or milieu (see Stiegler 2009). In fact, Stiegler sees the differences between certain aspects of Heidegger's and Simondon's philosophies precisely in Simondonian terms, that is, as two disparate fields, within a metastable environment, ready to transduce each other in a process of individuation. In this mode, Stiegler analyzes Heidegger's later thinking on technology in Simondonian terms, drawing parallels between Heidegger's notion of technology as the ultimate outcome, and end, of metaphysical thought – where technology is thought of only in instrumental terms of means rather than in its essence or process as way of revealing – and Simondon's idea of technical being.

Stiegler also takes seriously Heidegger's 'question of the question,' wanting to reevaluate, even restore, it and its possibility in the contemporary technical era. However, casting technology as the Derridean *pharmakon* – a term deriving from Plato, which designates simultaneously cure *and* poison – where hypomnesis apparently constitutes the condition of anamnesis, Stiegler thinks that Heideggerian thought is not capable of analyzing the relationship between calculation and the incalculable, and this is something that concerns us later in this chapter as a crucial aspect of any attempt at a DO (Stiegler 2013, p. 137). Countering the prospect of the end of metaphysics through technics, which may foreclose the possibility of the question, and responding directly in this to the notion of posthumanism, Stiegler wants to insist on Heidegger's *Dasein* as the question of being, by placing in question the very possibility of questioning, and this impossibility of questioning exposes beings as in contradiction with themselves. This brings the thought back around, in Stiegler's transductive process, to Simondon, for whom the subject's incompatibility with itself is fundamental to his ontogenetic philosophy of transindividuation.

Finally, it is worth briefly adding the importance of psychoanalysis in Stiegler's account, particularly regarding the bases and consequences of technics qua affect in the effecting of the human subject. For Sigmund Freud, modern humanity had become 'a prosthetic god,' that is, entirely dependent upon its technical extensions. Yet, as Freud points out, this delivers at least two further important features, in addition to the fact that human being is from the first a technical supplement. First, technology creates the problems to which it purports to be the solution, thereby driving innovations that necessarily obscure their own operative conditions and implications. Second, technology, even as it functions as a kind of libidinal 'extension of man' in ways that Marshall McLuhan would later examine, requires a certain form of organic renunciation in one's enforced submission to it. Here,

48　*Justin Clemens and Adam Nash*

Freud speaks of assemblages of original events such as the becoming-bipedal of the human animal being articulated to the mastery of fire through *not* putting it out by urinating on it (Freud 1961, p. 90). Whereas many if not most accounts of the history of technology provide fundamentally positivist examples for the co-evolution of the human and its tools, Freud emphasises how technology develops not only through an active working on the external world, but upon prior or coterminous forms of organic rejection and renunciation. In the aforementioned example, control of fire was (allegedly) achieved by *refusing* to either flee or put it out; that control required internal repression of a variety of instincts to be accomplished; that repression, in becoming embodied in psychophysical practice, was also simultaneously forgotten. Whatever one makes of the Freudian speculative anthropology, what matters in this context is that the forms of his arguments point to a certain self-occluding negation or negativity – creative sequences of forgotten repressions – as the decisive factor in the binding of disparate organic and artificial materials that is accomplished by technology. It is these aspects of the psychoanalytic anthropology that Stiegler takes up (see Howells and Moore 2013).

From applied science as computation to pure mathematics as ontology: Alain Badiou

Let us put momentarily to one side this strong Heideggerean, Simondonian and Freudian lineage in the thinking of technology in order to turn to a purely mathematical and logical ontology. For Alain Badiou famously declares that 'mathematics is ontology,' that is, that modern set theory as it stems from Georg Cantor and its subsequent axiomatisation and ongoing development by a host of mathematicians (including Gödel, Cohen, Easton and beyond) establishes for the first time a pure ontology that is at once infinite and not submitted to the (theological) reabsorption by a 'One' or Presence of any kind. It is crucial for Badiou that, following from Heidegger's realisations, one cannot think ontology according to kinds of taxonomy or hylomorphism (i.e., as a content/form or matter/shape relation). Rather, set theory is *pure*, that is, utterly independent of any empirical material; in its most popular axiomatisation (Zermelo-Fraenkel), it is founded, not on any thing or number, but on the empty set, whose 'nothing' undoes the one as a foundation and marks a suture to inconsistent multiplicity (Being); it also affirms infinite infinities as the basic, even banal, status of structured Being, to which it simultaneously gives a rigorous conceptual character for the first time (i.e., one that is not metaphysical or onto-theological; see Badiou 2006). For Badiou, set theory gives an absolutely rigorous way of discussing Being as 'founded' on the empty set (a set with no members and thus 'void'), yet essentially multiple.

Notably, psychoanalysis proves important in the construction of Badiou's system, this time deriving from two formulae of Jacques Lacan's. Above, we noted that Freud had already pointed to a kind of double negativity at the heart of all technology. Lacan further formalises this negativity, not only famously in terms of the linguistic signifier, but more precisely in terms that implicate formal logics. As John Cleary puts it in a recent study, these hold: "the real is inscribed as an impasse in formalisation; the real is the impossible" (Cleary 2018, p. 143). Badiou translates these desiderata in several ways. The real, Being, as impossible, is nevertheless seized by set theory under the heading of the empty set, which binds consistent multiplicity (the hierarchies of infinite infinities without totalisation formalised by the theory) to inconsistent multiplicity, Being as such. Yet, to do so, the mathematics itself has had to have made a *decision*, that is, has had to have *axiomatically* (decisively) declared the stakes of its enterprise. Perhaps unexpectedly, it is axiomatisation that bears the trace of subjectivity within any formal system, that is, a certain contingency, a certain thought, and the deliverance of a certain new version of necessity.

Precisely because contemporary technology is an *application* of regional forms of mathematics, it has to be considered by Badiou as downstream of the ontological, operationalising certain regional forms of Being, which, nonetheless, can be restituted in all their full materialist abstraction by recourse to such mathematics.[5] However, there are three aspects of this ontology which should be noted here. First, it still demands a minimal *technology*; in this case, a writing technology, an auto-securing of the letters that are required for all logical and mathematical proofs (see Clemens 2002; Clemens 2015). By definition, such a (technical) reliance cannot itself be fully thematised by what this reliance conditions. Second, this ontology can only consider the technologies of our time as derivative of the purity of the thinking of the void-infinites with which set theory deals. As such, Badiou has almost nothing cogent to say about such technologies beyond indicating their dependence upon this rationale. Third, the ontology is expressly Boolean, that is, dependent on classical logic, for which the two non-negotiable elements are the law of non-contradiction (LNC) and the law of excluded middle (LEM). LNC holds that something cannot be both true and false at the same time; LEM ensures that there is no third state between something and its negation.

Certainly, Badiou has subsequently extended his ontological account in *Being and Event* with what he calls the 'objective phenomenology' of *Logics of Worlds* (Badiou 2009). This phenomenology relies not so much on Boolean logic *per se* but on its extension and transformation according to a kind of intuitionist logic. We will say more about intuitionistic logic below; suffice it for the moment to say that it is one in which LEM does not *necessarily* hold. Badiou's phenomenology thereby provides a kind of general theory of the very variable ways in which different worlds allow different kinds of phenomena to appear with very different intensities. Moreover, this theory enables a comparison of intensities of appearing through a kind of transcendental indexing for which the negation of a negation (what Badiou

50   *Justin Clemens and Adam Nash*

calls its 'reverse') is not necessarily equal to the original intensity. This is not as recondite as it perhaps sounds: the point is that the objective structuring of the world(s) in which we find ourselves has to cohere to some extent (that is, not be contradictory), but also must enable both the proliferation of appearances (of a potentially infinite field of objects) and the relative intensities with which they appear. In such worlds, the 'negation' (or reversal) of the intensity of appearing of objects is not equivalent to their disappearance or destruction, but is rather a *modification* of that intensity.

Badiou acknowledges that this extension is not *ontological*, but bears on the structuring of the *apparition* of worlds, which, if they are ultimately *inscribed* in Being, are not entirely *circumscribed* by the laws of ontology. Nonetheless, the ontological prerequisite remains classical – to be or not to be – which, in being supplemented by a non-classical account of the worlds of appearing – to appear can be to appear a little bit, or alternatively very intensely – still relies upon a materialist synthesis in which 'every atom is real.' Ultimately, all appearance, however mutable, is founded upon an ontological base that is classical. In a word, Badiou's mathematical ontology retains both the ancient logical principles of non-contradiction and excluded middle. Yet, as we have seen, it is such a logic that Heidegger puts into question in his turn to the 'logic' of the poem, as indeed does Badiou himself regarding the status of phenomenological appearing.

Modulation and the end of questioning

We have now come to a critical moment in the attempt to think technology. Following a confrontation between a Kantian informatics as represented by Floridi and a virtual anthropological archipelagics as represented by Boellstroeff, we suggested that both versions remained too epistemologically-oriented, and, in a context in which the internet patently radically undermines established epistemologies, that it would perhaps be requisite to return to philosophies that attempted to think technology and ontology as indissociable, but without giving any priority to epistemology. We then proceeded, on the one hand, to elaborate a tradition which thinks 'technics and time' together, and on the other, we outlined a mathematical ontology which purports to break altogether with the apparitions of *techné* in the name of infinity.

There is a further difficulty, however. While the ontological interpretations from Heidegger to Badiou are extremely strong and profound, they radicalise the fundamental ontology at the expense of specific technical details, which can appear in their own frameworks as either *regional* ontologies or as giving merely 'ontic' or 'empirical' details; on the other hand, the very many approaches which attend to the technical specifications of the new technologies and media, reduce the ontological import to its *socio-technical* implications. In addition to those thinkers already cited, we could mention Gernot Böhme, Benjamin Bratton, Roland Capurro, Wendy Chun,

Alexander Galloway, Stamatia Portanova, McKenzie Wark, and Yuk Hui, among others (see Böhme 2012; Bratton 2016; Capurro 2006; Chun 2016; Galloway 2004; Portanova 2013; Wark 2015; Yuk 2016).

Our own 'solution' will therefore be as follows: to take up the ontological challenge in its fullest sense, but to do so through the salient technical requirements of the present. We have previously discussed in detail (Clemens and Nash 2015) how the *specific* processes of digital computing can be seen as a literal enacting of the Simondonian process of individuation via transduction. We call this *modulation*, for various reasons outlined elsewhere (Clemens and Nash 2015), but for our purposes here it is broadly understandable as 'transduction,' and we see it as fundamental for any attempt to think DO. We have shown that the digital has literally ended the concept of media, since media before the digital were actually differentiated whereas now they simply individuate as, in practical terms, simulations of differentiated media within a single metastable environment, i.e., the digital.

We have also shown that such an event, or process, unfailingly shines a retroactive light on the nascent tendencies within these prior media that were unable, for whatever reason, to emerge from within the restrictions of their differentiated state. This is Heidegger's *already-yet-only-now* character of the event-of-being operationalised in the digital, and we call this phase of undifferentiated media that nonetheless ostensibly appear differentiated in the world – the *post-convergent* world we inhabit now – that allows all sorts of aspirational or experimental tendencies to be enacted in the world (Clemens and Nash 2015). And we have also shown how operationalising a Simondonian understanding of digital networks allows certain neoliberal actors to perpetrate an unbalanced structuration that, while operating technically according to Simondonian processes, is simultaneously able to perpetuate an anti-Simondonian value system of individuality that results in a global anxiety amplifier, with the result that anxiety can be seen as the only true product of global digital capitalism (Nash 2016; Stiegler 2014).

All of these tendencies and acts, carried out digitally, have the seemingly extraordinary quality of both being and not being in the world. A social media update, for example, most certainly can be said to be in the world, and yet at the same it is impossible to say that it is in the world. In this sense, it is like music; music most definitely exists in the world, and yet it is impossible to say that it exists in the world. The sound itself is not the music, nor is its physical (mechanoelectrical transductive) perception via the eardrums and stereocillia of a listener, and nor is the person or computer playing the music. Does music exist only in the mind of the listener? If so, how is it possible that people can participate in music together? The same can be said of colour, and the same can be said of digital operations of any kind. We have shown how Simondonian thought (with some modification that we will discuss below), with Heideggerian, Stieglerian and Badiouan thought supplementing, can account for the operations of the digital, and for their perception and action in the world, by an ongoing transductive

52 Justin Clemens and Adam Nash

process of individuation and structuration within a metastable, or saturated, environment. This allows us to assert that, when using the digital, we are not passively participating in this process of becoming, but actively taking part in it, manipulating the process, as all participants in the transductive process must do, in a moment that Stiegler calls 'adoption,' as opposed to 'adaptation' (Stiegler 2013).

The digital is, then, at the same time as being an active participant in – also a *working model* of – the transductive process of becoming. We do not make this claim in the same manner as the digital physicists like Fredkin do, or such as Descartes did with clocks, in that we are not maintaining that the universe is a digital computer. Similarly, we are not maintaining that the digital is the *only possible* such participant/model, and we already pointed out music and colour as exemplary, to which list we could add, for example, religion (a fact of which Simondon was very aware), language and globalist economics (of which Stiegler is very aware). And we can make this claim largely with the help of a Simondonian world view. Must it be the case then that a Simondonian process of transindividuation is itself subject to this same process? Certainly, if we stay with Simondon, because for him there is no principle, only the process, so it cannot but be that the process is also in a constant reticulated process of individuation, always incompatible with itself. Since the digital is capable of simulating, or 'containing,' to refer back to Marshal McLuhan's notion of the individuating process of media, other prior but similarly exemplary systems as listed above, it would seem that the transductive process of individuation has transduced its self/other into a metastable environment that we all today call the digital.

So far so good, but we have not yet been able to account for *how* such a situation can not only come to be, but to come to be the condition for becoming. How is it that a subject is incompatible with itself, and yet can still be a subject? How is it that a calculation can be in the world by not being in the world? This brings us back to the problem of how to deal with DO when DO clearly shatters any unity of our knowledge of it. For us, it means there are not questions anymore. Heidegger always talked about 'questioning,' and we've shown how Stiegler has attempted to formulate the impossibility of posing questions as a question itself. We sympathise with this attempt at reformulation, and submit our own: not questions, but problems (i.e., with solutions), because, as we have shown, that's what the digital does to *questions* of being – like everything, it turns them into *problems* of being, in other words, *injunctions* that require a *solution*. If the digital means the instrumentalised end (and means) of metaphysics, then we must instrumentalise this very process to transduce this very process. This gives us a method: We take the shattering of unity of knowledge as key to the technology, and ask how it does this. It makes being itself subject to mathematised technology, but how? DO means the problem of ontology can precisely no longer be circumvented in experience since experience is now precisely the outcome of technology; but the problem of ontology can only be answered by returning to the abstract operations as to how this is done. So, against Floridi, we want to ask, is there a minimal difference, a pure binary, that must subtend yet condition any possible differentiation, even that of digital and analogue? Or is there an infinity of different differences, each a 'true contradiction'? For this, we will turn to the field of logics called *paraconsistency*.

A digital aporia

There is a point to mark that is crucial for any ontology: its integral binding to paradox and aporia. At one of the supposed inceptions of philosophy as such, we find the extraordinary character Socrates who is denominated by Plato as *atopic*, placeless or without place. As is well-known, Socrates pursues his various interlocutors with savage questions regarding their putative knowledge of this or that practice, until he has reduced them to silence, and the situation to *aporia*, impasse, deadlock, or loss. Such an impasse is the index of an irrationality that marks the impossibility of its being known under the current conditions of knowledge (Bartlett 2015). *Aporias* regularly prove catalysts to ontological thought.

Today, a new class of problems have emerged which constitute such an aporia for contemporary thinking. Moreover, they emerge in precisely the context we are discussing here: digital computing and modern logic. On the one hand, from Gödel, Turing and others, we know that there are certain kinds of problems which cannot ever be resolved, that is, they are logically impossible. On the other hand, there are certain problems for which no solution can ever be found, or, if found, ever proved. In between, there is a new kind of problem, neither impossible nor trivial. This new class of conceptual formal problems is usually phrased as 'the P versus NP problem.' It is one of the most significant open problems in contemporary mathematics, and is especially important for computer science. In the simplest terms, which hopefully maintain the core attributes of the problem, it poses whether every solution quickly verifiable by a computer is also quickly solvable by computer. There is a class of problems (called *P*) for which an algorithm exists (or can exist) which will solve the problem in polynomial time, meaning an amount of time that varies as a polynomial function of the amount of input. There is another class of problems (called *NP*) for which there is no known algorithm for solving the problem in polynomial time but for which any solution can be verified in polynomial time.[6] A popular method of visualising the difference, while not completely accurate, is the difference between listening to a piece of music and composing that piece of music. Listening (i.e., 'verifying') to the piece only takes as long as the length of the piece of music. Composing it, on the other hand, takes an indeterminate amount of time that quite possibly bears no relationship to the 'input size' of the problem. Whilst the prevailing assumption, which subtends all manner of contemporary digital operations like cryptography and networking, is that P does not equal NP, it has never been proved either way.

54 *Justin Clemens and Adam Nash*

This is an *essentially* contemporary problem. Having first been formalised in the early 1970s, specifically in relation to digital computing, it emerges in our time as *the* aporia of the digital era.[7] Not only did the problem not exist before the mid-twentieth century; it was previously unimaginable, let alone formalisable. The P v NP problem emerges *directly* as a result of the establishment of digital computing, a specific technical condition, yet currently seems irresolvable by the very means that have revealed it. For if digital technologies are today at once the conditions and the instruments for genetic, chemical, physiological, behavioural, situational, social and environmental manipulations – that is, for unprecedented power over beings – they open between verification and demonstration a gap which is essentially temporal. Certainly, this situation is also linked to a new priority of technology over science, not only in terms of financing and alleged utility, but insofar as technology can now be constructed, which works without anybody necessarily having the *knowledge* of how it works.

We wish to assert that it is this aporia which shows that *the one* of knowledge does not hold. Whether it is with the digital physicists, for whom in the end physics and metaphysics fuse or short-circuit at a certain point, or for the paraconsistent logicians who believe that ultimately true contradictions are the truth of being, or alternatively the epistemologists who believe that ontology is merely speculative in relation to what we can know, the aporias interrupt and challenge these convictions to show that *the one* cannot close upon itself. We've shown that Simondon, Heidegger and Badiou offer a perspective from which either the void or a constitutive disunity must subtend any attempt at an ontological unification via a *one* of knowledge.

This is why it is wrong-headed to begin with the assured new *knowledges* we have incontrovertibly gained from contemporary computing. Rather, it is the *limit* of these knowledges as expressed in an *aporia*, an impasse that afflicts knowledge as it opens a new phrasing of the problem of the grounds of this knowledge, to which we need to attend in the construction of any possible ontology. Indeed, we suggest that this aporia directs us towards a new ontology, which is that of the irremediable. For the digital is literally *irremediable*: its contradictions do not admit of correction, care, or cure but, on the contrary, establish the very grounds that enable its irremediability as both constitutive and constituting of our own knowledge economy.

A paraconsistent conclusion

At points throughout this chapter we have alluded to the field of *paraconsistent* logic. A general feature of paraconsistent logic is that consistency is not equivalent to the impossibility of deriving contradictions within a system. Unlike in classical and intuitionistic systems, contradiction is not necessarily 'explosive': some contradictions are tolerated, but such a system is nonetheless not trivial. A trivial system, in formal logic, is one in which everything is true. Another way of thinking of this is that paraconsistency admits inconsistency as potentially useful information. Yet this means that formal negation becomes, as Badiou says, 'more and more evasive' in the system.[8] Da Costa and Krause, in their attempt at formalising a logic of quantum physics, think that contemporary science's search for a grand unifying theory of everything would almost certainly need to be paraconsistent.[9]

In many ways, the idea of paraconsistency is keenly related to aporia, and in the case of the digital, we have mentioned that Simondon's philosophy of transduction and transindividuation seems to require that we dispense with the rule of the excluded middle, if we are to understand how transduction works, since the Simondonian philosophy apparently requires that anything both be itself and be different from itself. Clearly, LEM (there is no third state between something and its negation), does not allow this. Nor, apparently, does LNC, i.e., that something cannot be both true and false at the same time.

We would like to note here that, while Simondon was correct in noting how his theorisation of technology demanded a rethinking of classical logic, he felt that LEM should be dispensed with. Yet if it is possible to see his reservations as well-founded, we can modify some of his conclusions. At the time Simondon was writing, he only had the model of L. E. J. Brouwer's 'intuitionism,' dating from the 1920s, as the most rigorous formal attempt available to him to evade classical logic. Brouwer, disturbed by the results that were being generated by post-Cantorian transfinite set theory, noted that these results required the unrestricted application of LEM. For LEM underpins *reductio ad absurdum*: in the absence of a positive demonstration, one can assume the negation of the proposition one wishes to prove in order to show that, if its negation results in a contradiction, then that proposition itself must be true.

Brouwer, who was expressly Kantian in his theory, applied a Kantian-type discrimination to formal mathematical logic: while LNC must hold universally (it is tantamount to what Kant would call an 'Idea' of Reason), LEM is rather a regularity observed in finite mathematics (what Kant might call a 'concept' of the Understanding).[10] Brouwer's own ingenious formulation of the issues was, on the one hand, "the rejection of the thoughtless use of the logical principle of excluded middle," while, on the other, "the identification of the principle of excluded middle with the principle of the solvability of every mathematical problem" (Brouwer 1967, p. 401). As such, if the infinite 'exists,' it cannot be proven; any such proof must be able to be finitely and positively elaborated; therefore, the infinite parts company from mathematics as unwritable.

Paraconsistency, however, is a later development in formal logic, deriving from the work of the aforementioned da Costa and others. If paraconsistent logics seem to have first emerged in the 1960s, they have only taken off in a more public way decades later. This development enables us to reuptake Simondon in a form unimaginable to Simondon himself. Take, for example, a particular type of paraconsistent logic called *dialetheism*, as practiced by

56   Justin Clemens and Adam Nash

Graham Priest among others, which is able to accommodate *true contradictions* without 'exploding,' i.e., becoming trivial. According to dialetheism, true contradictions can and do exist in the world, not only in language or concepts, and dialetheism is capable of accommodating this (Priest 2006, pp. 52–53). We ourselves are routinely capable, especially when working with the digital, of extracting useful information from apparently contradictory sources. Juries are expected to extract useful information from contradictory witness accounts of the same event. Fictional characters both do and do not exist, as is true (or not true) of music, of colour, and of our ongoing interaction online, where we both do and do not exist. And those of us who live in Melbourne certainly consider its weather a true contradiction!

A transductive ontogenetic model implies paraconsistency in the world, so we must also accept that every 'thing' is dissimilar to 'itself,' and is constantly evolving, including the concept of truth. This allows us to assert that we humans both discovered *and* invented the digital, and offers some clue as to why we didn't discover/invent it at some previous time in history, since it seems reasonable to assume the potential was always there. But was it? Potential is a concept that can quickly become unworkable or trivial, especially when considered in the light of the digital.

Say we have a digital 'file' that we have explicitly prepared as an essay in a word processing document, but we open the file in a sound playing app. We have modulated that digital data into a sound in the world, and we cannot say that it is an essay. And yet, we can say that it is an essay, and everyone will know what we mean. Moreover, it would seem reasonable to say that the file had the potential to become an essay, except that the only proof we have of that potential is that it did *not* become an essay. Can we equally reasonably say that it had the potential to become an elephant because it did not become an elephant? Of course not, that would be ridiculous. Dialetheism attempts to formalise true contradictions without making everything true, and therefore may be useful in understanding the concept of potential in this sense. At the same time, we also restrain ourselves from a fully-fledged affirmation of dialetheism as practiced by Priest and others, primarily because it often presents itself as solving or resolving metaphysical problems by forever rediscovering the truth of their irresolvable contradictions. We, by contrast, emphasise that the irresolvability of aporias necessitates new ontological constructions.

Let us summarise. Taking up the Heideggerian thought of the poem as event but without the focus on the poem as such, with the Badiouan commitment to formalising ontology but without the commitment to classicism, along with the descriptions of individuation offered by Simondon and Stiegler, and, finally, the revelations of epistemic-breakage offered by new aporias in computation, we attempt to construct an ontology that exceeds the epistemic closures of the present. Our resultant ontological proposal can be schematised as a stack of three levels. The most basic is provided by LEM. LEM offers a pure principle of difference as such, difference prior to any content. At the next level, that revealed by the development of digital computing, we find that this introduces LNC as well, the Boolean logic that still governs all existing machinery. Third, we find the necessity of modulation of the restrictions that LEM and LNC require in the production of 'content.' Yet the necessity for modulation as a 'derivative' level opens up aporias that tie directly back to a situation that is 'pre'-contradiction: modulation exposes the radical instability of data as such.

In relation to DO, it would appear that we are required to engage with a system which is in fact constituted by inconsistency. The irremediability of the digital can only be understood in these terms, and we submit that DO means trying to understand that the digital literally enacts a form of paraconsistency, simultaneously constituting and being constituted by it. If paraconsistency can help us to think about the irremediality of the digital, we believe it opens a new issue: whether there is one minimal difference that underlies all the others (i.e., one pure, 'ultimate' binary) or an infinity of different differences, each a 'true contradiction.'

Notes

1 As mentioned, there were at least three versions available of Floridi's work on the first page of our results (again, note we overlook potential variations here, not to mention the significance of these variations), and restrict ourselves here to the version printed in *Synthese*.

2 Karen Barad's very influential work self-professedly seeks to produce a 'non-analogical' and non-representational account of 'agential realism' (the scare quotes are hers), "an epistemological-ontological-ethical framework that provides an understanding of the role of human *and* non-human, material *and* discursive, and natural *and* cultural factors in scientific and other social-material practices," p. 26. To do so, Barad offers tropes such as 'diffraction' and 'entanglement' in the service of her relational anti-dualistic processual thought. As she brilliantly puts it: "Quantum field theory allows for something radically new in the history of Western physics: the transience of matter's existence. No longer suspended in eternity, matter is born, lives and dies. But even more than that, there is a radical deconstruction of identity and of the equation of matter with essence in ways that transcend even the profound un/doings of (nonrelativistic) quantum mechanics" (Barad 2012, pp. 209–210). What is remarkable from our point of view is that Barad still takes an interpretation of the performativity of entangled relations as delivered by quantum theory as a guide to the *resolution* of "unresolved foundational problems" (Barad 2007, p. 248), according to her own *descriptive* metaphysics.

3 Simondon speculated that quantum mechanics would reveal the pre-individual: "Below continuity and discontinuity, there is the quantic and the complementary metastable, the more-than-one, which is the true pre-individual" (quoted in A. Bardin 2015, p. 39).

4 In various of his essays on technology, Heidegger returns to Aristotle's historically important theory of the 'four causes': material, efficient, formal and final. Standard interpretations render the silver of the jug the material cause, the action of the maker the efficient cause, the shape of the jug as the formal cause, and the end for which the jug is made as its final cause. In his analyses, Heidegger always seeks to confront Aristotle in several senses, not least to give a different

58 *Justin Clemens and Adam Nash*

sense to his thought (indeed, Heidegger carefully nuances this standard account), e.g., "what technology is, when represented as a means, discloses itself when we trace instrumentality back to fourfold causality" (Heidegger 1977a, p. 6). For Heidegger, Aristotle recognizes that these four ways together bring something to appearance; something comparable takes place today under the planetary reign of technology, in which very different scientific operations conspire to bring things to appearance: regulating, securing, challenging, etc., which subtract final and formal causes (and perhaps also the efficient).

5 In a somewhat passing critique of Heidegger on technology, Badiou remarks that it is not technology but *capitalism* that is globally dominant, and that the possibilities of/for technology is in fact limited by capitalism. This may be true, but it is worth adding: (1) this doesn't quite get at Heidegger's point, which concerns the essence of technology as disclosure of Being; (2) it shares with Heidegger the conviction that ontology is irreducible to any ontic requirement. See Badiou 1999. Although this is not the appropriate moment to discuss the issue in any detail, we do also need to note the deleterious political commitments of Heidegger to Nazism, which, as many have argued, are in a deep way articulated with his thinking of technology. For a recent overview, see Fuchs 2015.

6 Actually, the problem is framed in terms of Turing machines, but for simplicity's sake we have called them 'algorithms.' Strictly speaking, the P class describes problems for which a deterministic Turing machine can provide a solution in polynomial time, while the NP class describes problems for which a non-deterministic Turing machine can provide a solution in polynomial time.

7 Attributed to Cook 1972. Also described independently and simultaneously by Leonid Levin and now referred to as the Cook-Levin Theorem; formalized by Richard Karp the following year as P=NP? In 1989 a letter was discovered from Kurt Godel to John Von Neumann dated 1956, in which Godel suggests the problem.

8 See A. Badiou, *Logics of Worlds*. Trans. Alberto Toscano (London and New York: Continuum, 2009), p. 532.

9 N. da Costa and D. Krause, 'Physics, Inconsistency, and Quasi-Truth, I,' *Synthese* (2014) Vol. 191, Issue 13, pp. 3041–3055.

10 We owe this brilliant summation of Brouwer's method to John Cleary, personal communication.

Bibliography

Agamben, G., 2015. *The Use of Bodies*. Trans. A. Kotsko. Stanford, CA: Stanford University Press.

Andrejevic, M., 2013. *InfoGlut: How Too Much Information Is Changing the Way We Think and Know*. New York: Routledge.

Badiou, A., 1999. *Manifesto for Philosophy*. Trans. N. Madarasz. Albany: State University of New York Press.

Badiou, A., 2006. *Being and Event*. Trans. Oliver Feltham. London and New York: Continuum.

Badiou, A., 2009. *Logics of Worlds*. Trans. Alberto Toscano. London and New York: Continuum.

Barad, K., 2007. *Meeting the Universe Halfway: Quantum Physics and the Entanglement of Matter and Meaning*. Durham, NC: Duke University Press.

Barad, K., 2012. On Touching: The Inhuman That Therefore I Am. *Differences: A Journal of Feminist Cultural Studies*, 25 (3), 206–223.

Irremediability 59

Bardin, A., 2015. *Epistemology and Political Philosophy in Gilbert Simondon: Individuation, Technics, Social Systems*. Dordrecht: Springer.

Bartlett, A. J., 2015. *Badiou and Plato: An Education by Truths*. Edinburgh: Edinburgh University Press.

Boellstorff, T., 2016. For Whom the Ontology Turns: Theorizing the Digital Real. *Current Anthropology*, 57 (4), no page numbers.

Bohm, D. and Hiley, B. J., 1993. *The Undivided Universe: An Ontological Interpretation of Quantum Theory*. London: Routledge.

Böhme, G., 2012. *Invasive Technification*. Trans. C. Shingleton. London: Bloomsbury.

Bratton, B., 2016. *The Stack: On Software and Sovereignty*. Cambridge, MA: MIT Press.

Brouwer, L. E. J., 1967. Intuitionistic Reflections on Formalism. *In*: J. van Heijenoort, ed. *From Frege to Gödel: A Source Book in Mathematical Logic 1879–1931*. Cambridge, MA: Harvard University Press.

Capurro, R., 2006. Towards an Ontological Foundation of Information Ethics. *Ethics and Information Technology*, 8, 175–186.

Capurro, R. and Holgate, J. (eds.), 2011. *Messages and Messengers: Angeletics as an Approach to the Phenomenology of Communication*. München: Fink.

Chalmers, D. J., 1995. Facing up to the Hard Problem of Consciousness. *Journal of Consciousness Studies*, 2 (3), 200–219.

Chun, W., 2016. *Updating to Remain the Same*. Cambridge, MA: MIT Press.

Cleary, J., 2018. Subjected to Formalization: Formalization and Method in the Philosophy of Alain Badiou. *In*: A. J. Bartlett and J. Clemens, eds. *Badiou and His Interlocutors*. London: Bloomsbury.

Clemens, J., 2002. Letters as the Condition of Conditions for Alain Badiou. *Communication & Cognition*, 36 (1–2), 73–102.

Clemens, J., 2015. Can Mathematics Think Genre: Alain Badiou and Forcing. *In*: *Genre, Text and Language: Mélanges Anne Freadman*. Paris: Classiques Garnier, 203–226.

Clemens, J. and Nash, A., 2015. Being and Media: Digital Ontology after the Event of the End of Media. *Fibreculture Journal*, 24.

Cook, S., 1972. The Complexity of Theorem Proving Procedures. *Proceedings of the Third Annual ACM Symposium on Theory of Computing*, Shaker Heights, Ohio, 151–158.

Costa, N. da and Krause, D., 2014. Physics, Inconsistency, and Quasi-Truth, I. *Synthese*, 191 (13), 3041–3055.

Costa, N. da and Lombardi, O., 2014. Quantum Mechanics: Ontology without Individuals. *Foundations of Physics*, 44 (12), 1246–1257.

Dreyfus, H., 1992. Heidegger's History of the Being of Equipment. *In*: H. Dreyfus and H. Hall, eds. *Heidegger: A Critical Reader*. Oxford: Basil Blackwell, 173–185.

Dreyfus, H., 2004. Heidegger on Gaining a Free Relation to Technology. *In*: D. M. Kaplan, ed. *Readings in the Philosophy of Technology*. Lanham: Rowman & Littlefield, 53–62.

Dreyfus, H. and Spinosa, C., 2003. Further Reflections on Heidegger, Technology, and the Everyday. *Bulletin of Science, Technology & Society*, 23 (5), 339–349.

Floridi, L., 2009. Against Digital Ontology. *Synthese*, 168 (1), 151–178.

Floridi, L., 2017. The Logic of Design as a Conceptual Logic of Information. *Minds and Machines*, 27 (3), 495–519.

60 *Justin Clemens and Adam Nash*

Fredkin, E., *What Is Digital Philosophy?* Available at: http://digitalphilosopy.org (accessed: 12 September 2017).

Freud, S., 1961. *The Standard Edition of the Complete Works of Sigmund Freud, Vol. 21 (1927–1931)*. Ed. J. Strachey et al. London: The Hogarth Press.

Fuchs, C., 2015. Martin Heidegger's Anti-Semitism: Philosophy of Technology and the Media in the Light of the *Black Notebooks*. *Triple C*, 13 (1).

Galloway, A., 2004. *Protocol*. Cambridge, MA: MIT Press.

Hawking, S. and Mlodinow, L., 2010. *The Grand Design*. London: Bantam Press.

Heidegger, M., 1977a. 'Only a God Can Save Us Now': An Interview with Martin Heidegger. *Graduate Faculty Philosophy Journal*, 6 (1), 5–27.

Heidegger, M., 1977b. *The Question Concerning Technology and Other Essays*. Trans. W. Lovitt. New York: Harper.

Heidegger, M., 1996 (1927). *Being and Time*. Trans. J. Stambaugh. Albany: State University of New York Press.

Howells, C. and Moore, G. (eds.), 2013. *Stiegler and Technics*. Edinburgh: Edinburgh University Press.

Kittler, F., 2006. Lightning and Series: Event and Thunder. *Theory, Culture & Society*, 23 (7–8), 63–74.

Nash, A., 2016. Affect, People and Digital Social Networks. *In: Emotions, Technology and Social Media*. Amsterdam: Elsevier and Academic Press, 23–45.

Portanova, S., 2013. *Moving without a Body: Digital Philosophy and Choreographic Thought*. Cambridge, MA: MIT Press.

Priest, G., 2006. *Doubt Truth to Be a Liar*. Oxford: Oxford University Press.

Richardson, J., 2016. *Law and the Philosophy of Privacy*. Milton Park: Routledge.

Rovelli, C., 1996. Relational Quantum Mechanics. *International Journal of Theoretical Physics*, 35 (8), 1637–1678.

Schürmann, R., 1987. *Heidegger on Being and Acting: From Principles to Anarchy*. Trans. C.-M. Gros with the author. Bloomington: Indiana University Press.

Shannon, C., 1949. *The Mathematical Theory of Communication*. Champaign, IL: University of Illinois Press.

Simondon, G., 2016. *The Mode of Existence of Technical Objects*. Trans. C. Malaspina and J. Rogove. Minneapolis: University of Minnesota Press.

Stiegler, B., 1998. *Technics and Time, 1: The Fault of Epimetheus*. Trans. R. Beardsworth and G. Collins. Stanford, CA: Stanford University Press.

Stiegler, B., 2009. Theatre of Individuation: Phase-Shift and Resolution in Simondon and Heidegger. Trans. K. Lebedeva. *Parrhesia*, 7, 46–57.

Stiegler, B., 2013. *What Makes Life Worth Living: On Pharmacology*. Cambridge: Polity Press.

Stiegler, B., 2014. *The Re-Enchantment of the World: The Value of Spirit against Industrial Populism*. London: Bloomsbury.

Wark, M., 2015. *Molecular Red*. London: Verso.

Wheeler, J. A., 1995. Information, Physics, Quantum: The Search for Links. *In*: W. Zurek, ed. *Complexity, Entropy, and the Physics of Information*. Redwood City, CA: Addison-Wesley.

Wolfram, S., 2002. *A New Kind of Science*. Champaign: Wolfram Media.

Yuk, H., 2016. *On the Existence of Digital Objects*. Minneapolis: University of Minnesota Press.

2 Umwelt and individuation
Digital signals and technical being

Jonas Andersson Schwarz

Introduction

We are witnessing the rapid development of a technological ecology increasingly saturated by uncanny interactive designs. While entirely new kinds of artefacts (smartphones, digital platforms, etc.) throw us into "technologically enforced lifeworlds" (Lagerkvist 2017), media artefacts that were once familiar to us (broadcasting, news media, etc.) are also becoming increasingly governed by interactive computer-based systems, so as to provide personalized "user experiences." By bringing a set of philosophical theories about technological embedding into the fold, this article aims to critically assess what happens to subjects embedded in digital media environments. Media and communication studies have always drawn from an eclectic palette of societal, behavioral and technological subjects. By revisiting concepts primarily developed within cybernetics, evolutionary theory, anthropology and the philosophy of being, this chapter seeks to conceptualize the existential dimensions of online audiovisual and social media platforms. Since it is the primary exponent of these developments, my arguments will mainly be applicable to Facebook.

Contemporary, hyped phenomena such as "algorithmic decision making," "automated attention management" (Bucher 2012, p. 12), and "personalized media delivery" are all premised on cybernetic second-guessing of media users' preferences and desires (Bolin and Andersson Schwarz 2015; van Dijck 2014). But what notions of "knowing," "the individual," "the collective," and, for that sake, "being" would this second-guessing itself be premised upon? Cybernetics is an eclectic, often empirically grounded subject whose history is rife with examples of the ways in which human affairs become intermeshed with structural interventions. Situated behavior, social relations, and economic processes are integrated into systems large and small, and become governed through programmed assemblages and feedback loops. Everyday life becomes permeated with the technical means of mechanical conditioning. Thus, Kantian and Cartesian distinctions between 'pure' realms of human motivations and spheres of agency are continuously contested. There are no purely 'social' phenomena; all human activity involves some degree of technical integration.

62 Jonas Andersson Schwarz

Information theory stipulates that interactive systems adapt their behaviors to their individual users, based on information acquired about these users in their respective environments. This gives interactive mechanisms an uncanny, sometimes "disturbingly lifelike quality" (Pickering 2010, p. 7). For those interacting with them, they begin to appear quite like organisms. The concept of *Umwelt*, originally theorized by Jakob von Uexküll in the early twentieth century, is an early conceptualization of the ways in which organisms interact with their environments. The concept was later appropriated by prominent cyberneticists, e.g., Bateson, Luhmann, Maturana and Varela. While the space is lacking here to expand on the historiography of cybernetics,[1] Uexküll's biosemiotic philosophy has been very important for integrative, anti-dualistic philosophy, alongside its fertile links to media theory and attendant anthropological and phenomenological issues.

A key component of my discussion is the possible differentiation between the 'subjective' surrounding that the user finds herself immersed in (i.e., her phenomenological Umwelt, or associated milieu), and the more 'objective' notion of the surrounding, wider world, as it presents itself for another observer. Here, anthropological works on material culture, tool use, and dwelling (Gell 1998; Ingold 2000; Johansson 2003) have been instructive. In particular, the insight by Alfred Gell that "there is *isomorphy of structure* between the cognitive processes we know (from inside) as 'consciousness' and the spatiotemporal structures of objects in the artifactual realm" (Gell 1998, p. 222). Importantly, this is not to say that the self and environment *are* isomorphic (as, e.g., various interpretations of actor network theory might have it), but rather that the mediated environment prompts human self-understanding to take on *mental categorizations* that are isomorphic to this environment.

If the principal artefactual realm of our time is the world of digital media, impacting our experience "indirectly, sensorily, and at multiple scales" (Hansen 2015, p. 139), this material development is paralleled by an idealistic ideology of *dataism*, "a widespread belief in the objective quantification and potential tracking of all kinds of human behavior and sociality through online media technologies" (van Dijck 2014, p. 198). Strong ontological, epistemological and axiological trust in the (institutional) agents that collect, interpret and share data is imperative for this ideology.

In order to make for a more dynamic, progressive media theory, which enables us to account for algorithmic power while, at the same time, avoiding to reify the stagnant categorizations that many of these institutional "big data" (BD) agents are guilty of, I will try to enhance my biosemiotic understanding by turning to some theories of postwar French philosopher Gilbert Simondon (1924–1989), whose work is currently enjoying a renewed reception in the academic world (Barthélémy 2015; de Boever et al. 2012; Chabot 2013; Combes 2013; Galloway and Thacker 2007; Hughes 2014; Hui 2016; LaMarre 2012; Mackenzie 2002; Mills 2015, 2016). As we will see, this academic reaffirmation is hardly coincidental in an era of ubiquitous

Umwelt and individuation 63

computer networks. Notions like "social physics" (Pentland 2014) or "the social organism" (Luckett and Casey 2016) demonstrate that evolutionary metaphors are common also in business and management literatures on digitization. Simondon is emphasized not only as a "thinker of technics" (LaMarre, in Combes 2013, p. xxii), but equal prominence has been given to his previously overlooked theory of individuation – a theory that is radically different from virtually all of the more popularized sociological theories of individualization, as it is premised on a philosophy of being that is both non-anthropocentric and non-essentialist. By emphasizing the constant intermingling of external and internal realities, Simondon suggests a distinct, adaptive understanding of the human condition, vastly different from, e.g., Heidegger's; he never tries to excavate the phenomenological grounds for being, but rather explores ways in which beings relationally differentiate themselves from the surrounding milieu, *across* scales of existence. Hence, Simondon's non-essentialist theory of individuation applies to molecules, human beings, technical objects, and collective societies alike.

The surveillant profiling that takes place at the back end of digital media infrastructures has given rise to an imaginary of "datafied selves" or "data doubles." What is conjured is often akin to a "split" or "diffraction" of the classical, Cartesian subject. In his regrettably short, cryptic "Postscript," inspired by Simondon's writings on the nature of technical being, Deleuze's suggestion that today's individuals are "divided each within himself" (1995, pp. 179–180) is a truism, since the notion of a stable and authentic identity would always have acted as a veneer to mask inner cognitive incoherence. To think of datafication in this way is problematic since, ontologically and technologically speaking, there is little or no isomorphic connection between any alleged "digital selves" and our physical being (Day and Lury 2016). Surveillant digital infrastructures are negotiated at the level of *category*, not at the level of identity, subjectivity or individuality. According to our data, "we are temporary members of different emergent categories . . . Through various modes of algorithmic processing, our data is assigned categorical meaning without our direct participation, knowledge, or often acquiescence" (Cheney-Lippold 2017, p. 12).

Thus, another reason for me to synthesize Umwelt theory with Simondonian philosophy is to avoid the Cartesian mistake of imagining clear boundaries between the allegedly 'human' or 'social' and the allegedly 'non-human' or 'technical.' My investigation parallels that of Mills (2015, 2016) and Hansen (2012, 2015) in that I focus on informational, media-theoretical, and cybernetic aspects of Simondon. My own unique addition to this growing body of knowledge is the added emphasis that I put on the reflexivity of the knowing observer,[2] especially since so much of the contemporary BD landscape presupposes different forms of abductive knowledge (i.e., inferences from non-exhaustive, or even superficial, qualia to the most plausible explanations). Ultimately, I am able to outline some foundations of a complex and useful ontological theory of information, signal data, and digital mediation.

64 Jonas Andersson Schwarz

The Umwelts of personalized media environments

Jakob von Uexküll (1864–1944) was an Estonian-German biologist whose studies of animals in their cognitive environment have come to influence philosophers (Deleuze, Heidegger, Merleau-Ponty), semioticians (Deely, Hoffmeyer, Kull), and cyberneticists (Maturana, Bateson) alike (cf. Bains 2001). Uexküll proposed that the animal is co-constitutive of its own lifeworld (Umwelt), rather than its milieu being an external "given" (Umgebung). It is rarely illuminating to speak of "*the* environment" without making explicit *to whom* (or *to what*) it is an environment (Johansson 2003, p. 111), an ontological insight that was seminal to, e.g., Heidegger's "being-in-the-world." There are clear connections here to Gestalt psychology and, as we shall see, also to Simondon's ontology: Just as the environment and the organism form a dialectical unit – one cannot be thought without the other – the individual and its immediate setting form a unit, much like a figure and its background belong together. Importantly, Umwelt articulates the unity between beings and the aspects of the total environment *that they apprehend* (Johansson 2003, p. 115), meaning that beings can meet changes in their total environment through subtle changes in apprehension (i.e., subjectively), instead of modification of objective parameters.

By interacting with the world, conscious beings carve out their own Umwelts. When interacting with personalized digital media infrastructures, the Umwelt comes to manifest itself as it is performed. In the very act of using such infrastructure, users literally make their own material Umwelts. Does a world outside of these innumerable, discrete, singular events really exist, even for Google or Facebook? These corporate actors are often invoked as if they were god-like Leviathans, but every single act of observing the world that their employees make, would also be a situated one, consisting of instances of interaction, and shaped by them. When engaging with adaptive media systems like Facebook, you are constantly faced with the possibility that the system *does or does not feed you with things that resonate with your own individuality*. In order to keep users satisfied so as not to lose them, the data lords presiding over these digital platform sovereigns have to constantly test and upgrade their infrastructures in order to be as attuned to the users as possible. Such testing is essentially *operational responses to readings of the signals that users give off*. Once the user becomes aware of the principal way in which such a design operates, a potentially endless mental task presents itself: *Second-guessing the reading that the system makes of users' behavioural cues.*

In other words, the cognitive reflexivity of the media user directly intersects with the feedback-based technological system that (s)he uses. Media usage becomes a question of not only cybernetics (control), but of human ecology (interaction with the built environment) as well as questions of ontology (being), epistemology (knowledge), and axiology (values).

Alfred Schütz argued that an individual's social Umwelt is merely one component of her situated embeddedness in everyday life (Rasmussen 2014,

Umwelt and individuation 65

pp. 46–47). My interpretation differs from Schütz's in that I employ a much broader definition of Umwelt, seeing it as largely synonymous with the life-world – including also mediated social relations and relations to non-human entities. I posit that one could analytically differentiate between (1) one's lived, phenomenological Umwelt, (2) the individual *quasi*-Umwelt of each artefact or system that one interacts with, and (3) the surrounding "wider world," which Uexküll calls *Umgebung*.[3]

My lived Umwelt would be directly constituted by my body, my being there, my being-in-the-world (*Dasein*), or, as Husserl would emphasize, my subjective perception of my world, my lived experience. Still, as observed by, e.g., actor network theory, this realm can never be technologically 'pure'; it is always suffused by artefacts. Turner (2013) has theorized the twentieth-century notion of media *surrounds* – controlled "multi-image, multi-sound-source media environments" (p. 3) designated to foster democratic subjects. Twenty-first-century media surrounds are cybernetic systems of feedback and control, based on digital signals indexing physical phenomena, interfaces and algorithms translating abstract instructions into material being. Hence, the distinctions are blurred as to whether the conscious media user's own interaction with digital infrastructure is conditioned by categories by her own or not of her own making – that is, personalized quasi-Umwelts (2), which are supposed to reflect (1) but may or may indeed not reflect it. In every act of decoding (Hall 1980) and making sense of one's own media environment, an Umwelt is instantaneously made. At the same time, as an individual immerses herself in different personalized media experiences (e.g., Twitter, Facebook, Instagram), each of these can be said to constitute a ready-made, partial environment, fed back to her as a quasi-Umwelt, encoded with ontological, epistemological and axiological categories. Mediated Umwelt is highly recursive, as interpretation loops in two ways – users interpreting artefacts made by designers; designers interpreting user preferences. This generates numerous observer problems, underscoring what constructivist theorists of cybernetic environment (e.g., von Foerster, Luhmann, Schmidt) have been saying for a long time: Ask not what is allegedly 'subjective' or 'objective,' ask what is meant by *the act of observing*, how this act is constituted, and what the observer is like. Consequentially, the notion of an actual Umgebung (3) is highly idealistic, proposing an objective world 'in itself,' one that Husserl thought we should not worry about and that Kant thought we could only grasp through epistemological categories. In Simondon's parlance, which we will acquaint ourselves with further below, this realm would be thought of as "pre-individuated" being.

While Simondon's concept of individuation applies to beings of all sorts – animals, plants, crystals – Umwelt primarily refers to sentient beings, that is, beings that register and interact with their environment. Ordinarily, this requires consciousness, but not necessarily awareness. What a being is aware of might be an important ingredient in its Umwelt, but Umwelt cannot be restricted to awareness (Johansson 2003, p. 120). This is wholly synchronous

66 *Jonas Andersson Schwarz*

with the constructivist theories of cognition of, e.g., Maturana, Varela and von Foerster (cf. Schmidt and Hauptmeier 1984), the key hypothesis being that living systems are not primarily defined through the discrete qualities of their components, but through relations. A living system, as a unit of inter-actions, retains its stability and continuous existence through a circularity of (inner and outer) relations. Consequentially, when artefacts form quasi-Umwelts, this would only be so from the perspective of a conscious observer; the object comes to appear as if it generates an Umwelt.

The built environment is full of artefacts that come before us and to which we have to react. When understood as *extended artefacts* (i.e., including their human components), artefacts can be argued to have Umwelts too. They carry with them *their own unique ambiences* (Johansson 2003, p. 150). A stone axe is made with an intended Umwelt in mind, and is indeed embedded within it. The intended use – the ways in which artefacts prescribe behavior – is, however, never entirely finite; there is always room for aberrant uses.

> The artifact is or becomes an ecological entity by means of being attended to and used by human beings, but *only as long as it is being attended to and used*. As long as it is, however, the extended artifact, in the sense just defined, is as much an agent (co-agent) in the social ecol-ogy as is the organic human being.
>
> (Johansson 2003, p. 151, author's emphasis)

Proposing that artefacts have Umwelts requires an understanding of artefacts as interactive objects (in a sense, organisms) being embedded in sensemak-ing processes. As I understand it, Umwelt has less to do with an exchange of forces between two objects, as it has with the relations between a being that takes subject position and its objects (Bains 2001, p. 140). All sensemaking, scientific sensemaking included, always entails relationships with objects (any perceived entity becomes its object), yet such relationships are always dosed by experience (vision can never be wholly 'objective'). "An object, to be an object, requires a relation to a knower" (Deely 2001, p. 129).

> The relations in question concern above all how the limited and partial sensory aspects of the physical environment are connected among them-selves so as to constitute *objects of experience*, and this constitution depends above all on the constitution of the organism doing the sensing.
>
> (p. 127, author's emphasis)

Contending with the instrumentalist aspects of Umwelt ontology, the Christian philosopher Josef Pieper (1950) argued for a hierarchical differ-entiation of (plant/animal/crystal) sensation and (human) comprehension, where awareness of oneself and one's place in the world helps humans to detach themselves from the Umwelt in order to comprehend the actual Welt (Schumacher 2003, p. 120). This requires something much like the

Umwelt and individuation 67

"god trick" (Haraway 1988, p. 582) of imagining a wider Umgebung from arbitrary vantage points other than one's own, in other words, "knowledge encompassing everything that is knowable about the thing known" (Schumacher 2009, p. 13). Pieper maintains, in the vein of Aristotle and Aquinas, that the human mind is *capax universi* – it has the capability of knowing all things – yet this potential is hampered by the situatedness and empirical limitations of the lifeworld.[4]

It is now possible to broadly sketch out a range of synonyms, where the italicized terms will be introduced in Simondon's philosophy, as outlined further below:

- Umwelt = lifeworld = immediate setting, phenomenological environment = experiential/direct sensemaking (decoding) = *associated milieu*
- quasi-Umwelt = built, artefactual environment = affordances of the designed interfaces of digital platforms (immersive, prescriptive and formatted according to the designers' abductive assumptions about above and below) = intended/mediated (encoded)
- Umgebung = Welt = total environment = distant/non-overseeable = *pre-individuated being*

In biosemiotics, Umwelts are the generative processes in which all the semiotic processes of an organism are united into a whole. Semioticists like Kalevi Kull and Yuri Lotman thus emphasize semiosis as a living process, dependent on endless recursions of translation processes; "semiosis always requires a previous semiosis which produced the translator" (Kull 1998, p. 303).[5] The Umwelts of different organisms differ, which follows from the individuality and uniqueness of the history of every single organism. When two Umwelts interact, a *semiosphere* is created – not simply an adaptation to environment, but the creation of a new environment (Kull 1998).

Contemporary phenomena like automation, artificial intelligence and media personalization make this generativity all the more apparent, in that such technologies generate (quasi-)living systems. In the conventional mass media paradigm, the individual audience member would trust that, in principle, the text one sees would be the same as the one presented to everyone else. With personalized mass media, however, this expectation falls short: The text presented to you is expected to be different from the one your neighbor is seeing. Further, on the digital platforms for media delivery that are nowadays common, this personalization has an automated (and, most of the time, vastly accelerated and aggregated) element. The personalized experience fed to you is not based on a unique, manual selection; its composition is an algorithmic product based on patterns observed among vast amounts of viewers, an artificial composite of sequences of choices observed among innumerable users – you included! What is presented is therefore an artefact shaped by a plethora of dynamics: the design of the interface (and the behaviors it prescribes); the design of the selection mechanism (the algorithms and

68   Jonas Andersson Schwarz

databases involved); editorial choices made by data analysts; external pressures by stakeholders (copyright owners, infrastructural actors) who want to influence the range of content offered to customers, etc.

In other words, the personalized digital media experience is an upshot of its constituent networked interactions (Hansen 2015). It is not simply individual; rather, that which appears "individualized" is literally an assemblage conditioned by those who design the structural set up of the personalized media (Couldry et al. 2016). This structural set up is designed to balance several strong influencing forces. Because virtually all of this balancing takes place behind the surface of each user interface, the end result presented to viewers might appear rather arbitrary. Hence, many scholars now speak of a "black box" media experience (Pasquale 2015). Just as much as human media users treat their immediate[6] surroundings as Umwelts, only to imagine a larger Umgebung or Welt beyond these immediate stimuli, users read the perceptual signs of these surveillant digital systems and transform them into meaning, which in turn prompts meaningful behavior. At the same time, this behavior – enacted in and through usage of the digital artefacts in question – generates signals that are automatically fed into databases (the surveillant apparatus as Umwelt) that are subsequently read and translated into meaningful categories that shape the future design of the system in question (the system operators inferring a Welt from these signals). All this results in what could be called a semiosphere of the cybernetic system.

Dataism and its inadequacies

> I am never quite sure if Facebook's advertising algorithms know nothing about me, or more than I can admit to myself.
>
> (Anonymous Facebook user, in Watson 2014)

Gell (1998) proposes that users of artefacts constantly make *abductions* about the intentions of those who produced or brought forward these artefacts. Abductive reasoning is an analytical operation of logical inference from observations to the most plausible explanations, i.e., reasonably hypothesizing the causes of an event. For scholars who employ a constructivist understanding of technological media environments, it has long been established that media users intersubjectively second-guess the intentionality behind the human performances, habits and choices that they observe. It is also important to address the manners in which they reflexively anticipate the ways in which extended artefacts perform, act and cause things in the mediated environment. It is important to note that there is a substantial, continuously growing literature on how media users second-guess such phenomena, and how actual awareness is layered and distributed. Nevertheless, I omit that empirical question here, focusing instead on the theoretical potentiality of awareness.

Clearly, institutional actors like Facebook harness massive amounts of behavioural data, allowing for sophisticated pattern analysis on large aggregations.

Umwelt and individuation 69

Just as human beings act as intelligent subjects in their own immediate lifeworlds, weaving together all their sense data and abductively reasoning towards the most plausible conclusions, institutional data actors like Facebook act as collective intelligence agencies, weaving together signals into useable and financially valuable categories – or, at least, so the narrative of BD goes (boyd and Crawford 2012). Nevertheless, recent controversies, such as the role of BD intelligence agencies like Cambridge Analytica in US and UK elections, have reignited the debate on what such datasets really amount to. As Sauter (2017) inquires, how well do data objects align with the researchers' pre-made analytic categories? If we are to approach the formalized data platforms as sensory organs (harnessing signal data), and their attendant data agencies as intelligence (applying analytical reasoning on said data), what are the abductive capacities of such assemblages? The key question is not so much whether the categories are representative of individuals – but rather, whether they are useful and to what extent they correspond with lived experience.

In recent years, several scholars have explored a shift in corporate and public governance towards BD methods and epistemology. As many of the critical accounts (e.g., Boullier 2016; boyd and Crawford 2012; Cheney-Lippold 2017; Kitchin 2014; van Dijck 2014) have shown, while these new methods and epistemologies are accompanied by considerable idealism and underpinned by ideology, social media platforms make for capricious settings for estimations of quantities; user-generated data comes with all sorts of bias. Arguably, 'hard' data (numerical counts, census records, objective measurements, business data, e.g., sales and shipments) is generally more useful and reliable than the self-disclosed data found online (e.g., user-generated linguistic content), which is often more ambiguous and susceptible to all sorts of bias. Regrettably, due to the lack of transparency of virtually all corporate-engineered data environments, it is often hard to estimate exactly how biased the data might be (Pasquale 2015). Further, socially generated data tends to be highly context-dependent, which is a challenge for semiotic content analysis. Consequentially, BD approaches in the field of media management generally require various acts of translation (Bolin and Andersson Schwarz 2015). Many accounts that fixate on data (van Dijck 2014) tend to gloss over these complexities, as over-affirming the alleged objectivity of the quantification and tracking taking place, and exaggerating the capacities of the institutional agents involved.

Logically, the tailoring of each user's own information flow is never based on *the user's own phenomenological experiences*, but on *that which the platform providers perceive as preferences*. Is Facebook able to truly anticipate what I want, think and tend to do? To believe so would constitute a form of magical thinking – just like attributing to machines the ability to reason, it would in many ways constitute a massive overestimation of the capacities of the infrastructure. Rather, Facebook operationalizes a set of human-coded categorizations of the world that are programmed into infrastructure, thereby shaping its 'vision.' As long as this vision remains based

70 *Jonas Andersson Schwarz*

on an image of the world inhabited almost exclusively by consumer goods and consumers, this mode of vision will be limited, both technically and epistemologically. What is 'seen' by Facebook are detections, rather than measurements; the referent is not so much a human subject as it is a series of discrete signifiers triggered by the infrastructure in question. The mathematical pattern recognition operates on clusters of correlations spread out across populations – be it a topological mapping of relations (sociometrics), or a topical mapping of preferences or even personality types (psychometrics). Importantly, the data generated in such big data infrastructures can never be a one-to-one "data double." As we will see below, it is more instructive to understand data traces indexically, as fragmented concatenations of signals that are often ambiguous from the beginning.

All in all, this is not to say that dataism does not render actual, actionable analyses and results. Facebook-based data mining enables targeted persuasion on a massive scale, both commercially and politically; the whole purpose for its data resources is to allow actors to buy the means for highly targeted communication campaigns. What is more spurious, however, is the idea that such actionable data should be equated with objective knowledge.

Simondon amid the big data stalwarts

In his brief writings, Simondon presents a philosophy of being and of the nature of technology, postulating a stance of *living with* technology – not placing oneself above or outside of it. Not only do we find that the individual cannot be thought of without a consideration of the difference between individual and setting, Simondon also presents a process of *disparition*, or asymmetry between elements that requires a readjustment (Combes 2013, p. 111). This readjustment (which, importantly, operates internally as much as externally) he calls *transduction*: the source of change that characterizes all individuals. Even if we, as technical beings, *are with technology*, we are at the same time differentiated. There is a fundamental difference between an individual, a setting and the constitutive elements that form the interface or 'playground' where individual and setting come together. There is always readjustment, and this does not lead to totalizing synthesis but to individuation – which is the foundation for change and difference, a relational process that precedes actual individuals. Simondon's distinctive notion of individuation should be understood as a process of becoming (or, more specifically, through the biological concept of *ontogenesis*) in which the potentials of an entity are realized in its construction and maintenance, whether it is living or nonliving, human or non-human. Ontogenesis addresses *how something comes to be*, which is different from philosophical ontology, which addresses *what something is* (Mackenzie 2002, p. 17): "Anything that contributes to establishing relations already belongs to the same mode of existence" (Simondon 1992, p. 298). Individuation, in Simondon's parlance, should not be confused with sociological concepts like individualization (Beck and Beck-Gernsheim 2002). It strikes a more fundamental note that has momentous significance for phenomenology, as has been shown by de Beistegui (2005). While Simondon explicitly "says very little about perception, and simply ignores phenomenology" (de Bestegui 2005, p. 109), we can come to understand being's importance for phenomenology through Merleau-Ponty, who was in fact not only Husserl's student but also Simondon's doctoral supervisor.

At first glance, Simondon's concept of individuation appears to consider an even more fundamental mode of being and becoming than what von Uexküll presupposes, but that distinction is dependent on whether one puts cognition as a prerequisite for the latter's Umwelt ontology. Taken as a generative process, though, Umwelt and individuation can be thought as much the same, in that they constitute the primary mode of ontological distinction out of which beings (human *and* non-human) differentiate themselves from their environment, forming gradually more complex, interactive entities. Interestingly, in both theories differentiation presupposes relation, and *vice versa*.

Let us consider that which characterizes sentient beings – namely, cognition. Simondon's concept of "human energetics," which refers to the ways in which collectives arise as energy shifts within and through individuals, is akin to Gabriel Tarde's conception of the social as being borne by "imitative rays" flowing in and through individuals: "we imitate flows that traverse individuals, which are always flows of beliefs and of desire" (Combes 2013, p. 52). This means that collectives should also be understood in a non-essentialist way, never reducible to mere sums of their constitutive parts. Clearly, Simondon rejects substantialism and essentialism. He steadfastly maintains and explores the constitution of reflexive individuality as a decidedly *relational* activity (Combes 2013, p. 24); the transindividual hosts a mutual relation of one bundle of relations interior to the individual (defining its psyche) and one bundle of relations exterior to the individual (defining the collective).

Simondon's notion of "associated milieu" can also be thought of as synonymous with Umwelt: the environment which the technical being influences and by which it is influenced (Simondon 1980, p. 60), allowing technical objects to become more durable, more "concretized" over time (Simondon 1980, p. 31). Artefacts are conceptualized by Simondon as "technical individuals," that is, as individualized beings – but without cognition in the human or animal sense. Through the process of "concretization," the technical object *calls forth* an associated milieu that it integrates into its functioning (Barthélémy 2012, p. 213). *Function* is also central to the concept of "technicity," or *the practical inventive engagement with what is human in machines* (LaMarre 2012). Since he thinks of machines as technical individuals, ultimately Simondon calls for their liberation (Barthélémy 2012, p. 203), yet he does not fall into the simplistic trap of anthropomorphizing them. Similarly, the technical cannot be totally subordinated to the economic,

72 *Jonas Andersson Schwarz*

since it entails a "recurrent causality" between its elements – leading to friction, resistance, inertia and disparity of technical objects, but also durability (LaMarre 2012).

Digital technology has affordances that make it partially unpredictable, enabling a politics of possibility. For my purposes here, this mode of friction is similar to what the biosemioticians refer to as *semiospheres*, generative intersections between Umwelts. Just like semiospheres entail the creation of new environments, "the individualization of a technical individual as a coherent system means that its own operation partially determines the necessary conditions for its continuing operation" (Mills 2015, p. 62). Technical individuals clearly transform parts of the natural world and "operate with a level of indeterminacy which enables them to individuate further in relation to changes in the external environment" (p. 62).

The relation between online being and offline being is complex; the two realms are not simply separate entities that could either be fused or held separate. Rather, the online and the offline hold together like sign and referent, a relationship that is primarily *indexical*. A collapsing of the two would be like words literally becoming the same thing as that which they denote (Boellstorff 2012; Peters 2016). Since there always will be friction between digital representation and its referent, uncertainties and contradictions emerge. As we will see below, they can be both uncanny and productive.

Indication, correlation, calculation, abduction

The data economy, fueling the rise of Facebook, is directly premised on behavioural correlation: If quality A and quality B tend to correlate with each other beyond a critical statistical threshold of likelihood, chances are that if you have quality A you will be more likely than certain other persons to also have quality B. In pattern analyses like these, made by data analysts at the infrastructural back end, two things are privileged: *relationality* of being (as opposed to its identity) and its *potentiality* (as opposed to its actuality). While the conventional, linear information theory that underpins endeavors like Facebook is markedly different from Simondon's theory of information,[7] this emphasis on relationality and potentiality is remarkably consistent with Simondon's philosophy (Hansen 2012). The ontological schema of Facebook is based on an abstraction of the flows of information that take place in technical networks between nodes that are presupposed to represent real social actors (Couldry et al. 2016). The relations between individuals are, just as in the idealized data-driven "social physics" criticized by Mills (2015), thought "to relate to one another in accordance with the representations they have of one another as fully constituted individuals" (Mills 2015, p. 68). While consonant with conventional information theory, this functional relationship would, from a Simondonian perspective, lack certain features that would enable innovation among the end users themselves. For true social innovation to be possible, "individuals need to form a system with one another which brings them into a state of resonance by which fresh structuration can emerge" (Mills 2015, p. 68). From this point of view, proprietary, black box platforms like Facebook will always suffer from a lack of dynamism as their categories, imposed by BD analysts by means of abductive second-guessing, will remain static and out of touch with the users' own phenomenological experience.

Just like a solid crystal emerges over time out of a homogeneous solution, psychograms and sociograms can be patterned out of emerging webs of relational data, allowing for BD analysts to sketch out particular aspects of the human behavior recorded. Sometimes analysts even claim to be able to correlate these collective behavioural patterns with identifiable human beings – with the fundamental proviso that the aim of such analysis is to detect future potential behaviors by way of probability calculations. As Hansen concludes,

> today's media are able to access – and routinely operate by accessing – dimensions of our experience, of our open and ongoing individuation, that lie beneath the personal or individual level. This fact is absolutely crucial for appreciating the specificity of twenty-first-century media.
>
> (2012, p. 56)

When platform companies construct composite personas by aggregating discrete signals into viable "target groups," personhood is revealed to be "partible, constitutive of the relations it forges" (Nafus 2016, p. xxiii). Data traces are co-constitutive of being, albeit in an indirect, rarely straightforward or predictable way; the signals harvested are riddled with bias, the nudging that is fed back to users is never complete and is likely to conflict with lived experience.

Dataveillance is the continuous monitoring of citizens based on online data that they (unwittingly) give off, often as a result of continuous data tracking for not-as-yet defined purposes. Therefore, dataveillance goes well beyond the proposition of scrutinizing singular individuals, as it penetrates deep into the social fabric (Andrejevic 2012, p. 86). What is traced and recorded is not a capture of social reality, it is a continuous but limited capture of discretely defined and often arbitrarily configured sets of signals. By pointing *elsewhere*, the data is designated to index physical reality (Peters 2016), but, of course, the resultant datagram will always be underdetermined, since reality can never be reducible to such indexical signs.

> Sensors are designed to indicate. They are designed to point to a phenomenon as if data were like smoke to a fire – that is, an index in a straightforwardly Peircian way. In practice, indications are hardly straightforward or clear. A single sensor can indicate many things.
>
> (Nafus 2016, p. xx)

74 *Jonas Andersson Schwarz*

The reductionist nature of data gives rise to problems of indeterminacy of translation and thus precipitates an excess of abductive reasoning. Indexical relationships link the online and offline *through similitude and difference*, not by spatial metaphors of proximity and movement (Boellstorff 2012, pp. 56–57, author's emphasis), as if 'the online' would be in any way removed from 'the offline.' Instead of imagining a synthesis between the dual poles human–non-human, it is philosophically more rewarding to conceptualize social reality through the assemblage individuation–individual.

> The individual – the phenomenon in the narrow sense of the term – is not the whole of being, but only one of its phases, and actually the final one only. Far from constituting the origin and the completion of philosophical thought, then, the perception of the phenomenon, as the fully individuated thing we are for the most part familiar with, only provides a point of entry into the process that unfolds prior to it, and of which it is itself the completion.
>
> (de Beistegui 2005, p. 118)

Correspondingly, in digital assemblages, the value(s) of personhood "emerge in relations of division and connection, relations not of sameness but of self-similarity" (Day and Lury 2016, p. 61). That is, observations of properties are made, and the observer tries to infer how these are causally connected with other properties. For example, technological conditions now make it possible to sample things at much higher rates than surveys or conventional health registers. As Nafus (2016, p. xviii–xix) points out, it is no coincidence that the words "data" and "dated" are etymologically related: Biosensor data are, generally, time series data, and so are the autobiographical data of, e.g., Facebook. Pattern is usually detected by analyzing how different data co-vary over time ("When my steps increase, so does my heart rate"). However, there is also another type of correlation, independent of time, made by averaging all the data in each time series before correlating across a population ("People who take many steps also have high heart rates.") In both of these analytical operations, signals have to be translated into useable heuristics. For biosensory monitors, spikes in activity have to be explained by correlating timestamps with other events. For security agencies, probability modelling allows analysts to identify and funnel risk groups. For media economics and advertising, found sociograms or psychograms have to be translated into relevant, useable target audiences (Bolin and Andersson Schwarz 2015). Also the observations made are, in themselves, technological objects that are individuated through material-semiotic interventions.

Conclusion

It is beyond doubt that cybernetics, as an intellectual discipline, is rooted in biosemiotics as well as in Simondonian techno-philosophy. This chapter

Umwelt and individuation 75

shows the strong shared emphasis that these schools of thought have on theories of being, cognition and reasoning. They urge us to think in terms of ontogenesis (i.e., materially constituted becoming) rather than ontology (materially constituted being); they urge us to think not of materially constituted individuals as static beings, but of individuation as a primary dynamic, an ongoing process of relational differentiation; and, moreover, they urge us to think of cognition as itself relational to this emergent complexity, since not only does primary sensemaking develop over time, in each Umwelt, but also, simultaneously, in the generative friction between Umwelts that interact with one another.

It is also beyond doubt that most of us now live in cybernetically constituted realities. The most apparent example of this would be the increasingly adaptive, automated media surrounds that we inhabit, directly premised on signals processing, algorithms and feedback loops. Computer-based systems of conditioning and efficiency maximization are employed, where behavioural user data is gathered through various sensors, based on assumptions that these data are representative of actual psychological and social preferences and categorizations. What I argue in this chapter is that this form of technically mediated sensemaking can also be understood through biosemiotic and ontogenetic theory. To begin with, the signals intelligence that takes place in data processing centers necessitates calculative agents that make inferences from often patchy, by no means reliable or exhaustive, signals that users give off by using the data infrastructure. What is registered does not say much at all about any alleged 'true nature' of users' subjects; the data generated is always already a result of the user's own performance-as-interaction with the surveillant infrastructure as such – often prompted by nudges that the user got from the infrastructure, rather than based on any spontaneous, 'honest' impulses – and can be riddled with false information with the purpose being to obfuscate things (Brunton and Nissenbaum 2015). Arguably, when data analysts make inferences to a plausible state of affairs from such data, it is very similar to the abductive reasoning at play when sentient beings infer a distant Welt out of their direct Umwelts. Moreover, the notion that adaptive dataveillant systems of this kind tend to give you more sophisticated results over time, the more you use them, and the more detailed their mapping of your activity becomes, is an intellectual concept that is in many ways concordant with the concept of ontogenesis; the nest of relations, out of which being is individuated, becomes thicker, denser over time, the more one engages with it.

Let us not, however, confuse such ontological durability with epistemological reliability. "Algorithmic interpolation" (Cheney-Lippold 2017, p. 113) is a roundabout way of sketching out probable categorizations (that is, abductions) that come to inform the very infrastructures that now are co-constitutive of human, everyday subject-making. Algorithmic power "does not confront 'subjects' as moral agents . . . but attunes their future informational and physical environment according to the predictions contained

76 *Jonas Andersson Schwarz*

in the statistical body" (Rouvroy 2013, p. 157). This has more to do with ontology and axiology than it has to do with epistemology; the present data lords are less interested in seeking objective knowledge or perfectly aligning their built data infrastructures with users' actual lived experiences than they are in the shaping and nudging of pliant consumer subjects.

Operations of transduction allow individuals to momentarily come into being; when we interact with digital infrastructures, we temporarily achieve actuality from virtuality, permanence from immanence, difference from redundancy, while automatically generating new data traces that allow platform providers to enrich their structures, making them even more detailed. The cunning, sentient user has to rely on abductive reasoning, literally second-guessing the actual resources and intentions of the platform provider, in order to make the most out of the experience. Moreover, users constantly make reflexive abductions about the intentions and behaviors of *other* users (and their respective situatedness in their own semiospheres). In this sense, there seems to be the apparition of a "common logic" of usage, with one and the same relation (Combes 2013, p. 24) running through media users and data analysts, professional and non-professional alike. Each time the interactive system delivers you to you, how do you gradually re-formulate who you are? How are back end decisions resulting in socio- and psychometrics that condition "user experiences" co-constitutive of users' own modes of being?

Cheney-Lippold (2017) notes the often momentous epistemological and ontological chasm between lived gender and how, e.g., Google comes to define and operationalize algorithmic gender.

> And precisely because Google's gender is Google's, not mine, I am unable to offer a critique of that gender, nor can I practice what we might refer to as a first-order gendered politics that queries what Google's gender means, how it distributes resources, and how it comes to define our algorithmic identities.
>
> (p. 14)

The formative aspect of mediated social interaction is cut short, forbidding individuals to develop as they would wish: "When identity is formed without our conscious interaction with others, we are never free to develop – nor do we know how to develop" (p. 14). It is here where the current, corporate BD model, where categories are assigned to individuals without their genuine participation in the process, is most deeply problematic. Not only does it operate with conceptualizations of digital being based on remarkably linear, inflexible, static categorizations – it defines you from afar, thus infantilizing you, denying you your self-determination. In short, it *objectivizes* you.

Ultimately, the interactivity engendered in data-based media ecologies is more complex than mere human-machine relations. As noted above, when your observed preferences are correlated with those of hundreds of

Umwelt and individuation 77

thousands of other users in order to present you a tailored selection, 'just for you,' this personalized address is the result of a concatenation of entirely artificial simulations of transindividual relations, taking place throughout hidden back end infrastructures in server halls. By thinking this relation through biosemiotics and ontogenesis, a vista of potential new research opens up, allowing us to recalibrate our entire conceptual apparatus without having to resort to untenable dualism or brute monism, enabling a theory that is less inert, less static, and instead more dynamic, more vital, accounting for lived experience and phenomenology. The highly relational, pluralist and encyclopedic nature of this understanding promises considerable ontological and epistemological innovation.

Notes

I would like to thank my colleagues at the Department of Media and Communications, Södertörn University, for helpful comments and clarifications.

1 For an outstanding summary, see Pickering (2010).
2 While present in, e.g., Stafford Beer's and Gregory Bateson's cybernetics, reflexive epistemology is, regrettably, glossed over in much of cybernetic theory (see Mills 2015).
3 In Schütz' typology, the lifeworld has three additional components, extending beyond the Umwelt: the larger social world (*Mitwelt*), past relations (*Vorwelt*), and future relations (*Folgewelt*).
4 Especially so, Schumacher (2009, pp. 13–14) notes, with things like essence, totality and ontogenesis (the analogy between subsequent and antecedent form).
5 As we will see below, neither biosemiotics nor Simondon's ontology would be particularly compatible with Shannon's linear model of communication.
6 The term "immediate" is ironic, since its etymology indicates a *lack* of mediation. To my defense, what is referred to is the relation *preceding* that of the systematic mediation that the media user is exposed to; while one's relation to Umgebung/ Welt is always irrevocably mediated, one's relation to this mediation in itself is, phenomenologically speaking, more direct.
7 Simondon was in fact critical of the mathematical, linear formulation of information popularized by engineers like Claude Shannon, and challenged it. See, e.g., Mills (2015) for a longer exposé.

Bibliography

Andrejevic, M., 2012. Exploitation in the Data-Mine. *In*: C. Fuchs, K. Boersma, A. Albrechtslund and M. Sandoval, eds. *Internet and Surveillance: The Challenges of Web 2.0 and Social Media*. New York: Routledge, 71–88.

Bains, P., 2001. Umwelten. *Semiotica*, 134 (1/4), 137–167.

Barthélémy, J.-H., 2012. Glossary: Fifty Key Terms in the Works of Gilbert Simondon. *In*: A. de Boever, A. Murray, J. Roffe and A. Woodward, eds., A. de Boever, trans. *Gilbert Simondon: Being and Technology*. Edinburgh: Edinburgh University Press, 203–231.

Barthélémy, J.-H., 2015. *Life and Technology: An Inquiry into and beyond Simondon*. Trans. B. Norman. Lüneberg: Meson Press.

78   Jonas Andersson Schwarz

Beck, U. and Beck-Gernsheim, E., 2002. *Individualization: Institutionalized Individualism and Its Social and Political Consequences*. Thousand Oaks, CA: Sage.

Boellstorff, T., 2012. Rethinking Digital Anthropology. *In*: H. A. Horst and D. Miller, eds. *Digital Anthropology*. New York: Berg, 39–60.

Bolin, G. and Andersson Schwarz, J., 2015. Heuristics of the Algorithm: Big Data, User Interpretation and Institutional Translation. *Big Data and Society*, 2 (2). doi:10.1177/2053951715608406.

Boullier, D., 2016. Big Data Challenges for the Social Sciences: From Society and Opinion to Replications. Social Media Lab, EPFL Lausanne. arXiv:1607.05034.

boyd, d. and Crawford, K., 2012. Critical Questions for Big Data: Provocations for a Cultural, Technological, and Scholarly Phenomenon. *Information, Communication and Society*, 15 (5), 662–679. doi:10.1 080/1369118X.2012.678878

Brunton, F. and Nissenbaum, H., 2015. *Obfuscation: A User's Guide for Privacy and Protest*. Cambridge, MA, and London: MIT Press.

Bucher, T., 2012. A Technicity of Attention: How Software 'Makes Sense.' *Culture Machine*, 13, 1–23.

Chabot, P., 2013. *The Philosophy of Simondon: Between Technology and Individuation*. Trans. A. Krefetz and G. Kirkpatrick. London and New York: Bloomsbury.

Cheney-Lippold, J., 2017. *We Are Data: Algorithms and the Making of Our Digital Selves*. New York: New York University Press.

Combes, M., 2013. *Gilbert Simondon and the Philosophy of the Transindividual*. Trans. T. LaMarre. Cambridge, MA: MIT Press.

Couldry, N., Fotopoulou, A. and Dickens, L., 2016. Real Social Analytics: A Contribution towards a Phenomenology of a Digital World. *British Journal of Sociology*, 67 (1), 118–137. doi:10.1111/1468-4446.12183

Day, S. and Lury, C., 2016. Biosensing: Tracking Persons. *In*: D. Nafus, ed. *Quantified: Biosensing Technologies in Everyday Life*. Cambridge, MA: MIT Press, 43–66.

de Beistegui, M., 2005. Science and Ontology: From Merleau-Ponty's 'Reduction' to Simondon's 'Transduction.' *Angelaki: Journal of the Theoretical Humanities*, 10 (2), 109–122.

de Boever, A., Murray, A., Roffe, J. and Woodward, A. (eds.), 2012. *Gilbert Simondon: Being and Technology*. Edinburgh: Edinburgh University Press.

Deely, J., 2001. Umwelt. *Semiotica*, 134 (1/4), 125–135.

Deleuze, G., 1995. Postscript on Control Societies. *In*: M. Joughin, trans. *Negotiations: 1972–1990*. New York: Columbia University Press, 177–182.

Galloway, A. and Thacker, E., 2007. *The Exploit: A Theory of Networks*. Minneapolis: University of Minnesota Press.

Gell, A., 1998. *Art and Agency: An Anthropological Theory*. Oxford: Clarendon Press.

Hall, S., 1980. Encoding/Decoding. *In*: Centre for Contemporary Cultural Studies, ed. *Culture, Media, Language: Working Papers in Cultural Studies, 1972–79*. London: Hutchinson, 128–138.

Hansen, M., 2012. Engineering Pre-Individual Potentiality: Technics, Transindividuation, and 21st-Century Media. *SubStance*, 41 (3), 32–59.

Hansen, M., 2015. *Feed-Forward: On the Future of Twenty-First-Century Media*. Chicago, IL: University of Chicago Press.

Haraway, D. J., 1988. Situated Knowledges: The Science Question in Feminism and the Privilege of Partial Perspective. *Feminist Studies*, 14 (3), 575–599.

Hughes, J., 2014. The Intimacy of the Common: Gilbert Simondon Today. *Theory & Event*, 17 (2), np.

Hui, Y., 2016. *On the Existence of Digital Objects*. Minneapolis: University of Minnesota Press.

Ingold, T., 2000. *The Perception of the Environment: Essays on Livelihood, Dwelling, and Skill*. London and New York: Routledge.

Johansson, P., 2003. *The Lure of Origins: An Inquiry into Human-Environmental Relations*. Ph.D. Dissertation, Human Ecology Division, Lund University.

Kitchin, R., 2014. *The Data Revolution: Big Data, Open Data, Data Infrastructures and Their Consequences*. Thousand Oaks, CA: Sage.

Kull, K., 1998. On Semiosis, Umwelt, and Semiosphere. *Semiotica*, 120 (3–4), 299–310.

Lagerkvist, A., 2017. Existential Media: Toward a Theorization of Digital Thrownness. *New Media and Society*, 19 (1), 96–110.

LaMarre, T., 2012. Humans and Machines. *Inflexions*, 5 (March), 29–67. (Also published as 'Afterword' in Combes 2013.)

Luckett, O. and Casey, M. J., 2016. *The Social Organism: A Radical Understanding of Social Media to Transform Your Business and Life*. New York: Hachette Books.

Mackenzie, A., 2002. *Transductions: Bodies and Machines at Speed*. London: Continuum.

Mills, S., 2015. Simondon and Big Data. *Platform: Journal of Media and Communication*, 6, 59–72.

Mills, S., 2016. *Gilbert Simondon: Information, Technology and Media*. London: Rowman & Littlefield.

Nafus, D. (ed.), 2016. *Quantified: Biosensing Technologies in Everyday Life*. Cambridge, MA: MIT Press.

Pasquale, F., 2015. *The Black Box Society: The Secret Algorithms That Control Money and Information*. Cambridge, MA: Harvard University Press.

Pentland, A., 2014. *Social Physics: How Good Ideas Spread–the Lessons from a New Science*. New York: Penguin.

Peters, B., 2016. Digital. *In*: B. Peters, ed. *Digital Keywords: A Vocabulary of Information Society and Culture*. Princeton, NJ, and Oxford: Princeton University Press, 93–108.

Pickering, A., 2010. *The Cybernetic Brain: Sketches of Another Future*. Chicago, IL: University of Chicago Press.

Pieper, J., 1950. Welt und Umwelt. *In*: B. Wald, ed. 1997. *Werke in Acht Bänden*. Band V: *Schriften zur Philosophischen Anthropologie und Ethik: Grundstrukturen menschlicher Existenz*. Hamburg: Meiner, 180–206.

Rasmussen, T., 2014. *Personal Media and Everyday Life: A Networked Lifeworld*. New York: Palgrave Macmillan.

Rouvroy, A., 2013. The End(s) of Critique: Data Behaviourism Versus Due Process. *In*: K. de Vries and M. Hildebrandt, eds. *Privacy, Due Process, and the Computational Turn*. London and New York: Routledge, 143–168.

Sauter, M., 2017. Persuasion and the Other Thing: A Critique of Big Data Methodologies in Politics. *Ethnography Matters*, 24 May. Available at: http://ethnographymatters.net/blog/2017/05/24/persuasion-and-the-other-thing-a-critique-of-big-data-methodologies-in-politics/ (accessed: 11 November 2017).

Schmidt, S. J. and Hauptmeier, H., 1984. The Fiction Is That Reality Exists: A Constructivist Model of Reality, Fiction, and Literature. *Poetics Today*, 5 (2), 253–274.

80 Jonas Andersson Schwarz

Schumacher, B. N., 2003. *A Philosophy of Hope: Josef Pieper and the Contemporary Debate on Hope*. Trans. D. C. Schindler. New York: Fordham University Press.

Schumacher, B. N., 2009. *A Cosmopolitan Hermit: Modernity and Tradition in the Philosophy of Josef Pieper*. Trans. M. J. Miller. Washington, DC: Catholic University of America.

Simondon, G., 1980. *On the Mode of Existence of Technical Objects*. Trans. N. Mellamphy. Unpublished. London, ON: University of Western Ontario.

Simondon, G., 1992. The Genesis of the Individual. *In*: J. Crary and S. Kwinter, eds., trans. *Incorporations*. New York: Zone Books, 297–319.

Turner, F., 2013. *The Democratic Surround: Multimedia and American Liberalism from World War II to the Psychedelic Sixties*. Chicago, IL: University of Chicago Press.

van Dijck, J., 2014. Datafication, Dataism and Dataveillance: Big Data between Scientific Paradigm and Ideology. *Surveillance and Society*, 12 (2), 197–208.

Watson, S. M., 2014. Data Doppelgängers and the Uncanny Valley of Personalization. *The Atlantic*, 16 June. Available at: www.theatlantic.com/technology/archive/2014/06/data-doppelgangers-and-the-uncanny-valley-of-personalization/372780/ (accessed: 11 November 2017).

3 Thrownness, vulnerability, care
A feminist ontology for the digital age

Margaret Schwartz

This essay poses the question of embodiment in terms of its historical, ethical and existential stakes. It posits embodiment as central to the critical analysis of media and culture. Theory only fully engages the body if it accounts for the philosophical, technological and cultural forces that make it legible at particular moments, and in particular spaces.

The three terms in this essay's title name a philosophical situation (thrownness), a structure of feeling (vulnerability), and an ethical praxis (care). Each of these terms bears some relation to feminism, ontology and digitality. I argue that feminism is an ethical and theoretical praxis oriented towards vulnerability that practices care as it seeks to describe both lived and discursive constructions of sexual difference. I show that ontology from a feminist point of view is best described as thrownness – the fact of any being's situatedness in a place, and time, and social matrix. I use thrownness to construct a feminist ontology that is uniquely equipped to attend to the mutual determination of the biological and the cultural. A feminist ontology not only recognizes the complex relationship between technology and culture, but further, seeks to problematize the distinction between the two. A feminist ontology for the digital age, finally, critically re-examines the technics that characterize our contemporary moment with a special orientation towards their capacity to create vulnerabilities and offer modes of care. In keeping with this feminist ontology centered on thrownness, these vulnerabilities arise out of an assemblage of discursive and embodied elements, as do the practices of care available to attend to them. In sum, therefore, this essay argues for a specific philosophical orientation towards the question of media and the body, one that privileges practices of care as both feminist and ethical.

This argument is developed through the examination of two cases, themselves assemblages of texts, images, practices and bodily conditions. The first is female incontinence, and I discuss this issue as it is framed in online advertisements for Icon underwear, designed for women with this problem. The second case is that of reproductive health and gynecology as it is understood by a feminist collective in Spain known as the GynePunks. Through hacking, web publishing and collective action, these women and femmes

82 Margaret Schwartz

undertake practices of care to address the particular vulnerabilities of female and female identifying bodies. The GynePunks' collective praxis contrasts sharply with the neoliberal, individualized and ultimately commercial project of Icon underwear, which despite its rhetoric of sisterhood, works to shift the burden of care on to the backs of individual women.

I've chosen to discuss reproduction and toileting because these issues throw into sharp relief the matrix of biological and cultural forces that together construct sexual difference. Here we attend to bodies as they engage in their most intimate and vulnerable practices – making it crucial that meaningful critique engage with the body as a material entity and not reduce it to a discursive or philosophical construct. The discussion will center around two very different responses to the situated needs of female bodies: Icon underwear are a consumer product marketed online, and the GynePunks are an open source hacker collective.

In writing an ontology, I am sensitive to the danger of essentialism. Ontology as a philosophical tradition has sought to eliminate or ignore the very embodied particularities that give vulnerability its shape and pull. Why, then, even have congress with the ontological? Taking a critical perspective has often meant to adopt a social/discursive constructionist approach to the body. Postmodern criticism viewed materialism as naïve and outdated; media scholars viewed technological determinism with skepticism and scorn. Feminist theory has resisted essentialized notions of the feminine by asserting that gender is a social construct. Much of feminist and cultural studies has jettisoned the ontological in favor of the ontic. So why traffic in Being when the world is full of beings that require our care and attention?

These fields – which often operate from a premise of cultural constructionism – throw out the philosophical baby with the patriarchal bathwater. This strategy forecloses attention to the body in its materiality. How do we account for the physical realities of women's lives and bodies if we have rendered them purely textual? As violence towards cis- and trans women mounts, and reproductive rights are threatened, as access to trans health services remains a matter of privilege and child care costs soar while welfare is slashed, it is increasingly obvious that women's everyday lives are shot through with oppressions that they feel acutely in their material bodies. As Susan Hekman observes, feminism's political commitment requires an accounting for the real, for two reasons:

> First, feminists want to be able to talk about the reality of women's bodies and their lived experience in a patriarchal world. Extreme linguistic determinism precludes such discussions. Second, feminists want to assert the truth of their statements regarding women's status in that world. Embracing social constructionism and the relativism that it entails makes it impossible to make such truth claims.
>
> (Hekman 2008, p. 107)

Thrownness, vulnerability, care 83

The vulnerability that creates the stakes for this accounting for lived experience increases with intersectional bodies. These include, for example, bodies that are both trans and Black, or female and queer, or immigrant and poor: any hybrid or multiple identity (Crenshaw 1989). Each of these sociological categories is itself lived in the body of the category it names. Therefore, the embodied realities of intersectional bodies are here urgently at issue. I would add to Hekman's statement, then, that women of color need to be able to talk about the reality of Black and Brown women's bodies, and their lived experience in a racist, white supremacist world; that disabled women need to be able to talk about their realities, transgender women theirs, and so on.

Hekman proposes that some feminist writers are assembling a "new settlement" by redrawing the distinction between construction and reality. What I would like to suggest is that there is some worth in crafting an ontological discourse that is also feminist – a philosophy that, as Levinas advocated, places ethics before ontology (Levinas 2008). Further, such a feminist ontology would advance efforts to honor intersectional feminism by rigorously attending to vulnerability, here defined as the embodied, lived conditions of bodies in a variety of linguistic, cultural, architectural and digital spaces. A philosophy that places ethics before ontology necessarily responds, is called by, specific embodied vulnerabilities. In this way, it finds itself foundationally obliged to acknowledge and respond – however inadequately – to the special precarity that arises out of a physically vulnerable body in a structurally embattled social position.

If we cannot introduce the embodied vulnerabilities that mark the reality of people's lives into our philosophical discourse, then that discourse is broken. But I don't think we've truly tried hard enough to say that for sure. These feminists of the "new settlement" – many who, like Haraway, have a foot in media studies (Haraway 1987) – seek neither to abandon the insights of the discursive turn nor reject the irreducibility of the material.[1] What follows, then, is a tent pitched in the space cleared by that settlement, one that takes up the question of feminist ontology precisely in terms of the digital age. It is a bid for a "new settlement" outside of the binaries that still govern scholarly discussions of feminism, media studies, and critical theory. The three terms in this essay – feminism, ontology and digital – mark three fields for whom boundaries between nature and culture, the mind and the body, and the material object and the cultural construction have been constitutive arguments, marking disciplinary divisions and theoretical camps. My contention is that these boundary disputes are not useful to a nuanced understanding of any of these fields, and thus I seek a third path.[2] In particular, I want to consider the ways in which digitality – here defined as an assemblage of objects and practices articulated to networked technologies of counting and pointing – has complicated the question of the body in ways that, I argue, are fruitful for both feminism and for a philosophy of media. I hope to show that a feminist ontology for the digital age is not in fact a

84   Margaret Schwartz

narrow advocacy for one kind of body in one kind of environment, but an organizing principle for all the affairs of living and being in a networked age.

Vulnerable bodies move in new spaces, at new speeds, and are aggregated and analyzed on an outrageous scale thanks to the global expansion of digital technology. And, all the ancient questions about what it means to *be* unfold in the context of both this (radical feminist) embodiment and this digital, calculative sweep. Therefore: a feminist ontology for the digital age poses the body as an existential question in the context of digital media.

Thrownness as an embodied philosophy of media

To philosophize as feminists means to attend to the body as a material object that shapes and is shaped by the cultural and technological forces around it. The structuring affect of this feminist ontology is *vulnerability*, and the concept at its heart is *thrownness*. Its principle politics is one of *care*.

Amanda Lagerkvist uses Heidegger's notion of *thrownness* to describe the "vulnerable situatedness" of our digital existence. Thrownness names the particularity of a place and time, the irreducibility of the fact to exist means to be situated, to find oneself in a particular context that isn't of our own making, nor wholly bends to our wishes. It is to be "faced with a world where we are precariously situated in a particular place, at a particular historical moment, and among a particular crowd with the inescapable task of tackling our world around us and to make it meaningful" (Lagerkvist 2017, p. 2). Making our world meaningful is an existential task – a labor, in Arendt's sense of a life-sustaining striving – that does not necessarily produce any measurable results. Here, too, is precarity, because our meaning making is fleeting and must be constantly rebuilt. Different bodies will experience different kinds of challenges to this meaning making activity: though all of it is an act of maintenance, for some bodies the work of making existential sense of the world is infinitely more difficult, either nipped in the bud or erased as soon as it comes to fruition. Our existence is a never-ending care labor practiced from the particular confines of a body situated in place and time.

Throwness leads to vulnerability because it marks the limits of individual control: our situations shift without warning, and our footing is uncertain wherever we land. While this vulnerability is arguably an irreducible part of the human condition, our current political and historical moment puts precarity into sharp relief. Huge populations are displaced because of war and famine, as in Syria and the South Sudan. From South America to Europe, austerity policies force drastic cutbacks in state support for the most vulnerable. Political nationalism is on the rise in Europe and in the United States, throwing up racist and nativist barriers to the asylum sought by the populations displaced by war and famine. In late neoliberalism, the social supports for inevitable vulnerabilities like childbirth, aging and illness are disappearing, or available only to those who can pay a high price.[3] Hence the precarity

Thrownness, vulnerability, care 85

of such conditions is heightened as the burden of cost to the individual mounts, and social and communal responsibility is structurally eroded.

Care is the ethical response to vulnerability: it is the consideration, accommodation and even compensation required when bodies are vulnerable, precarious, or at risk. Care invokes bodies in their precarity, and often involves the gentleness of touch, soothing, bathing or holding. But care can also involve practices online such as posting or commenting, or linguistic practices designed to accommodate the fact that language can wound as well as heal. Many of the practices of speech labelled as "political correctness" or even "politeness" are just that – linguistic markers of care designed to honor and protect a vulnerability. Care may also involve the use of technologies, machines and digital computing: many if not all of our medical procedures are complex interminglings of human touch, machine technology, and the digital (cf Langlois, Chapter 7 in this volume). This is why I choose to delineate care as an ethical response to vulnerability rather than a finite set of practices. As we will see, implied in the terms "ethical response" and "vulnerability" is an acknowledgement of the body in its thrownness. I am "throwing" the discussion into the doctor's office, the exam table stirrups; I am throwing the discussion into the toilet – because that is where the proverbial rubber meets the material road. A feminist ontology for the digital age is a practice of theorization forged out of precarious situatedness in a particular body.

New practices of counting and pointing variously grouped under the term "digital" create new environments into which our selves are thrown, with new vulnerabilities and new exigencies for care. Online spaces where digital existence finds itself are not at all disembodied, but in fact give rise to complex vulnerabilities that confound traditional binaries between mind and machine or body and text (cf Miller, Chapter 8 in this volume). As Benjamin Peters writes in *Digital Keywords*, the digital is often assumed to be synonymous with particular electronic computing techniques. Hence a digital camera is one that makes use of a certain technology, rather than a set of practices more or less facilitated by different technological processes (Peters 2016). But Peters begins his definition of the digital with its conceptual origin in the "digit" – the numeral, or even the finger on the hand. Two major functions of digits, even at their most elemental,[4] are counting and pointing. In this sense, the digital is not new, nor is it strictly technological. What is new, Peters observes, is the scope and speed of counting and pointing functions facilitated by new technologies. So, one major function of digital technology is to render all things radically countable: Peters cites Turing's 1937 assertion that all information can be expressed, with some loss, via the binary system of 0 and 1. The coldness or reductiveness that we may poetically associate with the digital is precisely the result of this flattening: the phrase "with some loss" marks oceans of nuance left unrendered, even where information rendered in code is robust enough to be legible.

This countability leads to the pointing function: once converted into code, information is "mechanically reproducible," to use Benjamin's term (Benjamin

86   *Margaret Schwartz*

2006) or, to use Peters,' "computationally copyable." Peters identifies this as a pointing function because of the possibility of reference. A copy references an original, a representation references the world in some way. So much of our conventional notion of the digital – our online lives – entails living in representational spaces whose reference to the world we complexly navigate.

Peters' critique of the standard definition of digital echoes Sarah Kember and Joanna Zylinska's call to understand media as everyday, time-dependent, situated practices rather than static objects (Kember and Zylinska 2012). It also aptly echoes John Durham Peters' definition of media as "vessels and environments, containers of possibility that anchor our existence and make what we are doing possible" (Peters 2015). In our analysis, then, we want to keep in mind that the "digital age" is one characterized by enormous scales of countability and reference. At the same time, it may not be helpful to focus attention on particular technologies or machines, but on the possibilities created by the situated practices in which such technology is deployed. Information can be counted at breath-taking speed and in staggering numbers – that is how surveillance and marketing data are collected and processed, for example. And, worlds of computationally precise reproducibility can be constructed out of this data – worlds that constitute an important element of our contemporary "thrownness," and thus create the special conditions of our existence.

Peters emphasizes that reference relationships function by exclusion: as indeed semiology from Saussure on acknowledges, indexical meaning depends upon pointing to *this* and not *that*. I argue, echoing postmodern descendants of semiology like Barthes and Derrida, that this exclusion function is the space where ideology operates (Barthes 1964; Derrida 1977). One question we will want to keep in mind, then, is what is excluded in contemporary functions of counting and pointing where they index the female body or gendered existence? The vulnerabilities at stake in both toileting and reproductive health often go unnamed – excluded from what Irigaray called the "grid of intelligibility" (Irigaray 1993). These are taboo subjects, or subjects veiled by racialized feminine mystiques: "natural" childbirth becomes a status marker for the upper classes, while poor, immigrant, Black and Brown women are subjected to unnecessary or hasty caesareans with poor postpartum care. The adage "breast is best" serves to shame women who cannot or do not want to breast-feed by suggesting that there is a simple, unquestionable "natural" superiority to formula, the technical alternative. This adage is backed by big data driven studies that sloppily correlate breast-feeding with factors such as IQ and level of education. In short, contemporary attitudes about reproductive health and toileting support Peters' assertion that the "natural" exists only insofar as people have set it aside as so. The price of this setting aside goes unnamed – and here I would like to call it forth as vulnerability, and ask for a response in the form of practices of care.

This chapter engages the notion of care precisely in an environment (or a series of environments) where the digital is part of the world we're thrown

Thrownness, vulnerability, care 87

into – and one of the tools at hand to make sense of it. Next, I return to Hanna Arendt's distinction between *labour* and *work* in *The Human Condition* as a way to better understand what exactly practices of care entail for practices of meaning making in a digital world. This distinction, which Arendt excavates from the etymology of the terms in ancient Greek, also marks a social reality of exclusion. Insofar as we will see that practices of care are *labour* and not *work*, the feminist project will be to use the digital to make visible, rather than exclude, these practices – because they are the very core of the ethical response to the vulnerability of a thrown being.

The explication of these terms helps me make the argument that practices of care are in fact the appropriately ethical, feminist response to the precarities of digital existence. These practices of care, which respond to the vulnerability of human throwness, engage with the specificity and materiality of the body in its interactions with meaning making structures that have the potential to either heighten or alleviate vulnerability. Thus to offer care is to offer a nuanced assemblage of practices, caresses and representations in articulation with bodies whose situatedness leaves them in varying degrees of precarity.

Arendt's theorization of caring labour

The Human Condition presents Hannah Arendt's taxonomy of the social by dividing it into three activities, each of which has a corresponding condition. So the activities of *labour, work* and *action* correspond to the conditions of life itself, worldliness and plurality, respectively. Briefly, worldliness is that which outlasts individual beings – it is that part of the human condition that *lasts*, like culture, and may be handed down. Plurality is the condition of political life: the fact that "men, not Man, inhabit the world" (Arendt 1998, p. 7). Worldliness and Plurality correspond to the publicness of life. And because we are here talking about women, who have so long been confined to and associated with the private realm, they are not our main areas of concern.

Labour is the activity that supports the biological process of the human body. Labour brings forth human life, but it also cares for it through cleaning, cooking, sheltering and tending. It's condition is life itself, not world – for it creates no lasting monument, only a continual response to the needs of the body. As such, Arendt notes that in *Politics*, Aristotle associates labour with slaves and farm animals – "those who with their bodies minister to the necessities of life" (Arendt 1998, p. 80).

This meaning of the term labour has been lost with modern usage, and Arendt revives it so as to preserve the important distinctions between life and world, and between work and labour. Work creates lasting things in the world; labour produces human life. Labour is ephemeral and invisible: "what they [the slaves] left behind them in return for their consumption [the literal use of their bodies] was nothing more or less than their masters'

88 *Margaret Schwartz*

freedom or, in modern language, their masters' potential productivity." What is produced by labour cannot be heaped up and put away. And in fact, the rise of private property does even more to reinforce this distinction, even as it is buried by usage (Marx refers to labour as the waged labour of the worker). Labour contributes to no accumulation, and receives not even a pittance of remuneration. What it does produce, Arendt observes, is "the elemental happiness that comes from being alive" (Arendt 1998, p. 108). We might update that language for our purposes to say the meaning making practices of care that address the vulnerability of thrownness.

It is worth noting that the body plays a central part in Arendt's definition of labour, and not just because of its connection with bodily life. She writes,

> Nothing, in fact, is less common and less communicable, and therefore more securely shielded against the visibility and audibility of the public realm, than what goes on inside the confines of the body, its pleasures, its pains, its laboring and consuming. Nothing, by the same token, ejects one more radically from the world [recall that world is the space of works and culture and publicity] than exclusive concentration on the body's life, a concentration forced upon man in slavery or in the extremity of unbearable pain.
>
> (Arendt 1998, p. 112)

Reproduction – social or biological – and toileting all squarely fall within the bounds of labour. And indeed, as Arendt asserts, some of the taboo and exclusion we've discussed around these subjects may be attributed to the radical exclusion of labour from the public. It is interesting that Arendt does not mention housework or care work, most of which is still done by women, in this analysis. In some ways, we are left to assume she includes it under the category of "slavery." But what Arendt has done here is to illustrate very succinctly, and according to her own unique taxonomy, the quandary presented by the body in philosophy, in ethics, in feminism and in the study of digital media. The confines of the body are inaccessible in some radical way to the worldly strivings of analysis and politics. And yet I must reiterate: the time is ripe to try, and the only way to do it is to take that radical inaccessibility not as an isolated fact, but as a relation – a vulnerability that calls out for care.

In the rest of the chapter, I will analyze two very different relations in which a vulnerability calls out for and receives very different kinds of care. My contention is that practices of care that recognize, name and honor the vulnerabilities of bodies in their radical difference from one another are uniquely capable of performing a feminist ontology in the digital age.

Icon underwear: leaky bodies

Icon underwear is a brand name product that purports to solve the problem of mild female incontinence. They are attractive, even fashionable

Thrownness, vulnerability, care 89

underwear that can absorb a small amount of urine, but are also very thin and unobtrusive under clothing. The underwear is reusable and machine washable. Under the name Thinx the same company also makes underwear for menstruation that is similarly reusable and fashionable. It's an alternative to either the adult diaper, panty liner, or sanitary pad; adult diapers and thick sanitary pads are larger and considered unattractive, even taboo. The appeal of Icon underwear is that no one but you need ever know: hiding in plain sight, the underwear is attractive enough to "pass." In this, both Icon and Thinx are advertised as "life-changing," where the transformation in question presumably has to do with managing the shame and taboo connected to incontinence and menstruation.

But while Thinx underwear are advertised on subway platforms and billboards in New York City, Icon advertisements are restricted to online spaces. Specifically, they pop up in social media feeds based upon one's online profile. So for example, I learned about Icon underwear because it kept coming up in my Instagram and Facebook feeds. The reason it appeared there and not, for example, as a banner ad in fashion blogs or other websites I visit like Amazon is because my identity as a *mother* is most obvious in my social media feeds. While my online browsing profile might more easily portray me as an academic, a left-wing person, a Jewish person or someone interested in gardening, my Instagram and Facebook feeds are full of images of my children. I belong to a group called Academic Mamas on Facebook. My Instagram feed is almost exclusively pictures of my children, a shift I made consciously a year or so ago as Facebook became a more public, professional space. Wanting to keep my "mommy life" separate from my public life, I switched my image sharing with friends and family to a platform that didn't feel quite so public.

Why is Icon advertising triggered by my sharing of photographs of my children? Because many women who have given birth vaginally have minor incontinence issues.[5] Without directly criticizing the prevailing focus on impossible beauty ideals both as women age and as they recover from new motherhood, the brand advertises itself as a haven from this exhausting pressure to perform legible femininity, providing a kind of frank, "let's get real" sisterhood that will help women regain their self-respect in a world that does not understand, let alone accommodate, their bodies. The private and targeted advertising facilitated by digital computing – where data can be aggregated and analyzed with enormous speed and precision – forecloses the possibility of addressing the problem in a political or communal manner.

To illustrate the ways in which this example brings together what I am calling the 'discursive' and 'materialist' strands at stake in discussions of feminism, ontology and digitality, I'll turn to Judith Plaskow's work on toileting. Focusing on "bathroom issues" shows how the built environment enables or restricts different bodies' access to the public sphere. Moreover, toileting is *labour* in Arendt's sense: it is part of the cyclical striving needed to keep a body alive and thriving. Small children, the elderly, the ailing and

90 *Margaret Schwartz*

the disabled are all people for whom toileting might involve help or special technical innovations, from diapers to accessible toilets, to helpers and catheters and colostomy bags. Insofar as labour is "despised," to use Arendt's terminology, this crucial caring labour is effaced, shamed, or simply ignored. While groups like the P.I.S.S.A.Rs have successfully formed coalitions to advocate for gender-neutral and accessible bathrooms, toileting remains a largely untapped site of physical, embodied, yet also built and technological oppression. As Plaskow points out, female senators must cross through a gallery open to the public to reach a ladies' room, while their male counterparts run no such gamut (Plaskow 2008). The built environment thus both reinforces and reflects cultural ideas about which bodies belong where.

The need to eliminate is materially incontrovertible, but the spaces afforded for this need are culturally constructed. For example, Plaskow notes that gender segregation in bathrooms marks the boundary between public and private elimination: bathrooms in the home are rarely if ever segregated by gender, while public bathrooms almost always are. Incontinence or the inability to properly follow social norms concerning elimination leads to social stigma – either infantilization or ostracizing. Thus we use diapers for babies and for incontinent adults, and discipline and reject those who wet the bed or eliminate in public, whether due to illness, mental disability, homelessness or even exhibitionism.[6] Different bodies have different requirements for the universal human need for elimination, but *all* bodies require this accommodation in order to function in the public sphere.

Simply providing an equal number of toilet facilities for men and women effaces these important differences in what individual bodies may need. For example, 30 percent of women aged 15 to 64 suffer some kind of incontinence, in part because of the biological changes brought about by childbirth – while the rate among men in the same age range is at most 5 percent. This statistic implies that women require more ease of access to toilet facilities than men, while the universal joke in lines for ladies rooms everywhere is that precisely the opposite is chronically the case.

While access to bathrooms has been politicized in transgender rights and in disability rights, feminism has not politicized toilet access outside of solidarity with these issues, perceived here as marginal or ancillary. Plaskow notes that not only is there lack of proper toileting for women, but women also accept this as a normal part of life. Even the twenty-first-century feminist is so accustomed to sweeping biological femininity under the rug that she is unlikely to militate for accommodation. She simply does what she needs to do to survive the space (Plaskow 2008, 2016).

Icon underwear functions digitally both as a practice of pointing and as a practice of counting. As counting, digital computing and data mining allows its niche advertising strategy, which saves it from ridicule and allows women to discreetly take advantage of its offers. As pointing, the Icon underwear website and ad copy represent – point to – a world similar and adjacent to our own, a world we perhaps would like to live in, where women's problems

Thrownness, vulnerability, care   91

are a topic of frank and practical discussion. Below, a careful analysis of this world, which is constructed through text and image, with an eye towards critiquing the distance between what it promises and what it is actually able to offer in terms of *care* for vulnerable bodies.

The initial ad that appeared in my feed shows a couple of white women who look to be in their fifties or sixties standing together wearing black underwear. It does not look like a diaper, and indeed the fact that it's black and stylishly cut suggests, along with the women's state of undress, that not only is there "nothing to hide" here, but indeed there is something to show off or expose. Thus these women who are, in every element of the nominal content of the ad, flagged as incontinent to a greater or lesser degree, are by the visual rhetoric of the ad also framed as invulnerable – impervious not only an embarrassing toilet accident but also to the fear of appearing in public unclothed. Though manifestly unashamed of their aging bodies, the women's thin appearance and non-normative aging (these are bodies and faces of a certain tautness, as well as a certain slenderness) suggests that such confidence is only available to those for whom the laws of time and gravity seemingly do not apply.

Clicking through from the Facebook ad to the Icon website, a banner headline matter-of-factly declares, "Yep, it happens to 1 in 3 women, from spring chickens to silver foxes." The layout is stylish, with minimalist type, clean lines, and lots of white space. A pop-up invites users to "join the Tinklehood," and there are what look like emoji style avatar/icons that reinforce the idea that the "Tinklehood" involves women of all ages and ethnicities. The landing page offers a 30-day refund policy if not satisfied, explains how much liquid the undies can contain (six teaspoons), explains that they are designed to replace "pads and pantyliners," and concludes with the fact that the underwear are machine washable and "totally life changing." ("Icon: Pee-proof Underwear," n.d.)

The photographs accompanying this informal, girlfriend-to-girlfriend conversational copy are also emancipatory in their visual rhetoric. Women of a range of ethnicities, ages and body shapes are shown in the underwear. They are posed to suggest intelligence or strength and competence rather than sexual allure: three of the images show woman doing different athletic activities (yoga, Pilates, unself-conscious dancing). One shows a woman with silver hair staring contemplatively away from the camera while seated with her legs loosely crossed on a wooden chair. A full glass of water balances on the chair's slender arm rest, but the woman in the chair pays it no attention, markedly unconcerned about the risk of a spill. Water plays an important part in the euphemistic imagery of the brand, with another image showing simply several small glasses of water on a wooden table, one placed precariously on the edge. This hint of overspill is of course a metaphor for the out-of-control feeling of incontinence, the anxiety of feeling that one may at any minute "spill" and give oneself away as an embodied creature with particularities unique to one's individual body. The woman in

92 *Margaret Schwartz*

the photograph with the glass balanced next to her wears an expression of serene unconcern, thus advertising the "life-changing" confidence that wearing the Icon underwear brings.

Yes, Icon underwear do acknowledge and even validate the embodied reality of a woman's body. Indeed, in a move that mirrors Foucault's send-up of the "new Victorians" in *The History of Sexuality*, Icon all but congratulates itself on its boldness in addressing female incontinence. Where the digital returns, then, is also Foucault's point: in the distribution of power through (digital) networks whose practice as discipline links them explicitly – materially – to capitalist relations of production (Foucault 1978).

This invitation in the private space of the computer or smartphone screen, to come out of the closet, so to speak, and to proudly identify as one of those women by buying a product, seems revelatory in an age where women's menstruation and toileting issues are still widely shamed and hidden. Yet the very "life changing" nature of the underwear is that it doesn't look like what it is – a diaper. The fact is, Icon underwear mean you never have to come out of the closet – or search desperately for the nearest toilet.

And because the digital counting and pointing of social media are also consumer platforms, this promise of a changed life is linked to the purchase of a particular commodity. The thong runs $28 per pair, while the hi-waist style costs $34. While a woman might think twice about entering a store to purchase such a product, she can discreetly order them online, and in styles that wouldn't belie their practical purpose in the bedroom, under clothing, or at the gym.

Yet a feminist ontological perspective allows for an analysis of the ways in which embodied precarities translate and transmute in the digital space, and reveals the cost of relying on the current digital environment to facilitate a truly revolutionary feminist politics. The website's images, its affiliate marketers, and its branding as a progressive and social justice-oriented enterprise (a portion of every purchase goes to fund surgery for women with fistula, a rare and more extreme kind of childbirth-caused incontinence) all highlight the particular vulnerabilities at the sites where bodies meet the promise of connectivity.

The fact of reproduction, the essence of it, is still a source of shame, effacement and fetishization. It is not possible, rhetorically, theoretically or politically, to assert that this biological fact results in very different requirements for women's full participation in public life. Instead, the burden falls on those women who can afford it to manage their own participation without making an uncomfortable fuss for anyone else. As for those who can't afford to spend $30 on a pair of underwear, they'll just have to keep hiding in shame and running for a toilet that's always too far away, and with a long line.

What Icon underwear is offering the women who can afford to pay for their underwear is essentially an opt out of the body and of a communal responsibility for its care. For several hundred dollars a year (let's assume

Thrownness, vulnerability, care 93

these are pretty hardy undies), you can nearly buy your way out of your body. You can pretend for others and maybe even for yourself that for you, toileting is a simple matter. Moreover, you will perhaps feel less oppressed by the lack of proper facilities that can accommodate you: if there is an urgent need that cannot be immediately satisfied, it's no problem! Icon Undies are the life-changing solution that gets you out of the uncomfortable relation between your body's needs and the built environment upon which it relies.

Except of course, it won't. "Joining the Tinklehood" is about as public as joining a pornography subscription site – it's need-to-know only. It does nothing to honor labour, nor does it contribute to what Arendt's "elemental happiness" in being alive. It is another chapter in the ancient book that scorns labour and fetishizes work. I cannot stress enough that this book is written in the blood of the bodies that nurture and care and labour, no matter their gender.

As Arendt shows, the book is ancient. The tools Icon underwear uses are somewhat different than those Aristotle drew upon when he relegated labour to enslaved people. Hekman points out that feminist science studies makes use of Deleuze and Guattari's notion of assemblage to describe the imbrication of "science" or facticity and "culture" or the discursive (Hekman 2008). In an assemblage, different elements are non-hierarchically articulated, and this articulation is mobile and relational (Deleuze and Guattari 1987). In the case of Icon Undies, the facticity of the body and its gender specific toileting needs are articulated to late capitalist consumerism, to the affordances of niche marketing and narrowcasting via social media platforms, and to the rhetoric of body positivity and consumer activism. No life-changing valorization of labour is included in this assemblage, nor is any call for a communal undertaking of care. Instead, self-care and care for others is a lonely affair that takes place out of sight and sound of the public realm. The burden of care is thus squarely settled on the shoulders of individual bodies.

GynePunk: bodies honored, named, saved

The year is 1830-something, and in rural Alabama, a Dr. Skene is about to perform surgery on the body of an enslaved women named Anarcha. Dr. Skene is interested in learning more about the reproductive function in women, and so he will conduct over thirty operations on Anarcha, without the use of anesthesia. He justifies this abhorrent practice in the name of science, falling back on the cultural construction of the enslaved body as a feelingless tool for furthering of white knowledge and gain. Anarcha's sufferings under Skene's knife will earn him a lasting place in medical history: now known as the "father of gynecology," Skene's name is immortalized in the scientific nomenclature of the female anatomy. The gland that may be responsible for female ejaculation is named for him ("Skene's gland" 2017).[7] Every single person who goes to medical school to become an obstetrician or gynecologist, or who learns the anatomy of the female reproductive system,

94 *Margaret Schwartz*

learns his name. Without knowing it, every cisgender woman carries a map in her body of the brutal mining of black female bodies for knowledge, profit and gain. This maiming is in itself an extension of the historical context: white settler colonialism, plundering land for profit, saw the bodies enslaved on that land as yet another resource to exploit.

Anarcha's plundered and wounded body is the literal emblem of the ontological codetermination of the discursive and the material. Relegated discursively to the status of barely-human, her physical being yielded up information and knowledge that bore in its essence some mark of her pain.

Feminist activists and hackers who call themselves the GynePunk collective, critique this history by reinscribing it. In an effort to at least commemorate Anarcha's pain, these students of gynecology and researchers into alternative, queer- and trans-friendly reproductive care have renamed Skene's gland Anarcha's gland. It's a complicated move, because they don't have the power to make every anatomy textbook in the world reflect their critique. Yet their move acknowledges the power of naming and moves from this discursive space into a material space where women's bodies receive different care. This includes not only the actual laboratories and clinics where the GynePunks treat women and train practitioners, but also the online spaces where they describe their values and redraw their maps of the reproductive systems, with annotations that honor and commemorate the contributions of a once-effaced Black woman.

In closing, I'll offer this example of women working together with both analogue and digital tools to shift the burden of care from individually precarious bodies to communities structured by an ethics of care. In these communities, labour is indeed visible and audible to the public realm, and its honorable undertaking is the basis for the values of the community.

The GynePunk movement uses 3D printers, hacked lab equipment, recycled hardware and basic electronic components to create and disseminate the means for women to have safer and less violently intrusive gynecological exams. Some of this means remaking instruments such as the speculum so that they are safer, more comfortable, and more effective – for example, the GynePunk speculum has a hacked webcam inside it to facilitate close inspection of the cervix, as an alternative to the painful and intrusive practice of biopsy or scraping. All of their designs are open source: they are not seeking profit from their innovations, but instead serve the higher goal of making their world a less violent place for women's bodies, including queer and trans bodies.

Hacking – the subversive use of digital technologies – is central to their feminist communal ethos. "This hacker mentality, for me, serves as a new way to understand the world around us, and gives us many tools to develop and generate our own technologies," says Paula Pin, an early GynePunk.

> We understand our body also as a technology to be hacked, from the established ideas of gender and sex, to exploring the capacity to start

Thrownness, vulnerability, care 95

researching ourselves, to find our own ideas and technologies, to help us
be free, autonomous and independent from the system.
(https://motherboard.vice.com/en_us/article/qkvyjw/meet-
the-gynepunks-pushing-the-boundaries-of-diy-gynecology)

This understanding of the body as "a technology to be hacked" illustrates
several of the ideas under discussion in this chapter. First, if the body is a
technology, it does not represent some irreducible biological substrate independent of cultural and ideological forces. Instead, the body is a made object,
but its makers were "the system" and the tools to self-understanding and rec-
lamation of this body are stolen – hacked. One definition of hacking involves
using technology for a purpose other than the (corporate) one for which
it was designed. Here, the web camera, so often a source of surveillance
and voyeurism in mainstream society, becomes a tool for helping women
to understand their bodies in a less intrusive way. Secondly, the quote lists a
number of different *practices* of freedom that also involve "ideas and technologies," as well as "the capacity to start researching ourselves," which is a
reference not only to knowledge about the body but to the tools used to gain
that knowledge. In this sense, mediation and technology are not inert objects
or even an intervening layer between consciousness and the body, but a series
of situated practices. These practices unfold in real time and in particular
spaces, and they have transformative potential. As discussed earlier, in *Life
After New Media* Sarah Kember and Joanna Zylinska make the case for a
shift in understanding new media, not as a series of objects, but as a practice
of mediation (Kember and Zylinska 2012). In this, they dovetail with Benjamin Peters' assertion that the digital is not so much a particular kind of
technological interface as it is a process of counting and pointing. The Gyne-
Punks understanding of their own practices is very much in line with this
understanding of media, technology and the digital as practices undertaken
in time by particular bodies in particular spaces. As such, their specifically
feminist project highlights the ways in which this process-based notion of the
digital age is of a piece with an explicitly care-oriented ontology of media.

The GynePunk project is also inherently intersectional. Because theirs is a
practice of care, the GynePunk ethos recognizes the vulnerability of certain
kinds of bodies. Describing her own reasons for involvement, GynePunk
Klau Kinky says,

I came from a country where abortion is still illegal. I had myself a risky
illegal abortion in Perú 14 years ago. As a migrant I have been mis-
treated and insulted in Spanish gynecology rooms. I'm involved in this
work because it's something that my body needs, it's something vital,
as a political struggle about taking back technologies, taking my body
back and away from all this violence.
("Meet the GynePunks Pushing the Boundaries
of DIY Gynecology" n.d.)

96 Margaret Schwartz

The language here holds together the "vital" nature of the body and the "political" struggle against the violence enacted by hegemonic power structures that seek to discipline and disregard that body.

Notice, however, that despite the personal reasons for wanting to engage in political struggle, the GynePunks understand their struggle not as private, but as inclusive and community based. Their pooled knowledge and experience results in a world where trans, queer, disabled and any vulnerable body feels at home. It is a practice of radical care directed towards the precarity of those bodies for whom the "system" is an experience of suppression and violence.

Here the violence is not only that of experience, of the intrusive and sometimes assaultive scene of the exam room. It is also the implied violence that ignores or suppresses the pain, delicacy and great danger that women's embodiment imposes on their existence. In their practices of hacking, repurposing, redesigning and educating, the GynePunks radically honor the particular precarities of the female body. More: in so doing, they radically honor the particular precarities of *all* bodies. Their work is explicitly directed towards queer and trans health services, meaning that not every body that comes to them is engaged in cisgender reproductive activities. And, in renaming Anarcha's Gland, their scientific work involves a symbolic reclaiming of the body *of knowledge* from its racist roots. Here again, the body is both inextricable from but not reducible to the discursive networks that give it meaning. The GynePunks, thrown as they are into the vulnerability of their migrant, queer and female bodies, have engaged in material, technological practices to re-inscribe that meaning. ("GynePunk," n.d.).

A hybrid form of existence emerges as the linguistic and cultural practice of naming mingles with the communal living and working of young Spanish women (a country in the EU that's been hard hit with recent austerity measures in the economic downturn since 2008), and with the technological and scientific practices of hacking and laboratory testing. The being and the doing of feminism are here codeterminate, operate in assemblage with the repurposed technologies and the renamed anatomy of woman. The body being taken back is multiple: it is a body of knowledge and of practice, of flesh and of machine. The body produced is similarly multiple, and one of its incarnations is virtual: in Tumblr blogs and Facebook pages and websites like Hacketeria, the GynePunks make themselves known to others, disseminate their knowledge, and share art and writing dedicated to their political cause. If a feminist ontology for the digital age looks like anything, it looks more like a GynePunk than a pair of pee-proof underwear.

Conclusion

A feminist ontology for the digital age resists neoliberal capitalism's atomization of society and its rationalization of human care and striving. In recuperating the particulars of the body, I seek to write a radically intersectional

Thrownness, vulnerability, care 97

notion of the feminine, one that resists the essentialism of identity politics. In its best intentions feminism works against the hegemony of capitalist, white supremacist patriarchy. A feminist ontology thus understands being as enmeshed in overlapping structures of privilege that allow some bodies to thrive while relegating others to neglect, marginalization and outright genocide. More: a feminist ontology theorizes neglect, marginalization, appropriation, exploitation and genocide as the very condition of possibility for privilege – and seeks to overturn it. Within the context of a feminist ontology, the digital appears neither as a set of technologies neutrally, naturally expanding on given capacities – nor do we find historical determination manipulating reality to its own ends. Rather, we find a space of potential where the despised labour of care – the ethical response to vulnerability – might under some circumstances be represented differently. If the power of digital has until now been consolidated in the hands of a few, that is by no means a reason why it has to remain that way forever. Naming Anarcha's body and her vulnerability is a practice of posthumous care that has the potential to affect how bodies appear in the endlessly iterable space of the digital. It makes public a very private suffering, and that is an act of material reparation.

Notes

1 Tina Chanter's work is an excellent place to start for a feminist philosophy that deftly attends to both materialism and cultural constructionism. In her work on Heidegger and Levinas, Chanter both takes seriously the promises of both figures and takes no quarter in critiquing their failings. For example, on the question of Heidegger's Nazism, Chanter affirms that one can neither dismiss it as irrelevant biography – for it can be found to inform many of his central ideas – nor, given his stature and influence, is it useful to simply dismiss Heidegger altogether. Rather, Chanter follows Levinas in reading Heidegger as a serious thinker in need of serious revision – and in turn holds Levinas responsible for the ways in which his critique falls short, particularly with regard to the feminine. Chanter shows that the feminine is at work in Levinas' account of time in Heidegger's work, but that it is afforded an ill-defined, unfleshed status that replicates idealized and mystified notions of female bodies and experience. I don't mean to say – and this is part of why I've included this in an endnote – that Chanter's argument about Levinas' reading of Heidegger is central to what I'm exploring here. Instead, I would like to take Chanter's method and ethos as my model here, and think about what a feminist ontology would mean, precisely in the context of a philosophy of media.
2 I'll confess, too, that the political climate here in the United States (and its echo in right-wing nationalism in Europe) has me desperate to find coalition and inclusive resistance. It seems to me that the left defeats itself with infighting, and we have lost that luxury. This isn't to say that the concerns of those who have historically been marginalized by the left are unimportant – quite the opposite. It's a call to craft a position that hears these claims of marginalization, that precisely makes itself vulnerable to the charge of essentialism, exclusion or even racism, so as to move forward together. It strikes me that what the white supremacist right in this country feeds on is the fear of this vulnerability, the anxiety to not have to face the painful reality of social inequality, especially if one is already marginalized in some

98 Margaret Schwartz

other way (as, for example, poor rural whites who have supported Trump because they feel left behind by globalization).

3 A case in my home state of New York painfully illustrates this point. State funding for children with special needs stipulates that the child must be in public school to receive those funds. In one school district outside New York City, a large Hasidic population of ultra-orthodox Jews sends their children to private yeshivas – but also has a high proportion of children with special needs. A bitter feud over the distribution of these funds ensued between public school families, many of whom are Black and Latino, and the yeshiva families. Although their children do not attend the public schools, the Hasidic community rallied the vote to put a majority of their members on the school board. In a measure that seemed retaliatory to the public school families, the newly Hasidic majority board passed drastic budget cuts, driving two of the district's elementary schools to close. The bitterness overflowed into racial and ethnic hatred along the highly charged lines of the division between the Hasidic families and the public school families – both of whom, it should be noted, were relatively disadvantaged economically. My point is that this conflict might have been avoided had state funding to support children with disabilities been more readily available. The care of these children is expensive and hard to predict – it has no clear end date. It may range from teaching a blind child how to use a cane, to special tutoring or additional teacher training and support, to a fleet of aides required to assist a child whose mobility and communication require extensive support, as well as the purchase and upkeep of equipment. From the point of view of the Hasidic population, it was a human rights abuse to claim that their children should have to leave the linguistic (most Hasidic families use Yiddish as their primary language) and cultural/religious environment of the yeshiva, in which they felt comfortable, simply to qualify for these crucial services. The retaliatory act – to essentially starve the public school system – was misplaced because it was state support for disabled children that was already scarce and contested. Both populations were devastated by their reliance on an ever-shrinking pool of state support for the most vulnerable among them.

4 It's no accident that the theoretical engagement with the digital that speaks best to my project is one that traces its origins back to the body.

5 I actually had two C-sections, a fact that isn't particularly well-noted in my Instagram feed. But it's important here, because it means that my pelvic floor didn't suffer any damage when I gave birth. While researching for this chapter, I was teaching a class on Race, Class and Gender in Media for undergraduates and my rants on Icon underwear found their way into more than one lecture. It occurred to me that my students might actually wonder whether I had an issue with incontinence and just wasn't telling them – which itself became part of the joke of the topic. "I would totally tell you guys if I peed myself!" I told them, laughing, warning that a so-called "natural" childbirth is not always the preferable route. I might have had major abdominal surgery twice, but at least for now, I don't actually NEED Icon underwear. The point here is that it doesn't matter; as my students' and my own embarrassment indicate, the vulnerability and shame are the same.

6 I'd argue that uncontrolled or unconcealed incontinence is nearly universal grounds for social abjection. Homeless people and the mentally ill – those who smell like filth – are outcast in the most fundamental sense. Having no place to take care of one's elimination, conversely, condemns one to expulsion from human society.

7 There is some disagreement among GynePunks, historians and critics about whether the surgeries performed on Anarcha were done by Skene or by another so-called father of gynaecology, a Dr. Sims. I think the point stands nevertheless – that GynePunk reclamations of the female body are acts of resistance against patriarchal white supremacist medicine in the name of the enslaved female bodies that provided its grounds for knowledge.

Thrownness, vulnerability, care 99

Bibliography

Arendt, H., 1998. *The Human Condition* (2nd ed.). Chicago, IL, and London: University of Chicago Press.

Barthes, R., 1964. Rhétorique de l'image. *Communications*, 4, 40–51.

Benjamin, W., 2006. The Work of Art in the Age of Mechanical Reproduction. *In*: M. G. Durham and D. M. Kellner, eds. *Media and Cultural Studies: Keyworks*. Malden: Blackwell Publishing, 18–40.

Crenshaw, K., 1989. Demarginalizing the Intersection of Race and Sex: A Black Feminist Critique of Antidiscrimination Doctrine, Feminist Theory and Antiracist Politics. *University of Chicago Legal Forum*, 139–167.

Deleuze, G. and Guattari, F., 1987. *A Thousand Plateaus: Capitalism and Schizophrenia*. Minneapolis: University of Minnesota Press.

Derrida, J., 1977. Signature Event Context. na.

Foucault, M., 1978. We 'Other Victorians.' *In*: Hurley, R., trans. *History of Sexuality Vol. 1: An Introduction*. New York: Pantheon Books, 2–13.

GynePunk [WWW Document], n.d. Available at: http://gynepunk.tumblr.com/?og=1 (accessed: 15 December 2016).

Haraway, D., 1987. A Manifesto for Cyborgs: Science, Technology, and Socialist Feminism in the 1980s. *Australian Journal of Feminist Studies*, 2, 1–42. doi:10.10 80/08164649.1987.9961538

Hekman, S., 2008. Constructing the Ballast: An Ontology for Feminism. *In*: S. Alaimo and S. Hekman, eds. *Material Feminisms*. Bloomington: Indiana University Press, 85–119.

Icon: Pee-Proof Underwear [WWW Document], n.d. Available at: www.iconundies. com/ (accessed: 15 December 2016).

Irigaray, L., 1993. *An Ethics of Sexual Difference*. Ithaca, NY: Cornell University Press.

Kember, S. and Zylinska, J., 2012. *Life after New Media: Mediation as a Vital Process*. Cambridge, MA: MIT Press.

Lagerkvist, A., 2017. Existential Media : Toward a Theorization of Digital Thrownness. *New Media and Society*, 19(1): 96–110.

Levinas, E., 2008. Is Ontology Fundamental? *In*: A. T. Peperzak, S. Critchley and R. Bernasconi, eds. *Emmanuel Levinas: Basic Philosophical Writings*. Bloomington: Indiana University Press, 1–11.

Meet the GynePunks Pushing the Boundaries of DIY Gynecology [WWW Document], n.d. Motherboard. Available at: http://motherboard.vice.com/read/meet-the-gynepunks-pushing-the-boundaries-of-diy-gynecology (accessed: 15 December 2016).

Peters, B. (ed.), 2016. *Digital Keywords: A Vocabulary of Information Society and Culture*. Princeton, NJ: Princeton University Press.

Peters, J. D., 2015. *The Marvelous Clouds: Toward a Philosophy of Elemental Media*. Chicago, IL: University of Chicago Press.

Plaskow, J., 2008. Embodiment, Elimination, and the Role of Toilets in Struggles for Social Justice. *CrossCurrents*, 58, 51–64.

Plaskow, J., 2016. Taking a Break: Toilets, Gender, and Disgust. *South Atlantic Quarterly*, 115, 748–754. doi:10.1215/00382876-3656147

Skene's gland, 2017. Wikipedia. https://en.wikipedia.org/wiki/Skene's_gland

4 Digital unworld(s)

The Bielefeld Conspiracy

Yvette Granata

Introduction

The Bielefeld Conspiracy is an internet phenomenon that began on a bulletin board in the 1990s that claimed that the real German city of Bielefeld does not exist. Briefly, the story goes that this claim was posted to the newsgroup *de.talk.bizarre* on 16 May 1994, by a computer science student at the University of Kiel named Achim Held. The conspiracy includes a story that the city of Bielefeld was actually invented by a mysterious group known as 'THEM,' whose aims for inventing the city are unknown. Internet journalist Robert Boumis describes the phenomenon:

> Do you know anyone from Bielefeld? Have you ever been to Bielefeld? Do you know anyone who's ever been to Bielefeld? The city of Bielefeld is allegedly located in North-Rhine Westphalia in Germany. The population is supposedly about 323,000. But no one on the Internet has been able to substantiate the existence of this town . . . Little information is known about the purpose of this fake city. But a fake city would be attractive to a number of unsavory factions. Rumors of a CIA rendition facility, an alien crash cite quarantine zone, or a Mossad operating base have all been proposed as explanations for The City That Is Not There. But ultimately, Bielefeld is a mystery.
>
> (Boumis 2013, np.)

More than just a web prank, the effects of the Bielefeld Conspiracy have crossed into the space of the city over time, and into contemporary German politics. The reaction to the conspiracy produced dialogue and action plans in offline space that further added to the phenomenon. In 1999, the city put forth a press campaign called 'Bielefeld git es doch!' ("There really is a Bielefeld!") in order to increase awareness of the city. In 2012, Angela Merkel, while speaking at a town hall meeting, mentioned her own travels to Bielefeld, adding the joking comment "if it exists at all" and "I had the impression that I was there" (Boumis 2012, np.). Lastly, as Boumis points out in his article, due to several years of heavy construction that obscured most of the city from the Autobahn until late 2007, "it seemed somewhat plausible that there was no city on the other side of the construction" (2012, np.). The Bielefeld Conspiracy is not only an internet discussion, but involves a set of relations across bulletin board posts, the urban space itself, and the socio-political relations of the city, including the municipal economic expenditure for the production of a PR campaign. This digital conspiracy has not only reallocated some of the city's resources but, even if only in a small way, shaped socio-cultural relations to Bielefeld now for nearly two decades.

In the 1970s, Henri Lefebvre laid the groundwork for analysis of urban relations and social-economic production as understood through the manner in which physical urban infrastructures remake social relations, affirming and excluding segments of the social fabric (Lefebvre 1976). Lefebvre's city is a machine that produces and unmakes social relations, controlled by the dominant classes at the centre of the city, while those on the periphery are left out, forgotten and erased. In the last decade, critical software studies and human geography has tied the production of urban space to digital and software-based infrastructures, looking at the ways in which digital capture practices and software have become integral to the production of urban space (Thrift and French 2002). Urban software has been reframed as the machine that runs in the background of Lefebvre's city machine, through which certain urban features and social relations are newly captured, sorted, constructed and excluded by the software's structure (Graham 2005). Data is captured as material to build and structure the world, while data that is left out of this process becomes peripheral, erased from the world.

What then, about Bielefeld, the 'City That Does Not Exist'? In what way can we view the efficacy of a single bulletin board post that had an impact on an actual municipality? Implicit in the notion of digital capture models and software-produced worlds is a particular ontology of 'the world' itself – a constructivist world where what appears to the system is what counts and is what is accounted for, while what is left out of the system is what is forgotten and erased from 'the world.' To claim an exclusion from the world, however, one must take a certain ontological stance of what constitutes 'the world.' Rather than thinking through what is a part of or excluded from the 'world,' philosophically, this chapter shifts to think about the relation of contemporary internet culture, data and mechanisms of erasure through the lens of New Realism and Markus Gabriel's 'no world view.' In Gabriel's meta meta-nihilistic frame, the foregrounding of ontology rather than of metaphysics melts away the central impetus of metaphysical inquiry – thus removing the notion that reality is to be mined beneath the appearances of things (Gabriel 2015). Just as the internet claimed that 'Bielefeld does not exist,' Markus Gabriel's meta meta-nihilism claims that 'the world does not exist.' Beginning with the 'no world' premise of meta meta-nihilism then, there is no need to account for the mismatch between what 'appears' in the world and what does not. With the advent of a series of phenomena, from the widespread occurrence of 'fake news' across mainstream politics and

102   *Yvette Granata*

media, to the deletionist model of Wikipedia editing, to new forms of protest and intervention, such as the calls to 'delete your Uber account,' I claim that ubiquitous erasure is now a contemporary condition. How then shall we think of what is erased and deleted, if not within a frame of appearances; if not through what does and does not exist?

In this chapter, I look through the claims of the non-existence of Bielefeld and the non-existence of 'the world,' using the Bielefeld Conspiracy as just one example of contemporary digital culture that points to something other than the capture model and urban software-based infrastructures as producing erasures of the city and the world. Instead, I use Bielefeld as an example that relates to a wider conceptual frame for an ontology of deletions. Firstly, I give an overview of how critical frameworks of the capture model relate to the theoretical claims of the production and erasure of space, and then shift from the notion of data capture to identify various practical differences of 'erasure types' specifically focusing on how the Bielefeld Conspiracy operates as just one type – erasure as 'false data.' I then put forth that ubiquitous software also now reveals an ontology of ubiquitous erasure, or a 'digital unworld.' I seek ultimately to outline the notion of a 'digital unworld' as a case of how digital practices of erasure specifically produce an agglomeration, or a real database, of relational erasures. In other words, rather than viewing erasure solely as the effect of power and political exclusions, I explore the questions: Can erasure and deletion be framed as another form of digital existence? Do ubiquitous practices of deletion, rather than practices of capture and construction, reveal another ontology – the digital unworld – as now a part of our digital existence?

Background: production of space, erasure of the world

In 1994 Philip Agre charted models of data tracking systems in which the practices of 'capture' of information were implemented as "the deliberate reorganization of industrial work activities to allow computers to track [activities] in real time" (Agre 1994, p. 101). Agre traces the historical construction of data capture models that stem from industrial systems and that aided in the formation of other tracking systems such as surveillance systems, giving an account of the tracking of a FedEx package with barcode data as it travelled through production in order to observe the steps of delivery for maintaining efficiency and quality assurance. The seemingly innocuous data of the package's barcode is a specific data type that must be made relatable to other parts of the system further down the line. Such a beginning point of capture is the manner in which data types become integral for constructing the logic of other systems used to track information about human activities and production processes, or the manner in which each level becomes interoperable based on an initial data type. Rob Kitchin and Geoffrey Bowker, for example, both assert that the manner in which data is conceptualized helps to henceforth shape databases and data infrastructures which "fundamentally change the practices and organization of research" because "they tell us 'what we can and cannot say' by defining what is remembered and what is ignored and forgotten" (Kitchin 2014, p. 64, cited Bowker 2005). Tracey Lauriault (2012) resounds this in her work on the Canadian Census and Atlas of Canada as archives that develop recursively based on the data that constitute the 'institutional memory system.' For example, the archives are constructed via sensor-based data, web mapping standards, portals, metadata, open architectures and interoperability and affects the manner in which the data in the archive henceforth modulates the model of institutional memory. In other words, when a system is apt to capture a certain type of data, its expansion further structures other parts of a system to make use of that data according to a nested ability of readability, reinforcing the interoperability of the initial data into wider techno-social systems. What is left out is framed as simply forgotten and erased.

In 2002, Nigel Thrift and Shaun French noted a shift to the capture model of software systems – that data assemblages and software systems were no longer assistive in tracking production data within an urban infrastructure, but instead claimed that software has become the central force of production of urban space itself. They identified "the major change . . . taking place in the way that Euro-American Societies are run" as cities became fully interwoven with software, thus looking to "new landscapes of code" that began "to make their own emergent ways" (Thrift and French 2002, p. 309). For example, they noted how in the year 2000, the Y2K bug marked a new type of urban and social crisis that prompted audits of municipal computerized systems of all sectors of public life around the globe, including "the banking industry, gas, water and electricity supply, food retailing, the post office, the police force, the fire brigade, hospitals and emergency services" (2002, p. 315). For Thrift and French, Y2K revealed the shift of the pervasiveness of software and the infrastructural reliance upon its data assemblage as the very construction of urban space – of the urban world. In less than a decade from Agre's observations then, software-based systems quickly instilled and infused themselves into all forms of urban infrastructure like a deep digital cellulose, transforming every arm of production of urbanity, responsible for not only upholding and producing urban space but for the moulding of everyday life.

Along with the moulding of life, of course, comes the exclusions of life – or as Susan Leigh Star has said: "one person's infrastructure is another's difficulty" (Star 1999). Following Star's line of thinking, Stephen Graham points to the manner that software-generated infrastructures produce 'difficulties' not necessarily through what software systems actively capture and construct of the world, but instead, through the manner in which software and data sorting systems exclude parts of the world. 'Software-sorting' frames both what is tracked and coded into the infrastructure and what is left out of it; how one person's data captured is another person's data exclusion. For example, Graham analyzes Geographical Information Systems (GIS) and

104   *Yvette Granata*

how it can create a dynamic map based on the sorting of direct consumption information from data warehouses, store credit cards, direct marketing campaigns, internet activity, and so on (Graham 2005). Such a map is based on data from neighbourhood populations that spend the most money and where they spend it. In the GIS case, the neighbourhood is thus a map of consumer data, not a map of the multiple domains of the neighbourhood. Such a map lays out addresses for potentially lucrative company store-fronts – where you'll find your nearest Starbucks and where the next location for a Mac store will be. The streets of this map are populated only with spending potential. Lower income areas are excluded by the fact of their having less spending data. This type of data assemblage map produces what Graham calls a "software-sorted apartheid" (2005). What builds 'the world' via software sorting practices, in this case, is that which makes profit for a capitalist technocracy. As opposed to the production of space, software sorting here is Graham's turn of phrase for naming a software induced 'social unbundling,' or the production of an erasure of part of the world through the commercialization, privatization and digital commodification of the public sphere. Ubiquitous software and data assemblages in this case erase 'the world' by unbundling the social fabric through the virtual exclusions enabled by software.

Across the works of Agre, Lauriault, Thrift and French, and Graham, a particular framing is built: a cybernetic empire builds a spider-bot web of relations of production and seeks nothing else but to capture life as value into its world web. What is not captured remains invisible to the map and invisible in the database and is thus forgotten, left to decay, erased from 'the world.' We may see this as a critique levelled against the construction of a dystopian panopticon world, built in a way that affirms existence only through its perpetual capture and forceful silences. Rob Kitchin points outs that, while some modes of capture do in fact aid in discoveries, they nonetheless do so at the expense of producing silences and erasures, as he states,

> databases create silences, adding to the inherent gaps in the data, as much as they reveal relationships between data and enable some questions to be answered; they constrain and facilitate through their ontology, producing various presences and absences of relations.
>
> (Kitchin 2014, p. 64)

In Lauriault and Graham's critique, databases and software systems are framed as *equivalent* to the power of software to exclude and produce erasures from the world. In this analysis, the Foucauldian machine of non-apparent power accounts for both the ontology of the software database and the world. Data relations create and sustain power relations independent of the person or program that uses it, and what has not been made visible to it has not been given access to participate in the relations of the social economy. What is left out of the database and software therefore produces not only absences, but relational erasures. The ontology of the database and its software-based relations are construed as the world and the critique of its erasure, or as Jean-Luc Nancy puts it, "what forms a world today is exactly the conjunction of an unlimited process of eco-technological enframing and of a vanishing of the possibilities of forms of life and/or common ground" (Nancy 2007, p. 94). In this way, criticism of a constructivist capture model of computerized systems is a metaphysics of how the world is created through the 'appearances' of captured things, and as the confirmation that those certain things indeed exist. Non-capture and exclusion are thus the metaphysical explanation of how things are erased from the world. In other words, software-based systems framed in a constructivist manner, implies simultaneously that 'the map is not the territory' yet the data assemblage *is* nonetheless the metaphysical explanation of the world.

The above line of thought ontologizes only one data model paradigm as 'the world,' producing a theory of what happens when appearances are indeed taken as reality. In Michael Ferraris' terms, such a position is less about the ontology of 'the world' and more so an analysis of the ontology of power, which he calls the 'fallacy of knowledge-power' (Ferraris 2015). He indicts such a line of critique as a postmodernist renegade thought that "has cultivated the idea that reality is actually constructed by power for purposes of domination" – or that reality is actually isomorphic to power (2015, p. 143). This begs the question: are exclusions erasures of 'the world' due to a system's failure to capture pieces of that world into it? Or are these erasures the result of the conception of 'the world' itself? Put differently, through the critique of the capture model we have a notion of data as either related to inclusion or exclusion from a system, where exclusions then must necessarily function as the method of erasure by the power of those in control. In the post-truth digital world, however, erasures seem to have become just as pervasive as appearances. We participate daily in innocuous digital erasures of images, delete social media posts, filter out and delete more emails than read emails, drag file folders to garbage bin icons, sort through and discard fake news and fake friend requests, delete ourselves from social media accounts, and receive calls to action to erase mobile apps, such as Uber, in order to protest. Erasure is no longer an activity in the hands of hierarchal power, but a daily and populist activity. As such, digital erasure is also more than an accumulation of exclusions.

Ubiquitous erasure and the alt-deletion of the world

In order to think through another type of erasure model, I use the Bielefeld Conspiracy as a different category of data and digital erasure. My aim is to look through the manner in which Bielefeld reveals a specific active erasure mechanism at work rather than an implicit or explicit ontology that is isomorphic to power. Looking firstly to other frameworks, I bracket 'exclusions of data' as only one type of erasure mechanism. The shift towards deletion

106   *Yvette Granata*

has already been identified by some contemporary theorists, such as with the turn towards thinking 'digital death' as with the work by many writers in this volume. Such a reframing of erasure and deletion point us to the broad range of software supported practices of deletion: disconnection, denial and the various instances of digital 'death' of and in the digital world. Looking to other theoretical moves that expand notions of erasure not as merely the result of ubiquitous capture models nor as what does not appear to the system of power, we can see that there are already various forms of erasure enumerated.

Rather than as an escape from the trap of a high resolution panoptic prison and the torture of perpetual capture of presence that only stamps out social life, both Tero Karppi and Amanda Lagerkvist respectively look to the manner in which erasure is prevalent and necessary in digital culture. Without looking through the frame of valuations of 'good' and 'bad,' Karppi looks at the example of the 'Web2.0 Suicide Machine' as one example in digital culture that "point[s] out that there is a need and interest for digital suicide" (Karppi 2011, p. 4). Lagerkvist likewise describes the manner in which a "technologically enforced lifeworld" such as ours includes digital death and erasures that do not necessarily fall into the victimologic narrative of the powerless being erased, nor as the digital erasure of world. Instead, she frames capture as revealing how "our thrownness entails a fragility (intrinsic also to our originary human technicity)" and that "this fragility is at once a source of fecundity: it enables the opening of a space for productive *action*, in relation to the situation into which we are thrown" (Lagerkvist 2017, p. 3). Digital death and erasure framed in this regard includes not just the effects of the software infrastructure created by the state, the military, and the forces of capitalist corporations, but as Lagerkvist states, also "the meek, the mourners, the fainthearted and the sometimes resolute" (p. 4). Both Karppi and Lagerkvist couple erasure with the needs and rights of digital death as a part of human technicity on the one hand, and as building potentially new relations and altogether different forms of sovereignty on the other. We might call this 'alt-deletion' or the ability to erase as the right to deletion, the right to digital death, rather than the erasure of being forgotten by the powers that be. Such a right to deletion may be seen as similar in kind to the right to remain silent, rather than as being silenced. Lagerkvist's and Karppi's work are two examples in which digital erasure has begun to be framed as part of the normal practice of erasure, through digital death rituals, the maintenance of needs and the option of self-assigned silence.

Said differently: what is *erased* from the map can also be the territory. Such a view shirks the postmodernist habit of critique based on a zero-sum totality of power relations and the process of 'worlding' through capture in one direction. The call to erase the Uber app in protest of US anti-immigration policy decisions in late 2016 may be viewed as another example of the shift in the power relations of erasures, no longer solely in the hands of the state or data tracking systems, but literally in the hands of anyone with a cellphone. In his work on planetary computation, Benjamin Bratton likewise reframes

Digital unworld(s) 107

notions of erasure as no longer the 'bad object' but as multiple and reversible. He names sorting practices of data assemblages, including erasures, as the 'accidental megastructures' of 'the stack,' a model drawn from an in-depth analysis of how interoperability shapes a software development stack beyond the capture-control model. Rather than the unilateral power embedded in the notion of exclusions, he frames the paradigm of inclusion and exclusion as various forms of sovereignty "work[ing] by the normal sorting of what is and is not an externality" (Bratton 2016, p. 104). Bratton inserts the notion of verticality to accompany the erasure and production of worlds along an axis of 'reversibility' in order to replace the paradigm of unidirectional top-down powers of erasure controlled by the state or by capitalist production. The vertical lines of the stack "normalize the exception of reversibility, making the movement between inside and outside into a programmed function of infrastructural surfaces and interfaces" (p. 32). In other words, the 'world' and what does and does not appear within it is no longer the victim of the power of digital capture but a play of interactions of both capture and erasure as reversible processes, and even eventually outside of human control.

Taken as digital suicide, as a right to silence and closure from capture, and viewed along the vertical axis of reversibility, the relation of capture and erasure is no longer isomorphic to power nor framed as a unilateral determination. As such, power itself becomes the victim of the reversibility of both capture and erasure. If both presence and digital erasures now produce various political effects in their own right, or if they have been opened as a two-way street, then captured presence is no longer the digital norm that verifies and affirms existence. While Thrift and French named ubiquitous software as indicating the production of space itself, we might now name another shift. After software saturates the city and permeates our lives, its counterpoint arrives – the ubiquity of digital erasure.

False data as erasure type

A model of ubiquitous erasure requires a fuller enumeration of erasure types. While we have touched upon a few of the theoretical shifts that look at ubiquitous forms of erasure, from digital suicide and self-deletion, digital death as disconnection from capture, and verticality as the reversibility of erasure and capture, what we still lack is a comprehensive theory of digital 'erasure types' as to match that of data types and software structures, their various mechanisms, forms, illusions and effects. While out of the scope of this chapter to enumerate them all, I will look to a couple more examples. For example, one of the more innocuous and everyday forms of digital deletion is the erasure of digital objects, such as deleting a file. Yuk Hui describes the appearance of digital objects and states that,

> digital objects appear to human users as colorful and visible beings. At the level of programming they are text files; further down the operating

108　*Yvette Granata*

system they are binary codes; finally, at the level of circuit boards they are nothing but signals.

(Hui 2012, p. 387)

When we erase digital objects, we likewise move through these levels of appearance and remove the link to the colourful object, through commands to the circuit board signals, and through rearranging the binary code of the data. When we drag a blue folder icon from the desktop and place it in a digital trash bin icon, it is seemingly 'gone' with a click. In actuality the file is not gone, but unlinked or disconnected from the desktop interface. The memory slots assigned to it further down the system are unlocked and the memory previously allocated to that file is opened; it is no longer safe from being overwritten. As its memory storage is reallocated, it is overwritten by new files in various parts and at various times. The deleted digital object remains partially in existence (and retrievable) while, simultaneously, it is partially erased. The mechanism of erasure in this case is the unlinking of saved data from the interface and the unlocking of memory slots in which the file data is stored. As with the capture-production model, ubiquitous erasure includes all of these various levels of erasure types, albeit where erasures are types or modes of un-storage and non-retrieval, unlinking nested levels of connections through various mechanisms of overwriting, moving and deletion functions.

Despite the joking nature of the Bielefeld Conspiracy, I look to 'Bielefeld' as an example to speak through another type of erasure. On the one hand, I use it specifically for its seemingly apolitical nature, to look further at the manner that digital erasures operate on a different register and not necessarily as a 'bad object.' In keeping with Philip Agre's work, in which he traces the manner that capture models were further modelled from seemingly innocuous data, such as the FedEx barcode, I take the Bielefeld Conspiracy as a similar form of innocuous data, albeit of an erasure type. Furthermore, while digital suicide and unlinking are examples of mechanisms of erasure, the case of 'Bielefeld does not Exist' points to another kind of erasure mechanism that falls within the milieu of erasure types: false data.

For good reason, the notion of 'true' or 'false' data does not sit well with many critics. Similar to the critique of 'facts' within the archive of knowledge, Lisa Gitelman points out that data are 'always already cooked' by the structure that selects the data (Gitelman 2013). Rob Kitchin likewise points out that "data do not exist independently of the ideas, instruments, practices, context and knowledges used to generate, process and analyze them" (Kitchin 2014, p. 29). While helpful as criticism within the context of the production of knowledge, this line of thought may be seen as consistent with a philosophical constructivism, in which data are the *hyle*. Bits of amorphous information float around in the outside world, and are formed and shaped by the decisional structure of the software's functions and sorting practices. In other words, the concept of 'cooked data' here again repeats

Digital unworld(s) 109

the notion that 'the map is not the territory.' The critique remains that the data are not the representation of reality.

Looking at this notion through the lens of Markus Gabriel's meta metanihilism, we can call such a purview 'interface skepticism,' which perpetually reveals "that we mistake immediate access to the interface with immediate access to something else" and that with this mode of critique,

> all we might hope to show, therefore, is that the nature of the information available to the representational system (be it language, consciousness, thought, cognition, knowledge, justifiable belief-formation or what have you) might differ from the expectations inherent in the operation of the system.
>
> (Gabriel 2015, pp. 14–15)

Gabriel further identifies interface scepticism generally as the difference between metaphysics and ontology, where metaphysics always seeks only to explain the difference between appearances and reality. While critical data studies has identified that data – whether true or false – still operate as data, pointing to the divide between datum and factum, little scholarship has looked to the manner in which false data further differs from other types of data. In other words, while we have an in-depth analysis of true data as captured and sorted and data exclusions as a form of erasure, we do not have a theory of how the inclusion of false data produces and enables different functions. In the post-truth digital world, where falsity brings multiple immediate effects and potential disasters, locating the difference between appearances of false data and reality is not enough. The pervasiveness of false data in contemporary digital culture begs for further analysis.

As a specific type of data, 'false data' is made operative in a specific way within our software supported infrastructure. Looking at the effects of false data, rather than simply criticizing it as false, I argue that false data operate as an erasure mechanism precisely because they do something different than the intent of the system into which they are captured. While false data are supported by software in the same manner that 'true' data are, the effects of false data are noticeably different. Looking again at Thrift and French's example of Y2K as indicating ubiquitous software and the production of space, we may likewise reframe it as an example of how 'false data' are not only a part of the production of space, but equally part of a mechanism of ubiquitous erasure. Y2K was the scare that everything would reset computerized calendars to zero zero, causing systems to collapse, destroy and erase the world. The activity of structurally supported false data can thus indeed be extremely damaging. If the '00' were to be read by the computer as the year zero zero, such would be false and would erase the calendar's intended function, while the '00' read as the last two digits of two thousand would be correct and the intention of the computerized system intact. Although many systems were fixed before the year 2000, and 'the world' did not end,

110   *Yvette Granata*

there were nonetheless multiple consequences, including the incorrect risk assessments for Down syndrome sent to 154 pregnant women due to the miscalculation of the mother's age, with two abortions carried out as a result (Wainwright 2001). In light of this, instead of the production of space, we can reframe the possible and actual catastrophes of Y2K as indicating the global effects of false data that work to undo or erase the global intent of a system.

As a piece of data and a false statement, 'Bielefeld does not exist' is not merely a linguistic contradiction of a true fact. From the point of view of the computer system and the digital infrastructure that carries it across the internet, there is no difference between true and false data. As Kitchin points out, data are not 'facts' and "when a fact is proven false, it ceases to be a fact. False data is data nonetheless" (Kitchin 2014, p. 31). Data can thus be conceived differently at the outset than the role that facts play in knowledge formation and its critique thereof. With facts, what is true is seen as a statement of fact, and often tends to include a statement about what exists. Alexius Meinong's concept of 'non-existence objects' exemplifies this notion, for example, as it addresses the concern of the fact of existence of certain objects that are imaginary or intentional in the mind, such as unicorns (Findlay 1933). The statement that 'Pegasus exists' implies that it is true that an existent object of a 'unicorn' does in fact exist in the domains of thought and of imaginary creatures, whether or not it is possible as a biological horse-species by zoological standards. While the example of the unicorn falls into a wider discourse that relates to 'fictional objects,' Meinong's non-existent objects further addresses the logic of existence statements. For example, the notion of a 'round square' is framed as a non-existent object rather than as a contradiction. In this way, Meinong contests the law of non-contradiction as it is posed by Whitehead and Russell (1910), that a statement and its contradiction are mutually exclusive and exhaustive of the other. In classical logic, there are two sides of a contradiction and they cannot co-habitate. On the other hand, with Meinong's concept of the non-existent object, this law can be violated, as a 'square circle' may be a non-existent object without necessarily being an exclusive and exhaustive contradiction in total relation of one side to another. Such is relevant for the notion of 'digital false data,' as it also provides example for the manner in which contradictions may co-habitate.

The philosophical problem of identifying the difference between facts and statements of existence, however, does not enter into the picture in the same way when looking through the digital frame of 'data.' A digital unicorn is of course always already existing as digital data, and can be stored and retrieved in multiple forms, such as a JPEG or GIF. The existence of digital unicorns has never been posed as 'fictional data.' Within the context of data, data-assemblages, and software structures, fictional objects pose little problem and are quite easily supported and affirmed within digital existence. The Bielefeld Conspiracy, on the other hand, has a more complex status. It

Digital unworld(s) 111

is a false statement, 'Bielefeld does not exist,' and yet this false data is highly supportable and interoperable across digital bulletin boards, socio-political relations, and it has produced noticeable effects upon the city. The Bielefeld Conspiracy is thus neither merely a contradiction of fact nor a fiction, but instead points to how software can produce something else – an effectual deployment of false data supported by a digital infrastructure.

That false data do neither operate as a contradiction nor as fictional data aligns with Gabriel's conception of 'false thought,' where "the difference between true and false thought is that true thought holds good of its object(s) whereas false thought is in part or entirely dissociated from its object(s) by not holding good of it" (Gabriel 2015, p. 20). Thought that begins to dissociate from its object is one that no longer holds the object together – in other words, false thought is one that aids in erasing its object. Not 'holding good' of a digital object is quite literally the description of the process of digital erasure: unlinking a folder from the desktop and unlocking the memory slots that contain its data is a method of no longer holding the digital data together as a singular object. It is a scattering of its memory storage as open fields to be overwritten by various incoming digital requests. As such, false thought and false data are mechanisms that enable the unlinking of an object's memory-store, slowly and in parts, rather than exhaustively. Looking to the structures and methods of falsity in the digital realm means to no longer analyze falsity as an improper representation in the service of debunking a purported image of reality, and neither in the terms of the linguistic model of exhaustive contradiction, but instead at the particular erasure effects produced. The Bielefeld Conspiracy viewed as 'false data' allows us to further articulate what false data *do*.

False data is only one type of erasure mechanism that can be deployed to break an object apart. The contours of an object, such as the actual city of Bielefeld, are breached from a conspiracy statement and from the misreading of zeros as resetting the calendar. From within the domain of digital practices, erasure is itself a reality, just as all data are data. In other words, erasure is an existing thing itself which can affect various parts of objects rather than the notion that deletion is 'erasure of' the reality in the world. In the case of Bielefeld, we may further see the way that false data is not in opposition to reality, but performs a function similar to the one that the ubiquitous software and capture model does in the production of space. False data aid in the reallocation of working memory and city resources, and can quickly do so from little more than a single post on an internet bulletin board. Just as there is no 'raw deletion' that immediately removes something from the universe with a click, a digital erasure is composed of nested operations, methods, software practices, and fields where the erasure effects can and cannot further affect certain things. The erasure of urban space through software is therefore equally a multi-step process as the production of space, with its own set of erasure types, methods and functions that correlate to the operations of software-based infrastructures.

112   *Yvette Granata*

The digital unworld: Bielefeld, and the world, do not exist

Rather than different vying modes within a complete totality, true and false data only compete in certain domains of existence. This coexistence happens across different domains and problematizes the notion of a 'totality of the world.' Looking at these practices as ubiquitous erasure, I pose that we are moving toward a condition of erasures which are not merely symptoms of structural holes and political (dis)enfranchisement, but beyond that, are a type of production of the digital 'unworld.' Stepping away from interface scepticism requires the idea that there is indeed no 'world' or reality in totality that is constructed by either software systems or erased by it. The Bielefeld Conspiracy as a digital unworld reveals that both the actual city of Bielefeld and 'Bielefeld does not exist' structurally co-exist in certain domains but not others. They do not totally annihilate each other, but co-constitute, hold together and pull apart various parts of the social world. This ontology of the digital unworld aligns with what Deleuze, following Nietzsche, puts forth of the 'powers of the false' in his analysis of the cinema and the way in which mythological histories of the State presented in film can co-create the State. The powers of the false point to the notion that fiction and 'truth' co-mingle in a manner that does not induce the loss of reality. As Deleuze instead argues, "the 'true world' does not exist, and even if it did, it would be inaccessible, impossible to describe, and, if it could be described, would be useless, superfluous" (Deleuze 1985, p. 133). Markus Gabriel's meta meta-nihilism likewise resounds Deleuze with a similar rejection of the 'world,' that existence is not "to be one or a one, a unified object, be it unified in itself or unified by thought, language, discursive practices, the symbolic order, the neurochemistry of what we think of as intentionality or what have you." (Gabriel 2015, p. 105). To Gabriel's list and to Deleuze's cinematic powers of the false, I add that data capture, data-assemblages, software, digital infrastructures, and their exclusions and erasures are not the totality of the digital world.

While Deleuze's powers of the false necessarily employs Nietzsche's 'will to power' and thus incorporates political power as 'force' as part of its ontology, I stay close to the New Realism of Gabriel. This in order to move away from the notion of power as 'force,' and to instead keep a view on the mechanisms of erasure and false data that ubiquitous software allows us to further describe beyond the amorphous category of 'force' and 'power.' False data in action reveals a type of active meta meta-nihilism in which a map of 'the world' does not exist in effect. What exists is instead that which is made to be relational through the structural fields of objects and domains, whether real or fictional, true or false. False and true data intertwine and are deployed through networked software databases, producing various outcomes of both production and erasure, indicating that true and false data are not separate modes of existence within a single totality of a world, but that they simply perform different tasks.

Digital unworld(s)   113

True and false data can thus appear simultaneously wherever a field of sense is conducive for them to appear. Rather than a will to power, the false data of the Bielefeld Conspiracy appears in the field of the 'bulletin board' because the bulletin board is a field that enables its existence. It then appears along any subsequent field that supports its appearance, in the field of 'conspiracy theory,' the field of 'socio-political relations of the city,' and so on. Each of these fields are like database fields, which can store either false or true data, and can further appear in relation to other fields wherever possible. In other words, the actual city of Bielefeld and the notion that 'Bielefeld does not exist' are *actually* relational data across digital database fields, as opposed to contradictory. Framed in this way, the territory has never been the map, but rather both the map and the territory co-exist across multiple fields and structures. They need not be a unified whole to produce a complete picture of reality. The complexity of ubiquitous software includes the complexity of ubiquitous erasures – and a meta meta-nihilism that is not a totality but is a description of the set of fields that can host both true and false data simultaneously.

Such a paradigm shift might enable a mode for thinking through the processes of urban production and erasure differently, not only of the manner in which data sorting aids in the 'unbundling of the social,' but also for including an understanding of the 'bundling of false data.' The ontology of the 'digital unworld' as a bundling of false data, the fictional, the imaginary, and the unreal, structurally bundled across software systems – is as an active *part* of the social. In light of events occurring in the age of ubiquitous software, such as the global phenomenon of fake news and viral disinformation, and the speed of the political effects that alt-right conspiracies, meme mythologies, and superstitional science pose as a threat to, not 'the world,' but the planet, a paradigm shift that analyzes the abyss of false data and erasure as complex mechanisms may be fruitful and necessary for future research. Ubiquitous erasures as a contemporary condition points out that our software is not a totality, but rather, that we perpetually inhabit deletion. The Bielefeld Conspiracy reveals only one small door for thinking through the ontology of the digital unworld and the broad condition of digital deletion through false data. 'Bielefeld does not exist!' is thus a statement of an ontology of the digital unworld, a beginning for thinking through 'false data' and its effectual production, and for probing its mechanisms in order to provide for a wider theory of erasure. Bielefeld, and the world, do not exist!

Bibliography

Agre, P. E., 1994. Surveillance and Capture: Two Models of Privacy. *The Information Society* 10 (2), 101–127.

Boumis, R. J., 2012. Extra: Merkel Also Doubts the Existence of Bielefeld. *WELT*. Available at: www.welt.de/newsticker/news3/article111575893/Auch-Merkel-zweifelt-an-Existenz-Bielefelds.html (accessed: 1 July 2018).

114 Yvette Granata

Boumis, R. J., 2013. Bielefeld Does Not Exist? *Geek News Network*. Available at: http://geeknewsnetwork.net/2013/07/15/bielefeld-does-not-exist/ (accessed: 1 July 2018).

Bowker, G., 2005. *Memory Practices in the Sciences*. Cambridge, MA: MIT Press.

Bratton, B., 2016. *The Stack: On Software and Sovereignty*. Cambridge, MA: MIT Press.

Deleuze, G., 1985. *Cinema 2: The Time-Image*. Trans. H. Tomlinson and R. Galeta. London: Continuum.

Ferraris, M., 2015. New Realism: A Short Introduction. *Speculations VI: A Journal of Speculative Realism*,141–164.

Findlay, J. N., 1933. Meinong's Theory of Objects.

Foucault, M., 2012. *Discipline & Punish: The Birth of the Prison*. New York: Vintage.

Gabriel, M., 2015. *Fields of Sense: A New Realist Ontology*. Edinburgh: Edinburgh University Press.

Gitelman, L., 2013. *Raw Data Is an Oxymoron*. Cambridge, MA: MIT Press.

Graham, S. D. N., 2005. Software-Sorted Geographies. *Progress in Human Geography*, 29 (5), 562–580.

Hui, Y., 2012. What is a Digital Object? *Metaphilosophy*, 43 (4), 380–395.

Karppi, T., 2011. Digital Suicide and the Biopolitics of Leaving Facebook. *Transformations Journal*, 20.

Kitchin, R., 2014. *The Data Revolution: Big Data, Open Data, Data Infrastructures and their Consequences*. Los Angeles: Sage Publications.

Lagerkvist, A., 2017. The Media End: Digital Afterlife Agencies and Techno-existential Closure. *In*: A. Hoskins, ed. *Digital Memory Studies: Media Pasts in Transition*. New York: Routledge.

Lauriault, T. P., 2012. *Data, Infrastructures and Geographical Imaginations: Mapping Data Access Discourses in Canada*. Ph.D. Thesis, Carleton University, Ottawa.

Lefebvre, H., 1976. *The Survival of Capitalism: Reproduction of the Relations of Production*. New York: St. Martin's Press.

Nancy, J. L., 2007. *The Creation of the World, or, Globalization*. New York: State University of New York Press.

Star, S. L., 1999. The Ethnography of Infrastructure. *American Behavioral Scientist*, 43 (3), 377–391.

Thrift, N. and French, S., 2002. The Automatic Production of Space. *Transactions of the Institute of British Geographers*, 27 (3), 309–335.

Wainwright, M., 2001. NHS Faces Huge Damages Bill after Millennium Bug Error. *The Guardian*. Available at: www.theguardian.com/uk/2001/sep/14/martinwainwright (accessed: 1 July 2018).

Whitehead, A. N. and Russell, B., 1910. 1913. *Principia Mathematica*, 3.

Wood, D. and Graham, S., 2006. Permeable Boundaries in the Software-Sorted Society: Surveillance and the Differentiation of Mobility. *In*: M. Sheller and J. Urry, eds. *Mobile Technologies of the City*, New York: Routledge, 177–191.

Part II

Being human

Extension, exposure and ethics

5 You have been tagged

Magical incantations, digital incarnations and extended selves[1]

Paul Frosh

You have been tagged.

The first time I received this message, from Facebook – alerting me to the fact that I had been identified by name in an uploaded photograph – it was not, in fact, the first time I had been tagged. I had probably been tagged as a newborn baby in a maternity ward, and I definitely recall being tagged with a plastic bracelet on several other occasions in hospitals. More memorably, I had been tagged during military service: one metal dog tag hung on a chain around my neck, another was inserted into a special opening in my boot – a duplication designed to offset the difficulties that bodily dismemberment or severe trauma might cause in identifying me following a battle.[2] Surprisingly, however, none of these existentially significant instances of tagging, enforced by powerful social institutions (medical, military) tasked with managing the life, disease and potentially violent disintegration of my body or mind, caused nearly as much anxiety as the message from Facebook. This anxiety had nothing to do with the nature of the uploaded image, which was an unremarkable old photograph (that I had never seen before), of me, aged 15 or so, sitting next to a friend at school. What was disturbing was the mere fact of being tagged: by whom, for what purpose, and in view of whom was not immediately certain. All I knew was that somewhere out there, in the uncircumscribed vastness of 'the web,' a photograph was passing before unknown eyes; and it had my name on it.

Being tagged in uploaded photographs has today become a commonplace feature of digital culture, and this intense initial experience of ontological insecurity – the acute perception of exposure and disturbance to my sense of self-possession – has declined, though it has not vanished entirely. Indeed, the aftershocks of being tagged seem to persist as an ongoing yet manageable condition of mild unease. That the condition is both unsettling and manageable emerges from Martin Hand's brief but illuminating discussion of tagging as part of his research on students' photo-sharing practices. Hand observes that while tagging has become ubiquitous, many are highly selective about how – and of whom – they use it, remaining wary of the practice because it gives unauthorized (and not entirely predictable) access to others'

118 *Paul Frosh*

profiles and images, and because it is frequently interpreted as an assertion of ownership over an image of someone else (2012, p. 179).[3]

Admittedly, such wariness seems inconsequential when weighed against the existential gravity of non-digital forms of tagging in securing the integrity of the self at moments of supreme vulnerability. Being tagged in a Facebook photograph occurs in a lighter, more frivolous, sphere of the lifeworld than being issued dog tags to wear in battle. Nevertheless, in this article I will embrace Amanda Lagerkvist's contention "that the mundane and the extraordinary co-found (while often remaining separate fields of experience in secular cultures) the existential terrains of connectivity" (2016, p. 97). Tagging on social network platforms, I will argue, is deeply indebted to seemingly weightier practices for establishing and maintaining our being in the world, and the experience of being tagged provides a catalyst for reflecting on some of the existential conditions of digital media. Attempting to preserve the intensity of its initial occurrence, and despite its gradual routinization, I will explore the implications of being tagged as a 'limit-situation': a potentially life-defining moment where our circumstances of digital existence are "principally felt, and our security is shaken" (Lagerkvist 2016, p. 98).

Two existentially important practices which precede and inform being tagged will be at the centre of my discussion: the assigning of names to persons and the incarnation of bodies through photographs. These practices – each of which enjoys a venerable and diverse history – qualify as humanly significant in as much as while their particular forms and execution may vary widely between cultures and periods, there appears to be no human society that does not give names to persons or make figural images (or, at the very least, institute a taboo against making such images). Naming and figuration are also strongly connected to the life of the *self*, its presentation and extension in space and time, its entry into symbolic and imaginary psychic registers, and – as my opening comments on medical and military tagging suggest – to limit-situations of being such as birth and death. Naming and figuration combine to construct and extend the self through objects which instantiate, replicate and disseminate the individual subject discursively, visually and materially.

Digital tagging, moreover, reinforces and transforms practices of naming and figuration by virtue of an additional property. The digital tag is an operative sign whose use alerts those connected to the tagger and the named person to the latter's appearance in a photograph. This operative dimension not only means that social network systems such as Facebook repeatedly employ the powers of naming and figural incarnation, but that these powers are exercised as technological feats of magic – incantatory in the case of names, and sympathetic in the case of images – that animate the digital social network. By alerting our contacts to the fact of our being tagged every time it happens, by making being tagged a recurrent cultural rite of naming and incarnation that invites confirmation and assent (likes, comments), these systems flesh out the exchanges among contacts into the reflex responses of a social 'body' that is more than merely informational. The everyday existential condition that results reveals digital media as sensuously and symbolically entwined domains of individual and collective life that should not be reduced, in either thought or nomenclature, to abstract schemas of computation, information or networking.

The incantation of the name

With the rise of online social network services (SNS) like Facebook as key mechanisms for storing and displaying photographic images, new techniques for identifying, classifying and circulating images have become important. Tagging is perhaps the most prevalent of these techniques, though it is not restricted to photographs: 'Web-based *tagging systems*', Marlow et al. observe, "allow participants to annotate a particular *resource*, such as a web page, a blog post, an image, a physical location, or just about any imaginable object with a freely chosen set of keywords ('tags')" (Marlow et al. 2006, p. 31; original italics).[4] While tags can be algorithmically generated, for instance by using the metadata automatically embedded within an image file (e.g., geotags based on the camera's location), they are widely produced by users creating their own verbal associations and annotations, and especially through identifying others in images.

Indeed, social network services such as Facebook actively encourage the tagging of people since it helps to maintain and intensify connective activities via their platforms, to amass data about users and their social behaviour, and to develop automated face-recognition algorithms (Norval and Prasopoulou 2017).[5] The utility of tagging, both for social network platforms and for users, is not simply due to its role as a 'folksonomy' (Beaudoin 2007) – a bottom-up taxonomic procedure for creating new associations between images and labels – but, in the case of proper name tags, because tagging actively circulates photographs among the contacts of both those doing the tagging and those being tagged. For example, when you tag someone in an image on Facebook, it is seen by your own Facebook 'friends,' but it is also likely to be seen by 'friends' of the tagged – irrespective of whether they are also your 'friends'. Following the overall imperative to 'share' in social media (John 2016), this circulatory function is structured asymmetrically in the interests of platform connectivity rather than personal privacy: the default setting on Facebook, for example, is that you can be tagged without giving prior permission, though you can change this setting (and review all tags before they appear), and you can also remove tags of yourself post facto (though you cannot remove the image from Facebook itself without the cooperation of the person who uploaded it).

While tagging refers to the more or less unconstrained attachment of keywords to a range of digital resources, the experience of *being tagged* in uploaded photographs presents us with a special case: the allocation of one's name to the visual image of an identifiable body.[6] Tagging is therefore a kind

120   *Paul Frosh*

of deictic pointing – the name 'Paul Frosh' is given referential specificity by being bound to the body shown in a photograph. Names, however, are not merely linguistic designators.[7] To name is an expression of power. This is most obvious in the *assigning* of names: "By structuring the perception which social agents have of the social world", Bourdieu observes, "the act of naming helps to establish the structure of this world, and does so all the more significantly the more widely it is recognized. i.e., authorized" (1991, p. 105).[8] The assigning of personal names is usually undertaken by intimates (such as parents), where naming both expresses institutional power as well as interpersonal care, though it can also be undertaken by more formal and less personally invested agents (think, for example, of the renaming of migrants by immigration officials).[9]

Yet names are not only instruments of power. Names perform the 'entanglement' (Bodenhorn and von Bruck 2006) of the individual subject within the web of relationships, hierarchies, values and beliefs in a given society, simultaneously constructing the sense of singularity attributed to the named individual while establishing their relations to others (naming is thus important in the performance of subjectivation: the social production and reproduction of subjects). Nowhere is the importance of this entanglement clearer than in rituals of name-giving and naming ceremonies, which establish the name's symbolic and socially-legitimated attachment to the body of a particular person that in many cultures continues for much of their lives.[10] This entanglement of individual and group is far more significant than the assigning of an informational reference for functional or institutional use: "The law does not care if a name 'fits' the child. But it is a matter of great concern to name-givers across many cultures for whom names both express something of the child and reveal their relations to that child" (Bodenhorn and von Bruck 2006, p. 3). Moreover, such is their importance in bestowing, displaying and sanctioning a sense of self embedded in a particular social world, that, across cultures, personal names remain objects of profound psychological attachment and identification for the individuals they designate. Lévy-Bruhl's (1926) observation of so-called 'primitive societies' concerning the sacredness of the name as a concrete facet of one's person seems to apply much more broadly: names become almost physical appendages of the self, and to a significant extent "some people *are* their names" (Bodenhorn and von Bruck 2006, p. 9, original italics). This deep self-identification with and by virtue of our names becomes even more evident through the horror of losing one's name. To deprive others of their names, or forcibly to rename them, has become a byword for dehumanization, with the transatlantic slave trade and the Holocaust as the most extreme examples.

Names therefore produce, are attached to and secure the rich specificity of individuals in complex social and cultural contexts. However, names are also units of discourse, and they enable and perform the radical *detachment* between sign and object that characterizes language generally and technologically-mediated forms – such as writing – par excellence. 'Paul Frosh'

You have been tagged   121

can be articulated and circulated by others irrespective of my physical presence (as it is in this sentence and in this volume), as well as without my knowledge, permission or will, or indeed after my death. My name does not just fix me in place as a person; it also circulates *in place of me*, in my absence: where it travels, I need not be (this is, according to Derrida, part of the primary 'violence' of being named: 1976, p. 112). It refers to me, so to speak, behind my back: in absentia. That the authorized use of names is usually subject to regulation by law, norm or custom, and that various practices (for instance, the signature) struggle to restrain this detachment of the name from the guarantee of singular presence (Derrida 1988), only serves to emphasize the potentially radical threat to the integrity of the name-as-self that discourse promotes.

Clearly, being tagged in a photograph means that someone on a social network system like Facebook, whether they are a 'friend' or not, has used my name without my prior permission. Having our names uttered without our permission or our knowledge is an everyday, routine and unremarkable occurrence.[11] But this is not simply *any* use: there are several dimensions to this event which set it apart from ordinary conversational reference to me as a third party, whether in speech, writing, or even in posts on social media. It is, first and foremost, the result of a deliberate decision to put my name *into overt circulation*. Tagging on Facebook does not occur simply when one is mentioned in a post written by someone else (though Facebook does encourage one to tag by identifying a mentioned name as someone located on Facebook and offering a tagging option). A key characteristic of tagging is that one cannot be tagged unless one is a registered user of the particular social networking system in which the tagging is performed. You can be *mentioned* on Facebook even if you are not a member of Facebook, but you cannot be *tagged*: Facebook doesn't recognize you as a system element in respect of whom operations such as tagging can be executed.

Thus tagging interpolates me in Althusser's sense (1984). It hails me as the subject of an institutional-ideological system; specifically, as a *taggable individual*. Being tagged involves not only being addressed by others, but being addressed by them *as subjects of Facebook who are hailing another of their kind*. Note the significance here of being *hailed by name*. This differs from the example given by Althusser, where being hailed is compared to turning when a policeman shouts, "Hey, you there!" in the street (1984, p. 48). Social networking systems, in contrast, individuate as they tag: I am not hailed by the system as 'you there!,' but always as 'Paul Frosh'. In an age of increasing digital surveillance for purposes of profiling and target marketing (Turow 2012), I am more often than not already known by the apparatus hailing me as a named individual. While one is therefore tagged through the sociable actions of specific others, the conditions for this action are dependent on the technological infrastructure (and its own commercial commitments to datafication, network effects and economies of scale). It is not only the particular other who hails me through my name: it is the networking system itself as a constitutive social power.

122 *Paul Frosh*

Tagging, moreover, does not only address the person being tagged. As mentioned earlier, the tag is an 'operative' sign: "the application of a tag to an image sets in motion a causal chain of physical changes to binary data that exerts influence on the structure, processing and display of information" (Rubinstein 2010, p. 198). Like operative writing (Kramer 2003), it possesses functionality within a technical system independent of its ostensive semantic meaning. In the case of social network sites the tag is designed to alert others connected to both the tagger and the tagged person to the act of tagging. It executes hailing in a semi-public space, constituting the act of tagging as an observable communicative event in its own right, a performance of what Daniel Dayan calls 'monstration' (2009): the gesture of focusing attention and making visible. As in the Althusserian moment of being hailed in the street, attention is concentrated simultaneously on the one hailed and on the act of hailing itself. However, attention to the tagged is individuated *even beyond the name* of a given individual: there are many people called 'John Smith' listed on Facebook, but tagging hails only one of them. It does this not through some mystical access to the singular interior self of this or that particular 'John Smith,' but according to the distinctive pattern of social connections by which each individual is distinguishable: one is individuated *through the social* as it is systemically performed, traced, calculated and patterned by the apparatus (see Chapter 2, page 67 of this volume by Andersson Schwarz: the personalized media experience "is an algorithmic product based on patterns observed among vast amounts of viewers, an artificial composite of sequences of choices observed among innumerable users – you included!"). And, unlike being hailed in the street, the borders of the communicative event of tagging are radically extended in both space and time: a reverberation of responsive clicks translated into emoticons and comments from across the network, and – unless actively removed – available for perusal long after the tag has been created.

Lastly, tagging revitalizes the ancient magical power of *incantation*: the use of words to perform actions at a distance. While the performativity of language in general is often described (occasionally pejoratively) as magical (for instance, Bourdieu 1991), and the use of personal names in charms was a feature of magical practice in antiquity (Versnel 2002), contemporary social tagging seems distinctive. Thanks to the technical apparatus of the digital network, social tagging gives the articulation of the name the ability *to make images of the named appear instantly before others.*

My name, tagged, is thus the given symbol of my very own self that seeks me out as an incantatory power, calling into being images of me without my willing it so. This power hails me, makes me visible, and at the same time turns this hailing into a conspicuous staging of communication before numerous others. Part of the initial disturbance of being tagged, I submit, is the sudden sense of one's self being 'handled' not just by others whom one may or may not know, or by discourse as a system of language in social context, but by a new techno-cultural apparatus which also assumes the

You have been tagged   123

guise of magic. This apparatus handles my name (and grasps my 'handle') through others: real social actors who use the social network service and call out to me as an individual within it in acts of sociability.[12] But it also makes my name utterable according to its own designs; and for these designs my name is an operative signal with no purpose except the apparatuses' own functioning.

Social tagging, then, presents a new form of the power to articulate personal names. But this is only one aspect of its significance for our sense of being. It also presents a new kind of ability to give names flesh and to embody selves, repeatedly. In order to explore this further we need to turn to the second of the two fundamental powers involved in being tagged: the power to incarnate selves through visual images – specifically, photographic images.

Photographic incarnation

Ricouer says of the proper name: "singular denomination consists in making a *permanent* designation correspond to the unrepeatable and indivisible character of an entity, regardless of its occurrences. The same individual is designated by the same name" (1992, p. 29, original italics). Substitute the word 'visualization' for 'denomination' and 'image' for 'name' and an analogous claim could be made for the photograph's relationship to the individual body. Underpinning this analogy – though also undermining it as we shall see – is the concept of the indexical sign (Peirce 1958), which is a standard and still central claim of photography theory, even in the digital age, and even though indexicality is itself understood to be subject to ideological construction (Slater 1995).[13] Produced through contact with light emanating from the scene located before the camera, the photograph does not only represent me symbolically (by convention) or iconically (by resemblance) but indexically: it is a quasi-physical trace of my body's presence.

Indexicality provides a semiotic foundation for photography's epistemological and emotional power as a potential anchor of individual self-identity. In its evidentiary capacity, the photograph serves modern institutional forms of managing mobility and behaviour through the identification (and categorization) of individual bodies (Sekula 1989). Like proper names, photographs are treated as 'rigid designators' (Kripke 1980) of the person, and it is no accident that the photograph and the proper name together became central instruments by which the modern nation-state made individuals legible and recordable through documents such as passports and identity cards (Scott 1998). Additionally, personal photography has long been a primary means for the formation of autobiographical memory and identity – for picturing and narrating the self as a coherent entity along the axis of linear chronology, usually within the context of the family (Bourdieu 1990; Chalfen 1987). In this way photographs give figural form and putative evidentiary currency to the concept of identity that Ricouer calls 'idem,' or

124 *Paul Frosh*

sameness, and which is based on the principle of uninterrupted continuity or permanence in time (Ricoeur 1992, pp. 115–117): the photographed bodies designated as 'me' are held to produce a picture of the self's own distinctive integrity and identity as it unfolds, notwithstanding physical changes to the body, differences in the content and form of the photographs, and fluctuations in the way selfhood is performed (now smiling, now scowling) before the camera. Contemporary shifts towards reflexive self-representation (e.g., selfies), photo-sharing through social network sites (e.g., Instagram) and conversational 'live' photography (e.g., Snapchat) that have supplemented, though not replaced, the memory functions of personal photography, indicate the continued importance of photography to identity-formation (van Dijck 2008; Hand 2012; Keightley and Pickering 2014).

However, the indexical singularity of the referent is not to be confused with the purported singularity of the self, and the photograph can also disturb the identification of distinctive self and unique body which it has been utilized to anchor. For the photograph shows my body from external perspectives which I can rarely see with my own eyes. It presents 'me' but mediated through (and from the perspective of) another, whether that other is identified as the photographer, the camera, a hybrid institutional and technological apparatus, or a generalized 'scopic regime' (Jay 1988) that makes me an object of visibility. Hence the unease which we often feel when seeing ourselves in photographs.[14]

The experience of the photographed self as other, as an estranged apparition created by an alienated gaze, is famously described by Barthes as a kind of death through duplication: in the photograph "I am neither subject nor object but a subject who feels he is becoming an object: I then experience a micro-version of death (or parenthesis): I am truly becoming a specter" (2000, pp. 14–15). Photography theory frequently emphasizes that the photograph asserts its own presence through the *absence* of the body, describing the image as ghost, death-mask, even corpse. Indeed, for Christian Metz, the photographic snapshot "like death, is an instantaneous abduction of the object out of the world into another world . . . Photography is a cut inside the referent, it cuts off a piece of it, a fragment, a part object, for a long immobile travel of no return" (1985, p. 84). The photograph is more than an immobilization of life; it is an excision of the referent from the flesh of the world.[15] And photography (or at least photography after the daguerreotype) does not simply produce a *single* 'spectre' of the depicted object. It multiplies it, detaching the individual body from its specific spatial and temporal context and replicating it again and again for unfettered circulation in the body's absence.[16]

Anxieties over body-replication and the loss of control over self-representation have thus long been connected to the reproductive and spectacular powers of photography (Frosh 2001). However, for most of photography's history, two distinctive factors constrained these anxieties. The first is that the ability to control the circulation of photographs of oneself was overtly stratified according to political and socioeconomic power: privileged classes, social groups and nations exercised far more control over the creation and the circulation of images of themselves when compared to the powerless.[17] Second, until the late twentieth century, the technical, organizational and cultural divisions between domestic photography and mass media photography (documentary, news and advertising) meant that despite the technology's replicative potential, and barring exceptional circumstances, photographs from the personal realm usually remained there.

With the ubiquity of camera technologies embedded in smartphones and other networked devices, and the centrality of social network sites as forums for storing and displaying personal photographs, these constraints have been severely undermined. Thus being tagged in uploaded images magnifies the potential uncanniness of image-replication and intensifies the historical anxieties already connected to photography, distributing them liberally and democratically across social groups and classes – elites included – in the name of altruistic sociability. This happens in part because digital photographs in general are almost infinitely cheaper, easier and faster to reproduce and distribute than analogue prints, and the web and social network sites provide new arenas in which they can be publicly displayed. But it also occurs because tagging – an operative procedure, as we have seen – is an agent of replication. Tagging 'circulates' my photograph, placing it within the purview of others, not by passing it from one addressee to another, but *by multiplying it as a distinct digital object. My* own name, used as a tag, becomes fastened to singular, indexical images of *my* body (it is me, and no other, *there, then*), and at the very same time replicates those images in numerous separate newsfeeds across the social network. Tagging is a magical act of germination, whereby the incantation of a name generates multiple indexical body-images, making them materialize, unbidden, in heterogeneous spaces.

Being tagged also carries an imperative weight: the imperative of sociable responsiveness – of the liking, sharing and commenting that is integral to interactions on social network services. In this respect, it is similar to the use of the selfie for purely sociable interaction in that it turns the photographed body into a vehicle for *phatic* interaction – communicative behaviour whose main purpose is to make and maintain sociable contact with others (Malinowski 1923; Miller 2008). Selfies, however, are acts of self-representation (Frosh 2015); tagging, in contrast, treats *another's* photographed body as the substance for phatic operations, using it to send sociable signals to a relatively amorphous network of acquaintances and associates. Being tagged, one's body-image is used to perform sociability on one's behalf – not only in absentia, but according to the will of others and the logics of the apparatus. If the incantation of one's name on a social network system produces unease over one's self being 'handled' by a new social power, then the instrumental use of one's own body-image for unwilled sociability creates even stronger grounds for profound ontological disturbance.

126   *Paul Frosh*

Extended selves and the palpability of the network

Yet there is more. The imperative to respond to the act of tagging serves, by default, the purpose of identifying another's body-image which is increasingly distributed across numerous *different* photographs. Unless overtly articulated in opposition to a particular tag (as in the query 'is this really Paul Frosh?') or as a request to 'untag' the image, each 'like' or comment contributed by the network of responders implicitly confirms the original tagging. If names are first attached to bodies in what Kripke (1980) calls an 'initial baptism,' then – continuing the religious metaphor – being tagged is a condition of recurrent 'confirmation,' where the conjunction of one's personal name with different body-images is repeatedly authorized and performed in the presence of a congregation continually reassembled for that very purpose. Tagging thus fleshes out the body-image associated with the named self by linking it semi-publicly with numerous photographs, while also using those photographed bodies as a medium – in the elemental sense proposed by John Peters (2015) – for fleshing out the abstract schema of informational and functional connections characterizing social network systems. Tagging contributes to the palpability of social networks as sensuously experienced worlds, as *figural aggregations* of embodied individuals. It is a way of materializing and animating the social network as a connective social *body* that is fed by the continual proliferation, identification and confirmation of the named body-images of its own constituent members.

This systemic and social fecundity of tagging – its power of multiplication – raises an important question, as does the disturbance it can provoke. Does being tagged underscore the ideological conjunction of named person and photographed body that produces a unique unity of image and self – a potentially forced unity associated with the traditional power of photography? Or does it contribute to distributed understandings of the self, where the self extends beyond the confines of the body? The former possibility, that tagging reinforces the ideology of singular embodied personhood, seems to be the view of Daniel Rubinstein, for whom the tag "establishes complete identity between image and text and therefore strips the photograph of its concrete and untranslatable language. The unspoken assumption behind tagging is that images can be exhausted by description" (2010, p. 199). Yet why isn't the very reverse the case? Wherefore Rubinstein's own assumption that the attachment of the same word to innumerable *different* instantiations of a photographed body (each one in itself multiplied and dispersed across the network) produces 'complete identity between image and text,' rather than a heterogeneity of figures connected to the same name? Why privilege reduction *to* the name rather than propagation and proliferation *from* the name? Why insist that tagging establishes a total identity between names and images rather than an expansive, mutable 'family resemblance' among them?

Underpinning the critique of the tag as a mechanism for suppressing visual difference is, I suspect, an implicit privileging of the power of words over images. It also seems indebted to the assumption that personal photography aggregates multiple photographs into a single embodied image of the self through chronological narrative presentation. This is a strange debt given Rubinstein's own slightly earlier claim (made with Sluis 2008) that the 'networked image' obeys a database rather than a narrative logic (Manovich 2001): i.e., it does not follow or promote temporal sequences or hierarchies, but can be openly and variably configured in relation to other database elements. Yet even this claim requires revision: as Nadav Hochman (2014) astutely argues, the 'social media image' operates according to a dynamic logic of the transient data *stream* (think of the constantly updating Facebook news feed) rather than the more static, and less insistent, database. The consequences of this shift are compelling:

> As the data stream is a multiplicity of coexisting temporalities or 'worldviews' from many people and places, the experience of viewing the stream is a continuous *comparison* of temporal representations . . .
> The effect of this comparison is the resynchronization of our own living bodies' temporality with the temporalities of others.
>
> (Hochman 2014, p. 2, original italics)

Social tagging is an important mechanism for inserting images into the data stream; or, more precisely, for multiplying images as units-of-flow (the 'stream' metaphor threatens to constrain thought here: tagging does not work by treating photographs like paper boats launched on a current linking different users; it contributes to the formation of individual, idiosyncratic flows by multiplying the image-particles that constitute the stream itself). Given that these images are different from one another, and were taken at different times, uploaded at different times, and possibly tagged at different times – all by a variety of individuals, tagging reaffirms the figural heterogeneity of the bodies it incarnates and the temporal thickness of their mutual intersections. There is no overriding consecutive accumulation of photographed bodies whereby each image is positioned as a component of a larger, name-body amalgam that unfolds chronologically as a unified container of the self. Rather, the name becomes distributed across diverse photographs as they shift into and out of the data stream; each one, through the tag, socially confirmed as a unique, partial and ephemeral incarnation.

This distribution of the name across multiple photographic instantiations makes being tagged a means of routinizing and regulating the extended self (Belk 2013), whereby the self is embodied and materially distributed through objects (both digital and non-digital), and can also be recombined into aggregate formations by and with others. More specifically, being tagged fosters the heterogeneity of self-extension over four distinctive

128   *Paul Frosh*

frameworks: *visual*, as the named self is extended through diverse photographs of the body; *spatial*, as the locations of these photographs – and access routes to them – are distributed beyond the proximate control of the named individual depicted; *temporal*, as the origin and performance-times of images of the self and its identification through tagging, are distributed across diverse temporal frameworks; and *social*, as the power to extend the self through photo-tagging, is assigned to others on the network (including, through auto-tagging functions, to platform algorithms themselves), constituting "a joint project resulting in an aggregate self that belongs as much to the others who have helped to form it as it does to oneself" (Belk 2013, p. 488).[18] Needless to say, this extension also makes being tagged an ongoing site of negotiation and even conflict in each of these frameworks of extension, from struggles at macro institutional levels over the nature of the photograph as a legal possession and the right to privacy (Facebook is currently being sued over the alleged privacy infringements of its 'tag suggestions' technology), to the vulnerability felt at the micro level of the single user suddenly encountering photographs of their bodies in which they have been tagged. Being tagged thus reveals a new condition in which multi-scale fluctuations of dependence between self, other, name and body are continually performed in digital media.

Yet how can tagged digital photographs be characterized as materializations or embodiments of the self if, like analogue photographs, they are understood as images of spectral absence, and if, *unlike* analogue photographs, they are primarily virtual and informational entities? An initial response is that the characterization of photography as spectral tends to ignore its material dimensions. "The potential range of material practices and material objects that comprises the category 'photographs' is massive", Edwards notes (2012, p. 225), discussing a large anthropological literature. This is no less true of the digital era than it was of the analogue, although material forms and practices have shifted. As Hand reports from his research on photo-sharing,

> Not all photos had the same value, and significantly, nor did they all share the same fate. Some photographs were stored without much thought onto CDs, DVDs, memory sticks or external hard drives; others were instantly shared on Facebook or blogs and through e-mail. 'Special' moments were often kept in additional folders and/or printed and displayed in frames, albums or scrapbooks.
>
> (2012, p. 174)

These differential material practices suggest that digital photographs are also involved in processes of 'mattering' (Miller 1998), whereby objects come to be not just materially perceivable and semantically significant, but existentially valuable, giving meaning and shape to the lives of individuals and groups.[19]

You have been tagged 129

Photographs are not, of course, only material objects. They 'matter' as mimetic artefacts. Taussig, developing Benjamin's concept of the 'mimetic faculty,' emphasizes the duality of such artefacts:

> To get hold of something by means of its likeness. Here is what is crucial in the resurgence of the mimetic faculty, namely the two-layered notion of mimesis that is involved – on the one hand a copying or imitation and on the other, a palpable, sensuous, connection between the very body of the perceiver and the perceived.
>
> (1992, p. 16)

Taussig links this two-fold 'resurgence' of the mimetic faculty in modernity to the two types of 'primitive' sympathetic magic proposed by James Frazer (1950), which create attachments and effects between things that resemble each another (the law of similarity) and between those which were once in contact (the law of contagion). Like analogue photographs before them, digital photographs possess mimetic capacities thanks to their powers of producing visual likenesses (similarity), their indexical connection to depicted objects (contagion), and their appeal to viewers who do not just interpret them as images but perceive and encounter them as distinctive objects.

However, in the digital tagging of photographs, the character of this encounter – the "palpable, sensuous connection between the very body of the perceiver and the perceived" (Taussig, 1992, p. 16) – involves something more. Sympathetic magic is a magic of attachment between objects, whether through likeness or previous contact; digital tagging augments this attachment through novel kinds of technologically-enabled embodied relationship. Tagging photographs, as we have seen, turns viewers into responsive congregants potentially engaged in the 'confirmation' of an image generated by an incanted name. Yet these responses – likes, comments, etc. – are more than merely verbal or symbolic performances. They are embodied sensorimotor actions – pressing, swiping, clicking, typing, etc. – which are performed, semi-habitually, by our gesturing hands and scrolling fingers (under the guidance of our vigilant eyes) in direct contact with touch screens or graphic user interfaces on our digital devices. These 'ways of the hand' (Moores 2014, citing Sudnow 2001) are not simply functional skills; they are principal means through which we orient ourselves to and inhabit an environment. Though tagged photographs are not primarily integrated as discrete objects into the dimensions of physical space, they *are* sensuously apprehended and manipulated through an ensemble of kinaesthetic bodily and technological interactions, further making networked digital media a 'palpable' world in which we are somatically enmeshed. If, for Metz, the photograph 'cuts' the referent out of its world, then the tag re-attaches – through reference, symbol, figure and matter. To resurrect a term from film theory, tagging performs an act of *suture*: it repeatedly stitches together incanted names, incarnated images, extended selves and the bodies of viewers, turning digital networks and interfaces into entwined fabrics of existence.

130 *Paul Frosh*

Conclusion

Being tagged, then, is not only a habitual everyday experience produced by social networking services with implications for privacy, social interaction and the political economy of digital platforms. Being tagged, hyperbolic as the claim may seem, reveals itself as an existentially significant technique for mediating the attachments of the body and the self in the face of possible unravelling and disintegration. Like the tagging technologies employed in the past and to this day in medical and military contexts, it is deeply linked to naming and figuration – powers of specification, confirmation, identification and multiplication that accompany and shape selves from birth to death, and beyond. And like these other forms of tagging, it finds expression in a shape appropriate to the material substrate of the world in which it operates.

Three things, however, make being tagged in social networking services distinctive, and perhaps even more radically indebted to naming and figuration as magical arts: first, its increasing incidence and performance among ordinary individuals in everyday circumstances as opposed to the restricted institutional contexts and extreme limit-situations of physical tagging; second, its shift from the naming of physical bodies to the naming of mediated bodies in photographs; finally, its technologically-enabled germinative capacity that proliferates vehicles of the embodied self at the same time as it multiplies attachments to them.

These three features are intertwined, their connections assuming the familiar profile of a feedback loop. Tagging has become an everyday practice as individuals increasingly live their lives in and through digital media (Deuze 2011) – and hence in and through forces of replication, reconfiguration and dissemination (of discourse and images, but also of quantified data) which are fundamental to digital communication. In these conditions, self-extension shifts into high gear, raising the possibility not simply of heterogeneity and difference but also of disintegration, of an entity so overextended, so protean, that it loses the minimal degrees of attachment needed for being experienced or recognized as a self: the advent of 'identity theft' in the digital era is one obvious expression of this vulnerability. Tagging, then, goes against the grain of the more radical accounts of distributed or 'network' models of selfhood (Banks 2017) which decentre the body as the privileged 'host' of the self.[20] Though tagging promotes a heterogeneity of body-images, it returns constantly to the incarnation of the name, and the naming of the body, as central instruments in the perpetual maintenance of selfhood; a centrality it repeatedly asks its users to affirm, confirm and propagate through their own bodily responses every time they tag another or react to a tag. While tagging manages self-extension beyond the body, it is perhaps more the case that it actively extends names and bodies into the network, wrapping symbolic and figural flesh onto informational bones. It promotes a deeply sensuous but *parsimonious* germination of the self, channelling existential forces of

You have been tagged   131

mimesis, of symbolization and figuration, that were established long before the contemporary era and reconfiguring them to shape identity and sociality in digital times. These existential forces in turn flesh out the computational and operational systems which enable tagging to be performed, animating them as multidimensional spheres of living, as palpably inhabited worlds where embodied selves are continually affirmed and confirmed.

Tagging thus enables, and constrains, the possibilities for heterogeneously extended selves in contexts that continually threaten self-dissolution, and to which tagging – as an image-multiplier – itself contributes. Summoning the powers of the name and the body, hailing and individuating, incanting and incarnating, germinating and attaching, tagging invites us to rethink what constitute the 'limit-situations' of our digital lives, and the remarkable techniques by which we become habituated to their systemic recurrence: how, to return to Lagerkvist, we can comprehend the mutual immanence of the extraordinary and the mundane. For while being tagged was previously a distinctive event within our existence, it is rapidly becoming a perpetual condition of our existence. We do not live in the age of being tagged; we live in the time of tagged being.

Notes

1 This article is based on a chapter from my book *The Poetics of Digital Media* (Polity, forthcoming).
2 In the United States, private initiatives for military tagging of soldiers going into combat became common in the carnage of the civil war, as did demands for its compulsory state introduction (Labbe 2016). The latter occurred during the World War I. The precise course by which military tags became known as dog tags is hazy, however. Hearst applied the term in a newspaper scare campaign against plans of the Roosevelt administration to introduce social security identification, clearly drawing negative comparisons with the tagging of animals (Krajewska 2017, p. 99). On animal tagging, see Peters (2015, p. 349).
3 Findings such as Hand's are likely to vary across cultures and age groups. Miller and Sinanan, for instance, report that no teenagers in their English study (part of a comparative English-Trinidadian ethnography) opted to make private the photos they were tagged in, even if they would never personally post such images of themselves. "So although teenagers may cull tagged pictures, they clearly feel it would be wrong to be seen as someone who has failed to share" (2017, pp. 24–25).
4 Nevertheless, in this article 'tagging' will almost always be used as a shorthand for 'tagging people in photographs on social network services.'
5 Tagging utilizing face-recognition technologies has been in use on Facebook since 2010. Facebook's 'tag suggestions' identifies faces in images based on the analysis of previously tagged images (as well as profile pictures) in the Facebook database and a personal biometric profile created from them. Facebook's default setting is that tag suggestions are made and executed unless you opt out in advance in your overall user settings; otherwise, when suggested tags appear they can only be manually removed or edited on an individual image-by-image basis: www.facebook.com/help/122175507864081#How-does-Facebook-suggest-tags-for-my-friends?
6 Most social scientific studies of tagging focus on the reasons individuals have for tagging others rather than on the experience of being tagged. Mainly small-scale

132   *Paul Frosh*

interview-based investigations, these studies have identified a range of motivations for tagging such as social connectivity, gaining attention, maintaining relationships, altruism, play, status enhancement, memory, and identity construction (Ames and Naaman 2007; Dhir et al. 2017).

7   An extensive philosophical literature dealing with the nature of names and naming stretches back to classical antiquity, often characterized as a dispute over whether names work through pure 'denotative' reference and are largely devoid of semantic meaning (they endure even after losing any descriptive meaning they might have had), or whether they are 'connotative' and their meaning describes attributes of the thing they name. Modern proponents of the 'descriptive theory' include Frege, Russell and to a degree Searle. Their critics – most famously Kripke (1980) – propose an alternative 'causal theory' (Evans and Altham 1973), arguing that proper names refer to their objects by virtue of an original act of naming which creates a reference retained over time not through descriptive sense but through continued use among a community of speakers.

8   Power relations also govern the recitation of names, their utterance in diverse contexts. When successfully performed, assigning names and reciting names are different kinds of speech act. Assigning a name is a 'declaration' in Searle's (1975) schema – it brings into being the state of affairs to which it refers (I name you Paul Frosh; hence you are now called Paul Frosh). Uttering an already existing name rarely brings into being that to which it refers, and would more often be a 'representative' (concerning the truth of a state of affairs).

9   In many cases the seemingly 'free' naming power of intimates is ultimately underpinned by the coercive power of the state. For instance, in countries such as the United Kingdom, it is legally required to name newborn babies within a certain time period, and these names must be officially registered.

10 Butler (1993, p. 154) offers an important critique of the claim (proposed variously by Lacan and Zizek) that the stability of personal names produces a durable identity for the individual subject over time. She argues that this conceptualization elides the patriarchal 'social pact' that underpins naming in many cultures, since it is only men's names which are stable and enduring in patronymic systems. For women it is the obligation to change the (sur)name according to shifts in status (paternity, marriage) that are paramount.

11 Though in certain contexts, and in certain cultures, the unauthorized use of another's given name can be considered disrespectful (see Humphrey 2006 on Mongolian name usage) or hostile (see, for instance, Lévi-Strauss (1973, p. 270)) on the Nambikwara, and Derrida's discussion of Lévi-Strauss' analysis (1976, pp. 101–140).

12 Lack of space prevents me from considering the connections between being named and being *grasped* by others through the etymology of the term 'handle' used on CB (citizen band) radio – and before that, according to the OED – as a colloquial synonym for a publicly used personal nickname. The precise origin of this sense of 'handle' is obscure, though it implies physical contact through touch, and the idea that – in a technical system where one is called upon publicly – the name is also a way of 'getting hold' of a particular individual. The word 'tag' is also associated with bodily contact through the game of tag, also called 'touch.'

13 Slater describes this construction as 'ontological realism.' The supposed loss of photographic indexicality in a 'postphotographic' era of digital image simulation was loudly debated in the 1990s (Mitchell 1992). Recent revisions question the simple analogue-digital binary, with claims that the substitution of photoelectronic and computational processes for photochemical and darkroom ones need not have eroded – though it may subtly have altered – photography's indexical quality (Soderman 2007; Lister 2013).

14 This unease is connected to an understanding that the body alters itself before the camera. "I constitute myself in the process of a 'posing,' I instantaneously make another body for myself, I transform myself in advance into an image" (Barthes 2000, p. 10).
15 Or in the triumphant words of Oliver Wendell Holmes, predicting – around a 100 years before Metz – the seeming victory of form over matter in age of stereography and photography: "Every conceivable object of Nature and Art will soon scale off its surface for us. Men will hunt all curious, beautiful, grand objects, as they hunt the cattle in South America, for their skins, and leave the carcasses as of little worth" (1980/1859, p. 81).
16 The haunting quality of this replication of the singular body is frequently linked to the theme of the doppleganger in Freud's analysis of the uncanny. See Gunning (1995, p. 64).
17 The power asymmetries between institutions and social groups able to control photographic representations of themselves while creating and circulating images of others is manifest across diverse episodes in the history of photography. For instance, in the power of nineteenth-century colonialism to make visible 'primitive' peoples, such as Native Americans, at the very moment of their annihilation (McQuire 1998, p. 125) and in the power of the liberal state to exhibit the white and black poor as part of the 1930s Farm Security Administration photographic project (Tagg 1988).
18 Belk's formulation of the extended self is too complex to address in detail here. As this quotation makes clear, however, it should not be confused with a largely egotistical or narcissistic expansion of a 'core self' at the expense of otherness. Moreover, 'auto-tagging' functions – whereby the social network platform tags individuals through face-recognition technologies – mean that the 'others' who are involved in the extension of the self need not be human agents. Thanks to Gefen Frosh for clarifying this point.
19 These material practices invite us to refine, if not refute, the insistence that digital photographs are best understood as software-generated data structures whose defining obedience is to computational procedures (Rubinstein and Sluis 2013). Claims as to the 'mattering' of some digital photographs are further reinforced by research on 'virtual possessions' in general – digital objects to which individuals form strong emotional attachments (not just particular photographs, but also Facebook posts, emails, game avatars, personalized music playlists, etc.). See Odom and colleagues for an illuminating discussion (2014).
20 This includes to a degree Belk's own reformulation (2013) of the extended self.

Bibliography

Althusser, L., 1984. *Essays on Ideology*. London: Verso.
Ames, M. and Naaman, M., 2007. Why We Tag: Motivations for Annotation in Mobile and Online Media. *Proceedings of the SIGCHI Conference on Human Factors in Computing Systems (CHI '07)*, 971–980.
Banks, J., 2017. Multimodal, Multiplex, Multispatial: A Network Model of the Self. *New Media & Society*, 19 (3), 419–438.
Barthes, R., 2000. *Camera Lucida: Reflections on Photography*. London: Fontana.
Beaudoin, J., 2007. Folksonomies: Flickr Image Tagging: Patterns Made Visible. *Bulletin of the Association for Information Science and Technology*, 34, 26–29.
Belk, R. S., (2013) Extended Self in a Digital World. *Journal of Consumer Research*, 40: 477–500.
Beloff, H., 1983. Social Interaction in Photographing. *Leonardo*, 16 (3) 165–171.

134 *Paul Frosh*

Bodenhorn, B. and von Bruck, G., 2006. 'Entangled in Histories': An Introduction to the Anthropology of Names and Naming. *In*: B. Bodenhorn and G. von Bruck, eds. *The Anthropology of Names and Naming*. Cambridge: Cambridge University Press, 1–30.

Bourdieu, P., 1990. *Photography: A Middle-Brow Art*. Cambridge: Polity Press.

Bourdieu, P., 1991. *Language and Symbolic Power*. Cambridge: Polity Press.

Butler, J., 1993. *Bodies That Matter: On the Discursive Limits of 'Sex'*. London: Routledge.

Chalfen, R., 1987. *Snapshot Versions of Life*. Madison: University of Wisconsin Press.

Dayan, D., 2009. Sharing and Showing: Television as Monstration. *The Annals of the American Academy of Political and Social Science*, 625, 19–31.

Derrida, J., 1976. *On Grammatology*. Baltimore: The Johns Hopkins Press.

Derrida, J., 1988. Signature, Event, Context. *In*: *Limited Inc*. Evanston, IL: Northwestern University Press, 1–24.

Deuze, M., 2011. Media Life. *Media, Culture & Society*, 33 (1), 137–148.

Dhir, A., Chen, G. M. and Chen, S., 2017. Why Do We Tag Photographs on Facebook? Proposing a New Gratifications Scale. *New Media & Society*, 19 (4), 502–521.

Edwards, E., 2012. Objects of Affect: Photography Beyond the Image. *Annual Review of Anthropology*, 41, 221–234.

Evans, G. and Altham, J. E. J., 1973. The Causal Theory of Names. *Proceedings of the Aristotelian Society. Supplementary Volumes*, 47, 187–225.

Frazer, J., 1950. *The Golden Bough: A Study in Magic and Religion*. London: Macmillan. Originally published 1922.

Frosh, P., 2001. The Public Eye and the Citizen Voyeur: Photography as a Performance of Power. *Social Semiotics*, 11 (1), 43–59.

Frosh, P., 2015. The Gestural Image: The Selfie, Photography Theory and Kinaesthetic Sociability. *International Journal of Communication*, 9, 1607–1628.

Gunning, T., 1995. Phantom Images and Modern Manifestations: Spirit Photography, Magic Theater, Trick Films, and Photography's Uncanny. *In*: P. Petro, ed. *Fugitive Images: From Photography to Video*. Bloomington: Indiana University Press.

Hand, M., 2012. *Ubiquitous Photography*. Cambridge: Polity Press.

Hochman, N., 2014. The Social Media Image. *Big Data and Society*, 1 (2), doi:10.1177/2053951714546645

Holmes, O. W., 1980. The Stereoscope and the Stereograph. *In*: A. Trachtenberg, ed. *Classic Essays on Photography*. New Haven: Leete's Island Books, 71–82. Original essay published 1859.

Humphrey, C., 2006. On Being Named and Not Named: Authority, Persons, and Their Names in Mongolia. *In*: B. Bodenhorn and G. von Bruck, eds. *The Anthropology of Names and Naming*. Cambridge: Cambridge University Press, 157–176.

Jay, M., 1988. Scopic Regimes of Modernity. *In*: H. Foster, ed. *Vision and Visuality*, Seattle: Bay Press, 3–23.

John, N., 2016. *The Age of Sharing*. Cambridge: Polity Press.

Keightley, E. and Pickering, M., 2014. Technologies of Memory: Practices of Remembering in Analogue and Digital Photography. *New Media & Society*, 16 (4), 576–593.

Krajewska, M., 2017. *Documenting Americans: A Political History of National ID Card Proposals*. Cambridge: Cambridge University Press.

Kramer, S., 2003. Writing, Notational Iconicity, Calculus: On Writing as a Cultural Technique. *MLN*, 118 (3), 518–537.

Kripke, S., 1980. *Naming and Necessity*. Cambridge, MA: Harvard University Press.

Labbe, S. A., 2016. The Evolution of the Military Dog Tag: From the Civil War to Present Day. The Gettysburg Compiler: On the Front Lines of History. 176. Available at: http://cupola.gettysburg.edu/compiler/176 (accessed: 1 July 2018).

Lagerkvist, A., 2016. Existential Media: Toward a Theorization of Digital Thrownness. *New Media & Society*, 19 (1), 96–110.

Lévi-Strauss, C., 1973. *Tristes Tropiques*. London: Penguin Books.

Lévy-Bruhl, L., 1926. *How Natives Think*. London: George Allen & Unwin.

Lister, M., 2013. Introduction. *In*: M. Lister, ed. *The Photographic Image in Digital Culture*. Abingdon: Routledge, 1–21.

Malinowski, B., 1923. The Problem of Meaning in Primitive Languages. *In*: C. K. Ogden and I. A. Richards, eds. *The Meaning of Meaning*. London: Routledge and Kegan Paul, 296–355.

Manovich, L., 2001. *The Language of New Media*. Cambridge, MA: MIT Press.

Marlow, C., Naaman, M., boyd, d. and Davis, M., 2006. HT06, Tagging Paper, Taxonomy, Flickr, Academic Article, To Read. *Proceedings of the Seventeenth Conference on Hypertext and Hypermedia (HYPERTEXT '06)*, HT'06, August 22–25, 2006, Odense, Denmark, 31–40.

McQuire, S., 1998. *Visions of Modernity*. London: Sage.

Metz, C., 1985. Photography and Fetish. *October*, 34, 81–90.

Miller, D., 1998. Why Some Things Matter. *In*: D. Miller, ed. *Material Cultures: Why Some Things Matter*. London: University College London Press, 3–21.

Miller, D. and Sinanan, J., 2017. *Visualising Facebook: A Comparative Perspective*. London: UCL Press.

Miller, V., 2008. New Media, Networking, and Phatic Culture. *Convergence*, 14 (4), 387–400.

Mitchell, W., 1992. *The Reconfigured Eye: Visual Truth in the Post-Photographic Era*. Cambridge, MA: MIT Press.

Moores, S., 2014. Digital Orientations: 'Ways of the Hand' and Practical Knowing in Media Uses and Other Manual Activities. *Mobile Media & Communication*, 2 (2), 196–208.

Norval, A. and Prasopoulou, E., 2017. Public Faces? A Critical Exploration of the Diffusion of Face Recognition Technologies in Online Social Networks. *New Media & Society*, 19 (4), 637–654.

Odom, W., Zimmerman, J. and Forlizzi, J., 2014. Placelessness, Spacelessness, and Formlessness: Experiential Qualities of Virtual Possessions. *Proceedings of the 2014 Conference on Designing Interactive Systems (DIS '14)*, Vancouver, Canada, 985–994.

Peirce, C. S., 1958. The Icon, Index and Symbol. *In*: C. Hartshorne and P. Weiss, eds. *Collected Papers of Charles Sanders Peirce, Vol. 2: Principles of Philosophy and Elements of Logic*. Cambridge, MA: Harvard University Press, 274–307.

Peters, J. D., 2015. *The Marvelous Clouds: Towards a Philosophy of Elemental Media*. Chicago, IL: University of Chicago Press.

Ricoeur, P., 1992. *Oneself as Another*. Chicago, IL: University of Chicago Press.

Rubinstein, D., 2010. Tag, Tagging. *Philosophy of Photography*, 1 (2), 197–199.

Rubinstein. D, and Sluis, K., 2013. The Digital Image in Photographic Culture: Algorithmic Photography and the Crisis of Representation. *In*: M. Lister, ed., *The Photographic Image in Digital Culture*, 2nd edn., Routledge: London, 22–40.

Scott, J., 1998. *Seeing Like a State: How Schemes to Improve the Human Condition Have Failed*. New Haven, CT: Yale University Press.

136 *Paul Frosh*

Searle, J. R., 1975. A Taxonomy of Illocutionary Acts. *In*: K. Gunderson, ed. *Language, Mind and Knowledge*. Minneapolis: University of Minnesota Press, 344–369.

Sekula, A., 1989. The Body and the Archive. *In*: R. Bolton, ed. *The Contest of Meaning: Critical Histories of Photography*. Cambridge, MA: MIT Press, 342–388.

Slater, D., 1995. Photography and Modern Vision: The Spectacle of 'Natural Magic.' *In*: C. Jenks, ed. *Visual Culture*. London: Routledge, 218–237.

Soderman, B., 2007. The Index and the Algorithm. *Differences*, 18 (1), 153–186.

Sudnow, D., 2001. *Ways of the Hand: A Rewritten Account*. Cambridge, MA: MIT Press.

Tagg, J., 1988. *The Burden of Representation: Essays on Photographies and Histories*. London: Macmillan.

Taussig, M., 1992. Physiognomic Aspects of Visual Worlds. *Visual Anthropology Review*, 8 (1), 15–28.

Turow, J., 2012. *The Daily You: How the New Advertising Industry Is Defining Your Identity and Your Worth*. New Haven, CT: Yale University Press.

Van Dijck, J., 2008. Digital Photography: Communication, Identity, Memory. *Visual Communication*, 7 (1), 57–76.

Versnel, H. S., 2002. The Poetics of the Magical Charm: An Essay in the Power of Words. *In*: P. Mirecki and M. Meyer, eds. *Magic and Ritual in the Ancient World*. Leiden: Brill, 105–158.

6 Surveillance, sensors, and knowledge through the machine

Sun-ha Hong

Proliferation

Digital existence today is to live amidst a bewildering proliferation of data and data-emitting machines. The pattern of their appearance to human subjects is *hyperobjective* (Morton 2013). Seemingly ubiquitous in their vast distribution, these new technologies instantiate in innumerable local objects – a branded platform, a piece of hardware, a function – without being reducible to them. The modern word *technology* was itself born out of the sentiment that a new and broader system was emerging (Marx 2010). Today, as we will see, Silicon Valley bestows the newest predictive technologies totalising descriptions like the 'technium' (Kelly 2010) or the 'planetary nervous system' (Hernandez 2012). The corollary is that this expansive imaginary increasingly overshoots the phenomenological purview of the human subject. A constellation of black boxes, dramatic visualisations, collective fantasies and individual material tool-relations – each of these objects constantly put us in *touch* with the ever-expanding technological landscape, but in doing so, they further impress our inadequacy in grasping this ubiquitous non-human pulse, flow, hum.

This sense of *excess* is reflected in contemporary descriptions of life in the new media society as paranoia (Majaca 2016), sleepless fatigue (Crary 2013; Han 2010), a manic obsession with patterns (Steyerl 2016) and conspiracies (Andrejevic 2013) . . . in short, a subject driven to hyperactivity whilst constantly afflicted with anxiety about what is beyond its grasp. Yet it is also the same excess that animates the seductive promise that new technologies will augment human knowability in unprecedented ways. Proliferation undergirds both the uncertainty around informational excess and the fantasy of unprecedented predictive and calculative capacity.

Much of these hopes and fears revolve around the project of human knowing – a relation to the world that was elevated to a defining duty and capacity of the Enlightenment subject (e.g., Dean 2001). But to 'know' amidst the digital swarm is less a question of firm evidence possessed by the rational individual than a collective investment into deferred and simulated heuristics. Wittgenstein (1969) identified the curious masking work

138   *Sun-ha Hong*

performed by the innocuous phrase, 'I know this is a tree': to say so does not establish any comprehensive or objectively certain ground for my knowledge. Rather, it expresses my commitment to treat the proposition as *no longer requiring such proof*, and thereby use it itself as ground for other statements and actions (say, my decision to fell it for lumber). To say we 'know' about new technologies, or about the world and ourselves through new technologies, therefore expresses our ability to keep up with the flow of machinic emissions, and to produce and justify socially 'sufficient' ground for judgment and action.

This chapter examines the ways in which the generalised condition of data proliferation is rewiring the relation of knowing at a phenomenological level. The question here is not whether we know 'more' or 'less,' but how *knowing* as human subjects' mode of relating to the world out there is being reconfigured through new digital technologies as both the problem (of proliferation) and the solution (of data-driven predictivity). Two related scenes illustrate this pairing of proliferation/uncertainty and predictivity/knowledge, and the ways in which human subjects are enjoined to know through new technologies. The first – the controversial exposure of NSA surveillance in the 'Snowden Affair,' 2013 onwards – demonstrates a *recessive* relation: how technological knowing reassures the overwhelmed subject by withdrawing into the phenomenological background. The second – the empowering fantasies of better self-knowledge in the 'Quantified Self' community and self-surveillance technologies – then turns to a *protrusion* of objects, numbers, stimuli: how technological knowing appears into our most 'private' and domestic spaces of life, and seeks to pre-empt sense experience as a mode of self-knowledge.

These are sites for the public presentation[1] of technologies and claims to new knowledge. They chart the ways in which specific technologies of surveillance and data production were made object of debate, description, speculation, criticism. In other words, there is a certain 'politics of visibility' (Brighenti 2007; Flyverbom 2016; Thompson 2011) which governs the differential distribution of epistemic authority and information access. This chapter draws on news media, Snowden-leaked government files, interviews, field observations and more, over a three-year period (2014–2016) to sketch out the character of this publicised discourse.

Recession

The first sightings occurred on 6 June 2013. "NSA collecting phone records of millions of Verizon customers daily" (Greenwald 2013). In subsequent days and weeks, the single story would grow into an agglomeration, filling the public view with images of supermassive databases, conspiratorial secrets and futuristic Big Brothers. (George Orwell's estate would have an unexpected payday, with sales of *1984* rocketing by some 6,000% that month (Hendrix 2013).) Edward Snowden, suddenly the world's most famous living whistle-blower, called it the public's "right to know" (*NDR* 2014), the right to transparency.

But what kinds of things can secure the public's ability to 'know' when it comes to such vast, hyperobjective apparatuses? The NSA programs at the core of Snowden's revelations involve such vast volumes of material that its own analysts internally spoke of 'analysis paralysis'.[2] Their 'dragnets' fished from a wide variety of channels, from Skype video calls (Greenwald 2014) to video game chatter (Ball 2013), and their material footprint comes in tens of thousands of employees, housed in complexes the size of small towns (Fort Meade is larger than Cambridge, Massachusetts, in land area) as well as secret locations warded from photographic representation.[3] And in contrast to many traditional forms of surveillance, the surveillance activity itself is systematically withdrawn from the subject's experience – such that we might say, 'I know I am being watched, Snowden told me so – but I've never seen it happen'. How is the public supposed to secure any 'concrete' grasp of such knowledge?

The answer was apparently simple. That first report from *The Guardian* featured a rare scoop: a copy of the Foreign Intelligence Surveillance Court (FISC) order that addressed Verizon by name and demanded 'telephony metadata'. The slightly grainy text, a mysterious stamp-mark reading '13–80,' and the watermark TOP SECRET//SI//NOFORN (No Foreigners) attested to the materiality, secrecy, and (as if this followed naturally) authenticity of this document. PowerPoint slides, typically the object of fatigue and derision as the symbol of bureaucratic gesture without substance, were now respected as rare pieces of concrete evidence extracted from a secret domain. William Binney, a former NSA employee who had told the public much the same things Snowden did with much less impact, thought the documents made the difference: he now regrets that he didn't take documents himself, the "hard evidence [that] would have been invaluable" (Loewenstein 2014).

Yet these documents were also occasions for occlusion, speculation, simulation. Snowden's documents, the Snowden Files, make present surveillance as an uncertain and unknown world for public imagination. As such, they carry the secrets beyond lived experience, or the complex technological system 'out there,' back into the realm of knowledge-claims. Consider the following defense of the surveillance programs, raised by Dianne Feinstein a few days after the initial leaks (Knowlton 2013):

> Here's the rub: the instances where [surveillance] has produced good – has disrupted plots, prevented terrorist attacks, is all classified, that's what's so hard about this.

Feinstein had been Chairman of the US State Select Committee on Intelligence (also called the Senate Intelligence Committee), a major oversight body for state intelligence activities. In other words, this external auditor to the NSA's activities was arguing to the public that what one does not know (and what

140   *Sun-ha Hong*

one is not even sure exists) should overrule what one has learned. Feinstein's formulation asks the public to establish a sense of knowledge (that surveillance has done good) by simulating the knowledge of another, and transposing its results unto ourselves in what I have called elsewhere an *interpassive* movement (Hong 2015b). Here, the secret is the presumptive background that hems in and bleeds in on what is publicly visible, and thereby qualifies the knowledge of what is (apparently) transparent with an inexhaustible outside. Meanwhile, the pattern of the exposé, by now built into the media news cycle and the frenetic pattern of constant update in new media platforms (Chun 2011, 2016), produces the 'public's persistent feeling that "there is always something"' more behind the scenes (Horn 2012, p. 118).

Since surveillance by its very definition can never be fully transparent, its critics and defenders continued to find ways to stake claim to the nature of its hidden truth. The US government and its intelligence agencies produced its own set of figures and witnesses as stand-ins for what must, they argued, remain state secrets. President Barack Obama assured the public that a very specific number of fifty-four terrorist attacks had been thwarted, "saving real lives" (Elliott and Meyer 2013; Sterman 2014), through the surveillance programs in question. Yet soon after, the number was in doubt. NSA's defenders were forced to backpedal to just *one* case that could be presented with certainty: the 2009 bombing plot by Najibullah Zazi (Clarke et al. 2013; Angwin 2014; Schwartz 2015). Of course, the idea that metadata surveillance 'saves lives' would continue to circulate, even as specific evidence of such efficacy, positive or negative, remained withdrawn from public knowledge. We might say that the fifty-four was a silhouette, a stand-in; an object which renders political secret and technological complexity into something we can think and speak about, delivering a sense of knowability. Here, the specificity and certainty implied by the figure gives an appearance of objectivity to what is more explicit in Feinstein's request: the ultimately groundless choice of believing (that we know, that 'they' know in our stead, that it is 'known').

In short, what we find is not a contest of transparent proofs, but objects that present an appearance of epistemic solidity while referencing broader unknowns. The Snowden Files themselves provide a kind of silhouetted or bracketed presence, wherein the appearance of numbers and statistics function as anchors for imagining proliferation. A symbolic case: one month after the leaks began, journalists at *The Guardian* descended into their headquarters' basement, power drill and angle grinder in hand. Observed by two UK state officials, they proceeded to physically destroy the offending laptop containing leaked material (Rusbridger 2013). It was, of course, a purely ceremonial gesture; Snowden's files had already been distributed to a global network of journalists and activists (Farivar 2013), including *The Guardian*'s own offices in the United States. The pointlessness of the drill-and-grinder ritual reflects both the difficulty of catching up with proliferating data and the enduring desire to affix these new movements back onto old actors and identities.

The problem is that the Snowden Files were not only distributed; their very size, scope and location remains uncertain. Snowden himself has refused to give a firm number. In any case, he insists that he no longer even has access to the files, having turned them over to journalists; those journalists too have remained taciturn about the issue.[4] Meanwhile, the US government also tossed enormous numbers into the air, ranging from 900,000 from the Department of Defense (Leopold 2015) to the claim that Snowden 'touched' – a rather viral and visceral metaphor – 1.7 million files working for the NSA contractor, Booz Allen Hamilton (Kelley 2014). The secrecy archive Cryptome (2016) wryly noted that, as of October 2013, a mere 192 pages had been released, and that at current pace, it would take '20 to 620 years' for the public to actually receive the information it had been promised. The large variance in these figures, and the gap between technical availability and actual accessibility, actually reflects these 'insider' institutions' everyday difficulty in grasping the scope of their own proliferating secrets. Peter Galison (2008) reports that the US government as a whole has 'reportedly' classified 92,064,862 documents in the single year of 2011; not even 1.7 million scrapes the top of the iceberg. Meanwhile, the NSA had expanded massively following the September 11 attacks through internal hires, new infrastructure, and large outsourcing contracts to the private sector (e.g., Shorrock 2015) – such that, by 2010, it was lacking precise metrics for mapping its own surveillance apparatus and its total costs (Pasquale 2015, p. 13; Bamford 2008, p. 199).

Here, the wild numerical potshots work not so much to pin down the scope of the proliferation (of documents, of secret surveillance programs, of personal communications data), but to spray out a general horizon, a foreboding, the hyperobjective beyond – a function that is found more broadly in archives and databases as containers for epistemic fantasies.[5] After all, what difference does it make for public knowledge if there are 1.7 million documents, or 3 million, or 10? The complexity and size of the material guarantees that although the Files provide the idea of evidentiary availability to the public, few will be able to take the opportunity to 'know for themselves'.[6] Here, availability is a promise never taken up, but always present in theory. The Snowden Files thus presents itself as a concrete artefact and indisputable proof, but turns out to enact a kind of 'absent presence' (Frers 2013; Saury 2008). They make visible the withdrawn, opaque, secret, uncertain nature of the sociotechnical systems they propose to expose.

Numbers and documents: both faithful staples of modern epistemology, and privileged forms of evidence in that *regime du savoir*. Yet the contact-points where these objects meet human subjects and the amorphous body of the public entail a panoply of deferrals and as-ifs, designed to mitigate the withdrawal of 'actual' realities from the horizon of ordinary subjects. The objects thus maintain a certain presence – even as they cover for the nonappearance of the reality 'out there'. This is not to simply say that the information we had was not 'transparent' enough, which slips us back into

142 *Sun-ha Hong*

the rationalist fantasy that if we only knew enough/more then we would not need such 'tricks' (or that those who persist in employing such strategies of knowing are ignorant and/or irrational). The point is that 'to know' is a costly and limited affair, which constantly necessitates new techniques and conventions by which we can avoid some of the labour involved. If nonmodern societies produced myths of luck, chance, *mana* as a way to organise the world around them (e.g., Lears 2003), the digital age exhibits its own simulations of objectivity, correlation and predictive power in order to stabilise its grid of intelligibility. Amidst the proliferation of new media, the presence of statistical reason maintains the orientation towards objectivity and proof – even as the practices of knowing continue to defer the work of knowing onto someone else and something else.

The evidentiary objects involved in the Snowden Affair thus exhibit a *recessive* relation vis-à-vis the public's ability to 'know' new data-driven technological systems. Merleau-Ponty (2012) says that my pre-reflective awareness of my body and its relation of physical *doing* always already grounds all sense perception – that is, a body-schema. The problem of recession is the problem of grasping what is beyond the experiential purview established by that schema – or rather, what *appears* to the embodied perceiver as coming from that beyond. Clearly, this 'beyond' is not born with surveillance or digital technology. The hyperobjectivity of the Anthropocene reprises – albeit through very different parameters – the mythological function of the medieval cosmic order. And just as we sought to grasp the modern nation through populational statistics, or to know the strangers of the urban metropolis through the heuristics of physiognomy, we turn in the Snowden affair to traditional representatives of objective certainty: documents, numbers, journalistic truth. The recessive relation couples the search for a stabilising grid of intelligibility with the irreducible 'out there' – that which lies beyond ordinary subjects' lived experience or practical knowledge. The evidentiary objects, from the figure of the fifty-four to each of the Snowden Files, thus appear publicly in order to announce the non-/dis-appearance of the referent. The consequence is that the more we know, the less of the knowing is ours.

Protrusion

> For a certain type of person . . . data is the most important thing you can trust. Certain people think a feeling of inner certainty is misleading.
> (Gary Wolf, co-founder of the Quantified Self, Hesse 2008)

This contrast animates the Quantified Self, a community of experimenters in new self-tracking technologies (notably founded by two veterans of *Wired*, that singular hub for evangelising new technologies) – and more widely, the self-tracking industry that has grown in commercial and cultural prominence over the last decade. While there is a longer history of self-measuring

Surveillance, sensors, and knowledge 143

machines throughout the twentieth century (e.g., Crawford et al. 2015), and wearable technologies have been the object of futuristic imagination for decades, the confluence of miniaturised sensors and widespread wireless connectivity has resulted in a new generation of devices embraced by millions of consumers (e.g., Lupton 2016; Neff and Nafus 2016). These devices target problems of everyday living, of one's own body, that are so personal to the subject but never quite fully 'known': health, sleep, mood, sex, diet. Sleep trackers like Beddit generate numerical 'sleep scores' to grade each night's repose, and indeed, times its alarms to what it deems to be the right moment to wake the user. Each activity, each problem, is breached through its most discrete and measurable portions; hence the sex tracker Spreadsheets begins by yielding metrics like 'thrusts per minute,' though it is uncertain what this is supposed to tell us. The measuring machines themselves seek ever more persistent and intimate access to the subject, with experiments in tattoos, ingestible pills and miniature sensors dubbed 'neural dust' (see Mack 2016) as prospective heirs to present-day wristbands. The discursive foil around this new generation of devices expresses the hope that through smarter machines and their more intimate, persistent measuring, we will reach a degree of self-knowledge where *we cannot lie to ourselves anymore*; that prosthetics tracking mood, exercise, social relations, even sex will tell us what(/who) really makes us happy, how much we've really exercised, the hidden correlations between our eating and our productivity, the truth behind our illusions about our own habits and predilections.

And so, the technical and epistemic principles of data-driven surveillance are transposed unto the world of do-it-yourself datafication. Here, we find technical objects and machinic knowledge in *protrusion*. When we speak of recession, we think of things withdrawing out of my perception or reach; this in turn reflects the broader and older problem of locating 'knowledge' beyond lived experience and individual cognition. In protrusion, we may think of things that 'stick out' into notice, and coax the subject into interaction and engagement. The contrast is not between secretive uncertainty and democratised knowledge, but how claims to knowability are secured with regards to the world 'out there' or the me 'in here' (with the machines). Specifically, protrusion vis-à-vis self-tracking involves its promise to furnish savvy consumers with individualised and ultimately empowering access to the production of better 'self-knowledge' (that is, *their own* knowledge *about themselves*). Further, this is to be achieved through technologies which are literally in the home and on(in) the user's body. The McLuhanian vision of extension is emblematised by media coverage of early adopters, which plays up the trope of cyborg-like individuals dressed up in a conflagration of wires and gadgets.[7] Here, we find the intervention of new technologies into subjects' lived experience in their most private spaces and times – leading, it is claimed, to the subject's extended, upgraded, augmented capacity for knowledge.

Such protrusion should not be mistaken for any reduction in or elimination of mediation. It does not grant access to our 'true' selves, the nature of

144 *Sun-ha Hong*

which remains philosophically unclear and certainly anterior to the mediation of datafication. Instead, what we do produce, with greater fidelity than ever, is our *trace-bodies* (Hong 2015a): bodies reconstituted out of the debris left behind by our lived activity – whether in the form of a numerical sleep score, a mood emoji or a more complex set of metrics knitted together into visualisations. The many fissures between our trace-bodies and our everyday experience of ourselves, masked by the common reference to a 'self,' reflects the general trade-off in technological mediation of self-knowledge: we perceive ourselves precisely by having something else stand in for us. What appears to me as I gaze into a mirror is not simply 'myself,' for the me that I always already inhabit before any seeing is now actively visualising the self through this technologically produced apparition (which, as curved or otherwise warped mirrors make clear, is always subject to manipulation).[8]

The key here is that self-tracking machines produce trace-bodies through measurements that are typically too frequent, too persistent, too automatic, too closely attached to the body or home, for our consciousness to keep up. The sleep score on a Beddit is already distilled and ready as the user awakes – not to mention that his/her awakening was itself timed by the correlated conclusions of the algorithm. In this bid to constantly have us face off with our truths, these machines undercut the (alleged) traditional relation between the acting, experiencing subject and his/her truth. In other words, the promise is not only to know us better than we know ourselves, but to engage in this knowing *before* we are aware. Even as the trace-body looms larger the epistemic process, persistently connected to measuring machines that harvest its past to predict the future, the acting, experiencing, flesh-and-blood body in the present is nudged to the periphery.[9] These images of the self, generated by media whose workings we cannot consciously follow, are now celebrated as the path to empowerment and self-knowledge (Figure 6.1).

Such undercutting or bypassing of human consciousness explicitly calls out the phenomenological gap we saw in the problem of recession. If the gap between secrets 'out there' and the limited reach of the knowing subject was to be mitigated through deferrals and stand-ins, here it is the tracking device that stands in the gap between the thinking subject and its trace-body. This gap is not an artefact of the specificity of new media, but inherent in phenomenology's fundamental problem: how we derive meaning and sense about the world around us (including our selves as objects of sense perception). Thomas Sheehan (2014) has shown that the lessons of Heidegger's phenomenology have often been confused by the unfortunate terminology of *Sein/Dasein* (or, even worse, being/Being). Despite the metaphysical overtones of the words, Heidegger's problem is essentially a phenomenological one: What is the basis of intelligibility, of anything's making sense for us? In this context, Heidegger presents – in clear compatibility with Merleau-Ponty – what is variously described as *Geworfenheit* (a 'thrownness'), *die Lichtung* (the clearing), or even *das Offene* (the open):

Surveillance, sensors, and knowledge 145

Figure 6.1 Mood+Quantify, by Laurie Frick. CC BY-SA 4.0. "All that creepy surveillance will turn into an entirely new way to see yourself", exudes the artist.

to think or act dis-cursively entails 'running back and forth' (*dis-currere*) between the thing and its meaning, or the tool and the task, as we check out whether this thing actually does have that meaning or whether in fact this tool is suitable for that task . . . things do not show up directly as what and how they are, the way they might to a divine intellectual intuition. Rather, they appear only to a mediating and dis-cursive intellect, one that must "run", so to speak, from subject to predicate . . . and back again.

(Sheehan 2014, pp. 21, 126)

This gap, this distance between the experiencing I and the object of my experience, implies that our sense and meaning of the object does not inhere in the latter, and always retains a contingent and dynamic character. In other words, to render something intelligible is not to discover the *a priori* truth, but to take up the responsibility of becoming subjective. (Also see the analysis of *Geworfenheit* in Lagerkvist 2017.)

Now, this distance is itself not something we typically experience; when we perceive a vase, we do not experience our own perceiving, but have an impression of some direct contact with the object. And distance of another, analogous kind is masked by the phrase 'I know . . .,' as we saw through Wittgenstein. In contexts of recession, the object in question is removed from lived experience, challenging the illusion of direct or verifiable knowledge.

146 *Sun-ha Hong*

The subject's constant, *recursive* efforts at meaning making, relaying back and forth, and his/her reliance on various mediative figures, become more pronounced. In response, the spaces beyond the gap – the blind spots, the black boxes – are leveraged to restore a sense of access or contact.

In other words, even as the gap persists in every act of sensemaking, our techniques for making things sensible work towards a pragmatic closure that helps us get on with living. (As Wittgenstein says: we use 'I know' to establish a particular certainty, as distinct from 'I think that' or other such propositions.) Self-tracking technologies constitute the newest promise to eliminate this clearing, providing a direct injection of raw data and objective truth that dispenses with the meandering and distorted recollections of the experiencing subject. In this respect, what I call recession and protrusion are not opposites; they are variant forms of a common process by which the uncertainties built into the way we connect with the world out there and the us in here is problematised, solutionised. And in doing so, what we mean by 'knowing,' what kinds of dependencies, reductions to standardised form, faith in intermediaries are employed, is being reconfigured.

To understand such 'reconfigurations,' let us return to the promises of self-tracking. What exactly is being changed at the level of the phenomenological relationship between the experiencing subject and the 'self' as object of his/her knowing? A clear contrast may be drawn when we consider some pre-modern techniques of self-knowledge, some of which also grapple explicitly with the consequences of technological intervention.

Knowledge's subject

> Monday evening, I ate a cabbage and an omelet. Tuesday evening, I ate one half of the head of a kid and soup. Wednesday, fasted. Saturday, I went to the tavern: salad and omelet, and cheese, and I felt good.
>
> (Pontormo, cited in Pilliod 2005)

In January 1554, the Italian painter Jacopo Pontormo began to write. His topics: food intake, social calls, bowel movements, self-diagnosed psychological states. A few decades later, the physician and inventor Sanctorius of Padua would track his weight, his food (input) and excretions (output). Both would later be duly referenced as early precursors to twenty-first-century self-tracking (Swan 2013; Crawford et al. 2015, Urist 2015). Benjamin Franklin, with his thirteen virtues, also made frequent cameos in journalistic coverage of self-tracking (Kronsberg 2013). Self-trackers of the twenty-first century were not left wanting when it came to historical precedents. To narrow the vast historical scope, we might take the cue from the Quantified Self community's adoption of the old Delphic maxim – *know thyself* [γνῶθι σεαυτόν] – and turn to Antique practices of self-knowledge. Here we are guided by Michel Foucault, who positioned these techniques in terms of

Surveillance, sensors, and knowledge 147

parrhesia and avowal – that is, techniques of truth-telling (Foucault 1986, 1997, 2001, 2011, 2014a, 2014b). Rather than take the vast difference in technological capacity as the primary point of comparison, I emphasise how the relation of knowing, and the technical mediation of the 'gap' therein, is managed across the two groups.

'Know thyself'. γνῶθι σεαυτόν was immortalised through Plato's texts on Socrates – and these texts made clear that to know oneself was a methodology for living. The subject would come to know oneself through the challenge of the speaking interlocutor, and in one's dialogic, experiential encounter with that challenge. In *Laches*, Socrates is described as an excellent interlocutor – that is, a human *medium* and indeed 'technology' for others' pursuit of self-knowledge. Notably, Socrates is qualified for such a function not due to his erudition, but a certain relationship he has cultivated between his actions and speech – that is, his conscious 'I' – and his *self*:

> Laches does not say: Socrates is qualified to talk about courage because he is courageous. [Rather, he does so] because there is this symphony, this harmony between what Socrates says, his way of saying things, and the way in which he lives.
>
> (Foucault 2011, p. 148)[10]

This harmony is encapsulated by the term *basanos* [βάσανος]. The term originally referred to a silicon-based 'touchstone' which the Greeks used as a base to test the purity of precious metals. Here, it is Socrates who functions as a touchstone for others like Nicias and Laches, cross-examining them with his questions. If contemporary self-tracking tests users according to its (often pre-designed) algorithms and classifications, the 'test'[11] here is intersubjective and dialogic. Socrates' subjects are not *told* any clear answer; there is no informational transfer in that sense. Instead, there is a lived, communicative, asymptotic process by which the way one considers courage, the way one should approach such a problem, and the way one reflects upon oneself, is transformed.

This centrality of human experience is in marked contrast to modern self-tracking machines, whose promise of better self-knowledge is predicated on a certain externalisation of the knowing process away from the thinking, feeling subject. Socrates makes this point in *Phaedrus*, where he warns of the dangers of writing as technology. He argues that such a radical increase in external mnemonic objects will take away from people's ability to remember 'of themselves'. But what is remembering 'of ourselves,' anyway? Once again, the problem comes down to the role of experience and cognition in the lived present.

> I cannot help feeling, Phaedrus, that writing is unfortunately like painting; for the creations of the painter have the attitude of life, and yet if you ask them a question they preserve a solemn silence. And the same may be said of speeches. You would imagine that they had intelligence,

148   *Sun-ha Hong*

but if you want to know anything and put a question to one of them, the speaker always gives one unvarying answer. And when they have been once written down they are tumbled about anywhere among those who may or may not understand them, and know not to whom they should reply, to whom not: and, if they are maltreated or abused, they have no parent to protect them; and they cannot protect or defend themselves.

(Plato 1899, p. 581 [275d-e])

Here, the chief sin of writing as a technology for instruction and knowledge is its ossifying quality: wisdom, unmoored from the process of becoming-wise, is abused through indiscriminate circulation. Socrates asks: do we not already know a better way to know and remember – "an intelligent word graven in the soul of the learner, which can defend itself, and knows when to speak and when to be silent"? In this formulation, writing's production of stable, unchanging information is analogous to self-tracking's reliable, autonomous facts: the solid, data-driven assertion that you are depressed, or that chocolate makes you more productive, that does not change and transform with the caprice of my own perception or mood. But it is precisely such stability that Socrates warns against.

This is not to say that technologies like writing invariably push us towards a non-experiential mode of knowing. A host of writing-based techniques for self-examination in late Antique and early Christian periods sought precisely to produce its own kind of dialogic, transformative experience. Here, as in *Laches*, the critical element in self-knowledge is not the factual content of the written text, but the experience of the writing subject. Seneca writes in *De Ira*:

"What bad habit of yours have you cured to-day? what vice have you checked? in what respect are you better?" . . . I daily plead my cause before myself: . . . I pass the whole day in review before myself, and repeat all that I have said and done: I conceal nothing from myself, and omit nothing: for why should I be afraid of any of my shortcomings, when it is in my power to say, "I pardon you this time: see that you never do that anymore"?

(Seneca 2012, Book III, XXXVI)

Foucault (1986, p. 61) notes that these sessions were held in an 'administrative' spirit rather than guilt-wracked penitence. The point was to produce a reliable and accurate – it would be anachronistic to say 'objective' – form of self-knowledge. And so, with such self-writing, we find: the temporal and procedural regularity of the examinations; the model of the pseudo-rational, controlling I; the 'administrative' attitude as an affective regulator. These elements were designed to substitute the figure of the interlocutor with a relationship where I, in a specific sense, become other to myself. The emphasis is squarely on cultivating a subject that is then in a position to properly

Surveillance, sensors, and knowledge   149

perceive and internalise their own truths. Again, it is not the specific content of the experience that is conserved across these cases, but the centrality of *human experience, and the reflective (conscious) subject*, to the process of knowing. The experiencing I – as *basanos*, as 'administrator' – acts as a clearing house for producing, curating and analyzing data about the self. It is this function that contemporary self-tracking attempts to bypass and undercut in its promise of automated objectivity.

In short, there is a certain contrast between the integral ideal, where the experiencing subject *avows* the truth of the self, and a distributed network, where the subject is constantly reliant on and empowered by externalised input. Self-tracking's pursuit of the latter, which I have depicted in terms of protrusion, entails two specific shifts in the phenomenal process of 'knowing'. First, the experiencing, conscious subject is *displaced*; as 'knowledge' increasingly becomes understood as the achievement of stable, objective fact rather than a subject's reflective transformation, the various powers of judgment concentrated in the subject become challenged and dispersed. Second, the externalisation of this self-knowledge into discrete and standardised forms of data, from sleep scores to heart rate variability readings, means that the aspects of knowing and judging the self that was previously internal to the subject now become available for scrutiny, optimisation, rationalisation – by myself, by my employers (who are increasingly the consumers of new self-tracking technologies), and more. The subject now faces a wider frontier where his/her truth is open to another's scrutiny, and indeed, is exposed to scrutiny *before* the conscious subject can catch up.

Future-forward

Recession and protrusion describe two felt tendencies in which new technological knowing appears to the human subject. They write new chapters in the long history of how things other than ourselves come to tell us what we are. They reconfigure which aspects of what we call 'knowing' becomes externalised, available for prediction and judgment, reduced to quantification and populational correlation; which aspects increasingly pre-empt human cognition and prefigure it; which aspects are secured by collective faith in statistical reason or the still-enduring aura of the state.

To be sure, what we are charting here is at the order of instructions, prescriptions, fantasies. These technologies are, in many ways, *imaginary media* (see Kluitenberg 2011): imperfect and flawed objects that orient us towards a currently impossible end, and in doing so, open up a certain mediated access to that impossible. Their present function is to produce effects of the real that authorise their claims towards actually delving into the real, and thereby build an informational paradigm where the effect can 'count'.

The stakes in such future-forwarding are clear. Recession and protrusion describe problems of 'knowing' technological complexity and knowing *through* complex technology. In a more immediate sense, these problems

150 *Sun-ha Hong*

manifest as widespread cynicism in the political sphere; the continuing fetishisation of exposing secrets (Dean 2001); the normalisation of machinic conditioning of everyday self-experience. In the longer term, as rhetoric, investment and invention continues towards the already labelled vision of the 'data-driven society,' these phenomena signal a progressive demotion of the human subject and his/her lived experience to the periphery of what is able to count as 'knowing'.

Notes

1 My use of 'public' thus aligns with what has been called 'publicly oriented' (Warner 2002) or 'publicised' (Habermas 1991): discourse intended for, and circulated to, a wider community of indefinite strangers.

2 Internal NSA memos leaked by Edward Snowden (see Maass 2015) speak of 'analysis paralysis' and 'too many choices,' and featured titles such as "Data Is Not Intelligence" and "In Praise of Not Knowing."

3 Trevor Paglen (2009) has documented the locations which have been rendered 'blank spots' on the map – excepted from visual and cartographic capture for fuller withdrawal from public imagination. In the NSA's case, we might point to the windowless skyscraper in the heart of Manhattan at 33 Thomas Street – quite literally blacked out in both its solid façade and in the black-striped redactions in declassified documents (Gallagher and Moltke 2016).

4 Glenn Greenwald, Snowden's primary journalist contact, has refused to give a firm number; the closest he came was in an obscure New Zealand television appearance, where he referred to 'hundreds of thousands' of documents (*The Nation* 2014). Janine Gibson, the Editor-in-Chief of *The Guardian* US, claimed 'over 58,000 files,' but apparently only once – at an event at Columbia University (Bell et al. 2014). In fact, the figure 58,000 only appeared in mainstream news outlets as part of the false rumour that David Miranda, Greenwald's partner, was detained in Heathrow with that number of documents (Greenwald 2015).

5 This fantasy is epistomized in Borges' "The Library of Babel" (1998) – and of course in Jacques Derrida's *Archive Fever* (1998).

6 A survey, addressing news habits in the first four days of the Snowden leaks (6–9 June 2013), suggested that 50% of the Americans followed the news 'not too closely' or 'not at all closely' (*Pew Research Centre* 2013); we might well expect public attention to have declined in subsequent weeks.

7 For example, consider the media coverage of Chris Dancy, widely labelled the 'most connected human on earth.' His symbolic position is anchored through descriptions of 'up to 700 sensors,' and the many gadgets extracting data from his body at all times (See Griffiths 2014; Kelly 2014; Wainwright 2014).

8 Analogously, consider Merleau-Ponty's analysis (2012, pp. 94–96) of the double sensation phenomenon (i.e., the feeling of the right hand touching the left hand, or vice versa).

9 Comparing self-tracking to the familiar science fiction fascination for bodies that 'jack in' to another space, Rebecca Lemov (2015) describes "the curious status of the body that serves as the passively patient platform for a self's 'remote' activity or as the hooked-up object of endless measurement and observation – or indeed as both." Especially since the flesh remains a privileged source of information for self-tracking's claim to knowledge, it seems more appropriate here to contrast the body primed for machinic communication (the trace-body) with the thinking, experiencing subject (including his/her embodied, lived sense of self).

Surveillance, sensors, and knowledge 151

10 In the original text, Laches says: "I have no acquaintance with the words of Socrates, but . . . have had experience of his deeds, and there I found him a person privileged to speak fair words and to indulge in every kind of frankness" (Plato 1920, p. 64 [188e]).

11 Foucault (2011, p. 145) notes that *basanos* is derived to give *basanizesthai* [βασανίζεσθαι], a verb for being examined or tested. The latter form appears in Laches, most clearly in the Jowett translation: "To me, to be cross examined [βασανίζεσθαι] by Socrates is neither unusual nor unpleasant" (Plato 1920, p. 64 [188a]).

Bibliography

42 Years for Snowden Docs Release, Free All Now, 2016. *Cryptome.* Available at: http://cryptome.org/2013/11/snowden-tally.htm (accessed: 16 February 2016).

Andrejevic, M., 2013. *InfoGlut: How Too Much Information Is Changing the Way We Think and Know.* New York: Routledge.

Angwin, J., 2014. *Dragnet Nation: A Quest for Privacy, Security, and Freedom in a World of Relentless Surveillance.* New York: Times Books.

Ball, J., 2013. Xbox Live among Game Services Targeted by US and UK Spy Agencies. *The Guardian.* Available at: www.theguardian.com/world/2013/dec/09/nsa-spies-online-games-world-warcraft-second-life (accessed: 1 February 2015).

Bamford, J., 2008. *The Shadow Factory: The Ultra-Secret NSA from 9/11 to the Eavesdropping on America.* New York: Doubleday.

Bell, E., Abramson, J., Gibson, J., Schulz, D. and Sunstein, C. R., 2014. Journalism after Snowden, Columbia Journalism School. New York, 30 January.

Borges, J. L., 1998. The Library of Babel. *In*: A. Hurley, trans. *Jorge Luis Borges: Collected Fictions.* New York: Penguin Books, 112–118.

Brighenti, A. M., 2007. Visibility: A Category for the Social Sciences. *Current Sociology,* 55 (3), 323–342.

Chun, W. H. K., 2011. Crisis, Crisis, Crisis, or Sovereignty and Networks. *Theory, Culture & Society,* 28 (6), 91–112.

Chun, W. H. K., 2016. *Updating to Remain the Same: Habitual New Media.* Cambridge, MA: MIT Press.

Clarke, R. A., Morell, M. J., Stone, G. R., Sunstein, C. R. and Swire, P., 2013. *Liberty and Security in a Changing World.* Available at: https://obamawhitehouse.archives.gov/blog/2013/12/18/liberty-and-security-changing-world (accessed: 18 December 2013).

Crary, J., 2013. *24/7: Late Capitalism and the Ends of Sleep.* London: Verso.

Crawford, K., Lingel, J. and Karppi, T., 2015. Our Metrics, Ourselves: A Hundred Years of Self-Tracking from the Weight Scale to the Wrist Wearable Device. *European Journal of Cultural Studies,* 18 (4–5), 479–496.

Dean, J., 2001. Publicity's Secret. *Political Theory,* 29 (5), 624–650.

Derrida, J., 1998. *Archive Fever: A Freudian Impression.* Chicago, IL: University of Chicago Press.

Elliott, J. and Meyer, T., 2013. Claim on 'Attacks Thwarted' by NSA Spreads Despite Lack of Evidence. *ProPublica.* Available at: www.propublica.org/article/claim-on-attacks-thwarted-by-nsa-spreads-despite-lack-of-evidence (accessed: 21 March 2016).

152 Sun-ha Hong

Farivar, C., 2013. Snowden Distributed Encrypted Copies of NSA Files across the World. *Wired*. Available at: www.wired.co.uk/news/archive/2013-06/26/edward-snowden-nsa-data-copies (accessed: 16 February 2016).

Flyverbom, M., 2016. Transparency: Mediation and the Management of Visibilities. *International Journal of Communication*, 10 (1), 110–122.

Foucault, M., 1986. *The Care of the Self*. New York: Random House.

Foucault, M., 1997. *Ethics: Subjectivity and Truth*. New York: The New Press.

Foucault, M., 2001. *Fearless Speech*. Los Angeles: Semiotext(e).

Foucault, M., 2011. *The Courage of Truth: Lectures at the Collège de France, 1983–1984*. Basingstoke: Palgrave Macmillan.

Foucault, M., 2014a. *On the Government of the Living: Lectures at the Collège de France, 1979–1980*. Basingstoke: Palgrave Macmillan.

Foucault, M., 2014b. *Wrong-Doing, Truth-Telling: The Function of Avowal in Justice*. Chicago, IL: University of Chicago Press.

Frers, L., 2013. The Matter of Absence. *Cultural Geographies*, 20 (4), 431–445.

Frick, L., 2013. *Mood+Quantify*. Available at: www.lauriefrick.com/mood-quantify/ (accessed: 1 May 2017).

Galison, P., 2008. Removing Knowledge: The Logic of Modern Censorship. *In*: R. N. Procter and L. Schiebinger, eds. *Agnotology: The Making & Unmaking of Ignorance*. Stanford, CA: Stanford University Press, 37–54.

Gallagher, R. and Moltke, H., 2016. Look inside the Windowless New York Skyscraper Linked to the NSA. *The Intercept*. Available at: https://theintercept.com/2016/11/19/nsa-33-thomas-street-att-new-york-photos-inside/ (accessed: 19 November 2016).

Greenwald, G., 2013. NSA Collecting Phone Records of Millions of Verizon Customers Daily. *The Guardian*. Available at: www.theguardian.com/world/2013/jun/06/nsa-phone-records-verizon-court-order (accessed: 14 February 2016).

Greenwald, G., 2014. Microsoft Handed the NSA Access to Encrypted Messages. *The Guardian*. Available at: www.theguardian.com/world/2013/jul/11/microsoft-nsa-collaboration-user-data (accessed: 12 July 2013).

Greenwald, G., 2015. The Sunday Times' Snowden Story Is Journalism at Its Worst—and Filled with Falsehoods. *The Intercept*. Available at: https://theintercept.com/2015/06/14/sunday-times-report-snowden-files-journalism-worst-also-filled-falsehoods/ (accessed: 22 January 2016).

Griffiths, S., 2014. Is This the Most Connected Human on the Planet? Man Is Wired up to 700 Sensors to Capture Every Single Detail of His Existence. *Daily Mail*. Available at: www.dailymail.co.uk/sciencetech/article-2588779/Is-connected-man-planet-Man-wired-700-devices-capture-single-existence.html (accessed: 26 March 2014).

Habermas, J., 1991. *The Structural Transformation of the Public Sphere: An Inquiry into a Category of Bourgeois Society*. Cambridge, MA: MIT Press.

Han, B.-C., 2010. *Müdigkeitsgesellschaft*. Berlin: Matthes & Seitz.

Hendrix, J., 2013. NSA Surveillance Puts George Orwell's '1984' on Bestseller Lists. *Los Angeles Times*. Available at: http://articles.latimes.com/2013/jun/11/entertainment/la-et-jc-nsa-surveillance-puts-george-orwells-1984-on-bestseller-lists-20130611 (accessed: 11 March 2014).

Hernandez, D., 2012. Big Data Is Transforming Healthcare. *Wired*. Available at: www.wired.com/2012/10/big-data-is-transforming-healthcare/ (accessed: 29 March 2016).

Hesse, M., 2008. Bytes of Life. *The Washington Post*. Available at: www.wired. com/2010/11/mf_qa_ferriss/ (accessed: 29 March 2016).

Hong, S., 2015a. Presence: The Sense of Being-There and Being-with in the New Media Society. *First Monday*, 20 (10).

Hong, S., 2015b. Subjunctive and Interpassive Knowing in the Surveillance Society. *Media and Communication*, 3.

Hong, S., 2016. Data's Intimacy: Machinic Sensibility and the Quantified Self. *Communication + 1*, 5.

Horn, E., 2012. Logics of Political Secrecy. *Theory, Culture & Society*, 28 (7–8), 103–122.

Kelley, M. B., 2014. Snowden Has One Very Important and Potentially Devastating Question to Answer. *Business Insider*. Available at: www.businessinsider.com/ snowden-and-military-information-2014-3 (accessed: 16 February 2016).

Kelly, K., 2010. *What Technology Wants*. New York: Viking.

Kelly, S. M., 2014. The Most Connected Man Is You, Just a Few Years from Now. *Mashable*. Available at: http://mashable.com/2014/08/21/most-connected-man/# I60SjAremkqw (accessed: 14 April 2016).

Kluitenberg, E., 2011. On the Archaeology of Imaginary Media. *In*: E. Huhtamo and J. Parikka, eds. *Media Archaeology: Approaches, Applications, and Implications*. Berkeley: University of California Press, 48–69.

Knowlton, B., 2013. Feinstein 'Open' to Hearings on Surveillance Programs. *New York Times*. Available at: http://thecaucus.blogs.nytimes.com/2013/06/09/law maker-calls-for-renewed-debate-over-patriot-act/?_php=true&_type=blogs&_r=0 (accessed: 1 July 2018).

Kronsberg, M., 2013. Know Thy Quantified Self. *The Wall Street Journal*. Available at: www.wsj.com/articles/SB10001424127887324000704578388680077749540 (accessed: 1 April 2016).

Lagerkvist, A., 2017. Existential Media: Toward a Theorization of Digital Thrownness. *New Media & Society*, 19 (1), 1–15.

Lears, J., 2003. *Something for Nothing: Luck in America*. New York: Viking.

Lemov, R., 2015. On Not Being There: The Data-Driven Body at Work and at Play. *The Hedgehog Review*, 17 (2). Available at: http://iasc-culture.org/THR/THR_ article_2015_Summer_Lemov.php (accessed: 30 March 2016).

Leopold, J., 2015. Inside Washington's Quest to Bring Down Edward Snowden. *Vice News*. Available at: https://news.vice.com/article/exclusive-inside-washingtons-quest-to-bring-down-edward-snowden (accessed: 16 February 2016).

Loewenstein, A., 2014. The Ultimate Goal of the NSA Is Total Population Control. *The Guardian*. Available at: www.theguardian.com/commentisfree/2014/jul/11/the-ultimate-goal-of-the-nsa-is-total-population-control (accessed: 14 February 2016).

Lupton, D., 2016. *The Quantified Self: A Sociology of Self-Tracking*. Cambridge: Polity Press.

Maass, P., 2015. Inside NSA, Officials Privately Criticize 'Collect It All' Surveillance. *The Intercept*. Available at: https://theintercept.com/2015/05/28/nsa-officials-privately-criticize-collect-it-all-surveillance/ (accessed: 15 February 2016).

Mack, E., 2016. Beyond Fitbit: 'Neural Dust' Puts Invisible Cyborg Tech Deep Inside You. *Cnet*. Available at: www.cnet.com/news/beyond-fitbit-neural-dust-puts-invisible-cyborg-tech-deep-inside-you/ (accessed: 3 August 2016).

Majaca, A., 2016. Little Daniel before the Law: Algorithmic Extimacy and the Rise of the Paranoid Apparatus. *e-flux*, 75.

154 *Sun-ha Hong*

Marx, L., 2010. Technology: The Emergence of a Hazardous Concept. *Technology and Culture*, 51 (3), 561–577.

Merleau-Ponty, M., 2012. *Phenomenology of Perception*. London: Routledge.

Morton, T., 2013. *Hyperobjects: Philosophy and Ecology after the End of the World*. Minneapolis: University of Minnesota Press.

Keall, C., 2014. RAW DATA: Lisa Owens interviews Glenn Greenwald. *National Business Review*. Available at: https://www.nbr.co.nz/article/raw-data-lisa-owen-interviews-glenn-greenwald-ck-162378 (accessed: 15 May 2018).

Neff, G. and Nafus, D., 2016. *Self-Tracking*. Cambridge, MA: MIT Press.

Paglen, T., 2009. *Blank Spots on the Map: The Dark Geography of the Pentagon's Secret World*. New York: Dutton.

Pasquale, F., 2015. *The Black Box Society: The Secret Algorithms That Control Money and Information*. Cambridge, MA: Harvard University Press.

Pew Research Centre, 2013. *Majority Views NSA Phone Tracking as Acceptable Anti-Terror Tactic*. Available at: www.people-press.org/2013/06/10/majority-views-nsa-phone-tracking-as-acceptable-anti-terror-tactic/ (accessed: 10 June 2013).

Pilliod, E., 2005. Ingestion/Pontormo's Diary. *Cabinet*. Available at: http://cabinet magazine.org/issues/18/pontormosdiary.php (accessed: 22 May 2015).

Plato, 1899. Phaedrus. *In*: B. Jowett, trans. *Dialogues of Plato* (Vol. 1). New York: Charles Scribner's Sons, 515–586.

Plato, 1920. Laches. *In*: B. Jowett, trans. *The Dialogues of Plato* (Vol. 1). New York: Random House.

Rosenberg, D., 2013. Data before the Fact. *In*: L. Gitelman, ed. *Raw Data Is an Oxymoron*. Cambridge, MA: MIT Press, 15–40.

Rusbridger, A., 2013. The Snowden Leaks and the Public. *The New York Review of Books*. Available at: www.nybooks.com/articles/2013/11/21/snowden-leaks-and-public/ (accessed: 16 February 2016).

Saury, J.-M., 2008. The Phenomenology of Negation. *Phenomenology and the Cognitive Sciences*, 8 (2), 245–260.

Schwartz, M., 2015. The Whole Haystack. *The New Yorker*. Available at: www.newyorker.com/magazine/2015/01/26/whole-haystack (accessed: 15 February 2015).

Seneca, L. A., 2012. *Minor Dialogs Together with the Dialog 'on Clemency.'* London: Forgotten Books.

Sheehan, T., 2014. *Making Sense of Heidegger: A Paradigm Shift*. London: Rowman & Littlefield International.

Shorrock, T., 2015. US Intelligence Is More Privatized Than Ever Before. *The Nation*. Available at: www.thenation.com/article/us-intelligence-is-more-privatized-than-ever-before/ (accessed: 16 February 2016).

Snowden-Interview: Transcript, 2014. *NDR*. Available at: https://web.archive.org/web/20140128224400/www.ndr.de/ratgeber/netzwelt/snowden277_page-1.html (accessed: 24 November 2016).

Sterman, D., 2014. Infographic: How the Government Exaggerated the Successes of NSA Surveillance. *Slate*. Available at: www.slate.com/blogs/future_tense/2014/01/16/nsa_surveillance_how_the_government_exaggerated_the_way_its_programs_stopped.html (accessed: 21 March 2016).

Steyerl, H., 2016. A Sea of Data: Apophenia and Pattern (Mis-)Recognition. *e-flux*, 72.

Swan, M., 2013. The Quantified Self: Fundamental Disruption in Big Data Science and Biological Discovery. *Big Data*, 1 (2), 85–99.

Thompson, J. B., 2011. Shifting Boundaries of Public and Private Life. *Theory, Culture & Society*, 28 (4), 49–70.

Urist, J., 2015. From Paint to Pixels. *The Atlantic*. Available at: www.theatlantic.com/entertainment/archive/2015/05/the-rise-of-the-data-artist/392399/ (accessed: 29 March 2016).

Wainwright, O., 2014. Rise of the 'Inner-net': Meet the Most Connected Man on the Planet. *The Guardian*. Available at: www.theguardian.com/artanddesign/architecture-design-blog/2014/mar/19/inner-net-most-connected-man-earth-fitness-trackers-data (accessed: 19 March 2014).

Warner, M., 2002. *Publics and Counterpublics*. New York: Zone Books.

Wittgenstein, L., 1969. *On Certainty*. New York: Harper Torchbooks.

7 Social media and the care of the self

Ganaele Langlois

Mediation and the care of the self

This chapter asks the following question: what is the state of the relationships between the networked digital self and the embodied, feeling self in a context saturated with corporate social media logics? I start from the obvious premise that one central use of social media is to reflect on and shape our selves. By this, I mean that we commonly engage with social media to explore where we stand in the world, with regards to pressing issues, to the social context surrounding us, to how our personal desires and wishes could become reality. Reflecting on ourselves should not be understood as an de facto egocentric gesture: it is about our engagement with the world and with others, about our openness to the world and to others, including non-humans and inanimate beings (Haraway 2016).

It would be a mistake to think about the mediated exploration of the self in the world – in other words, the search for meaningfulness through engaging with media – only in terms of information gathering and consumption of content. Indeed, one of the key characteristics of digital media is the capacity to craft different modes of engagement with mediated objects and subjects, some of which informational of course, but others affective (Hillis et al. 2015), emotional and existential. As well, it is crucial to acknowledge that having ourselves out there on social media networks, which increasingly takes place whether we want it or not, does not simply result in the creation of a kind of clone or mirror image of ourselves. Being digitally mediated means being turned into a series of digital network objects that can be combined and disaggregated almost instantaneously based on the data traces left behind. Furthermore, this digital self – or rather, this modulable collection of self objects, links us to multiple planes of existence: a mundane selfie at the gym, for instance, articulates personal desires with social expectations, and engages into a new kind valuation of the self that subjects itself to the gaze and judgment of others.

Overall, social media platforms have taken the existentialization of the self through its mediation as their focus and business model: their key job is to help organize and make sense of our place in the world. Our constant use of and growing dependency on social media to find all kinds of emotional, cultural, affective and political meanings has ushered in new types of techno-human intimacies. Why, then, are contemporary corporate social media routinely decried for fostering all kinds of anti-social traits such as narcissism, bullying and isolation? Indeed, new media scholar Sherry Turkle (2015), who used to celebrate the promises of digital media with regards to crafting new identities through self-mediation, now argues that we should turn away from networked technologies and rediscover the practices of face-to-face conversation, which allow for empathic listening, hearing and being heard, and consequently for vulnerabilities to be expressed and shared. Notably as well, philosopher Bernard Stiegler (2016) argues that current social media technologies are part of a context that mostly fails to mediate the relationship between self, others and the world, resulting in widespread disaffection, unhappiness and loneliness. He describes the loss of the self through digital technologies as one of deindividuation, where the capacity to find meaningfulness and possibilities of becoming to and in the world is curtailed and ultimately destroyed. This deindividuation has repercussions at both the individual and collective level: the fabric of the social, the capacity for people to come together to imagine and craft new conditions and possibilities of being together is curtailed as well. The consequence is that current social media technologies are part of a context that mostly fail to mediate the relationship between self, others and the world, resulting in widespread disaffection, unhappiness and loneliness.

This chapter agrees that social media technologies have promises that have been undermined, underdeveloped and co-opted, and argues in turn that we need to develop a critical ethics of the relationships between embodied self and socially mediated self. To do so, we should adopt a pharmacological approach to the question of social media, which entails examining the capacity for that which is poison to become a cure when used judiciously and carefully (Stiegler 2016). Such pharmacological approach involves identifying where social media fails with regards to mediating the relationship between self, world and others. The list is long in that regard, and involves not only questions surrounding privacy and commodification of personal data, but also the design of algorithms, the safety of networks, the for-profit goals of most social media platforms, pervasive surveillance and manipulation of users, the interest of big corporations, to name but a few.

This chapter focuses on the question of the care of the self (Foucault 1987, 1988) as an entry point to both critique and rethink the potential of social media. The care of the self is indeed closely related to the search for meaningfulness described above: it is an important concept to explore the relationships between the embodied self and the socially mediated self. While the concept of care or *sorge* is particularly examined in depth in Heidegger's work, I focus specifically on Foucault's approach which examines the actualization of such a concept of care through everyday practices of existence

158   *Ganaele Langlois*

(McNeill 1998). The care of the self involves a critical reflection on one's conditions and possibilities of existence. In Ancient Greece (Foucault 1988, p. 42), the care of the self involved "the intensity of the relations to the self, that is, of the forms in which one is called upon to take oneself as an object of knowledge and a field of action, so as to transform, correct and purify oneself, and find salvation". For Foucault, practices for the care of the self are practices of freedom: in exploring ourselves, questioning our ethical stance and finding new spaces for change, we can experience freedom from power formations.

I further base my analysis of practices of the care of the self through the concept of being-with (Nancy 2000; Miller, Chapter 8 in this volume) and through critical psychoanalytical explorations of relationality (Benjamin 1998, 2004, 2013): despite conjuring images of asceticism and withdrawal from the world, the care of the self is not a self-centred pursuit done in complete isolation. Rather, the care of the self entails techniques for rethinking and refashioning the relations one has to the world, to others, and to the self. In that regard, it entails some form of mediation that could be provided by social media technologies. In Foucault's work on the practices of the care of the self in Ancient Greece and Rome, the care of the self is not primarily an exercise in solitude, cut off from others (1988, p. 106). On the contrary, practices of the care of the self involved the development of modes of living with others and the world, from attitudes to practices of engagement: talking to mentors, for instance, and developing friendships and alliances in both non-institutional and institutional settings (1988, p. 91). Interestingly enough, the practices of the care of the self that Foucault analyzed also involved the use of existing media technologies: writing letters and keeping journals, in particular (Weisgerber and Butler 2015). And these practices, one might add, are exercises in mediating the self and its engagements in the world to develop a reflective space that opens up new possibilities of becoming. Such mediation is not only about representation: it is not simply a question of testimonial, of building either a personal memory or adding to a collective archive. Rather, when one is engaged in the mediation of oneself and therefore in the externalization of one's self, one opens up a space between the self as subject and the self as object. In mediating one's self, in turning the self into an object, one engages with a new relationality between self and the world that should be described, following Winnicott (2005), as transitional, where transformative potentials can emerge. The transformation of one's self through self-mediation is thus a crucial, although under-studied aspect of the care of the self. While Foucault showed that the care of the self involves at its core a process of ethical socialization, it is interesting in turn to look at the care of the self as a mediated process that must include some sort of critical, ethical and creative stance towards media technologies. Such a stance requires first understanding the role of specific media technologies in mediating the self.

The production of meaningful relations

Social media are not neutral conduits for communication: rather, they have become central regulators of the relations between self and others, between self and the world and between self and self. It is important here to distinguish social media from other kinds of digital media technologies, even though social media platforms host and are folded into many different kinds of networked and information technologies. In particular, social media should not be confused with participatory media, even though social media have incorporated and, I argue, undermined the participatory media ethos. The purpose of social media is different than participatory platforms, which are focused on enabling anybody with an internet connection to express themselves. Social media use participatory technologies in order not to have to produce content, a job that is delegated to users and other content-based media. In turn, social media technologies are specifically about collecting all kinds of information to foster meaningful relations among informational objects. These meaningful relations currently obey a logic of personalization. That is, networks of meaningful relations are specifically established for each social media user. Such a model of meaningful connectivity now dominates all digital networked communication, so much so that all aspects of online existence have been imbued with what we can call a personalized social media logic. Google search, for instance, has moved away from identifying universal results to contextualizing results to one's profile, and video repositories such as YouTube keep track of their user's behaviors to curate recommended videos.

To establish these meaningful relations, social media platforms require linking together, via software and hardware infrastructure, the following components: data, algorithms and responsive visual interfaces. Let's have a look at these in turn to understand how technological systems such as social media can generate meaningful relationships. Informational objects are made up of data. They can be based on human users: a social media profile, for instance, is made up of pieces of information about somebody. But there can also be non-human informational objects: for instance, a media object such as a video. Informational objects constantly evolve and change: they can be disaggregated and re-aggregated. My social media profile, for instance, is constantly augmented every time I am online: what I do, see and interact with is recorded and added to my profile's database. This is the first step in the process of establishing meaningful relationships: social media enable the creation and tracking of ever-evolving informational objects through the collection, sorting and aggregation of all kinds of data.

Second, social media facilitate and establish connections among these informational objects. Connections, or 'edges' in the technical parlance, can be initiated by users and enabled by a social media platform's user affordances: when I click "like", "share", or "join", for instance, I establish a connection between my profile and another informational objects. However, the

160 *Ganaele Langlois*

vast majority of connections or edges are the results of technical processes rather than human choice. These involve embedding all kinds of supplementary information into informational objects, or in technical terms, metadata. Typically this type of operation takes place when data is being collected and compared with other kinds of data. For example, when I upload a picture on Facebook from my smartphone, it is not only the picture that is being transmitted, but also the time it was taken, the brand of my smartphone, the software used for taking the picture, whether the picture is of a view or of faces that are then scanned for automatic recognition and so on. Metadata can then be used to identify matches and therefore create connections among informational objects. For instance, in my profile on a social media platform, I might indicate what kind of music I like to listen to and as a result get a set of recommendations for some other music to listen to. The connection is simple to establish in that case: the algorithm identifies keywords in metadata associated with the kind of music I like and then scan a database of music to locate which piece of music contains in turn, in their metadata, those keywords.

The third step is to make these connections among informational objects meaningful: in that regard, the success of social media is based on transforming informational connectivity into relationships that make sense to us. This shift from quantitative (connection based on measuring diverse criteria) to qualitative (meaningfulness) requires the development of complex algorithms. A common logic to all these social media algorithms to establish meaningfulness is to identify the weight of different connections, or edges. For instance, if there is another user I interact with often on Facebook, my connection with them will be weighted heavier than someone on my friend's list that I have never interacted with. Because there are many different kinds of informational objects that are part of one's constantly evolving networks, the calculation of weights becomes quickly complex. It has been speculated that the proprietary Google PageRank search algorithm, for instance, deploys upwards of 200 types of metrics that have then to be correlated to obtain personalized search results (Dean 2016). As well, the news feed ranking for the Facebook algorithm has as many as 100,000 individual weights (McGee 2013). The proprietary, and therefore secretive, algorithms deployed by social media platforms play a key role in establishing meaningful relationships among informational objects. It is literally a case where the algorithm, the non-human, surpasses the human in making sense of connections. Elsewhere, I have argued that there is a profound shift in meaning making practices with the arrival of social media (Langlois 2014). Finding meaningfulness has always been considered as an intrinsically human process, but social media, and in particular algorithms, have inserted themselves in this process so that the making sense of the world increasingly displaces the human element. Indeed, in the social media context, it is the platform that increasingly organizes our world for us.

Social media and the care of the self   161

Finally, all this work in the background of the platform has to be given some kind of recognizable shape for us users. This is where responsive visual interfaces intervene. The message "you might be interested in X" is an example of meaning being attributed to a connection between my profile and another informational object. In this specific instance, I, as a user, am invited by the platform to participate in making sense of the connection. In other cases, the social media platform decides what is meaningful. The Facebook news feed, for instance, curates and ranks news items based on its proprietary algorithmic logic and gives me the result without much of my direct input. It is key here to remember that the process of fostering meaningful relations takes place constantly: we never have a finished picture, but a constant evolution. As Bucher (2015, p. 1) pithily puts it:

> being social in the context of social media simply means creating connections within the boundaries of adaptive algorithmic architectures. Every click, share, like and post creates a connection, initiates a relation. The network dynamically grows, evolves, becomes. The network networks. The social in social media is not a fact but a doing.

In that sense, social media take even further the idea that technology is not a means to an end, but rather imposes ways of being in the world. The question is, of course, about how specifically do different sets of technologies come to be accepted as the very ontological ground that generates the conditions through which the world can make sense to us, and usually in specific and limited ways. Typically, understanding the shaping of the meaningfulness of the world through technical mediation is divided into two camps: those who argue that the technical system itself takes precedence as fostering an ontological ground through which meaningfulness can arise, and those who argue that the specificity of communication technologies is the production of meaningfulness through signs and texts that are mostly driven by human intervention. However, in an environment where most meaningful relationships are not only managed, but produced by the system itself, there is not difference between signification and technique: the first is altogether produced and managed by the other. In other words, the social media dynamic is about enfolding everything into its "adaptive algorithmic architectures".

The impossible care of the self on social media

The fostering of meaningful relations makes it possible for social media to intervene in the very relationship of the self to itself, as well as between self and other and between the self and the world (Lagerkvist 2016). It is useful here to briefly pause and think further about the question of the self. The self is not a coherent, definite being separate from the world. On the

162   *Ganaele Langlois*

contrary, we should follow Felix Guattari here and understand any question related to the self involves a never-ending process of "putting into being" (my translation, Guattari 1989, p. 36). Such putting into being takes place through encounters between multiple and discording processes of subjectivation: socioeconomic ones, informational, cultural, political, subconscious ones, technological ones and so on. That is not to say that the self, even though it is a "terminal" that receives all these dynamics of subjectivation, is passive and completely shaped by them. As Guattari argues, the "interiority" of the self, one's capacity to be able to differentiate oneself from processes of subjectivation, "establishes itself at the crossroads of multiple components" that are each autonomous and sometimes even in open conflict (p. 36). This is an important point to remember: the defining characteristic of a "self" – its interiority and capacity to differentiate and even singularize itself by disrupting dominant processes of subjectivation and creating new modes of existence – can only take place in relation to these very processes of subjectivation. The critical task, for Guattari, is to cultivate the capacity to identify and provoke disruptions into dominant processes of subjectivity, so as to craft new possibilities of existence. We find in this an echo of Foucault's care of the self, where the retreat from the everyday world created a disruption that made it possible to create distance and potential for differentiation between the self and dominant power formations. The options available to develop new modes for the care of the self, then, include refusal of engagement with processes of subjectivation, but not only. The crafting of new encounters with processes of subjectivation, of new modes of existence, of new alliances with others to transform collective conditions of existence are also key to the care of the self.

The subsequent question is about how existing dominant social media technologies prevent that kind of care of the self from happening. The answer is to go back to the image of the self as a terminal: we could say that social media technologies are about connecting this very terminal to processes of subjectivation. By creating meaningful relationships, existing social media technologies define the scope and characteristics of the encounter between the self and processes of subjectivation. Social media technologies intervene in the sphere of memory, taking over and decentering human agents from practices of making sense of the past and the present, and imagining future possibilities. Stiegler (2016) describes this process as one of retention – the selection of what is consciously and subconsciously remembered, including both personal and collective memories – and protention – the capacity to embrace potential becomings. With regards to retention, social media differ from previous media technologies of memory in that through their capacity to create meaningful connections at the very intimate and microscopic level, they intervene in the individual psyche in minute ways that were previously impossible to achieve (Thomas 2013).

By taking over processes of protention – the capacity to imagine and project oneself into a future – social media technologies insert themselves in the

Social media and the care of the self 163

sphere of what we usually see as the interiority of our selves. With social media, we do not have to question ourselves about who our future friends should be, or about how relevant information we receive is anymore: the technology makes sense of it for us, and we only have to trust it. The key difference between social media technologies and other media technologies is that they do not simply intervene in processes of retention and protention, shaping them according to their capacities, limitations and affordances. They do not bend these processes, but make them possible in the first place. In other words: social media technologies are now becoming the ground, the very condition for the possibility of processes of retention and protention (Hansen 2015). And hence the main issue with social media technologies as they are currently designed: they have become opaque machinic systems that aim to take over the "doing" of existence.

The key problem is that the process of automated, non-human production of meaningfulness has been hijacked by capitalist imperatives. That is, the making sense of the world has not only been turned into a technical process rather than an activity of the so-called human spirit, but also into a capitalist enterprise. The repercussion of this new "semiocapitalist" enterprise, as Berardi (2009) would call it, are far reaching. Because they are for-profit enterprises, social media corporations have very little interest in empowering users beyond granting them the limited ability to post and share content: they deprive users of control over their data, and keep algorithms secret. Any kind of public scrutiny and therefore input over the vast amount of personal data that is routinely processed on social media is almost impossible. Second, social media corporations have in turn invested and injected economic interests into the very process of formation of the self, of the self with others and of the self with the world. In other words, the characteristics of social media corporations is to not only have the capacity to create conditions of existence, but also to work to make these conditions of existence indistinguishable from their very own for-profit imperative. As a consequence, the self is not only a new market to be tapped into, but also a resource to be mined. Here, we can see the question of the self in social media resurfacing through the concepts of attention economy (Terranova 2012) and reputation economy (Hearn 2010).

As a market, the socially mediated self offers a way to tap into a whole set of emotions, affects and psycho-social capacities that fosters states of attention that can in turn be directed towards the consumption of both material and immaterial commodities. The capacity to pay attention – both intentionally and subconsciously – is a key precondition to the ability to recognize something or someone as meaningful. Most social media corporations and associated advertising and marketing corporations have intensively developed online strategies to awaken, shape and manage attentional capacities. Increasingly, the social media algorithms that create meaningful relations for us are devoted to matching one's interests with specific informational commodities. In other words, the algorithms are not neutral anymore – trying

164   *Ganaele Langlois*

to identify connections among informational objects – but are rather tasked with giving preferences over some informational objects (typically commodities) over others. The process at stake here is one of tapping into the self's propensity to seek meaningfulness to establish new consumer habits. Ultimately, in this new attention economy, being a consumer and living a meaningful life tend to become indistinguishable. With corporate social media, the self is not only a set of attentional capacities to be mobilized, but becomes a new valuable resource in turn that requires one's constant investment into a new reputation economy. The attention economy is not only about tapping into attentional capacities, but also about measuring and tracking them. The reputation economy is based in turn on valuing the amount of attention – be it positive or negative – that an informational self receives. The contours of this new reputation economy still have to be fully studied and include a wide range of phenomena, from social media celebrity, whose success is primarily based on being able to capitalize on their reputation to attract large amounts of attention, to personal reputation scores (Gerlitz and Lury 2012) that enable people with high social media following to receive free consumer objects that they can then advertise.

A lot of us now regularly spend time monitoring our informational selves: we Google ourselves, for instance, to figure out how we fare in the world. The kinds of result we get, the self that emerges online is often somewhat disconnected from our personal perception of our selves. We get to see what other people think about us, and what kind of information about us has been collected without our knowledge, and what has been omitted. This goes contrary to popular discourses surrounding social media that claim that thanks to instantaneous communication we can freely shape ourselves through connecting, exploring and discovering. The reality is more that our relationship to our online selves is increasingly made up of responses and adaptations to the information networks that mine both our personal data and the kind of attention from other users it receives. This new form of subjectivation is what is meant when we talk about the rise of a reputation economy. Such valuing of digital selves strongly encourages us to engage in a new set of relationships with our online selves, ones that often entail us trying to adapt to the logics of ranking and to adopt strategies to attract positive attention. It is mostly for this reason that we often hear, in the mainstream media, commentaries about how social media is turning us into narcissists. But rather than moralistic blaming, it might be more useful to consider that so-called narcissist behavior is a direct product of the new reputation economy, where our social and economic well-being is increasingly tied to the type of informational self that is presented online. The socially mediated self – the self that is presented to others when they search for our name on Google, for instance – is the one that is often used to decide whether we can get a coveted job position and whether we can have an opportunity to make other meaningful connections, from romantic ones to ones linked with increased social status. As a result, digital existence through social media requires that one adopts marketing and PR tactics in order to foster more positive conditions of existence. Overall, the social media self joins together algorithmic processes, capitalist incentives and psychic modes of existence. This kind of commercialization of the self is not without its consequences. The injection of capitalist imperatives into social media technologies result in a never seen before disruption of the processes through which the self emerges. Through social media, the risk is that processes of consumer subjectivation intervene directly in the formation of the interiority of the self, negating the capacity to differentiate and singularize oneself. Hence the numerous forms of deindividuation experienced by social media users and mentioned above: disaffection, isolation and alienation.

Redesigning social media for the care of the self

Deindividuation through corporate social media stands in stark contrast to the kinds of promises offered when the internet became accessible to the public back in the 1990s. Internet media technologies were perceived to enable new modes of being, particularly in relation to so-called virtual reality. While virtual reality is commonly understood as a radically different space, as an alternate and completely fabricated world most linked with gaming, it actually raised the possibility of new modes of being in the world. Drawing on Deleuze's discussion of the virtual, the actual, and the real (1990), there was hope that online mediation could be a way to become aware of potentialities, or in Deleuzian terms, virtualities (Shields 2003, 2006). Mediation, here, was a way to identify and enact alternatives by changing parameters of existence. These included, mainly, the ability to try out new identities – Second Life is a key example in this case (Martey and Consalvo 2011). We could now say that the internet was imagined as a kind of new transitional space – neither a completely imaginary place of one's invention nor a place in the actual world, but imbued by qualities of both: this new mediation troubled common perceptions, opening up the possibility of new modes of existence. As a bridge between the interiority of the self and the external world, such mediation could enable new disruptions and negotiations, and new encounters and modes of engaging and understanding others. Such a reflection on the link between mediation and the care of the self can serve as a basis to think about how to reinvent social media technologies.

Of course, there is already a significant amount of work being done on regulating, transforming or reinventing social media. With regards to regulation, there has long been a great outcry against violations of individual privacy on social media. More recently, with the intensification of reputation economies, we see attempts, at least in some jurisdictions like Europe, to regulate personal data flows and empower citizens to control use of personal data through the "right to be forgotten" (Rosen 2012). Privacy advocates and critics of reputation economies work towards empowering individuals to have some form of control towards their digital selves. In contrast to

166 *Ganaele Langlois*

attempts to regulate existing social media corporations, alternative social media models, on the other hand, aim to challenge and create other social media spaces that do not answer to the constraints, dangers and limitations of the for-profit model. Typically, alternative social media are focused on developing network infrastructures to support specific communities. Communities with common interests and values gather around to create network communication systems and platforms that embody these specific values such as non-commercial use of data, respect of privacy or complete anonymity (Gehl 2014; Gehl and Synder-Yuly 2016; and Schwartz, Chapter 3, this volume). A bulk of the work is therefore being done at the level of infrastructure and regulation to empower users to design network communication systems that enact more transparent, democratic values against corporate interests. However, such attempts tend to be popular with activist communities while failing to reach a broader public. Alternative social media platforms encounter the difficult and almost impossible task of overturning mainstream's social media's network effects: as it is impossible for users to move their social media data from one platform to another, there is very little incentive to embrace alternatives. The common theme between regulation and alternative approach is about the respect of the integrity of individual users. However, the question is also about the engagement of the self with others and with the world. In other words, and to go back to the discussion at the beginning of the chapter, redesigning of social media should entail thinking of the mediation of the relationships between self, others and the world. While giving control back to the individual is a useful first step, there are limitations in ignoring the relational aspects that are necessary to the care of the self.

The question of mediation of the relationalities of the self brings us back to the three levels that are central to social media described at the beginning of this chapter: data, algorithms and interface. In the first place, we should develop new ways of relating to personal data and the shaping of informational objects. The collection and use of personal data should not only be controlled, it should also be made more transparent. Consequently, we should foster new relationships with our personal data, and with personal data sharing and exchange. In Yuk Hui's words, we should become our own personal digital archivists (2015). As Hui argues, the personal digital archive offers new practices for taking care of self and others, and for the preservation and transmission of personal memories to enable new processes of transindividuation, of the mediated becoming of self and others:

> The call for an archivist culture is a proposal to regain the knowledge and skills of living with digital objects. At this level, we need both technics and technologies to "take care" of archives and the self. Such humanism integrates rather than expels technologies from our life.
>
> (2015, p. 245)

Social media and the care of the self   167

Such vision of reciprocal care between digital objects and the self can take the form of a greater attention to what kind of data is collected and for what purpose. Potentially, it would require giving agency back to users through new regulations. It would require cataloguing all the different types of personal data that could potentially be shared: biometric data, geographical data, data related to emotions, engagements with others, and so on. It would also entail participating in cataloguing and curating our own data, being able to decide under which conditions it could be shared, whether it should be made anonymous or not. Such new forms of digital archiving would also entail choosing what kind of knowledge and related applications of knowledge should be derived from personal data. This could be made in a similar way to creative commons licensing in which users can define the conditions under which their creative work can be copied, shared and modified (IF 2015).

The intervention of social media into practices of care of the self also involves algorithms. There is a need to reflect and design new algorithms that help produce different types of meaningful connections among informational objects. Of course, such concerns with technically assisted production of meaningful relations go back to the origin of digital network communication, particularly in Vannevar Bush' concept of "trails of association" (1945). In such conception of technically assisted production of meaningful relations among objects, the relationship between user and technology differs completely from the kind of black boxed automation so familiar to corporate social media (Pasquale 2015), positing instead a readability and transparency of the technical system assisting processes of association so that a certain form of intimacy and trust can be established between human users and technologies of association. The challenge is therefore to develop not only tools but also processes to enable the collaborative and transparent development of new social media algorithms. Such an idea is not new, and is indeed at the core of open source software communities, which strive for collaboration, transparency and exchange to create software that benefits all. The task is in turn to develop these kinds of recursive publics to decide on and create new types of social media algorithms. Social media algorithms could potentially enable this sort of mediation that allows for the formulation of transitional spaces that in turn allows for reflection over and potential transformation of one's relationship with oneself, others and the world. Social media algorithms should be developed with a transitional ethics in mind, allowing for a new form of playfulness, combining data with potential scenarios to explore complex issues, for instance. The development of alternative social algorithms could in the first place foster new relationships between technologies of mediation and our selves.

In that regard, we can refer back to alternative processing and visualizing complex data for inspiration. We could go back to Matthew Fuller's alternative web browser "Web Stalker", which radically refashioned hyperlink network visualization to disrupt both the dominant design and common

168   *Ganaele Langlois*

perceptions of the World Wide Web (2003). Such disruption opens us up to the possibilities of alternative interactions with a technology, asking us to recognize other potential relationships and intimacies with technologies of mediation. One could also refer here to artist Zach Blas' work on data collection and surveillance. In the *Facial Weaponization Suite* (2014), Blas worked with homosexual participants to collect their biometric data and create a "Fag Face Mask". Mashed together, such data were shaped into masks that had no recognizable facial characteristics. In so doing, the masks challenged gay stereotypes and therefore disrupted common preconceptions as well as the problematic ways in which personal data can be used to target and segregate individuals. Both these instances show the kind of disruption that can be fostered when data is given another shape through algorithms and visualization. This new rendering of the relationships between self and others raises a challenge with regards to commonalities and differences between selves through showcasing the distorted views of dominant power formations.

Conclusion

There were two questions raised in this chapter: one, is mediation necessary for the care of the self? The answer was that indeed, mediation is necessary, and that it is not simply either an egocentric act or something that we are forced to do with the development of corporate social media. Mediation allows for the creation of transitional spaces, where the encounters between processes of subjectivation and capacities for the self to individuate and develop its own interiority can be examined, played with, refashioned and challenged. Mediating the self is not an artificial need, but entails practices that are essential to the care of the self. The second question was: what kind of mediation can be achieved through social media technologies, which are about extracting data to foster all kinds of meaningful information? The current risk with mainstream corporate social media is that processes of relational individuation – of defining one's self in relation to the world – are hijacked and subsumed to capitalist imperatives, resulting in deindividuation. Refashioning mediation of the self through social media requires reinventing how we collect and archive personal data, transparency and playfulness in reinventing algorithms, and new modes of visualizing the actual and potential relationalities of the self.

Bibliography

Berardi, F. "Bifo", 2009. *The Soul at Work: From Alienation to Autonomy*. Trans. F. Cadel and G. Mecchia. Los Angeles: Semiotexte.

Blas, Z., 2014. Facial Weaponization Suite. *Digital*. http://www.zachblas.info/works/facial-weaponization-suite/.

Benjamin, J., 1998. *Like Subjects, Love Objects: Essays on Recognition and Sexual Difference*. New Haven, CT: Yale University Press.

Social media and the care of the self 169

Benjamin, J., 2004. Beyond Doer and Done to: An Intersubjective View of Thirdness. *The Psychoanalytic Quarterly*, 73 (1), 5–46.

Benjamin, J., 2013. *Shadow of the Other: Intersubjectivity and Gender in Psycho-analysis*. New York: Routledge.

Bucher, T., 2015. Networking, or What the Social Means in Social Media. *Social Media + Society*, 1 (1), doi:2056305115578138

Bush, V., 1945. As We May Think. *Atlantic Monthly*, 176 (1), 101–108.

Dean, B., 2016. Google's 200 Ranking Factors: The Complete List. 5 November. Available at: http://backlinko.com/google-ranking-factors (accessed: 1 July 2018).

Deleuze, G., 1990. *Bergsonism*. Trans. H. Tomlinson and B. Habberjam. New York: Zone Books.

Dienlin, T. and Trepte, S., 2015. Is the Privacy Paradox a Relic of the Past? An in-Depth Analysis of Privacy Attitudes and Privacy Behaviors. *European Journal of Social Psychology*, 45 (3), 285–297.

Foucault, M., 1987. The Ethic of Care for the Self as a Practice of Freedom: An Interview with Michel Foucault. *Philosophy & Social Criticism*, 12 (2–3), 112–131.

Foucault, M., 1988. *Technologies of the Self: A Seminar with Michel Foucault*. Cambridge: University of Massachusetts Press.

Foucault, M. and Faubion, J. D., 2000. Ethics Subjectivity and Truth: The Essential Works of Michael Foucault, 1954–1984.

Fuller, M., 2003. *Behind the Blip: Essays on the Culture of Software*. Brooklyn: Autonomedia.

Gehl, R. W., 2014. *Reverse Engineering Social Media: Software, Culture, and Political Economy in New Media Capitalism*. Philadelphia, PA: Temple University Press.

Gehl, R. W. and Synder-Yuly, J., 2016. The Need for Social Media Alternatives. *Democratic Communiqué*, 27 (1), 78.

Gerlitz, C. and Lury, C., 2012. Self-Evaluating Media: Acting on Data. *In: New Numeracy Workshop*. London: Goldsmiths University.

Guattari, F., 1989. *Trois écologies*. Paris: Galilée.

Hansen, M. B. N., 2015. *Feed-Forward: On the Future of Twenty-First-Century Media*. Chicago, IL: University of Chicago Press.

Haraway, D. J., 2016. *Staying with the Trouble: Making Kin in the Chthulucene*. Durham, NC: Duke University Press.

Hearn, A., 2010. Structuring Feeling: Web 2.0, Online Ranking and Rating, and the Digital 'Reputation' Economy. *Ephemera: Theory & Politics in Organisation*, 10 (3/4), 421–438.

Hillis, K., Paasonen, S. and Petit, M., 2015. *Networked Affect*. Cambridge, MA: MIT Press.

Hui, Y., 2015. A Contribution to the Political Economy of Personal Archives. *In*: G. Elmer, G. Langlois and J. Redden, eds. *Compromised Data: From Social Media to Big Data*. London: Bloomsbury Academic, 226–246.

IF. 2015. Data Licenses. http://bigbangdata.somersethouse.org.uk/artist/if/.

Lagerkvist, A., 2016. Existential Media: Toward a Theorization of Digital Thrownness. *New Media & Society*, Online first, June 7, 2016.

Langlois, G. 2014. *Meaning in the Age of Social Media*. New York: Palgrave Macmillan.

Martey, R. M. and Consalvo, M., 2011. Performing the Looking-Glass Self: Avatar Appearance and Group Identity in Second Life. *Popular Communication*, 9 (3), 165–180.

170 *Ganaele Langlois*

McGee, M., 2013. EdgeRank Is Dead: Facebook's News Feed Algorithm Now Has Close to 100K Weight Factors. August 16. Available at: http://marketingland.com/edgerank-is-dead-facebooks-news-feed-algorithm-now-has-close-to-100k-weight-factors-55908 (accessed: 1 July 2018).

McNeill, W., 1998. Care for the Self: Originary Ethics in Heidegger and Foucault. *Philosophy Today* 42 (1), 53–64.

Nancy, J.-L., 2000. *Being Singular Plural*. Translated by Robert Richardson and Anne O'Byrne. Stanford, CA: Stanford University Press.

Pasquale, F., 2015. *The Black Box Society: The Secret Algorithms That Control Money and Information*. Cambridge, MA: Harvard University Press.

Rosen, J., 2012. The Right to Be Forgotten. *Stanford Law Review Online*, 64, 88.

Shields, R., 2003. *The Virtual*. New York: Psychology Press.

Shields, R., 2006. Virtualities. *Theory, Culture & Society*, 23 (2–3), 284–286.

Stiegler, B., 2016. *Dans la disruption*. Paris: Liensliber.

Terranova, T., 2012. Attention, Economy and the Brain. *Culture Machine*, 13 (1), 1–19.

Thomas, N., 2013. Social Computing as a Platform for Memory. *Culture Machine*, 14, (2013), 1–16.

Turkle, S., 2015. *Reclaiming Conversation: The Power of Talk in a Digital Age*. New York: Penguin Press.

Weisgerber, C. and Butler, S. H., 2015. Curating the Soul: Foucault's Concept of Hupomnemata and the Digital Technology of Self-Care. *Information, Communication & Society*, 1–16.

Winnicott, D. W., 2005. *Playing and Reality*. London: Routledge.

8 The ethics of digital being
Vulnerability, invulnerability, and 'dangerous surprises'

Vincent Miller

Introduction

For roughly a year (around 2015/2016), about once a month, my mobile phone would ring in the middle of the night. Waken from a deep sleep, without the presence of mind to screen the call, my answer would be greeted by a frantic voice shouting at me in French. Not being a French speaker (and particularly not in the middle of the night), the only word I would recognise in these tirades was 'alarm'. Each call followed the same frustrating pattern of French tirade on their end, English tirade on mine, then me hanging up. More often than not, another call would follow shortly after which I wouldn't answer, but the call logs listed these calls as either originating in France, or numbers that were 'unknown'.

Over the following months, these calls continued periodically, and became progressively more annoying to me. I would angrily answer the calls, then, if the number was listed, send back Google-translated French language text messages saying not to call this number again and that I would call the police. The last call I received was in April 2016, when I was at a conference in San Francisco. Again it was a late night call. With all the bravado of someone 5,500 miles away from their potential adversary, my end of the conversation consisted of a string of expletives followed by the statement, 'Do not phone me again, for the last time, you have got the wrong number!'

'I don't have the wrong number, Vince. . .'.

Vince. Not Mr. Miller, Dr. Miller, or even Vincent, but Vince. Suddenly, these first words spoken in English in this set of exchanges changed them from something mildly annoying, to something more sinister and disturbing. How did this person from a place I haven't visited in years know my name and number? Who do I know in France? What else do they know about me? What do they want? I hung up immediately with a heavy feeling in the pit of my stomach. This person, this stranger, located somewhere 5,000 miles from me, had made me feel vulnerable. The calls have seemingly stopped now. But even as I write this in the late Autumn of 2016, I still wonder how these people in France got my number, let alone my name, and put the two together.

172   *Vincent Miller*

With a bit of academic reflective hindsight, one interesting thing for me about this set of interactions was the speed at which my state of being changed from an arguably hyper-aggressive stance enabled by a technology which placed me 3,000 miles from my adversary, to a somewhat intense experience of vulnerability where that adversary seemingly knew a lot more about me than I knew about him. I felt somehow exposed and susceptible to something unknown, unexpected and beyond my control.

Corporeal existence, some would argue, is defined by a stance of vulnerability and the anticipation of 'dangerous surprises' (Dreyfus 2000; Merleau-Ponty 1962). This is the understanding that the material world around us is full of potential hazards; that things can happen to us. Some of these, such as falling off a nearby cliff, or drowning in a river we are crossing, are more evident to us than others. However, part of having a body means possessing a background awareness that something, even something unexpected, could happen which we need to be ready for. The dangerous surprise could be a falling tree, a wild animal, or a lunatic waiting in the bushes, but having to look after a body means, to a certain extent, expecting the unexpected, to look for potential immediate threats.

A world of digital communications and digital presences at a distance complicates this. On the one hand, a world of far-reaching, mediated, often anonymous interactions can give us the impression of a lack of embodied vulnerability. When people are far away, we can become more brave, more willing to defend ourselves and others, become 'keyboard warriors'. We can be more confident, more expressive or our opinions or our creative talents, or more brazen, by more actively pursuing flirtatious, romantic or sexual interactions, and even more aggressive and abusive, by engaging in acts of trolling, bullying, or other forms of harassment.

At the same time, our continuous, archived, digital presence, distributed in a multitude of networks, archives, databases and servers, opens us up to exposure to others of which, because they are not embodied or immediate, we are only partially aware. Indeed, the confidence, forthrightness and sense of invulnerability common to digital interactions belie a host of unknown 'dangerous surprises', created through an extension of exposure, both bodily and virtually, to unknown scales. These vulnerabilities become more apparent to us when we hear of, or are the victims of, a data breach, hacking scandal or other forms of 'dangerous surprises'.

Using the work of Heidegger and other phenomenological, existential theorists, I argue that a defining feature of digital being thus consists of a contradictory stance to the world. First, there is a mediated, metaphysical outlook which encourages a stance of invulnerability in online social interactions. Such an outlook misapprehends our presence and fails to grasp our ontological status as both *Dasein* (beings in and of the world) and *Mitsein* (beings with and of each other). Secondly, and paradoxically, there is an increased, yet less apparent, ontological vulnerability resulting from our continual, omnipresent online presence, manifest in constant connection

The ethics of digital being 173

to others and the ceaseless archiving of our data, actions and interactions. This means that we are increasingly, yet ambiguously, vulnerable to others through a continual 'being with' which has no time, space, or embodiment.

Using the examples of the five-year trolling of Nicola Brookes, and the recent 2015 'Ashley Madison hack', this chapter will investigate the notion of *vulnerability* as one-way to investigate being in the digital age (cf. Lagerkvist 2016). In particular, it will propose that the misapprehension of invulnerability online leaves us inevitably open to periodic 'dangerous surprises' which ultimately demonstrate the vulnerabilities we all share as part of digital human existence.

Vulnerable being

As Harrison (2008) points out, vulnerability is largely unthought of within the social sciences. Indeed, vulnerability, when it is discussed, is conceived of as both a weakness and a contingent state which needs to be overcome or rectified. Thus, much effort in social science research is spent identifying 'vulnerable people' and how to protect them or change their vulnerable status in a given situation. This, of course, is compared to a kind of ideal state of 'invulnerability', or autonomy, which arguably refers back to the legacy of Descartes-inspired modern philosophy and its conception of 'being' as a rational, autonomous, self-contained, metaphysical subject actively engaged with the 'objective' world around it (Harrison 2008). In such a conception, the subject (as a 'mind' or 'psyche') stands apart from the physical world of objects and bodies, and imposes its intentional, rational 'will' upon that world through the possession of a body. This view, labelled variously 'mind/body dualism', 'metaphysical presencing' or 'essentialism' was of course famously critiqued by Heidegger, Merleau-Ponty, Nietzsche, Derrida, Dewey and many others from phenomenological, existential and pragmatic traditions throughout the twentieth century. Heidegger, Merleau-Ponty, and Nancy in particular argued that 'being' as such needs to be conceived of in inter-relation with, not in opposition to, the physical and social world in which we find ourselves. It is in such an inter-relation, where our being is open to the world and yet constructed in connection with that world, where vulnerability can be seen as part of the ontological experience of being human (see Butler 2004).

Being as existential exposure

> The world of Dasein is a *with-world*. *Being-in* is *Being-with* Others.
> (Heidegger 1962, p. 155, original emphasis)

Although Heidegger is largely given credit for associating the essential relationship of 'being-with' to 'being', Pyyhtinen (2009) points out that Simmel (1908/1992) actually preceded Heidegger in suggesting that

174   *Vincent Miller*

being-with-others was constitutive of 'being' itself. He quotes Simmel: 'The human being is in one's whole essence determined by the fact that one lies in reciprocal interaction with other people' (Simmel 1992, p. 15, cited in Pyyhtinen 2009). For Simmel, even being 'alone' is a form of social interaction which invokes the lack of another's presence where there has been previous meaningful and influential contact. Thus the being of an individual is something always and already constituted by others, thereby making others crucial in the structure of being (see also Lagerkvist 2016).

Shortly after, in *Being and Time*, Heidegger argued that 'being-with' (*Mitsein*) was part of the ontological existence of *Dasein*, or 'being-in-the-world'. This formed part of his overall critique of metaphysical thinking in which he argued against the notion dominant in Western philosophic traditions of a self-enclosed, self-referential view of being as a transcendental thinking subject, or *res cogitans*: a 'thinking thing'. Heidegger argued that humans are not these kind of abstracted 'thinking things' which stand apart from the world and contemplate it. Indeed, to conceive of humanity in this way is to misunderstand 'being'. Instead, he posited that humans are 'doing things' that exist in and through bodies which have a relationship with the world and the things and beings in it. Selves and the world are thus co-constructed, and the world, far from a series of 'objects' to be contemplated from a distance by an abstract 'subject', transcendental 'mind' or 'psyche', is something in which beings are *thrown*, and something in which they *dwell* in a relationship of openness to, and engagement with, the world.

The logic, that an 'individual' should not be understood as something in isolation from the material world (in terms of ego, psyche, etc.), also applies to our relationship with other Beings in the world. The individual should not be understood in isolation from other Beings (*Daseins*), but as a part of the social world in which we are thrown and with which we continually engage (Cohn 2002; Heidegger 1987). The world is something that is shared with others in the sense that people (*Daseins*) exist in these spaces in propinquity; they dwell together in the same 'Being-here', not as one subject to another, but as co-dwellers opened up unto the world. So 'being-with' (*Mitsein*) is an 'existential characteristic of Dasein' (Heidegger 1962, p. 155).

When we fail to acknowledge our being as something dependent on others, the meaning of being for Heidegger is obscured, but importantly, so is the relationship to the world and the others encountered in it (Sorial 2004). The problem then becomes one of the kinds of 'being-with' we achieve with one another. When we (encouraged by Cartesian-esque metaphysical thinking) see ourselves as self-enclosed subjects or 'I's' not really a part of that world, we become alienated from ourselves, others and the world. The obscured relationship to others that results from terms of their being-with, Heidegger (1962) referred to as a 'deficient' form of solicitude, where we engage in a 'being against or without', 'passing by', or 'not mattering' towards one another (Bauer 2001, P. 136; Cohn 2002, p. 37).

The ethics of digital being   175

Mitsein provides a contrast with the alienated, metaphysical 'I', with a recognition of fellowship and mutual dependence, but with a tension of potential subsumption of one's unique authenticity into what Heidegger calls 'das man' ('the they'), where we can lose ourselves in the undifferentiated will of masses, or fail to be recognised as unique beings in our own right (Bauer 2001).

Recognising this tension, Jean-Luc Nancy (2008) argues that Heidegger never fully articulated the 'with' in 'being-with', even though that had been characterised as essential for *Dasein*'s existence. Nancy (2008) squarely addresses this 'shortfall in thinking' in Heidegger's notion of 'being-with' by using Heidegger's being-with ontological status as a springboard to develop his notion of 'being-singular-plural'. For Nancy, this is a way of conceptualising the complex relationship between unique individual beings and their communal co-construction with others (2008, 2000).

Nancy (2000) uses this concept to retain the idea that the uniqueness or alterity of each bodily being matters, and that each being is unique in terms of their face, voice, gestures, comportment, yet at the same time acknowledging that what it is to 'be' as a human by necessity exists as something that is shared, because meaning itself is something that can only come into existence through sharing or exposure. According to Willson (2012), the essence of being-singular-plural is the inevitable and transient exposure to one another. Willson herself suggests the terms 'exposures' or 'events' as in many ways preferable to 'being' as they more accurate depicts Nancy's conception of what it is to exist in common with others.[1] It is that mutual exposure to one another which preserves the existence of an 'I' in the face of the commonality of a 'we'. Thus 'being-with' for Nancy, is 'the exposure of singularities' (Nancy 1991, p. 30).

Emmanuel Levinas also emphasises the fundamentally relational character of human existence and the entangled condition of inter-relation with other humans as one of exposure and vulnerability. Levinas (1985, 1969) argued, to be human is to always already find oneself connected in relationships with others which we cannot define or control (Groenhout 2004). Indeed, it is the intersubjective encounter of the other, an exposure to the other, which, for Levinas, is the first and primary human encounter which ultimately constitutes human subjects. In this respect, it is our relational existence which makes vulnerability to others an ontological part of the human condition. For Levinas, this vulnerability is manifest in terms of a fundamental burden of ethical responsibility. That is, exposure to the 'face' of the other 'calls' or 'makes moral demands' of the subject to acknowledge and care, or to abandon or harm:

> There is a commandment in the appearance of the face, as if a master spoke to me.
>
> (Levinas 1985, p. 89)

176   *Vincent Miller*

Indeed, the face of another is something which presses upon us. Where we generally engage the presence of, say, rocks or trees or other objects in the world with a 'passing-by' (to use Heideggerian terminology) because they do not present 'face' to us, by contrast, other humans tend to bring us into engagement. We are drawn to them because their uniqueness as other persons brings their ultimately unknowable and uncontainable otherness to us. It demonstrates to us our limitations, that we share the world, that we are not able to do simply as we please, that we are connected.

Being as embodied exposure

For Nancy, both the singularity of being and the commonality of meaning centre around the body, as it is the traits and capacities of the body which mark us out as singular within the proximity of other embodied beings which recognise its meaningful singularity through apprehension of a unique body, thereby bringing it into existence. Levinas, refers to the embodied, face-to-face encounter as the primary encounter constitutive of human subjectivity. The face of the other, on whom our being is dependent and who we are called to responsibility for or to care for, is a physical entity with physical and emotional needs (Groenhout 2004). As a result, human existence is not only defined relationally, but is dependent on that embodied relation to others.

To be a human body is to be physically vulnerable, and awareness of such vulnerability is part of our ontological condition. Of course, all bodies themselves are vulnerable to the physical hazards and threats encountered in the material world as well as the potential hazards involved in being in proximal relations with others. For Butler (2004, p. 29), the vulnerability of bodily life is the realisation of vulnerability to a 'sudden address from elsewhere'. As beings with bodies, we have a sense of exposure to the unpredictable, the unchosen, and the unforeseen. Such a sense is part and parcel of our encounter with others (Harrison 2008). We need others to exist, yet this exposes us to them. This understanding of our limits and vulnerabilities affords us a certain wariness as we make our way through the world. Indeed, as Dreyfus (2000) suggests, the sense of risk, endemic to embodied life, provides us with a sense of the 'realness' of the world around us. Borrowing from Merleau-Ponty's use of *urdoxa* as a kind of 'background readiness', it is this constant readiness towards things such as 'dangerous surprises', or a general readiness to 'get a grip' in any particular situation[2] which helps us make sense of the reality of the world.

However, while vulnerability may be a part of the human condition, what constitutes a 'threat' and the awareness of vulnerability itself is less universal. Feminist scholarship explores vulnerability further by, on the one hand, acknowledging the shared, ontological and existential vulnerability of humans as living beings exposed to potential harm, injury and inevitable death, and, on the other, by highlighting the fact that while it may be a state

The ethics of digital being   177

shared among all humans, the experience of vulnerability is not equal (Page 2016, p. 25). As Butler (2004) suggests, vulnerability is a universal condition with an uneven distribution (see also Schwartz, in Chapter 3 of this volume).

These scholars emphasise the distinction between universal conditions and particular circumstances (Fineman 2008; Page 2016), or similarly the difference between 'precariousness' and 'precarity' (Butler 2004), or between the 'possible' or condition of vulnerability, and the 'actual' or experience of, vulnerability (Gilson 2014). In this way, feminist scholars are able to discuss vulnerability as an ontological condition, but also the specific political and social contexts in which vulnerable bodies are a site of politics (Bergoffen 2003). This allows them to emphasise the uneven nature of vulnerability for women, LGBT persons, and ethnic minorities.[3]

Online *Mitsein*, digital urdoxa and dangerous surprises

The ontological notion of being as embodied and relational means that vulnerability is not a weakness or a condition to be overcome, but is part of the ontological condition of human existence (Harrison 2008; Lagerkvist 2016). Indeed, vulnerability 'is the inherent and continuous susceptibility of corporeal life to the unchosen and unforeseen . . . its inherent openness to what exceeds its abilities to contain and absorb' (Harrison 2008, p. 427). As embodied, corporeal beings, we are always left exposed, susceptible to the natural and social world of other humans around us to which we are intimately connected, but yet exceed our capabilities of control.

Through existential connectedness to others, and through having bodies which are open to the world and its dangerous surprises, vulnerability is an inherent part of the human condition. But what happens online when our social encounters are more numerous and interconnected yet separated from our embodiment?

Clearly, the notion of 'being-with' takes on a new relevance in digital culture. With a little thought, the co-construction of self and world becomes more evident when we recognise the complex, structureless, interconnecting, indeed rhizomic machinations of our digital existence as articulated by writers such as Bernard Stiegler (1998, 2008) (in terms of, for example, the exteriorisation of desire into digital technologies) and Brian Rotman (2008), who both conceive of the contemporary human being as an assemblage of bodies and technologies which include data, profiles, avatars, images, databases which are stored on a vast array of networked servers and distributed around the world. As Rotman suggested, 'it is harder and harder to say where the world stops and the person begins' (Rotman 2008, p. 8).

Our being is data-encumbered, and in that sense, conceptually at least, we can imagine the collapse of the metaphysical Cartesian self which separates the subject from object. As Coté (2014) suggests, 'the capturing of data is not something that happens to us; it is constitutive of our being as digital humans' (Coté 2014, p. 14). Our digital selves exist in and through relationships with

178 *Vincent Miller*

other digital things and beings. A social networking profile, for example, cannot be meaningfully conceived of in isolation as an individual, self-contained 'thing', given that its existence is dependent on connection and interaction with other profiles, as well as the networked databases, image banks, hyperlinks and even material bodies which are assembled into what we perceive as the singularity or continuity of 'the profile'.

Mitchell (2014) argues that the spatial technologies of connection and the temporal technologies of archiving have created a digital lifeworld of archival subjects, giving the things and beings present online a perpetual ready-to-hand quality in Heideggerian terms, defying both space and time. The temporally fleeting contact of the embodied proximal or face-to-face interaction in terms of touch, gesture, gaze, conversation, becomes a matter of record in online contexts. For example, the timelessness of archival subjects, their actions, and their interactions (constituted in the form of both known and unknown presences, such as profiles, databases, conversations, search histories, purchase histories, browsing histories and the like) marks out a fundamental difference between online and offline in terms of Being or 'being-with'. Whereas our embodied exposures to others are usually tied to the moment of encounter, a moment circumscribed in time and space, our archived presence extends the digital moment of encounter to any time or any place. Thus we are always already present to others in the networked traces of ourselves. We therefore potentially and unknowingly encounter any other, anywhere, all the time.

Indeed, I have suggested elsewhere (Miller 2016), one key problem in contemporary culture is that the Web, as currently manifest with its distanced, mediated and (largely) disembodied interactions, plays into the hands of metaphysical thinking by allowing us (through processes of networking and archiving) to achieve a kind of omnipresence in time and place which is beyond the body as we currently understand it. This, I argue, encourages a metaphysical outlook which is more akin to the self-enclosed, self-referential, and, ultimately, alienated 'thinking thing' of Descartes' *res cogitans*. Such an 'I' tends to set the world and the things and people in it at a distance from itself, and ironically, such an outlook juxtaposes a world in which we are increasingly interconnected through technologies. Thus, I suggested that digital culture is paradoxically potentially moving us further away from understanding ourselves ontologically as interconnected with the world[4] (*Dasein*) and each other (*Mitsein*), and that this misunderstanding or alienation has articulated itself in a series of ethical crises (such as controversies around abusive behaviour, privacy, speech) which have become endemic to the internet.

In what follows, I will present two online incidents which demonstrate how this misunderstanding of our ontological status manifests itself in terms of a heightened impression of invulnerability in online social encounters with others, yet paradoxically led to intense experiences of vulnerability to a host of unexpected 'dangerous surprises'.

The ethics of digital being 179

The trolling of Nicola Brookes – or 'Happy Christmas to a dog'

In early November 2011, Frankie Cocozza, a teenage contestant on the popular UK talent show *The X-Factor*, left the program amidst allegations of drug use. *The X-Factor Facebook* page soon filled with hostile comments and criticism of Mr. Cocozza. Dismayed by what she had seen, Nicola Brookes, a 45-year-old mother from Brighton, United Kingdom, decided to intervene with some words of encouragement: 'Keep your friends and your family close, Frankie. They'll move on to someone else soon' (Carey 2012).[5] This proved to be both a prophetic and pivotal moment in Ms Brookes' life, as this intervention turned the focus of attention onto herself, with personally devastating consequences.

Within hours, over a hundred abusive messages were directed at her on the *X-Factor* page, her own Facebook page had been cloned and was sending abusive and paedophilic messages to young women on Facebook in her name. Other fake accounts were set up in both her and her daughter's name, filled with photoshopped, sexualised images of them both. Websites were created which warned the public of her 'fake' battle which Crohn's disease, as well as accusing her of being a drug dealer, prostitute and paedophile. Such claims drew in others (under false pretences) to join in the malicious comments and threats, escalating the intensity and scope of harassment, as well as the wider damage to her reputation. Months later, her home address was published online, prompting worries about physical threat (she began to sleep with a knife under her pillow). She subsequently received 'snail mail' harassment as well, including a Christmas card featuring a picture of a dog, and the caption 'Happy Christmas to a dog'. In the card, there was a post-operative photo of her taken from her daughter's Facebook page (Naked Security 2013), neatly tying together the relationship between her digital and embodied vulnerability.

In her own personal and legal accounts of the unfolding events, it was Nicola Brookes' desire to 'answer back' which helped to escalate a minor trolling incident into a fully-blown campaign of online harassment which lasted for five years and spread into offline contexts. Indeed, the UK Crown Prosecution Service refused to bring charges to her assailants, as they suggested that, against police advice, she actively engaged with trolls and thus there was no realistic chance of prosecution (Naked Security 2013). No charges have ever been brought against any of her harassers.

On the one hand, this can be seen as 'blaming the victim'. People should have a right to defend themselves and others. However, in offline, embodied contexts, such disputes usually dissipate as both parties possess an *urdoxic* awareness of one's vulnerability to a 'sudden address from elsewhere', or 'a dangerous surprise', should things escalate. Bodies encountering each other in such circumstances would be guarded by the realisation of a potential escalation to a physical altercation. Women, being familiar with their ontological vulnerability to physical threat from men, would (for better or worse)

180 *Vincent Miller*

likely be more wary of intervention. Men, perhaps more aware of the social stigma and recrimination of a physical altercation with a woman in public, would likely be more wary of escalation.

The Nicola Brookes case demonstrates where things can go when there is no embodied vulnerability in an encounter. It demonstrates a misunderstanding of online existence, which continually exposes us, not just to a presence tied to the time and place of encounter, but to an always already presence with others in the networked traces of ourselves across multiple locations and contexts. Thus, Ms Brookes' dispute with her antagonisers would not be contained to the *X-Factor* Facebook page, but would follow her online presence across the Web, to her family, and eventually to her home address over the course of five years. At the time of her first encounter, such a life-changing potentiality would have been difficult to imagine.

Online *Mitsein and vulnerability: the Ashley Madison hack*

> Hello [name redacted], you don't know me but I know you very well. As you likely know, the Ashley Madison website was hacked a little while back and in the process some personal information from tens of millions of their clients was compromised. As scary as that sounds, most of their families will never find out. First, they would have to actively seek out the information. Second, the files containing the information are multiple gigabytes in size and are not all that convenient to access if you don't know how. There will be some spammers who shoot out mass threatening emails to those on the lists but they can safely be ignored. Only the unlucky few will draw the attention of a true blackmailer willing to actually research a target's family and acquaintances. Unfortunately, [name redacted], you are one of the unlucky ones.
>
> Yes, I know about your secret, that you paid for services from a company that specializes in facilitating adultery. But what makes me a threat to you is that I have also spent several days getting to know about you, your family and others in your life. All you have to do in order to prevent me from using this information against you, [name redacted], is to pay me $2000. And before you ignore this letter consider this: You received this via first class mail. It wasn't a spam email some Nigerian sent to thousands of people. That means I spent money on it. It means I took extensive counter-forensics measures to ensure the Postal Inspector would not be able to track it back to me via post marks or via prints and DNA. It means I paid cash for a printer that couldn't be traced back to me. I have spent considerable time and money on you, [name redacted]. So if you decide to ignore me, you can be certain that I sure as hell won't ignore you.
>
> (Sample blackmail letter from Cluley 2016)

Ashley Madison is dating website which specialises in bringing together married persons who are looking for illicit liaisons outside of their marriage or relationship. The premise of its business is that it provides a safe, discreet and confidential means for engaging in such activities without risking ones

The ethics of digital being   181

relationships, family life and reputation, which is more likely to be the case if one attempts such activities among members of their own community or immediate social circle.

On 12 July 2015, employees of Avid Life Media, owners of Ashley Madison, turned on their office computers and were greeted by the familiar chords of the AC/DC song 'Thunderstruck', and a message from a hacker group calling itself the 'Impact Team':

> We are the Impact Team. We have taken all systems in your entire office and production domains, all customer information databases, source code repositories, financial records, e-mails . . .

It went on to say that if Ashley Madison and partner website Established Men were not shut down immediately, the hackers would release to the public all customer records, including profiles, sexual preferences and fantasies, chat records, pictures and credit card data (including real names and addresses), as well as employee documents and e-mails, causing irreparable harm not only to Avid Life Media, but to the millions of customers (mostly men) who, under assurances of discretion and anonymity, had used the site.

The ethical reasoning behind the attack was two-fold. First, the Impact Team took offence at the idea that Ashley Madison was engaged in the morally dubious business of encouraging extra-marital affairs. Secondly, the Impact Team took issue with the ethically reprehensible business practices of the website, for example, in not properly encrypting customers' data and financial transactions, and also falsely offering a $20 'full delete' service (in which all of their data would be deleted from Ashley Madison databases) to customers which was never fulfilled. In addition, the website was actively engaged in grossly exaggerating the number of female users on the site by creating fake profiles ('bots'), which encouraged men to join and pay for the service under false pretences. In the eyes of the Impact Team, the fraudulent behaviour of Avid Life Media was as morally problematic as the idea of a 'cheating website' itself.

The moral and ethical questions around these events are intriguing and complex, and a discussion of these larger questions remains outside the remit of this chapter. What we do know is that in mid-August, when Avid Life Media refused to shut down Ashley Madison, the Impact Team followed up on their threat and posted large amounts of the leaked data on the 'Dark Web'. From this point on, those who had data on the site now faced the threats of exposure, embarrassment, blackmail, threats to employment and marital breakdown.

This is exactly what happened. Soon after, search sites sprang up where one could simply type in an e-mail address of a partner, friend, neighbour, or work colleague and would indicate whether or not that e-mail had been associated with a profile on the site. This did not necessarily mean that the person in question had contacted anyone or even actively used the site, indeed, since

182   Vincent Miller

Ashley Madison did not utilise e-mail verification, so anyone could have used any e-mail address to create a profile, but the implication of at least an interest in infidelity was there. Famously, one Australian breakfast radio program provided that service live on air, letting one female caller know that her husband's e-mail had come up on their search (Guardian 2015).

Local blogs, newspapers and Twitter feeds, particularly in the US 'deep south' engaged in 'name and shame' campaigns published the names of local residents found on the database, sometimes ordering them by postcode so anyone could know who in the vicinity was a potential cheater. The damage to reputations and the amount of marriage break-ups resulting from the hack goes unmeasured and untold, as does the amount of persecution received by those in countries such as Saudi Arabia, where adultery and homosexuality are illegal and punishable by severe sentences, even death. However, we do know that Toronto police linked two suicides with the data leak in Canada (Mansfield-Devine 2015). A police officer in Texas and a pastor in New Orleans had also taken their own lives as a result (Segall 2015; Waugh 2015).

Many of those fortunate enough not to have been publically 'outed' faced blackmail, and through the latter months of 2015, dozens of nefarious groups and individuals e-mailed extortionate messages to those on the database demanding bitcoin deposits under threat of exposure to friends and family (Brown 2015a). Several security websites reported thousands of dollars in bitcoins collected by blackmailers. One website (Meulle 2015/2016) listed eight bitcoin wallets used in blackmail attempts, and a check by this author counted 108.2 bitcoins collected across these eight accounts, equating to roughly $44,000 USD,[6] proving that, at least some of the time, crime does pay. Several months later, defying expectations and the conventional wisdom that internet blackmailers never make good on their threats, some in America followed through, sending 'snail mail' letters to the home addresses and wives of some men on the list, exposing their secret (Murgia 2016).

Conclusion

> I still am looking over my shoulder, and know that it will never go away.
> (Brown 2015b, e-mail correspondence with Ashley Madison
> hacking victim[7])

The world, when it includes the online, truly is a 'with-world', as our selves are always ready-to-hand for others in a kind of continual online *Mitsein* which continually exposes us to others, yet is also the fabric of online being. Such exposures often occur without our knowledge, as a lack of embodied urdoxic awareness of such connections obscures the exposures and vulnerabilities which are part and parcel of our existence.

The ethics of digital being 183

Feminist critiques, such as those encountered earlier in the chapter, demonstrate that while we are all vulnerable to 'dangerous surprises', it is women who are particularly aware of the ontological status of vulnerability as a condition of life. Nicola Brookes' experience as a trolling victim demonstrated how these 'dangerous surprises' can emerge from the most innocuous circumstances. Circumstances that, nonetheless, would have played out in a completely different manner had they involved the interaction of material bodies. If Dreyfus (2000) suggests that the sense of risk, endemic to embodied life, provides us with a sense of the 'realness' of the world around us, the lack of risk perceived in online encounters puts us in a position where we not only distance ourselves from the 'reality' of our actions online, but lose the 'wariness' of embodied life. The perceived lack of embodied vulnerability in the interactions of both Nicola and her tormentors allowed a minor dispute to escalate into ridiculous proportions, eventually spilling out from the virtual to the material and embodied.

By contrast, the men on Ashley Madison joined a site advertising discretion and confidentiality, providing them the assurance that they could safely engage in activities that were outside the ethical and moral codes of their immediate relationships and communities. The presence of their data, perhaps lying dormant for over a decade, would have hardly occurred to them outside of their own use of it. They had no reason to expect that their actions would make their way into the public realm, connecting them to a world of hacktivists, bloggers, news agencies and blackmailers, ultimately returning to their own doorsteps in some cases. Many of those who have not been publically exposed still carry the feeling of vulnerability and angst, as epitomised in the epigraph to this section. The hack, and the events that followed, demonstrated that vulnerability does not just apply to traditionally 'vulnerable' groups, but illuminates the wider ontological vulnerability at the core of digital existence itself: the openness inherent in a connected world, where selves extend in unforeseen directions, creating unanticipated presences which bring contact and exposure with unimagined others.

The theme of vulnerability not only speaks to the specific instance of men caught using an infidelity website, but is something that is endemic to all of us in a contemporary digital culture. Ceaseless networking, archiving and leaks of data mean that we are all connected and thus exposed, in a myriad of profiles, accounts, archives, databases and servers, and in a multitude of unexpected ways. Ohm (2010) refers to the potential harm caused by the worldwide accretion of data as a potential 'database of ruin'. He suggests that:

> Almost every person in the developed world can be linked to at least one fact in a computer database that an adversary could use for blackmail, discrimination, harassment, financial or identity theft.
>
> (Ohm 2010, p. 1748)

184 *Vincent Miller*

The vulnerability of these online aspects of self become more present at hand to us when we hear of, or are the victims of, a data breach, identity theft, extortion, late night phone calls from France, or a gang of internet trolls. Incidents such as these illustrate the contradictory stance of digital being: of heightened invulnerability in our social encounters with others, alongside a heightened vulnerability to a host of unknown 'dangerous surprises' or 'sudden addresses' from elsewhere.

Notes

1 For Willson, the 'singular' being ends at the moment of encounter with other beings. This is the point where a single being has cause to question and acknowledge its own and other's existence (Willson 2012, p 286).
2 This is, for example, articulated in the heightened awareness of potential threat we might feel in a dark alley or walking past a group of overly intoxicated people on a night out.
3 This allows Bergoffen (2003), for example, to challenge cultural and legal assumptions of the body (particularly in terms of the idea of 'consent') as autonomous and invulnerable as part of a kind of fallacious, masculine cultural ideal (Page 2016).
4 For another discussion of the role of social software in the becoming of oneself and encountering the world, see Langlois, Chapter 7, this volume.
5 Other articles have varying versions of this statement.
6 In November 2015 value as depicted by *Yahoo UK Finance*. Retrieved from https://uk.finance.yahoo.com/quote/BTCUSD=X?ltr=1
7 Brown (2015b).

Bibliography

Bauer, N., 2001. Being-with as Being-against: Heidegger Meets Hegel in The Second Sex. *Continental Philosophy Review*, 34 (2), 129–149.

Bergoffen, D., 2003. Mourning the Autonomous Body. *In*: J. J. Cohen and G. Weiss, eds. *Thinking the Limits of the Body*. New York: State University of New York Press.

Brown, K., 2015a. What Happens When the Internet Shame Machine Gets Names and Zip Codes. *Fusion.net* [online] 28 August 2015. Available at: http://fusion.net/story/190277/ashley-madison-public-shaming/ (accessed: 20 January 2017).

Brown, K., 2015b. Scared, Dead, Relieved: How the Ashley Madison Hack Changed Its Victims' Lives. *Fusion.net* [online] 12 December 2015. Available at: http://fusion.net/story/242502/ashley-madison-hack-aftermath/ (accessed: 20 January 2017).

Butler, J., 2004. *Precarious Life: The Powers of Mourning and Violence*. London: Verso.

Carey, T., 2012. The Mother Who Took on the Trolls. *Mail Online*. Available at: www.dailymail.co.uk/femail/article-2158408/Nicola-Brookes-The-mother-took-trolls.html (accessed: 23 May 2017).

Cluley, G., 2016. Here's What an Ashley Madison Blackmail Letter Looks Like. [online] GrahamCluley.com. Available at: www.grahamcluley.com/ashley-madison-blackmail-letter/ (accessed: 20 January 2017).

Cohn, H. W., 2002. *Heidegger and the Roots of Existential Therapy*. London: Continuum.

Coté, M., 2014. Data Motility: The Materiality of Big Social Data. *Cultural Studies Review*, 20 (1), 121–149.

Dreyfus, H., 2000. Telepistemology: Descartes Last Stand. *In*: K. Goldberg, ed. *The Robot in the Garden: Telerobotics and Telepistemology in the Age of the Internet*. Cambridge, MA: MIT Press, 48–63.

Fineman, M., 2008. The Vulnerable Subject: Anchoring Equality in the Human Condition. *Yale Journal of Law and Feminism*, 20 (1), 1–23.

Gilson, E., 2014. *The Ethics of Vulnerability: A Feminist Analysis of Social Life and Practice*. London: Routledge.

Groenhout, R. E., 2004. *Connected Lives: Human Nature and an Ethics of Care*. Oxford: Rowman & Littlefield.

Guardian, 2015. Radio Hosts Tell Woman Live on Air Her Husband Has Ashley Madison Account. *The Guardian*. Available at: www.theguardian.com/technology/2015/aug/20/radio-hosts-tell-woman-live-on-air-her-husband-had-ashley-madison-account (accessed: 8 January 2017).

Harrison, P., 2008. Corporeal Remains: Vulnerability, Proximity, and Living on after the End of the World. *Environment and Planning A*, 40 (2), 423–445.

Heidegger, M., 1962. *Being and Time*. New York: Harper & Row.

Lagerkvist, A., 2016. Existential Media: Toward a Theorization of Digital Thrownness. *New Media & Society*, 19 (1), 96–110.

Levinas, E., 1969. *Totality and Infinity: An Essay on Exteriority*. Pittsburgh, PA: Duquesne University Press.

Levinas, E., 1985. *Ethics and Infinity: Conversations with Philippe Nemo*. Pittsburgh, PA: Duquesne University Press.

Mansfield-Devine, S., 2015. The Ashley Madison Affair. *Network Security*, 9, 8–16.

Merleau-Ponty, M., 1962. *Phenomenology of Perception*. Trans. C. Smith. London and New York: Humanities Press.

Meulle, E., 2015/2016. Bitcoin Wallets Used for Ashley Madison Blackmail Attempts. *Weblog of Evert*. Available at: https://evert.meulie.net/2015/09/28/bitcoin-wallets-used-for-ashley-madison-extortion-attempts/ (accessed: 20 January 2017).

Miller, V., 2016. *The Crisis of Presence in Contemporary Culture: Ethics, Privacy and Speech in Mediated Social Life*. London: Sage.

Mitchell, L., 2014. Life on Automatic: Facebook's Archival Subject. *First Monday*, 19 (2), Available at: http://firstmonday.org/article/view/4825/3823 (accessed: 15 August 2015).

Murgia, M., 2016. Wives of Ashley Madison Users Receive Blackmail Letters at Home. *The Telegraph*. Available at: www.telegraph.co.uk/technology/2016/03/02/wives-of-ashley-madison-users-receive-blackmail-letters/ (accessed: 20 January 2017).

Naked Security, 2013. Troll Victim Upset as Tormentor Escapes with Written Warning. *Naked Security*. Available at: https://nakedsecurity.sophos.com/2013/12/06/facebook-trolling-uk-cop-gets-off-with-wrist-slap-following-closed-door-hearing/ (accessed: 23 May 2017).

Nancy, J. L., 1991. *The Inoperative Community*. Minneapolis: University of Minnesota Press.

Nancy, J. L., 2000. *Being Singular Plural*. Stanford, CA: Stanford University Press.

Nancy, J. L., 2008. The Being-with of Being-there. *Continental Philosophy Review*, 41 (1), 1–15.

Ohm, P., 2010. Broken Promises of Privacy: Responding to the Surprising Failure of Anonymization. *UCLA Law Review*, 57, 1701–1777.

186 Vincent Miller

Page, T., 2016. *Unspectacular Events: Researching Vulnerability through the Localised and Particular*. PhD Thesis, Centre for Cultural Studies, Goldsmiths College, University of London.

Pyyhtinen, O., 2009. Being-with: Georg Simmel's Sociology of Association. *Theory, Culture & Society*, 26 (5), 108–128.

Rotman, B., 2008. *Becoming beside Ourselves: The Alphabet, Ghosts, and Distributed Human Being*. Durham, NC: Duke University Press.

Segall, L., 2015. Pastor Outed on Ashley Madison Commits Suicide. *CNN Online*. Available at: http://money.cnn.com/2015/09/08/technology/ashley-madison-suicide/ (accessed: 28 January 2017).

Simmel, G., 1908/1992. Soziologie, In: *Georg Simmel Gesamtausgabe*, Band 11. Frankfurt am Main: Suhrkamp.

Sorial, S., 2004. Heidegger, Jean-Luc Nancy, and the Question of Dasein's Embodiment: An Ethics of Touch and Spacing. *Philosophy Today*, 48 (2), 216–230.

Stiegler, B., 1998. *Technics and Time: The Fault of Epimetheus* (Vol. 1). Stanford, CA: Stanford University Press.

Stiegler, B., 2008. *Technics and Time: Disorientation* (Vol. 2). Stanford, CA: Stanford University Press.

Waugh, R., 2015. Two Suicides Linked to Ashley Madison Hack. *Metro*. Available at: http://metro.co.uk/2015/08/24/policeman-kills-himself-after-being-exposed-in-ashley-madison-leak-5358396/ (accessed: 28 January 2017).

Willson, M. A., 2012. Being-Together: Thinking through Technologically Mediated Sociality and Community. *Communication and Critical/Cultural Studies*, 9 (3), 279–297.

Part III

Transcendence

Beyond life, death and the human

9 The internet is always awake
Sensations, sounds and silences of the digital grave

Amanda Lagerkvist

Facebook is always awake.
> (Interview with Margareta, age 39, mourning daughter, November 2015)

I just feel I can connect so much easier with Emil on Facebook than by the grave.
> (Interview with Rickard, age 52, mourning father, November 2017)

Introduction

The tombstones are ever so still and silent. I pause from writing this piece on the abundance of the digital dead and the buzz of the network that never sleeps, and glance out from my desk through the window across the street. Always a fixture in my view, these tombstones captivate me as I see them on the other side of the stonewall of the Woodland Cemetery in Stockholm. Sturdy fir tree trunks, like quiet guardians of the stones, stand tall in this landscape inspired by Nordic burial archetypes. The cemetery is on the world heritage list. Designed by the Swedish architects Gunnar Asplund and Sigurd Lewerentz, it opened in 1920 and then consecutively opened up new areas, chapels and quarters between 1923 and 1940. The beautiful site, which combines the pristine sense of Nordic nature with functionalist architecture, is described on the UNESCO website as "evoking a primitive imagery" and as having unique artistic and cultural value for humanity. What distinguishes this place for me, for whom the place is part of my everyday environment, is how minimally cultural regimentation seems to have intervened in this unique space. It is not loudly heralding a concept; instead, it delivers a message of silence.

One might typically assess the serene tombstones' aim at eternalization as they sit there among the evergreens. But as I gaze at them, I feel not just soothed, but also saddened. There is something forlorn, paradoxical and vain about the human will to preserve the dead in the first place (cf. Kneese and Peters 2017). Any preservation is bound to be transient, as the dead are preserved in loving and *living* memory, which subjects them to a process of change. And preservation is futile, since commemorating the dead occurs

190   *Amanda Lagerkvist*

through various externalized media forms that will inevitably decay. For despite the fact that stone archetypically symbolizes permanence, a medium enabling long-term civilizations and the cultural transmission of memories that are meant to last, the stones on the cemetery are aging, eroding, even evaporating. Some are covered in moss, many are leaning just a bit, abandoned and deteriorating, to be replaced when no one is there to remember, honour and mourn the dead.

In representing the final resting place and site of memorialization (and imagined 'eternalization') of someone departed, a grave is in fact also, as John Durham Peters has argued, an age-old communication medium and a meaning storage device (2015, pp. 83, 145–146, 310). It is or can be an enabler of (perceived) connections. Today, as the statistics from the Swedish Funerary Directors' Association (SBBF) reveals, the number of people who choose a grave and gravestone continues to drop.[1] But there is also a growing number of people in Sweden who choose to have no ceremony at all for their departed relatives. The so-called *direktare* (that is: 'those who go directly into the ground') are simply cremated, a procedure followed by their ashes being spread out on a memorial hill by a maintenance person. This service can be purchased online through the funeral home. This is, for many, a disquieting circumstance: no one is there to bid the recently deceased farewell, no one ritually acknowledges them having existed, their passage and conduct through life, and their contribution (if only slight or subtle) to their family, community or to humanity in general. No medium, not even language, is used to intervene; no "earth to earth, ashes to ashes, dust to dust" is uttered. And there is no one reaching out to them, one imagines, in the afterlife either. In light of the fact that the experience of adjusting to a state of bereavement is profoundly social – always achieved in *conversation* with both the living and the dead (Klass 2006) – one could further surmise that no one, in fact, mourns these dead. Instead, as oblivion settles on them without intermediaries, we observe absence-qua-absence. This way of reckoning in this new situation once more invokes the tomb as a communication device, a transmitter of thoughts and sentiments to the dead. As with all existential phenomena, it constitutes an irresolvable paradox: due to its very quality of being silent, it can be perceived as a receiver of 'sound' of sorts from the other side. The grave, as much as the dead, or the corpse, in addition, is thus not inert, not an agentless object, not lacking a message (cf. Ariès 1981; Verdery 1999; Young and Light 2013; Walter 2016).

In *Dead Matter: The Meaning of Iconic Corpses*, Margaret Schwartz (2015) astutely argues that communication with the dead is necessary, because the dead have things to teach us and things to say. But their message is different; it's about embodiment and evaporation: "Their bodies hold secrets of disappearance and flux. When we banish them, we banish these things with them. We also banish our own sadness" (p. 105). Talking to the dead is crucial, but it can never be a dialogue between presences, and it is therefore a mere striving:

The internet is always awake   191

Communication with the dead is the classic case of incommensurate dialogue. They cannot speak back to us in the same language we use to speak to them. The dead speak to us in dreams, if they speak at all; we speak to them silently and in prayer. When we light candles or visit gravestones or tend a garden or visit a favorite spot, we are *seeking them in the places that are ritually marked with absence.*

(p.105, emphasis added)

The grave is hence a medium of absence. As I notice in the November twilight, the stones all seem to be asleep, sitting there inanimate and literally 'silent as the grave.' But, following Schwartz, this does not mean that they are not 'speaking' to us. I ponder them further: Are they in fact indexically referencing surrender before the inevitability of death, loss and the end itself? Are they in that sense 'existential media' (Lagerkvist 2016), marking out the antinomy of life and death, as spaces and media of absence? Or, perhaps rather, as media that mark out what is present in the absent, and absent in the present?

Our contemporary digital environment by contrast – never sleeping and always awake – is overloaded with traces of the dead. Highly standardized digital memorials are re-presencing the dead in abundance, constituting a new vernacular and perhaps even acting as surrogates for the dead (cf. Maddrell 2012; Veale 2004). Can these ever be *existential media*? If not, where do they fail? And if they succeed, by what merits and virtues?

Proper ghost effects

My concern in this chapter is to offer a way to begin to describe the particularities and peculiarities of the digital dead, as these are present on online memorials where mourners (of the Global North) are in the habit of speaking directly to them (cf. Ryan 2008; Walter et al. 2011; Brubaker et al. 2013; Graham et al. 2015). This chapter is mainly a theoretical intervention supported by a few illustrative examples from my fieldwork on the Swedish NGOs VIMIL ("We who lost someone in the middle of life"), VSFB ("We who lost a child") and the memorial site Minnesrummet.se, as well as examples from international scholarship.[2]

First of all, one must note that the dead are no doubt present online, or within the digital ecology, in a multi-mediated manner. They are there, primarily through an abundance of *photographs*, but also quite often through their digital afterlife in online *textual* post-mortem memorialization and after death communication – a feature I will delve into further in this chapter. They are also increasingly present through *algorithmic agency* itself: their digital traces are often still 'alive' in the network despite their passing. And in automated farewell messaging and other features of the transcendence industry, they are making themselves known as acting in and upon the present from the grave (Tucker 2014; Bollmer 2016; Gibson 2015; Lagerkvist

192   *Amanda Lagerkvist*

2017). The dead are thus seemingly alive, when buzzing us from the grave, when emailing us on our birthdays, when they appear through reminders or updates in our feeds. This is even more apposite if we project ourselves into futuristic visions where the dead are soon to be given a holographic gestalt, a digitally animated body with a voice for us to chat with. On this techno-logical front, the latest media presence of the dead is the *griefbot*, which as a vision includes physical features as well as a digital voice impersonating the dead person.

Despite all the visual and textual enunciations of the dead, I will put par-ticular emphasis – heuristically, metaphorically and concretely – on the audi-tory and sensory faculties in order to map how the dead become present: as *sensation, sound* or *silence*. In this pursuit, I will also provide examples of, and a theoretical reflection on, how/when digital technologies assume a *transcending* role. In this way, the chapter also promises to offer important new insights into discussions on the technospirituality of after death com-munication online, which scholars have been paying attention to lately (cf. Brubaker et al. 2013). It thereby aims to chart new dimensions of the rela-tionship between digital technology and vernacular religiosity, beyond what scholars have mapped before such as the magic of network agency, the mys-terious capacity of media to erase time and compress space, the supernatural sense in which technologies create doppelgangers and an ethereal sense of disembodiment (cf. Sconce 2000; Chun 2011; Stolow 2013a).

Focusing on how subjectivity has been forged differently in different media epochs, Brian Rotman (2007) is interested in how media produce *ghost effects*, that is, psychic entities and objects of belief. Rotman delib-erately discusses these ghost effects without any reference to the originary ghosts, *the dead*. Here I draw inspiration from his definition, but dismiss his disclaimer. The dead, I submit, could also be described as "hypostatized effects of communication media" (Rotman 2007, p. 58), or as their literal and *proper ghost effects*. To argue that the digital dead are media ghosts means quite straightforwardly to say that their emergence and character-istics depend on the medium through which they are perceived to be con-nectable. This way they can teach us something crucial about our media. By reading the technology off the dead and the dead off the technology, I will suggest that the dead 'mimic' the leading medium (and, in particular, the dominant social media platform) of our age. This pursuit necessitates a revisiting of imaginaries of electronic presence, and the presence of the dead, throughout history.

Media presence and ultimate absence: histories and perspectives

One way of conceiving of existential media, as I have suggested elsewhere, is to stress that they profoundly engage with presences and absences (Lagerkvist 2016). This is also why there is such a deep connection between death and

The internet is always awake 193

media. The dead – those ultimately absent – have made themselves felt and heard throughout history precisely through media, and new media have given the dead social presence (Walter et al. 2011, p. 294; Walter 2016; see also Graham and Montoya, Chapter 12, this volume).[3] As is well documented the dead have also been sought and sometimes summoned by the living, by various means and media across history. The written word itself has often been connected with the idea of a voice from beyond the grave. The dead literally make themselves present when their words act upon us, which represents a life after death of sorts (Ruin 2015). Early in the twentieth century, the film medium was seen to animate the dead and bring them back to life; film was the art of revenants, and as such was considered demonic and monstrous. Cinema was not only "a spectral medium but one animating dead bodies: what we see flickering on the screen are visual effects of presence" (Bronfen 2017, p. 18). Electronic media, as I will return to below, revolutionized the relationship between time and space, and was perceived as a substance that could animate both body and soul. But, in addition, such media provided enhanced forms of mystical presence – also of those departed.

John Durham Peters posits, as the first key "existential fact about modern media," the ease with which we can mingle with communicable traces of the dead. And he argues that "indeed, all mediated communication is in a sense communication with the dead, insofar as media can store 'phantasms of the living' for playback after bodily death" (Peters 1999, p. 142). In the modern and late modern ages of media, the dead are seemingly all around – they are mediated, remediated and made present through a vast array of technologies with a number of different characteristic features. They are ubiquitously represented and replayed in photographs, videos and words. For Peters, there is an existential challenge in the abundance of traces, effigies, pictures and sounds of the dead.

Others have argued that the mediated dead can potentially punctuate our humdrum existence and remind us about our finitude. Photographs, as famously stated by Roland Barthes, are connected to death, because they stand in an indexical relation to the *what-has-been* (1981). The existential punctum of the photographic dead does not bring back the past but presences the absent and reminds us of death. Just like the tomb, the photograph is still, and may be described as a static connective enabler with the dead. And precisely through the silent re-presencing of the dead, the photograph powerfully evokes their absence in the present or presence as absence. By capturing finitude itself, the potential of photographs is to bring us a 'deadly' message.

As some scholars have argued, this is also the case of the web memorial that enables lavish visual and immediate presencing of the dead, "in tension with the very pastness of the person it represents" (Ryan 2008, pp. 173–174). Instead, for Peters, it is this very overexposure of representations that may distort the profundity of communication with the dead. Similarly for Schwartz, instead of being existential lighthouses, these recordings of the dead are in effect *undead media*, that is, nauseating repetitions that haunt

194   *Amanda Lagerkvist*

us. Schwartz argues that communicating with the dead is in fact radically different from these other forms of communication, and from our general relationship to, and consumption of, various media forms that often record and replay the dead in harrowing detail. Connoting presence and imagined fullness, modern communication media achieve, perchance, something other than existential communication, in which breakdown, interruption and absence are key, and in which "'speechlessness' may be both the medium and the message" (Lagerkvist and Andersson 2017, p. 552). And through their aspirations for fullness and exhaustiveness, it seems that they are in fact too 'perfect,' and thus insufficient for communicating with the dead.

The second key existential fact about modern media is for Peters the strong potential conflation in human experience between reaching out to living or dead others, in acts of communication. For instance, talking to the dead may easily be confused with communicating with someone at a distance (see also Stolow 2013b, pp. 96–97). Observing this affinity between those distant and those dead, in an equally circumspect assessment of how the dead seem to be present, to *live on*, in the contemporary digital culture of social media, the British author Zadie Smith articulates amazement quickly followed by levelheadedness before the practices of commemorating the dead online. She succinctly asks: "Do they genuinely believe, because the girl's wall is still up, that she is still, in some sense, alive? What's the difference, after all, if all your contact was virtual?" (2010). Smith critiques the types of relationships social media *really* foster, and she warily questions whether these *really* matter, implying that the dead will suffer the same virtualizing fate as the living.

By contrast, Graham et al. also highlight the benefits of online memorials as they "mark a less bureaucratic, more individualized and neo-modern approach to memorialization where the dead, once again, become part of everyday social interactions and so are given an existence" (2015, p. 38). Yet they simultaneously problematize the medium, pointing to a profound dearth of concreteness, sincerity and substance at its core, while underlining that it activates the key issue of presence and absence:

> we suggest online memorials support the wider engagement of a grieving public, that is, like the deceased, both present and absent: present in its abstract engagement with the emotion produced through the memorial, absent in its lack of concrete engagement with the living.
>
> (p. 38)

Importantly, they furthermore maintain that despite this lack and the "strangely unincorporated" nature of web memorials (p. 51), there is also a type of fullness through "*the engagement of the senses*" and this "means less exertion of the imagination by the living when memorializing, mitigating the lack of proximity between the physical body and the memorial" (p. 39, emphasis added).

In similarly stressing such vital fullness of the medium itself, Elaine Kasket argues (more unequivocally) that compared to a physical grave, online memorials provide more accessibility and a "comparative vividness of the deceased individual's presence" (2012, p. 13). She further notes that "Facebook could be experienced as a particularly effective way of communicating with and feeling close to the deceased person, more so than graveyard visits, visits to the home, thinking thoughts, or writing letters" (p. 66). And the continuing bonds paradigm in scholarship on grief seems to have been given renewed relevance through social networking (Klass 1996; Klass and Walter 2001). As Kasket argues, all four processes of grief are facilitated by the medium: sensing the presence of the dead, talking with them, experiencing their guidance and talking about them (2012, p. 67). But if the medium enables unprecedented presencing and continuing bonds, how does this differ from other media in the past? In order to be able to analyze how the digital dead become present, how they are connected to or communicated with (or not), they need to be contrasted with the analogue dead, or the way the dead have been presenced in other media environments and epochs. This also requires insight into the phenomenon of media presence itself.

In *Haunted Media: Electronic Presence From Telegraphy to Television*, Jeffrey Sconce (2000) argues that the advent of electronic media engendered powerful imaginations. He distinguishes between three consistent cultural fantasies and fictions across the various electronic media he investigates: the fiction of *disembodiment*, which is the enabling of leaving the body to transport the soul to a distant location; the fiction of *the sovereign electronic world* into which subjects can be immersed; and the *anthropomorphizing of media technology* through cyborgs and androids. These all rely on a utopian discourse of the self-importance of electronic transformation, and imagined endless possibilities for technological change and development. These fantasies, and especially the miracle of electronic simultaneity, which portended "the possibility of live contact with distant frontiers, making early media presence an avenue of wonder bound to the exploratory social deployment of these early technologies" (p. 11), may also have played a role in how computers were understood when they were introduced. Some of these imaginings may still linger.

Sconce maps four types of electronic presence that also have bearings on the presence of the dead, and on communication with them. They all seemingly echo in perceptions of the digital dead, which is why I rehearse them at some length. The first was the telegraph, introduced in 1844, and the Modern Spiritualist movement that it spurred. In séances directed by gifted "mediums" – someone who could hear messages and sounds from the other side – the belief was that one could receive transmissions from the dead through 'the spiritual telegraph,' which enabled conversation with the dead through point-to-point transmissions via spirits that conveyed their communications (see also Peters 1999; Stolow 2013b).

196 *Amanda Lagerkvist*

The second innovation was wireless radio, which signalled a radically different vision of electronic presence. It replaced the concept of the individuated stream with a vast etheric ocean: "Disembodied consciousness of the living and the dead no longer traveled a fantastic wire that connected the mundane here with the transcendental 'there,'" Sconce (2000) argues. Instead: "Wireless replaced the comforting and often utopian ideal of extraordinary interconnection with a more bittersweet presence, one that evoked a no less marvelous yet somehow more melancholy realm of abandoned bodies and dispersed consciousness" (p. 61–62). Accounts of wireless were anxious and pessimistic; the technology was about loss of communion, estrangement, alienation and despair. Such anxieties, it could be argued, can also be found in realm of the digital, where they are to some extent replayed.

The third form of electronic presence was the development of networked radio in the 1920s, when radio became "the omnipresent telecommunicative blanket covering the nation" (p. 15), which changed both the experience of radio, as well as the quality of electronic presence itself. "With the growth of broadcasting," Sconce argues, "the once spectral presence of radio no longer appeared as the 'mysterious voice from the void' becoming instead the familiar 'live' and 'living' voices of the national networks" (p. 93). In light of this understanding, Sconce sees the panic broadcast of the 'War of the Worlds' as a mass psychological reaction against the suffocating presence of mass broadcasting. Electronic presence became 'omnipresence,' which caused anxieties (p. 123).

The fourth form of electronic presence emerged with the advent of television, which demonstrated a continuity with the occult powers of radio and wireless and telegraphy (p. 127). Television, however, fostered fantasies of paranormal contact, of televisual ghosts that did not speak through the technology, but *resided within the technology itself*. Television generated, Sconce argues, an autonomous spirit world. And it played on the ambiguous and indeterminate relationship to space and time: it was able to transport viewers to a different place; it allowed for experiencing being in 'two places at once' and to teleport oneself, to *be there*, as well as to move into a 'perpetual present' on the other side of the screen – that is, to be immersed into the program's liveness (p. 130). The television set both talked and could see, which made it seem more than inanimate.[4]

Sconce traces a shift in the history of electronic presence from point-to-point communication (as in telegraphy and wireless radio) to mass broadcasting (network radio and television). Through this gradual transferal "presence became less a function of engaging an extraordinary yet fleeting entity across frontiers of time and space and instead assumed the forms of *an all-enveloping force*" (p. 11, emphasis added). The internet works today precisely as a transcendental and 'environmental force' in the world (cf. Floridi 2014). This feature of the medium – described by one of my informants as being 'always awake' – also reflects back on the digital dead in interesting

The internet is always awake 197

ways, as I aim to show below. In the following, I offer a provisional analysis that probes the presence of the digital dead. I will show that they in some ways represent continuity rather than a clean break from other, older forms of electronic presence (of the dead), but there are also distinct features of their presencing.

The dead are online and are getting the message

As has been noted by several scholars in the emergent field of study called 'death online,' talking directly to the dead in online mourning environments is widespread. People speak directly to them, in writing messages on their walls, or in commentary fields and in blogs (see e.g., Kasket 2012; Brubaker et al. 2013; Staley 2014). Talking to the dead occurs both in memorial groups on social media sites, on web memorials on personal homepages, in closed support groups for the bereaved, and on sites where one may post condolences and light a digital candle. These memorials appear in the shape of private homepages, similar spaces in the hands of the funerary sector, or organized by an NGO or enabled by the key players of the platform society, such as Facebook and YouTube, etc. Typically it is next-of-kin, close relatives and friends who set up these spaces and post, but sometimes this involves strangers who write to the dead person as well (cf. Graham et al. 2015; Gibson 2016). On the contemporary Swedish internet, speaking to the dead online may look like this thread on a public memorial site, set up by the funerary sector:

> From: SABINA
> I don't get it. I have no idea what happened to you. How you passed. We lost touch lately but you were my best friend in elementary school. In *(name of city deleted)*. Despite this I have to say that I was deeply touched to hear that you are gone. I really hope you are in a much better place. Where you are now. Rest in peace!

> From: MARIA
> Johanna my darling fighter and friend! I can't believe it's true, that I will never see you again. But I hope we meet again in heaven ❤

> From: MALIN
> My beloved kid and friend ❤
> Am gradually realizing that you are not coming back – that we won't run into each other anymore. It hurts so much – tremendously so but in my heart you have a very special place and I wish you – with all my heart – PEACE

> From: TORA
> Miss you beautiful Johanna and thinking of you every day and hoping that you're doing great wherever you are now ❤

198 *Amanda Lagerkvist*

From: NENNE

I can hear your gorgeous laughter within and I feel warm inside . . . I know that you are the strongest and most lovely star in the sky waking over your loved ones . . . you are the most beautiful angel in the Kingdom of heaven.!! You are missed

From: SAGA

It's so hard to understand that you do not exist anymore, I will always remember our crazy days on the horseback, both when we were on the road, in the ditch and in the forest. You had an angel's patience and looks. Rest in peace Johanna the best

From: MARIE-LOUISE

Johanna! Wonderful Johanna! One never forgets a person like you! Your presence, your amazing kindness and warmth made everyone feel seen and liked. We will always miss you!

(Condolence book www.minnesrummet.se/minnesplats.as,
retrieved 16 January 2015)

This thread represents several features belonging to the contemporary practice of talking to the dead online. As it exemplifies, when their personalities are praised through after death communication, the dead are given eulogies. In this example, there is the strong notion or presumption that the dead girl is awake, that she possesses some kind of agency, and that she is silently watching or hearing. Hence, and importantly, the dead person is believed to be somewhere right now. There seems to be a form of vernacular religiosity or a post-Christian sentiment discernible here: despite the alleged widespread secularism in Sweden, there are also references to 'angels' and to 'heaven.' There is also one posting that is about seeing each other again in the afterlife in an embodied reunion (cf. Lagerkvist 2014).

As I will discuss in the following sections, the implied presence of the dead online may also reveal something important about the digital itself. Reverberating the broader affordances of the technology, these practices may reflect the above discussed 'liveness' of the medium, as observed by Jeffrey Sconce. In order to understand better the distinct features of the digital dead and how they are present through the medium of the internet, we may begin by placing them in the context of late modernity, where there is a dismantled boundary between the living and the dead (Howarth 2000). Today the dead are not conceived to be in a complete elsewhere, but in an *in-between space*. Contemporary beliefs about death and how the living should engage with the dead envision the dead in familiar or longed-for places, and as doing similar things as in life, which brings them closer to the living (Kellaher and Worpole in Graham et al. 2015, p. 38).

Following this thesis, we could imagine that the dead are, in fact, in that familiar yet in-between space we can only partially know, but connect to and inhabit all the time: they are *online*. Hence, they resemble the televisual dead and seem to be residing *within the technology itself*. A striking feature of the commemoration of the dead, given expression in forms of after death

The internet is always awake 199

communication that I have studied, is not only that the dead are online but that for some mourners, this is the key interface through which they feel to be connected to them. One example is Rickard, who mourns his dead son Emil, who died at the age of 22 in a skiing accident a few years earlier: "I just feel I can connect so much easier with Emil on Facebook than by the grave" (Interview November 2017). The same goes for Sara, who has mourned her brother Niklas online for over ten years:

AL: Can you describe in a little more detail how you know that Niklas can hear you on the digital memorial and not by the physical grave?
SARA: It's very difficult to explain, but I think the written word becomes so definite, it remains, but spoken words disappear into nothingness (an empty void), they land nowhere. Although sometimes I think he can actually hear my thoughts . . . and it feels good to think that way.
(Interview April 2016)

Sara built a web memorial on a homepage in memory of her dead brother who died in an accident on a vacation trip abroad in 2005. Writing a diary there directly to him has meant a great deal to her in her grief process. Her feelings and perceptions about this digital space corroborate findings in other contexts. Kasket cites a British mourner saying: "I feel she will see it if it's on her wall. If I were to leave a letter for her at the gravesite . . . when I can't see what I wrote to her, I feel like she won't be able to see it too" (2012, p. 66). There is also an explicit belief that the dead are *getting the message* on Facebook or on other memorial sites (DeGroot 2012).

The dead are thus alert to the communications. Recent studies on vernacular religion online (in the British context) have identified that in social networking, the dead are described as angels, rather than souls, with *agency* (see Walter 2011, 2016). But whatever agency the dead may have, I will add, they are at once mute. In line with Schwartz' observation, there is of course an inevitable asynchronicity here, and maybe that is just a simple fact. But as I will discuss, whilst the dead remain silent receivers of our commemorations, they can still be *connected to*, and the internet is then a place of *full and total connection*. How come, and what are the bearings of this? Grant Bollmer gives one clue to this sense of full presence through the medium, and he suggests that the existential consequences may be grave:

> Recordings have always animated traces of the deceased. What is new about network technology is the belief that the amount of data recorded and externalized gives a nearly full representation of the authentic identity of the human being. *It is not simply the presence of the deceased that causes anxiety, but the supposed fullness of that presence, formed by near-totalized recording, networked and beyond the control of the user.*
> (2016, p. 121, emphasis added)

In addition, I suggest the backdrop for this is the sense of *always-thereness* of the internet as such. As one of my informants, Margareta, puts

200   *Amanda Lagerkvist*

it: "Facebook is always awake" (2015). In the following, this liveness of the medium will be related to broader debates on transcendence in technology. My intention is to dissect the potential cluster of meanings contained in this statement. The internet is *awake*, which I understand as animate and animating. But I will also expand beyond liveness. I suggest, in addition, that 'awake' can also imply ever-present, everlasting, all-encompassing, ubiquitous and always watching. Before delving further into the peculiarities of the digital dead, I will also ponder what type of communication this awakeness fosters.

Always awake: a medium of lifeline communication

What could 'awake' mean in this context? Awake is easily read as in *alive* and thereby enabling instant connections. This resonates with Sconce's idea about the larger cultural mythology of the living quality of television, which suggests that television is "'alive . . . living, real, not dead' even if it sometimes serves as a medium of the dead." He continues to say that all television programming is discursively 'live' "by virtue of its instantaneous transmission and reception" (2000, p. 2). This feature of television is even more strongly articulated by the internet, which operates through the temporality of instantaneity. Sconce thus notes that: "the computer (and other operators) can now speak directly to us (and we to them) in an immediate electronic interface" (p. 3).

Could we infer from these immediacies that awake also means *benevolently watching over us*? As discussed above, liveness sometimes means that electronic media are "animate and perhaps even sentient" (p. 2). Could this imply that we are dealing with a watchful network that is a conscious presence, a deity of sorts? This is the sense of presence evoked by Laurence Scott in his discussion on what validation by text messages means to him, and he calls the sensations of the network a promise of a "Messenger God" (2015). The network is somehow awake and aware. It also possesses infinite knowledge. As Dr. Debra Campbell (a psychologist blogging for the *Huffington Post*) notes, for her technospirituality of the web is "like a great unseen Deity of techno-joy and a hub of infinite wisdom" (Campbell 2017). This resonates with Peters' idea of an omniscient Google God that sits and waits for our connecting acts of searching (2015, pp. 315–376).

Another rendition of this alertness of the net may suggest that *awake* means *always there. Always-thereness* may be conceived on a temporal axis: the internet is awake, as in 24/7, mirroring the neoliberal digital economies of flexible accumulation that never sleep and demand that we do the same. But, on reflection, it could also mean *always there* in the a-temporal sense, as in *at the end of time*, which is in infinity. I have argued elsewhere that in the age of temporal instantaneity, the eternal seems to make a forceful return, or to manifest its long-term place in human culture, precisely through a netlore of the infinite (2014).

The internet is always awake 201

When Facebook is always awake, as Margareta senses, moreover, it may then invoke the promise of being *forever* there, of being an eternal archive, which draws on the mythology of digital media as something that will outlast humans and remain for eternity (Chun 2011). Always-thereness may also be on a synchronous axis. It brings omnipresence to mind in terms of a synchronous absolute present, and it is then always there, like the air or oxygen (hopefully). This echoes philosophical approaches that emphasize media as an enabler of life, an infrastructure of being, media as elemental and atmospheric (Peters 2015).

In fact, this understanding of awakeness as everywhereness, or "everwareness" (Greenfield 2006), is closely related to one form of meaningful existential communication that is occurring through digital media. As I have argued at length elsewhere, and in the introduction to this volume, our media are existential both because of their ordinariness, and due to their importance in relation to extraordinary, transformative, or traumatic events that transcend the everyday (Lagerkvist 2016). By providing crucial means in the important work of restoring the world and recreating life after loss, and in allowing for mediating continuing bonds with the dead, social media environments and online memorials afford a sense of "existential security" in the face of bottomless grief and suffering. It is in this context, when meaninglessness holds sway, that people turn to the internet as a *literal lifeline*, providing a medium of what we have recently called 'lifeline communication' (Lagerkvist and Andersson 2017). This is a key example of when digital media, in all their awakeness and semiotic overload, are in fact *existential media*, which offer mourners a complex and fulfilling presence that entails, importantly, both silence and interruptions within. Lifeline communication is, namely, *existential communication*, which puts emphasis on *being there* through connective presence (Lagerkvist and Andersson 2017); that is simply locating and confirming each other through echoes or 'echo-location' (Markham 2017). In this type of communication the mutual respect for silence is key, since there are mourners who seldom post but collect strength by silently watching other mourners do so. For others the lifeline is crucial as an outlet, and this is the case for some who mourn in anonymous guest books and chatrooms:

SOFIA: . . . I'm right now in the wave of grief and hope it abates so I can sleep. It helps a bit to briefly write for a while *straight out into Vimil's net*. You know what this means. A comfort in the misery. Life is like this. Now it feels a little bit better.
(Vimil's Guestbook 2017, emphasis added)

Here writing straight out into the net of this association, which is available around the clock, means a lot and can be a resource for getting through the night. Two other online mourners communicating and debating in the guestbook of VIMIL express this sense of the importance of the lifeline, and of the net presence of their support group, but they have different perspectives

202   *Amanda Lagerkvist*

on anonymity versus personalization, and about what the medium affords and what the needs are in grief:

EVA: It's too bad you have bad experiences of Facebook, I can warmly recommend our Facebook group. We are all going through the same difficult phase in our lives. And I can confirm that we dare to talk for real. *The responses feel more true, when you have the person behind.* And we can keep people away who are posting in anonymity with the purpose that does not match what Vimil is. Both outlets are needed but don't be afraid of the Facebook group. Warmly welcome.
LENA: I'm not afraid of FB on my part and have no bad experiences either but in mourning it's better for me to speak to strangers. *The most important thing is to pour out your thoughts. Not to know who is listening . . .*
      (VIMIL, Guestbook, summer 2014, emphases added)

Eva represents a mourning self who goes online to be able to both give away and dispense of something, and it is important for her to know there are real persons, with faces and names, on the listening end. What matters for Lena is, by contrast, to have the opportunity to anonymously share her vulnerability through connectivity, and to thereby release herself, if only temporarily. It is not so important to know *who* is listening, since someone is always listening. And by consequence, the network itself is listening: the internet is always awake.

The digital dead: silent lurkers

So what of the dead when the medium through which they are perceived is sleepless? As discussed earlier in this chapter, scholars have recently suggested that in the online context the dead are described as angels (rather than souls) with agency (see Walter 2011, 2016).[5] Even if the dead can be inferred as having agency online, and even if they are present through an over-abundance of visual and textual traces, I argue that, at least on the Swedish internet, they are also *mute*: a bunch of lurkers loitering about. The analogue dead were interactants contacting us through the mediums of spiritual telegraphs, or ghostly presencing themselves in radio transmissions or in the liveness of televisual agency. They were *communicated with* through the spiritual telegraph or *brought to life* through the film medium. But the digital dead are silent receivers of our commemorations. The internet and social media thus establish one-way communication with the dead. As opposed to other forms of technospirituality, such as the case of the spiritual telegraph, there is palpably no expectation of receiving an *answer* from the grave.[6] This way, they to some extent remediate the reticent gravestones. But, moreover, it is actually as if the bereaved are satisfied and content with being heard (or seen) themselves. The corollary to social media in general seems clear, and one may speculate about whether this reflects an aspect of the platforms at large:

The internet is always awake 203

that while validation (someone responds/likes/sees/loves me!) is essential in social media practice, it is perhaps not so important to listen to others and to truly *communicate*. It is perhaps more important to be seen than to hear out, to showcase the self (and thereby amplify value, skills and connections) than to interact with fellow humans? In a similar assessment, for Graham et al. (2015), something is in fact lacking in these hyperpublic spaces of commemoration. They hold that the

> doomed attempts to converse with the dead are strangely more private than public, more individualistic than common, more subjective than objective, more performative than structural, more transient than obdurate and more emotive than restrained. For although the assembled publics can empathise and emote, they are spectators, doomed to be absent from the dialogue and true understanding.
>
> (2015, p. 52)

Contrasting with our studies of lifeline communication, which primarily focused on support, this view holds that strivings of after death communication online reflect a shallow culture of narcissism, bereft of true communal engagement.

But beyond hyperindividualism, something else also seems to be going on. Here it must be noted that although the dead remain silent receivers of our commemorations, they can, however, be *connected to*, and the internet is then a place of full and complete connection. The network is always there, awake, rattling and watching. In relation to the history of electronic presence, digital media seem to embody the transcendent and to exemplify forms of 're-enchantment,' by enabling *connective presence* as such. The dead are, as ghost effects of the medium, a sensation of connectivity itself: they can be logged on, and the internet is then a place of full and complete connection. This in fact echoes a broader development traced by Jeffrey Sconce. He discerns a transition from a fascination with fantastic media technologies of communion in the past to fantastic textuality in the late 1990s world of cyberspace:

> Whereas discourses of presence were once dominated by the varieties of contact and communion to be achieved through the discorporative powers of telecommunications, such discourse is now most often concerned with the *extraordinary and seemingly sovereign powers of electronic textuality itself*.
>
> (2000, p. 10, emphasis added)

This movement is in important ways resonating in, yet also furthered by, the most recent developments of the internet. Today, digital media covers the spectrum of life and death. But even more importantly, what seems sovereign is connectivity itself, including its imponderable infrastructural

204   *Amanda Lagerkvist*

backstage; the algorithms, protocols, bits and data that enable the world we see and inhabit through our digital devices, but hide from us at the same time (see Hong, Chapter 6, this volume).

I propose once more, that this can be related to the fact that the internet is always awake: a presence-qua-presence in the world. The network thereby becomes a ritualistic 'totem' – a numinous and all-enveloping force – that is always there, attentive and watching. Hence, it represents a kind of techno-spirituality that turns the network itself into a seemingly universally presenced "device of divinity" (Peters 2015, p. 334), which promises to spawn full and complete connection. This scope of digital media as an all-encompassing force – spanning the magical as well as the mundane (cf. Frosh, Chapter 5, this volume) – thus affects their imagined transcendent scope, which in turn informs the idea of fullness in connecting with the dead.

Conclusion: sensations of connectivity, sounds of silence

The internet is always awake, and as such it is a medium of fullness and of ultimate presence. Through the highlighted practices of mourning and connecting to the dead online, I have in this chapter shown that they can tell us something about the texture of the digital terrain more generally: that it is a space of sensational connective awakeness, and of chatter, but also of silently lurking and listening. The latter is manifestly the case when virtual mourners, who bring important dimensions both to the debate on vernacular religiosity in the digital age and to the emergent understanding of existential communication, engage in lifeline communication in support groups online. This is a form that foregrounds existential needs and offers a rich ethics for being there for one another online, thanks to the net that is always awake – and yet with respect for silences and withdrawal. But if we once more turn our attention to the particularities of after death communication in the online context, we may wrap up these deliberations by returning to my initial question: can web memorials ever be *existential media*?

In this chapter, I have suggested that digital media embodies the transcendent, by enabling connective presence per se, and *one-way communication* with the dead. As opposed to the case of the spiritual telegraph, for instance, in after death communication online there is rarely an expectation of interacting with and receiving an answer from the grave. The digital dead in social media are essentially 'silent', in terms of not being expected to talk back. We simply know they are listening. At the same time, I have discerned a sense of fullness in connecting with the dead, because there are vibrations, sounds and sensations of the network as a transcendent presence that animates the world. As ghost effects of the medium, the dead are importantly like the web itself, awake and seemingly attentive. And they are, like the internet, *all-pervasive* (cf. Walter 2018). Hence, while the dead are ultimately as mute as they have always been in the physical grave, importantly, the digital memorial is *not evacuated of presence*: it is not a space and medium

The internet is always awake   205

of absence. We are thus faced with the silence of the dead, in the midst of the buzz of the overloaded network.

The question is whether the effectiveness and fullness of digital mediation, and its excess of images and traces and sensations, is conducive to, and may therefore enable existential communication, or if it mainly produces an obscuring, an obfuscation, a stifling virtualization, as Schwartz, Peters and Smith advocate. Since there is no room given for a caesura, a pause, one may venture to suggest that these are echo chambers that are full but existentially empty, loud but inaudible. And it could be argued that in this very sense, these media are therefore not existential. The jury is also still out on whether the surplus of traces will be helpful in the collective work of producing a durable biography of the dead person, which is the purpose of grief itself (Walter 1996), or whether it will prevent this process.

Fullness is unremittingly chased in yet new ways by the designers. On the bleeding edge of technology, a new necromedium is being developed: the *griefbot*. Beyond being mere surrogates of the dead, these technologies may soon become, even more profoundly, digital bodies of substitution. They aim to bring the fullness of the dead person to life, first in text-based forms but potentially also in the shape of androids.[7] Here, the future may promise beyond Sci-Fi, a different fully embodied robotic presence of the dead, with recorded or simulated voices, and with capabilities to learn and develop.[8] At least at face value this may complicate this discussion of when the dead may actually 'speak,' and how we may interact with them, and whether they may offer something beyond mere sensations of connectivity. Perhaps such technologies, as is often suggested by technophiles, will even alter the human relationship to the dead and death altogether? And perhaps the nature and shape of existential needs themselves, may fundamentally change, due to technological change? Would the advent of full-blown griefbots force me to then revise this chapter and talk about the potentially meaningful sounds of the digital grave, through the interactive affordances of the sentient robot?

Who can properly foresee and second-guess the implications of such a fantastical scenario – one in which technologies have overcome the aporias of life and the abyss of loss? Let me close by suggesting a different possibility in the face of the seemingly relentless developments of AI. To offer these a balance I propose – as is indeed the key incentive for this entire project and volume – we invoke *other* tenacious voices from the grave, stemming from the tradition of existential philosophy, who have posited the indispensable and indeed productive role of recognizing finitude in human of existence (for instance, those of Kierkegaard, Jaspers and Heidegger, cf. Lagerkvist 2016, 2017). Their presence will remind us that the existential could also, and as likely, offer up the digital some defiance. Listening to them may thus allow us to stubbornly reclaim a bedrock of existentiality, solid as the rock from which the serene tombstones of old were chiselled. Embracing such a

206   Amanda Lagerkvist

perspective means to retain a richness to the prospects of being and becoming human. And since it will place, I submit, unwavering stress on *paradox* and *limits* – by emphasizing a value of the void – it will continue to demand both media of absence and sounds of silence.

Notes

1 Ulf Lernéus, CEO of SBBF, interview October 2017. The reasons may vary: there are other means of commemoration (such as memorial hills, or spreading the ashes in the ocean). According to Lernéus, though, there is no correlation between not having a physical grave and setting up a web memorial instead. In my study, there are cases when parents who chose not to have a physical grave testify to the importance of other spaces, or indeed, to the web memorial, in its place. See Graham et al., who also discuss such multiplying options for memorializing the dead, both offline and online (2015, p. 37).

2 This research has been conducted within the research program that I am heading as Wallenberg Academy Fellow: *Existential Terrains: Memory and Meaning in Cultures of Connectivity*, funded by the Knut and Alice Wallenberg Foundation, the Marcus and Amalia Wallenberg Foundation and Stockholm University. In line with the approval of the Regional Ethics Board of Stockholm, the study has been undertaken without participant observation in any of the studied groups. All participants have been anonymized and permission to quote those who have been interviewed has been granted.

3 Tony Walter (2016) shows that media technologies have played a significant role throughout history for how the dead are 're-presenced.' In every society, the presence of the dead partially depends, he argues, on available communication technologies. These include speech, stone, sculpture, writing, printing, photography, and the mass media, but also today the internet. According to Walter, the dead have had an important function in legitimating the social world, but in addition, they need media technologies to perform this function. Each communication technology affords possibilities for the dead to justify particular social groups and institutions: "from the oral construction of kinship, to the megalithic legitimation of the territorial rights of chiefdoms, to the written word's construction of world religions and nations, to the photographic and phonographic construction of celebrity-based neo-tribalism, and to the digital reconstruction of family and friendship" (2016, p. 215).

4 Other fantasies instead projected onto television an electronic nowhere (as echoed perhaps in Zadie Smith's worries about a virtual hollowing out of true human connectedness, authentic sociality and presence): "these more ominous portraits of the medium saw television as a zone of suspended animation, a form of oblivion from which viewers might not ever escape." Television was in this imagination fated to produce a cultural void and to place audiences in suspension which implied the inauthentic position of the mass consumer (Sconce 2000, pp. 131–132). The real world, in this perspective, would collapse into the voids of televisual nothingness, a vast wasteland.

5 According to Walter, one contextual background for the dead becoming angels is the popularity of angels in the 1990s Anglo-American context, which exemplified "playful new discursive engagements with the supernatural" (Walter 2016, p. 16). This has also taken hold, Walter argues, following Howarth, because of the fact that there is a dismantled boundary between the living and the dead in today's world. This is thematized in popular culture in the West, which is overpopulated by vampire sagas and other dead and undead creatures, engendering discussions on the re-enchantment of the West (Partridge 2005).

The internet is always awake 207

6 And yet it must be noted that this observation is fraught with ambivalence, since many mourners also report on answers from the grave through other media: birds, cats, flowers in a jug that don't wither, a voice cutting through the air from nowhere, and a strong conviction that the dead youngster is "actually in here right now, listening" (cf. Interview with Malena, mourning mother, Spring 2016).

7 Godfrey (2018).

8 See my analysis of one such fictional scenario (in Lagerkvist 2017).

Bibliography

Ariès, P., 1981. *The Hour of Our Death*. New York: Vintage Books.

Barthes, R., 1981. *Camera Lucida*. New York: Hill & Wang.

Bollmer, D., 2016. *Inhuman Networks: Social Media and the Archaeology of Connection*. New York: Bloomsbury.

Bronfen, E., 2017. Gothic Wars: Media's Lust: On the Cultural Afterlife of the War Dead. *In*: F. Bottin and C. Spooner, eds. *Monstrous Media/Spectral Subjects: Imaging Gothic from the Nineteenth Century to the Present*. Oxford: Oxford University Press, 15–28.

Brubaker, J. R., Hayes, G. R. and Dourish, P., 2013. Beyond the Grave: Facebook as a Site for the Expansion of Death and Mourning. *The Information Society*, 29 (3), 152–163. doi:10.1080/01972243.2013.777300

Campbell, D., 2017. Is there Techno Spirituality? *The Huffington Post*. December 6, 2017. Available at: https://www.huffingtonpost.com/debra campbelltunks/post_10149_b_8143744.html (accessed: 12 September 2017).

Chun, W. H. K., 2011. *Programmed Visions: Software and Memory*. Cambridge, MA: MIT Press.

DeGroot, J. M., 2012. Maintaining Relational Continuity with the Deceased on Facebook. *OMEGA: Journal of Death and Dying*, 65 (3), 195–212.

de Vries, B. and Rutherford, J., 2004. Memorializing Loved Ones on the World Wide Web. *OMEGA: Journal of Death and Dying*, 49 (1), 5–26.

Floridi, L. (ed.), 2014. *The Onlife Manifesto: Being Human in a Hyperconnected Era*. Berlin: Springer Open.

Gibson, M., 2015. Automatic and Automated Mourning: Messengers of Death and Messages from the Dead. *Continuum: Journal of Media and Cultural Studies*, 29 (3), 339–353.

Gibson, M., 2016. Youtube and Bereavement Vlogging: Emotional Exchange between Strangers. *Journal of Sociology*, 52 (4), 631–645.

Godfrey, C., 2018, The Griefbot That Could Change How We Mourn, *The Daily Beast*, January 12. Available at: www.thedailybeast.com/the-griefbot-that-could-change-how-we-mourn (accessed: 1 February 2018).

Graham, C., Arnold, M., Kohn, T. and Gibbs, M. R., 2015. Gravesites and Websites: A Comparison of Memorialization. *Visual Studies*, 30 (1), 37–53.

Greenfield, A., 2006. *Everyware: The Dawning Age of Ubiquitous Computing*. Berkeley: New Riders.

Howarth, G., 2000. Dismantling the Boundaries between Life and Death. *Mortality* 5 (2), 127–138.

Kasket, E., 2012. Continuing Bonds in the Age of Social Networking: Facebook as a Modern-Day Medium. *Bereavement Care*, 31 (2), 62–69.

Klass, D., 2006. Continuing conversations about continuing bonds. *Death Studies* 30 (9), 843–858.

208 *Amanda Lagerkvist*

Klass, D. and Walter T., 2001. Processes of grieving: how bonds are continued. *In:* M. Stroebe, R. Hansson, W. Stroebe, & H. Schut, eds., *Handbook of Bereavement Research: Consequences, Coping, and Care.* Washington DC: American Psychological Association, 431–448.

Kneese, T. and Peters, B., 2017. Afterlife Imaginaries 1844/2044: Technologies for the Future in Silicon Valley and Mormon Theology. Paper presented at the DIGMEX Conference 'Digital Existence II: Precarious Media Life,' The Sigtuna Foundation, Sweden, October 30–November 1, 2017.

Lagerkvist, A., 2014. The Netlore of the Infinite: Death (and beyond) in the Digital Memory Ecology. *The New Review of Hypermedia and Multimedia*, 21 (1–2), Online first December 10, 2014.

Lagerkvist, A., 2016. Existential Media: Toward a Theorization of Digital Thrownness. *New Media & Society*, Online first June 13, 2016.

Lagerkvist, A., 2017. The Media End: Digital Afterlife Agencies and Techno-Existential Closure. *In:* A. Hoskins, ed. *Digital Memory Studies.* New York: Routledge, 48–84.

Lagerkvist, A. and Andersson, Y., 2017. The Grand Interruption: Death Online and Mediated Lifelines of Shared Vulnerability. *Feminist Media Studies*, Online first June 7, 2017.

Maddrell, A., 2012. Online Memorials: The Virtual as the New Vernacular. *Bereavement Care*, 31 (2), 46–54.

Markham, A., 2017. Echolocating the Self: A Granular Metaphor for Digital Technology as Tool, Place and Way of Being, Paper presented at the DIGMEX-conference 'Digital Existence II: Precarious Media Life,' The Sigtuna Foundation, Sweden, October 30–November 1, 2017.

Partridge, C., 2005. *The Re-Enchantment of the West, Vol 2: Alternative Spiritualities, Sacralization, Popular Culture and Occulture*, London: T&T Clark International.

Peters, J. D., 1999. *Speaking into the Air: A History of the Idea of Communication.* Chicago, IL: University of Chicago Press.

Peters, J. D., 2015. *The Marvelous Clouds: Towards a Philosophy of Elemental Media.* Chicago, IL: University of Chicago Press.

Rotman, B., 2007. Ghost Effects. *Differences*, 18 (1), 53–86.

Ruin, H., 2015. Life after Death, Paper presented at the conference Human Existence as Movement, Patočka's Existential Phenomenology and Its Political Dimension, IWM, June 3–5, 2014. Available at: www.iwm.at/transit/transit-online/life-death/ (accessed: 5 November 2017).

Ryan, J., 2008. The Virtual Campfire: An Ethnography of Online Social Networking. MA diss., Wesleyan University. Available at: www.thevirtualcampfire.org/virtual campfire.htm (accessed: 3 December 2013).

Schwartz, M., 2015. *Dead Matter: The Meaning of Iconic Corpses.* Minneapolis: University of Minnesota Press.

Sconce, J., 2000. *Haunted Media: Electronic Presence from Telegraphy to Television.* Durham, NC: Duke University Press.

Scott, L., 2015. *The Four-Dimensional Human: Ways of Being in the Digital World.* New York: W.W. Norton & Company.

Smith, Z., 2010. Generation Why? *New York Review of Books* [online] 25 November 2010. Available at: www.nybooks.com/articles/2010/11/25/generation-why/ (accessed: 16 May 2016).

Staley, E., 2014. Messaging the Dead: Social Network Sites and Theologies of Afterlife. *In:* C. M. Moreman and A. D. Lewis, eds. *Digital Death: Mortality and beyond in the Digital Age.* Santa Barbara: Praeger, 9–22.

The internet is always awake 209

Stolow, J., ed. 2013a. *Deus in Machina: Religion, Technology and the Things in-between*. New York: Fordham University Press.

Stolow, J., 2013b. The Spiritual Nervous System: Reflections on a Magnetic Cord Designed for Spirit Communication. *In:* J. Stolow ed. *Deus in Machina: Religion, Technology and the Things In-between*. New York: Fordham University Press, 83–113.

Tucker, A., 2014. Virtually Dead: The Extension of Social Agency to Corpses and the Dead on Facebook. *Honors Theses*. 53, College of Saint Benedict/Saint John's University. Available at: https://digitalcommons.csbsju.edu/honors_theses/53 (accessed: 1 October 2017).

Veale, K., 2004. Online Memorialisation: The Web as a Collective Memorial Landscape for Remembering the Dead. *Fibreculture*, 3. Available at: http://three.fibre culturejournal.org/fcj-014-online-memorialisationthe-web-as-a-collective-memo rial-landscape-forremembering-the-dead/ (accessed: 10 November 2017).

Verdery, K., 1999. *The Political Lives of Dead Bodies, Reburial and Post Socialist Change*. New York: Columbia University Press.

Walter, T., 1996. A New Model of Grief: Bereavement and Biography. *Mortality*, 1 (1), 7–25.

Walter, T., 2011. Angels Not Souls: Popular Religion in the Online Mourning for British Celebrity Jade Goody. *Religion*, 41 (1), 29–51.

Walter, T., 2015. Communication Media and the Dead: From the Stone Age to Facebook. *Mortality*, 20 (3), 215–232.

Walter, T., 2016. The Dead Who Become Angels: Bereavement and Vernacular Religion in the 21st Century. *OMEGA: Journal of Death & Dying*, 73 (1), 3–28.

Walter, T., 2018. The Pervasive Dead, *Mortality*. doi:10.1080/13576275.2017. 1415317.

Walter, T., Hourizi, R., Moncur, W. and Pitsillides, S., 2011/2012. Does the Internet Change How We Die and Mourn? *OMEGA: Journal of Death & Dying*, 64 (4), 275–302.

Young, C. and Light, D., 2013. Corpses, Dead Body Politics and Agency in Human Geography: Following the Corpse of Dr. Petru Groza. *Transactions of the Institute of British Geographers*, 38 (1), 135–148.

10 Digital rituals and the quest for existential security

Johanna Sumiala

The Charlie Hebdo attack as a disruption of existential security

The attack on Charlie Hebdo that occurred in Paris in 2015 was instant global news and consumed the digital media landscape, as the massacre in the office of this satirical magazine brought the horror and terror of the world to the mobile screens of the global public. This realization was forced on us only minutes after the tragic event unfolded at 10 Rue Nicols-Appert. During the following three days, digital media outlets were devoted to news of the attack, to the ensuing manhunt and eventually to the killing of the shooters. This digitalized horror, which interrupted people's everyday routines on a global scale, also shook their sense of existential security (Lagerkvist 2013, 2016) and turned them into digital witnesses (see, e.g., Chouliaraki 2015; Frosh and Pinchevski 2008) who felt vulnerable in the face of mad, terroristic violence. In this context, a ritual response developed within the digital media environment, as professional news sources and ordinary media users alike began to publish, post, share and circulate messages of public mourning and commemoration; through these messages, people sought to pay tribute to the victims and expressed support for the value of freedom of expression, which many felt was threatened by the attack (Niemeyer 2016; Sumiala et al. 2016).

In this chapter, I build on the premise that death rituals performed and experienced in the digital media play a significant role in the social construction of death in the present mediatized world (Sumiala 2013). In this new circumstance of what we may term "media death" (Sumiala forthcoming), old social theories on death, developed in the pre-digital age, are insufficiently equipped to grasp the current condition (cf. Hviid 2017; Walter 2007). In media and communication studies, research on journalism, popular culture and death online has provided valuable empirical knowledge on death in the media; however, existing literature typically lacks any comprehensive theory on the role or place of death rituals in today's media-saturated life (cf. Van Brussel and Carpentier 2014).

The aim of this chapter is to contribute to the study of death in contemporary mediatized society. I apply a media anthropological approach to the analysis and place special focus on the ritualization of death in digital media.

In brief, media anthropology is best described as an approach that takes the middle ground between media and cultural studies and anthropology of modern societies, often using the tools of ethnography to study the interplay between the media, symbols, rituals and myths, as well as people who use the media (Sumiala 2013, p. 2). Media anthropologists, thus, are interested in the role and place of media in producing, shaping and maintaining symbolic order in contemporary mediatized societies, as well as in the role and place of individuals within that process. Furthermore, media anthropologists want to understand how media connect people or drive individuals apart in today's digital condition, or how people use and interpret media in building an understanding of the present media-saturated world. Many media anthropologists emphasize symbolic dimensions in the present media life (see, e.g., Rothenbuhler and Coman 2005). This media life, according to media anthropologists' understanding, is constructed around sharing, circulating and following rituals, media events, images, myths and stories constructed and mediated by the digital media. Through their analyses of these rituals, events and images and stories, media anthropologists aim to understand how media produce and shape social reality and how we share in that reality.

In what follows I will examine those ritual practices that emerge in relation to media death. As anthropologist Nigel Barley (1995, p. 151) argues, "Death does not just exist. In order to have coherence and to find its place, it has to be integrated into a wider scheme of things". Elsewhere, he claims, "death is always part of a more general vision of life. The opposite is less often true. What is supposed to be a window on eternity becomes a looking glass in which we see ourselves" (Barley 1995, p. 11). Rituals, I argue, are the key cultural and social practice through which individuals and communities process, negotiate and integrate mortality in life. The rich anthropological literature on death rituals in society provides valuable tools for rethinking, elaborating on and reflecting upon those fundamental processes in the present digital world and for helping us to better understand how death is constructed in the present digital life (e.g., Metcalf and Huntington 1997; Myerhoff 1984).

In "Death in Due Time: Construction of Self and Culture in Ritual Drama", Barbara Myerhoff (1984) describes the complex interplay between ritual and death; this interplay is, she writes, a response to the sense of fundamental uncertainty that we experience in the face of death. Myerhoff (1984, p. 151) further underlines the importance of ritual in "all areas of uncertainty, anxiety, impotence, and disorder"; in her view, the repetitive nature of ritual provides "a message of pattern and predictability". Ritual invites individuals and communities to engage with symbols and symbolic communication, thus bidding people to participate in spreading messages that we might not otherwise even conceive of or believe. Consequently, our "actions lull our critical faculties, persuading us with evidence from our own physiological experience until we are convinced" (Myerhoff 1984, p. 151).

212 Johanna Sumiala

In these moments, rational order gives way to the symbolic, the mythical and the spiritual. At the heart of Myerhoff's argument is the idea that in situations of uncertainty rituals provide emotional, symbolical and mythical tools that can be used to cope with the existential fear of annihilation that is triggered by thoughts of death (see also Metcalf and Huntington 1997).

To further develop Myerhoff's ideas in light of the present digital age, we need to better understand the interplay between ritual and digital media. Drawing on Amanda Lagerkvist's (2016) work on 'existential media', I approach digital media in this chapter as a type of *momentous media* (Lagerkvist 2016, p. 11) – a form of existential media that is created in those exceptional moments "when people share and explore existential issues in connection with loss and trauma online" (Lagerkvist 2016, p. 2).

This is to say that I am interested in the inner workings of the death ritual in a Janus-faced context, in which digital media simultaneously thrust the horrors of Paris into the mundane realities of the public while also providing them with a platform, a means of coping with this condition and of helping people to regain a sense of existential security during such a dire situation. However, as Lagerkvist (2013, p. 5, cf. 2014) reminds us, existential security is never unconditionally realized and thus should be thought of as a *quest* rather than as an actuality. To this end, Lagerkvist (2013, p. 5) maintains:

> Set within a liquid modern frame of the digital age, where constant flux is the norm, existential security adds to this emphasis on the social, individual and material the prospects for individuals to integrate their being-in-the-world into a meaningful unity, involving a sense of purpose or direction in life or a sense of cohesion and dignity. In other words, existential security involves the extent to which experiences can be integrated into a functional meaning-making system, which can involve both this-worldly and other-worldly experiences of profundity *or* spirituality . . . In addition, existential security is not solely an individual quest (although it can be), but also a matter of seeking meaning and continuity through/as inspired fellowship – that is, through communitas.

This mode of thinking about existential security in a digital age invites us to reframe our conception of death rituals in a digital context, prompting us to view them as processional rather than unchanging or stable (hence the concept of ritualization, which to my understanding refers to the death ritual as a process), as collective rather than individual, as forever ambivalent rather than ultimately fixed and closed in meaning and outcome.

In the seminal works of van Gennep (1909/1960) and of Victor Turner (1969), death rituals are thought of as *rites of passage* or *life crisis rituals*. Whereas van Gennep emphasized ritual as a *process* rather than a representation, Turner expanded upon this idea and viewed death rituals as manifestations of *transformative practice*. Contemporary ritual scholar Bruce Kapferer (2004, p. 38) maintains that Turner understood the ritual process

Digital rituals 213

as something more than merely a machine for social reproduction or for maintaining the cultural categories of meaning (Turner 1969). Instead, Kapferer believes, Turner concentrated on the process of ritual as the generative source of the invention of new cultural categories. Kapferer (2004, p. 38) explains:

> The powerful argument that he [Turner[1]] began was that processes observable in ritual action – especially those that are creative, generative and innovative – are constantly repeated (regardless of whether or not they are recognized as being ritual) in the contexts of major moments of social and political change. Furthermore, they often dramatically appear at transformative moments.

When considering death rituals according to this Turnerian framework, we find that in those exceptional moments when momentous media are called into being (e.g., Lagerkvist 2016, p. 11), digital death rituals are seen as transformative cultural and social practices that have the potential to create new meaning in the midst of chaos caused by the loss of life; such rituals may bring people together (in liminal communitas; see, e.g., Turner 1969) and help the living to transfer the deceased into a new category of social life, whether that be as ancestors, spirits, angels, memories or immortals. In helping to reorganize the social relationships between the living and the dead, death rituals can create a new social life around death and can thus help the public to cope with the unpredictability and vulnerability of life (see Metcalf and Huntington 1997; Davies 2002).

The idea of ritual as a transformative practice resonates with Kapferer's (2004) work on ritual, imagination and phantasmagoric spaces. Kapferer (2004, p. 47) explains:

> A phantasmagoric space [is] a dynamic that allows for all kinds of potentialities of human experience to take shape and form. It is, in effect, a self-contained imaginal space – at once a construction, but a construction that enables participants to break free from the constraints or determinations of everyday life and even from the determinations of the constructed ritual virtual space itself. In this sense, the virtual of ritual may be described as a determinant form that is paradoxically anti-determinant, able to realize human constructive agency. The phantasmagoric space of ritual virtuality may be conceived not only as a space whose dynamic interrupts prior determining processes but also as a space in which participants can reimagine (and redirect or reorient themselves) into the everyday circumstances of life.

In Kapferer's thinking, the creative grounds of the phantasmagoric open to the imaginal, to the imaginaries through which worlds are made, but also to the imaginaries through which worlds are altered in concert with the living

214 *Johanna Sumiala*

(Handelman 2004b, p. 214). In this way of thinking about death rituals, a scholarly focus is first dedicated to the actual ritual work in digital media; only after that is focus shifted to its meanings or functions in a given context. Handelman (2004b, p. 213) calls this perspective a phenomenological approach to the study of ritual. Such an approach places special emphasis on the phenomenality of the phenomenon itself and not on its surroundings; it requires us to study ritual in its own right, if you will (Handelman 2004a, pp. 3–4).

In digital media, the phenomenality of ritual cannot be considered without also contemplating the concept of the virtual. Kapferer draws a distinction between his use of the concept of the virtual in studies of ritual and "the virtuality of cyber technology" (Kapferer 2004, p. 37). However, I would like to suggest an approach in which digital media considers the potential of the phantasmagoric space – in which it is open to the phenomenality of ritual and the related imaginal dimension of the digital ritualization (e.g., those ritual processes) that surrounds death. According to this line of argument, the rituals of death are perceived to be activities that are profoundly spatial and imaginal. Inspired by the work of Tom Boellstorff (2008, p. 5), I wish to argue that not only do digital rituals borrow assumptions from 'real life' rituals, digital rituals can also show us how our 'real life' rituals have been 'virtual' all along (cf. Grimes 2014).

In this chapter, I draw on these perspectives – that death rituals are motivated by a fear of annihilation (Myerhoff 1984) and that rituals have significant transformative and imaginal potential to help individuals and communities cope with that fear and to create new life (Turner 1969; Kapferer 2004) – in light of the framework of existential media (Lagerkvist 2016, 2013). I illustrate the existential dimensions of the inner workings of death rituals by investigating the ritual practices of mourning and by paying tribute to the victims, as identified in digital media, of the Charlie Hebdo attack. In this digital ethnographic analysis, I focus on the rituals of mourning and commemoration, and analyze in detail the ritual performances involving memes, slogans and hashtags (e.g., *Je suis Charlie*) that spread across a variety of digital media platforms.[2] These types of rituals (mourning and commemoration) and the associated example (*Je suis Charlie*) were selected based on their prominence and status in the empirical material. The analysis of this empirical material consisted of three interconnected phases: (1) digital ethnography collected at the time of the incident provided the initial outline of the event; (2) automated content analysis and social network analytics of the available quantitative social media data were used to construct the digital field for this research (Boumans and Trilling 2016); and (3) digital ethnography allowed for an in-depth interpretation of what (substance/content) had been circulating and how this material constituted links and connections between the participants and the digital media platforms (cf. Sumiala et al. 2016, p. 8). This chapter draws on the findings of the third phase and places special emphasis on the ritualization of public

Digital rituals 215

mourning by examining the prevalent memes, slogans and the *Je suis Charlie* hashtag. In conclusion, I seek to rethink the dilemma of existential security and the ritual search for order and predictability in the context of liquid digital media.

Death rituals in digital media

In this chapter, I view digital death rituals as life-crisis rituals (see, e.g., van Gennep 1909/1960, Turner 1969). In this line of thinking, digital death rituals share many similarities with the death rituals that were performed in previous 'offline' contexts. Both online and offline death rituals consist of elements of symbolic communication, require participant involvement, are carried out in certain times and spaces and, when successful, have an impact (ritual efficacy) on the lives of participants (see, e.g., Sumiala 2013). What is characteristic of the digital death ritual is that it appears in a very particular context, which causes us to expand our conceptions of time, space, participation and scale into something more fluid, mobile, multi-temporal, multi-sited and, hence, rather heterogeneous (Sumiala 2014).

However, we can still identify certain elements of linearity when thinking of digital death rituals as life-crisis rituals. The first phase of such a ritual is rupture – the sudden, violent public awareness of an unexpected loss of life (Turner 1969). In terms of digital media, this sense of rupture is brought to the public in the form and shape of terrorist-related news. Such news travels rapidly from one digital media platform to another, thus affecting mainstream media and social media alike. In the digital media world, our sense of existential security (Lagerkvist 2013) is shaken by the speed of circulation and the volume of such news. Digital media thus makes disruption a digitally shared social reality, though it also begins to provide a means of coping with the situation; this brings us to the second phase – the liminal stage. During this phase, emotionally laden symbolic responses are activated within the digital media landscape; these responses, in turn, begin to affect the global news media and ordinary media users alike.

One significant aspect of recent digital death rituals concerns how professional media outlets report on the ways in which people in different parts of the world ritualize the death event (Sumiala 2013). Moreover, during this phase, media users typically gather together in digital media forums to express the emotions that have been stirred in them by the news of terror. This gathering can come in the form of posting, sharing and circulating still and moving images of symbols of grief, such as flowers, candles, condolence notes, stuffed animals and pictures of the deceased (e.g., Brubaker et al. 2013; Gotved 2014). Formulations such as RIP (rest in peace) or 'tribute' are typically added to the images to communicate a sense of mourning. Additionally, ritual practices of commemoration are closely tied to mourning in the digital media environment. One particular cultural form of commemoration (and mourning) is to create YouTube videos that feature the deceased.

216 *Johanna Sumiala*

These videos typically tell the story of the life of the deceased by highlighting certain moments in his or her life's narrative.

However, the liminal phase is not only about expressing emotions of solidarity and empathy for the victims as a form of mourning, paying tribute or commemoration. As a transformative period, the liminal phase can also offer one the opportunity to express anger or even malicious enjoyment at another's death (see, e.g., Sumiala 2014). In fact, rituals of resistance often apply the communication strategies of other ritual forms, such as posting images and messages and making videos, though this content is transformed to indicate the opposite of mourning and tribute; instead, these practices are intended to mock and disrespect the deceased. The liminal phase has its climax in the ritual performance of a funeral, which in the case of considerable public interest can become a globally ritualized media event (see, e.g., Dayan and Katz 1992).

The funeral moves the life-crisis ritual into a third phase. It is a ritual performance that helps the public to transform the deceased into a new form. The deceased is buried and given a new identity in the social reality of the community; this identity can manifest in the form of a memory, spirit, ancestor or immortal (Davies 2002; Metcalf and Huntington 1997). In the digital media landscape, funerals might be performed publicly, and multiple actors may be involved. In short, the mass media broadcasting notion of communication as 'from one to many' (e.g., a funeral is broadcast by a national television agency to a national audience, which watches the ritual unfold on their TV screens) has been transformed into 'from many to many' (Castells 2009). Thus, not only the mainstream media, but also those people who participate in a funeral, either at the site or in other physically or virtually connected locations (on streets, outside the space where the ceremony is being held or anywhere that is digitally connected to the funeral site) may contribute to this ritual performance by posting and commenting on the event via their mobile gadgets. This multiplication of the number of ceremonial participants able to take part in the event also brings about a polyphony of interpretations regarding what is occurring and what it signifies. Not all voices have similar power, but the potential for contradictory interpretations of this ritual act of granting the deceased a new identity also makes the rite unpredictable and difficult to control. In the following sections, I empirically analyze the inner workings of these three phases (e.g., rupture, liminality and regaining a new order) in the context of the Charlie Hebdo attack.

Ritualization of mourning following the Charlie Hebdo attack

First phase: disruption

The Charlie Hebdo attack disturbed the routine order of life in Paris in a violent manner, thus triggering disruption. The attack occurred at approximately 11:30 A.M. on 7 January 2015; on that Wednesday morning, French-Algerian brothers Said and Cherif Kouachi attacked the headquarters of the satirical newspaper *Charlie Hebdo*, killing 12 people (including cartoonists, columnists and other workers and visitors who were present in the building at the time) in the resulting massacre. This attack was followed by a massive three-day manhunt, which involved hostage situations and an additional attack in a Jewish supermarket (which left four people dead) perpetrated by another gunman named Amedy Coulibaly. Eventually, the police special forces killed all three perpetrators.

The brutality of these attacks, and the breakdown of daily order in the lives of Parisians, caused anxiety among the people who witnessed these events unfold in Paris; however, unease was also felt in the digital media world. News of the attack broke almost immediately. Live material of the shootings began to circulate within digital media, as ordinary media user Jordi Mir had been at the site and had witnessed the killing of Muslim police officer Ahmed Merabet, and had captured the scene with his mobile phone camera. Mir recorded the progress of events and relayed how the perpetrators escaped the building, executed Merabet and drove off in their car. Mir posted the video on Facebook, though he quickly came to regret his decision and removed the video. His removal, however, came too late, as the video had immediately gone viral; his live recording of the killing spread throughout professional mainstream media and social media platforms alike. The widely circulated killing of Merabet provided visual evidence of the horrific nature of terrorism for the eyes of a global audience. Moreover, the resulting hostage situations inspired heavy digital mediatization; people were able to witness live reporting on the hostage drama, as both the perpetrators and those taken hostage utilized digital media to make contact with the 'outer world' and its reporters (Sumiala et al. 2018, forthcoming). Concurrent with the attacks, various ritual responses began to emerge in the digital media landscape.

Second phase: liminality

One of the most deeply ritualized messages found in the immediate public response to the attack was a slogan and a meme: *Je suis Charlie*. French journalist and artist Joaquim Roncin first created this meme for *Stylist Magazine* less than 20 minutes after the attack; his creation featured the words *Je suis Charlie* written against a black background (see Figure 10.1). According to BBC News (3 January 2016), this image was used 1.5 million times on the day of its publication and roughly 6 million times during the next week on Twitter, Instagram and Facebook. Additionally, the hashtag #jesuischarlie became the most tweeted message in the history of Twitter (Sumiala et al. 2016). The meme and related hashtag travelled quickly from one digital platform to another, and both were used by a countless number of media users, professional and non-professional alike, for diverse purposes in relation to the attack.

218 *Johanna Sumiala*

Figure 10.1 Roncin's first tweet.

Characteristic of digital media, the meme was transformed during its travels across various digital platforms, and it soon became associated with various actors, messages, symbols and images that were used to comment on the assaults and the resulting public reaction. I argue that this meme, with its slogan and related hashtag (#jesuischarlie), was the most powerful element in the digital ritualization of death in the case of Charlie Hebdo (see also Todd 2015). The digital rituals of mourning, grief, paying tribute and commemoration were applied, used and centered around this very meme, slogan and hashtag.

The content of these symbols and the meanings associated with this meme, slogan and hashtag varied massively across digital media. Some repetitive connections were made to other symbols, including a pen, the French flag, the Eiffel Tower and popular cultural figures such as the cartoon character Charlie Brown (see e.g. Figure 10.2). Additionally, the meme was typically posted along with symbols of grief and mourning such as candles and flowers; moreover, pictures of the deceased (of the cartoonists in particular) were given visibility during the circulation of the ritual message of *Je suis Charlie*.

Digital rituals 219

Figure 10.2 The *Je suis Charlie* meme makes reference to Edvard Munch's famous painting *The Scream*.[3]

The message travelled quickly from one digital media platform to another and thus led to the advent of multiple ritual encounters with numerous digitally connected media users. A Facebook community named *Je suis Charlie* was established to commemorate and pay respect to the victims. On this site, people shared images and messages of solidarity with the victims. Indeed, the *Charlie Hebdo* magazine itself featured the slogan on its website. The search

220   Johanna Sumiala

term "Je suis Charlie" results in a rich variety of YouTube videos that feature the slogan. The mourning videos that were created around *Je suis Charlie* typically include musical compositions that feature still and moving images of the various sites of commemoration as well as messages of condolence. One can also find news items written by professional media houses as well as vlogs made by ordinary YouTubers that feature this slogan. Many of these videos circulated materials of public mourning, but some also commented on the events. The tone of these news videos and commentaries varied from relatively neutral reporting to explicit expressions of solidarity and compassion to criticisms of the event and its ritualized media coverage. One of the most prominent ritual images that circulated across multiple digital media platforms was an image of people gathering in public places such as the Place de la Republique in Paris, Trafalgar Square in London, Brandenburg Gate in Berlin and various French embassies across the world; across these images, the placate "Je suis Charlie" was written in many different ways, styles and languages.

Although heterogeneous in their associations, we can identify a particular emphasis on the death of the cartoonists. In numerous news stories tied to the meme, slogan and hashtag of *Je suis Charlie*, the murdered cartoonists are associated with special values. These individuals were made into iconic symbols, into advocates of the French Republican values of *liberté, égalité, fraternité* (freedom, equality and brotherhood); they were also recognized as embodying European culture and Western heritage. Throughout French history, political satirical newspapers and magazines have played an important role in maintaining the value of freedom of expression by pushing boundaries and testing the limits of this freedom using the tools of humor and laughter (cf. Todd 2015). The *Charlie Hebdo* magazine was granted a special position within this tradition as a result of the news stories that followed the attack. For example, on the day of the attack (7 January 2015), the *Guardian* published an article titled "Charlie Hebdo attack: cartoonists show solidarity with Paris victims" and circulated posts featuring tweets of solidarity that were written by cartoonists across the world. On 3 January 2016, on the eve of the first anniversary of the attack, the BBC interviewed Roncin, who first created the meme and put it into circulation. He was asked to reflect on why he posted the *Je suis Charlie* image and to offer an explanation for the massive public reaction that followed:

> "I was deeply shocked, but I wasn't frightened" . . . The slogan took off because "we're trying to feel a community," he says. "It is very reassuring to be all together whenever something horrible happens." . . . for . . . Joaquim Roncin, the meaning of his slogan is still straightforward. "*Je suis Charlie* is just an expression of solidarity, of peace," he says. "And that's all".[4]

However, not every public voice agreed with this interpretation. For example, *Al Jazeera English* published an article (on 10 January 2015) on its opinion page titled "Charlie Hebdo and western liberalism: Islam has been unfairly criticized and ridiculed in the west for centuries"; in this article, the author condemns uncritical attempts to defend freedom of expression in the West, stating that these efforts are conducted in such a manner that only serves to underline the West's long history of racism against Muslims. The author, Abdullah Al-Arian, argues:

> French society – and indeed, the global reaction – has been united in its condemnation of the attack, and French authorities mobilised the full strength of the state's law enforcement agencies to track down the assailants, who were killed after a standoff with police on Friday. As with most incidents of violence involving Muslims, however, the ensuing public discussion has revolved largely around resolute vows to uphold a fundamental value of western civilisation – the freedom of expression – and degenerated into recriminations about Islam's purported assault on that very freedom. As a result, the natural expressions of grief and sympathy on behalf of the victims have taken on the added quality of high-minded liberal support for the content of the Charlie Hebdo cartoons, irrespective of the publication's history of racism towards Muslims and people of colour.[5]

In global news stories and comments regarding the attack, the *Charlie Hebdo* magazine was sometimes perceived as a racist and misogynist outlet that often used its mandate to mock, offend and harm groups and people who do not hold positions of power in society, such as ethnic and religious minorities (cf. Todd 2015).

What is more, the widely shared ritualization of the *Je suis Charlie* message underlined not only the importance of this death event per se, but also the distinct significance of particular victims (namely the cartoonists) as compared to other casualties of the attack. Although slogans such as *Je ne suis pas Charlie*, *Je suis Juif*, *Je suis Ahmed* and *Je suis Kouachi* were also ritualized in digital media following the attacks, the slogan *Je suis Charlie* was clearly the most popular message to be found in the ritual activity of tweeting. Figure 10.3 illustrates the explicit difference in the popularity of several of the aforementioned hashtags.

With regard to the liminal phase that followed this violent attack, we may argue that the massive ritualization surrounding the meme, slogan and hashtag *Je suis Charlie* transformed the moment into an "existential momentous condition", to use Lagerkvist's (2016) terminology. In this exceptional, highly intensified moment, the practice of posting, sharing and commenting on this meme, slogan and hashtag opened up a possibility for the public to participate in what Kapferer (2004) describes as a phantasmagoric and imaginal space in which participants can reimagine and reorient themselves to a new condition after their everyday order has been violently disrupted – and after this disruption has been brought into their own reality via their digital

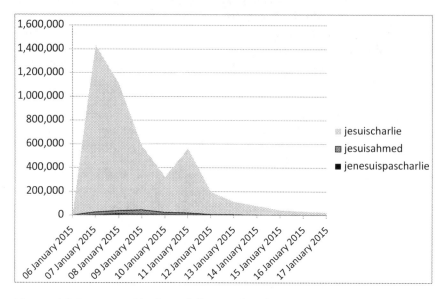

Figure 10.3 Instances of hashtags following the Charlie Hebdo attack.

screens. In such a condition, the ritualization of mourning, grief, paying tribute and commemoration that was performed via the sharing and circulation of the *Je suis Charlie* message can be best characterized as a multisited (simultaneously addressing many digital platforms) and heterogeneous practice (involving a variety of activities and associated meanings). As a fluid and mobile space, the digital media environment both encourages this type of multitude and volume in ritual activity and also causes the practice of ritualization to become unstable and unpredictable, as there is no single ritual pattern or fixed interpretation available to all. This, I argue, may have consequences for the third phase of digital mourning as a life-crisis ritual – that is, to regain existential security and confirm the continuity of life.

Third phase: regaining existential security

The digital ritualization surrounding the Charlie Hebdo attack was carried out on multiple levels and served various purposes. Digital media material suggests that the rituals of mourning and commemoration that were symbolized by the posting, sharing and circulation of the slogan, meme and hashtag *Je suis Charlie* achieved special significance in this digital ritualization process in the wake of the attack. I argue that those digital practices played an important role as cultural communicative responses to the fear, anxiety and disturbance that was spawned by the unexpected and violent deaths. The intense and highly performative circulation of the *Je suis Charlie* message functioned as a transformative practice, as the public and the professional news media attempted to cope with the violent situation and bring order to the disorder and confusion. In the liminal moment after the killings and before the publication of a new *Charlie Hebdo* issue (called the "survival issue"), public mourning and commemoration helped audiences to engage symbolically with the emotions that were triggered by terror and to develop a means of overcoming those fears. These ritual actions also gained more significance as funerary rituals were, in many cases, held in private, hidden from the global public eye.

And yet, we should not assume any simple unity in this attempt to regain existential security and order. In the digital media landscape, this attack touched a highly fragmented global audience that was affected by the event in different, and even contradictory, ways. As previously discussed, counter voices also appeared in the discussion; many of these voices claimed that the ritualization surrounding the death of the cartoonists served to bring about unfair criticism of the world's Muslims (see, e.g., Al Jazeera English 10 January 2015).

Furthermore, we should not accept any simple harmony, nor a unanimity in interpretation or *meaning*, regarding the ritualized *Je suis Charlie* message that circulated in the wake of the killings. The multitude of voices active in these death rituals must be understood in light of the fluid, mobile and ever-changing nature of digital media as an existential site of ritualization. Accordingly, we are left in a state of ambiguity concerning the digital ritualization of death (the Charlie Hebdo attack is a case in point here). Even considering the phantasmagoric and imaginal condition of digital ritualization, in which new creative practices and forms are created to respond collectively to violence and shock, we must acknowledge that the idea of regaining order may, at times, conflict with the liquid condition of digital media, which is constantly in flux.

Conclusions

This dilemma – a ritual search for order in the unpredictability of digital media – is at the very core of this issue as we attempt to understand the quest for existential security in our present digital age. As per this mode of thought, the quest for existential security via the digital ritualization of death is constantly embedded, in one way or another, in the horror, pain and suffering experienced by people as they attempt to search for meaning and to cope with the vulnerable reality of life that has been thrust upon them via their digital devices. As Nigel Barley (1995, p. 151) puts it: "Death does not just exist. In order to have coherence and to find its place, it has to be integrated into a wider scheme of things" (p. 151). Speaking of intellectual schemes, media anthropology provides one key framework for the analysis. It encourages us to remain attentive and sensitive to those signals of vulnerability in the digital media and the ways in which we symbolically try to manage them in digital ritual practices. It is in this way that media

224 *Johanna Sumiala*

anthropology keeps us vigilant in our search for meaning in the present condition of fluid social life.

Notes

1 Added by JS.
2 The empirical material for this analysis was collected for a research project titled *Je suis Charlie – The symbolic battle and struggle over attention*. The project combined quantitative big data analysis with qualitative digital ethnography. The digital data consists of 5,159,097 tweets, of which 28.83% were original tweet posts and 71.17% were "engagements" (which here refers to re-tweets and/or comments). The hashtags used to collect data were: *je suis Charlie, je suis Ahmed, je ne suis pas Charlie, #jesuischarlie, #jesuisahmed, #jenesuispascharlie*; the languages included in the selection of data were French, English and Arabic. The collected empirical material covers the period between 7 January and 16 January 2015, which marks the timeframe between the beginning of the attack on the *Charlie Hebdo* headquarters (which occurred on 7 January) to two days following the publication of the first *Charlie Hebdo* issue after the attack (which was issued on 14 January). This survivors' memorial sold a total of 795 million copies (the typical circulation of a *Charlie Hebdo* paper is roughly 60,000 copies).
3 Paris 16, Wikimedia Commons CC BY-SA 4.0, via Wikimedia Commons License. Retrieved from http://creativecommons.org/licenses/by-sa/4.0.
4 M. Devichand, Mukul, 'How the World Was Changed by the Slogan "Je Suis Charlie",' *BBC News* (3 January 2016). Retrieved from www.bbc.com/news/blogs-trending-35108339
5 A. Al-Arian, 'Charlie Hebdo and Western Liberalism: Islam Has Been Unfairly Criticised and Ridiculed in the West for Centuries,' *Al Jazeera* (10 January 2015). Retrieved 25 January 2017 www.aljazeera.com/indepth/opinion/2015/01/charlie-hebdo-twilight-western-201511063740106115.html

Bibliography

Al-Arian, A., 2015. Charlie Hebdo and Western Liberalism: Islam Has Been Unfairly Criticised and Ridiculed in the West for Centuries. *Al Jazeera* [online] 10 January 2015. Available at: www.aljazeera.com/indepth/opinion/2015/01/charlie-hebdo-twilight-western – 201511063740106115.html (accessed: 25 January 2017).

Barley, N., 1995. *Dancing on the Grave: Encounters with Death*. London: John Murray.

Boellstorff, T., 2008. *Coming of Age in Second Life: An Anthropologist Explores the Virtually Human*. Princeton, NJ: Princeton University Press.

Boumans, J. W. and Trilling, D., 2016. Taking Stock of the Toolkit. *Digital Journalism*, 4 (1), 8–23.

Brubaker, J. R., Hayes, G. R. and Dourish, P., 2013. Beyond the Grave: Facebook as a Site for the Expansion of Death and Mourning. *The Information Society: An International Journal*, 29 (3), 152–163.

Castells, M., 2009. *Communication Power*. Oxford: Oxford University Press.

Chouliaraki, L., 2015. Digital Witnessing in Conflict Zones: The Politics of Remediation. *Information, Communication & Society*, 18 (11), 1362–1377.

Davies, D., 2002. *Death, Ritual and Belief: The Rhetoric of Funerary Rites*. London: Continuum.

Dayan, D. and Katz, E., 1992. *Media Events: The Live Broadcasting of History*. Cambridge, MA: Harvard University Press.

Devichand, M., 2016. How the World Was Changed by the Slogan 'Je Suis Charlie.' *BBC News* [online] 3 January 2016. Available at: www.bbc.com/news/blogs-trending-35108339 (accessed: 5 May 2017).

Frosh, P. and Pinchevski, A. (eds.), 2008. *Media Witnessing: Testimony in the Age of Mass Communication*. Houndmills: Palgrave Macmillan.

Gani, A., 2015. Charlie Hebdo Attack: Cartoonists Show Solidarity with Paris Victims. *The Guardian* [online] 7 January 2015. Available at: www.theguardian.com/world/2015/jan/07/charlie-hebdo-attack-cartoonists-show-solidarity-victims (accessed: 5 May 2017).

Gennep, A. van, 1909/1960. *The Rites of Passage*. Chicago, IL: University of Chicago Press.

Gotved, S., 2014. Research Review: Death Online-alive and kicking! *Thantos*, 3 (1), 112–126.

Grimes, R. L., 2014. *The Craft of Ritual Studies*. Oxford: Oxford University Press.

Handelman, D., 2004a. Introduction: Why Ritual in Its Own Right? How So? *Social Analysis*, 48 (2), 1–32.

Handelman, D., 2004b. Epilogue: Toing and Froing the Social. *Social Analysis*, 48 (2), 213–214.

Hviid, M. (ed.), 2017. *Postmortal Society: Towards a Sociology of Immortality*. London: Routledge.

Kapferer, B., 2004. Ritual Dynamics and Virtual Practice: Beyond Representation and Meaning. *Social Analysis*, 48 (2), 35–54.

Lagerkvist, A., 2013. New Memory Cultures and Death: Existential Security in the Digital Memory Ecology. *Thanatos*, 2 (2), 1–17.

Lagerkvist, A., 2014. A Quest for *Communitas*: Rethinking Mediated Memory Existentially. *Nordicom Information*, 36 (2), 205–218.

Lagerkvist, A., 2016. Existential Media: Toward a Theorization of Digital Thrownness. *New Media and Society*, 19 (1), 96–110.

Metcalf, P. and Huntington, R., 1997. *Celebrations of Death: The Anthropology of Mortuary Ritual*. Cambridge, MA: Cambridge University Press.

Niemeyer, K., 2016. Les unes Internationales du 8 Janvier 2015. Entre Uniformité et Singularité. *In*: P. Lefébure and C. Sécail, eds. *Le Défi Charlie. Les medias à l'épreuve des attentas*. Paris: Lemieux Éditeur, 19–48.

Myerhoff, B., 1984. Death in due time: Construction of self and culture in ritual drama. *In*: J. J MacAloon, ed. *Rite, Drama, Festival, Spectacle: Rehearsals Toward a Theory of Cultural Performance*. Philadelphia, PA: Institute for the Study of Human Issues.

Rothenbuhler, E. W. and Coman, M., 2005. *Media Anthropology*. Thousand Oaks, CA: Sage.

Sumiala, J., 2013. *Media and Ritual: Death, Community and Everyday Life*: London: Routledge.

Sumiala, J., 2014. Mediatized Ritual: Expanding the Field in the Study of Media and Ritual. *Sociology Compass*, 8 (7), 939–947.

Sumiala, J., forthcoming. *Media Death: The Social Life of Public Loss in Ritual Events*. London: Routledge.

Sumiala, J., Tikka, M., Huhtamäki, J. and Valaskivi, K., 2016. #JeSuisCharlie: Towards a Multi-Method Study of Hybrid Media Events. *Cogito: Media and Communication*, 4 (4), 97–108.

226 *Johanna Sumiala*

Sumiala, J., Valaskivi, K., Tikka, M. and Huhtamäki, J., 2018. *Hybrid Media Event: Charlie Hebdo Attacks and the Global Circulation of Terrorist Violence*. Bingley, UK: Emerald.

Todd, E., 2015. *Who Is Charlie? Xenophobia and the New Middle Class*. Cambridge, UK: Polity Press.

Turner, V., 1969. *The Ritual Process: Structure and Anti-Structure*. London: Routledge and Kegan Paul.

Van Brussel, L. and Carpentier, N. (eds.), 2014. *The Social Construction of Death*. Houndmills: Palgrave MacMillan.

Walter, T., 2007. The Sociology of Death. *Sociology Compass*, 2 (1), 317–336.

11 Cybernetic animism
Non-human personhood and the internet

Devin Proctor

Being things

You and I have often been things among other things. If you have spent any time in the internet,[1] you may have experienced what I am calling *cybernetic animism*, a process whereby many in Western societies—children of Empire and Science—become accustomed to an ontology shared by many in the world, but denied by our own foundational systems of belief. Though there are myriad understandings of the term (see below), I am defining *animism* for our purposes as the recognition of some animating presence in non-human entities. Internet use places users in a context similar to animist experience: they occupy a meeting-space with others separated by physical space and often by time; furthermore, some of these others are *bots*—programs made to impersonate humans in digital settings—or self-running algorithms exerting agency and acting in supposedly "human" ways. Within these non-bodied spaces, self-identification does not depend on a biologically predetermined model.

In what follows, I will argue that participating in internet sociality allows users to experience and internalize an animistic mode of being-in-the-world. I explain this mode through the dual processes of autopoiesis and ontological filtering. But first, I will describe what I mean by cybernetic animism in the Heideggerian terms of this larger volume. Being-in-the-internet involves the internet's own *interneting* as an *existential a priori* (Heidegger 1996, p. 183), just as the world is constantly *worlding* and the things in it are constantly *thinging*. To *thing* as a verb is to Be in a way that fulfils the thing's part of the larger *worlding*.[2] This same concept applies to internet things. The affordances[3] constantly *afford*, and that is the manner of their *thinging*. Buttons are *buttoning*, pictures are *picturing*, and drop-down menus are *dropping-down* and *menuing*. At the same time, bots and algorithms are Being-in-the-internet in their own botic and algorithmic ways, *sorting, conversing, calculating, running, buying, selling, impersonating*. That said, bots and algorithms are usually understood as things, but not as things that can Be. This is the core of the cybernetic animist's environment. It involves the confluence of *thinging* and Being—the recognition that things are actively Being-in-the-internet around us, while also *thinging* as a part of the internet.

228 *Devin Proctor*

And so are we. As a parallel to the non-human persons of animist experience, we are among (and in fact are ourselves) Being things.

Otherkin

The concept of cybernetic animism comes out of my anthropological fieldwork with the Otherkin, a community of folks who identify "as non-human on a non-physical level, be it spiritually, psychologically, or both" (Therian-Kin Corner 2017). They recognize that their bodies are biologically human[4] but argue they also contain non-human aspects, manifest in non-material forms such as urges, dreams and memories. The entities represented in these forms can be native to the body, but can also come from external sources, both spatial and temporal: past lives, other dimensions, and works of fiction. The label Otherkin is often used as an umbrella term, but the community splits into two subsets: otherkin (lowercase "o"), who identify as beings that do not exist on Earth[5] (elves, dragons, demons, angels, fae, etc); and therians, who identify as animals that exist (or previously existed) on Earth such as wolves, sharks, saber-toothed cats, and otters (Lupa 2007). The Otherkin espouse an approach to existence at odds with contemporary modes of Being, marking a stark disavowal of the Cartesian mind/body dualism on which the West bases much of its understanding of what it means to be human. Current academic work either views Otherkin identification as a religious belief system based in fiction (Kirby 2008, 2013; Davidsen 2013, 2016; O'Callaghan 2015; Cusack 2016); as a neurological abnormality (Gerbasi et al. 2008; Probyn-Rapsey 2011; Grivell et al. 2014); or as an exercise in alternate epistemological formation (Laycock 2012; Robertson 2012, 2013; Johnston 2013; Shane 2014). I understand it, rather, as a form of animism. In an indigenous animist culture, the idea that a person is a wolf or demon might be taken as a matter of course. In the contemporary West, however, it is seen as cause for alarm, ridicule and pathologization, which explains why most Otherkin choose to keep their identification "in the closet" to colleagues, friends and often family. Being situated within societies that do not support animist ontologies leads the Otherkin toward mediating technologies (namely, the internet) to find others like themselves. Thus, most Otherkin sociality occurs in digital spaces.

The Otherkin have found each other and formed groups across the internet landscape, from text-based Internet Relay Chat (IRC) and newsgroup forums to 3D virtual environments to social media platforms. Affiliation with these groups has been growing at an increasing rate in the current digital paradigm of ubiquitous social media. The website *The Otherkin Community* [otherkincommunity.net] provides a relevant example, as it is a well-known and frequently visited site within the community, and, unlike social media networks or password-protected chat areas, it posts a tally of its membership. By the end of 2006—the year the site went live—it had 47 members. When I started working with the Otherkin in 2011, it was up to

1,500 members. As I am writing this in 2018, membership is over 5,500. This may seem like an exaggerated number of people who identify as fundamentally non-human, yet interlocutors of mine have estimated Otherkin membership as over 10,000, spread across different platforms and sites. The sharp increase in number has caused some friction within the community. Participants who self-identified as Otherkin before the rise of social networking sites like Reddit, Facebook and Tumblr bemoan how the younger, "Tumblr era" kin are "far too tolerant of people and don't stop to consider that some people really are lying about their experiences" (Dreamsinger 2012). While the Otherkin contest boundaries of viability and authenticity from within, they also must defend themselves from the apex predators of the internet: trolls. As the internet has facilitated communication between Otherkin and offered an outlet for community, it has also opened them up to criticism and outright aggression from many who question the validity of the concept of Otherkinity. Issues with griefing and trolling are not exclusive to the Otherkin community, but Otherkin griefing is particularly pervasive, dismissive and regularly violent—often saying the Otherkin should kill themselves.

Why have so many internet users recently self-identified in this way, in the face of such precariousness and aggressive opposition? Those dubious of Otherkin identification say that people want to believe they are "special snowflakes" and will say anything to be considered different. To Otherkin, though, it's not a choice at all. Likening Otherkinity to trans identity, many explain that, "species dysphoria[6] sucks," and, "until the advent of the internet and the veils coming down, we didn't know there were others like ourselves" (BloodyKitten 2014). This claim provides a few answers: (1) it is not a choice, and, if it was, many would not choose Otherkinity, and (2) there were many Otherkin all along, but they did not have an avenue through which they could build community until the internet opened one up. It seems perfectly logical that the community grew out of the increased global exposure social media has introduced, but I assert that there is something deeper at play in their (and our) use of these technologies. The internet not only offers a means of sociality for the Otherkin, but also creates the very conditions through which these non-human identifications can become available via the process of *cybernetic animism*. Untangling this process first requires a discussion of our understandings of animism and of the roots of cybernetics, revealing how both have come to act upon and through us, largely unnoticed.

Animism

While animist experience may seem incompatible with contemporary frameworks of thought, many of animism's underlying components could be seen in Europe at the formation of modern Western science and philosophy. German chemist Georg Stahl first used the term *anima* in 1708 to describe a

230   Devin Proctor

physical element of "living stuff" that vitalized matter, along with *phlogiston*, or "burning stuff" that escaped during combustion (1708). Stahl's work is often referenced in the transition from alchemy to chemistry, suggesting the idea of animating forces occupies an important place in Western scientific development. It is important to note that, although Stahl gave us the terminology for an understanding of animism, *anima* only applied to 'vital' matter (living things) and that 'inert' matter (dead things) did not contain any, and thus his concepts were not truly animistic (Harvey 2006). Though not using the term, David Hume anticipated in 1757 what would be called "animism" over a hundred years later when describing how humans tend to see the world around them in human terms: "There is a universal tendency amongst mankind to conceive all being like themselves, and to transfer to every object those qualities with which they are familiarly acquainted, and of which they are intimately conscious" (1889, p. 11). Anthropology, begotten of enlightenment and empire itself, coined the term *animism* with Edward Burnett Tylor's description: "the general doctrine of souls and other spiritual beings in general" (1871, p. 260). This definition is extraordinarily broad, and far from the current understanding of the word, but it served as a point of departure for anthropologists to negotiate the slippery concept for the next century and a half.

Animism is "one of anthropology's earliest concepts, if not the first" (Willerslev 2007, p. 2). Thus, while anthropologists have generated a wealth of data and theory through animist beliefs and practices, the earliest of these theories are founded in the colonial and patronizing language that typifies the field in the late nineteenth and early twentieth centuries. Many Victorian anthropologists were interested in comparing indigenous cultures around the world to the triumphs of the scientific mind in the West, and found differing worldviews—animism chief among them—to be a denial of science's truths. The Western world had put the superstition of religion behind it, in favor of progress and rationality. Tylor considered animism to be the foundation of all religious thought, the "primitive," non-scientific "belief in Spiritual Beings" (1871, p. 424). Since indigenous cultures represented humankind in a childlike state, the "primitives" were not at fault for believing this way, merely mistaken. Lévy-Bruhl considered animism to be the product of a pre-scientific, thus pre-logical mind, not a childlike version of Western intelligence, but something else entirely he called "primitive mentality" (1926). Even those who saw an inherent logic behind animist frameworks blatantly regarded animists themselves as possessing lesser intellects. Durkheim, for instance, saw totemism as a logical way of making sense of the world and maintaining social solidarity, but argued that totems were chosen because the clan itself "is too complex a reality for such unformed minds to bring its concrete unity into clear focus" (1912, p. 222). Even when searching for logic within animist concepts, anthropology up to the mid twentieth century distanced animist practitioners from modern (i.e., scientific) minds. Anthropologists focused on separating animist beliefs from their spiritual aspects to

Cybernetic animism   231

uncover their social meanings and functions. While this allowed scholars to discuss indigenous belief without Tylor's gloss of superstition, it prohibited any engagement that took the *experience* of animism seriously. As Leach phrases it, spirits are "nothing more than ways of describing the formal relationships that exist between real persons and real groups" (1954, p. 182). The experiences are false, but they serve true social functions. Lévi-Strauss, for instance, explained the totemic system not as a tradition of large-scale superstition, but instead part of a larger complex structural classification system; however, he still viewed the beliefs as symbols rather than real experiences (1963). Even when Evans-Pritchard revealed the rationality underlying Azande witchcraft, he did so through the Western scientific method's logic of observation and replication rather than viewing the system of belief through its own logics (1951).

The move toward taking the animist experience seriously came about through Hallowell's work with the Ojibwe, introducing the concept of "other-than-human persons" (1960, p. 22). The division of "human" and "person" here is important. In this understanding, a human is purely a biological designation: "To be a person does not require human-likeness, but rather humans are like other persons" (Harvey 2006, p. 18). These other persons can be animals, trees, or rocks, as long as they can show some sort of personhood. Building on these ideas, Bird-David argues animism is a "relational epistemology," meaning that humans do not personify non-humans in order to socialize with them, but rather see human-likeness in them because we *already* socialize with them (1999). In this sense, animism is seen in the contextual experience of human and other-than-human persons, following Ingold's argument that animism is a lived experience of Heideggerian "Being-in-the-World" (1986). A focus on experience has influenced the so-called ontological turn in anthropology—a group of theorists who argue for understanding existence as the experience of completely different realities, rather than simply differing epistemological views on a single reality. Philippe Descola—a part of this "turn"—explains the world not as a "complete and self-contained world waiting to be represented according to different viewpoints, but, most probably, a vast amount of qualities and relations that can be actualized or not by humans according to how ontological filters discriminate between environmental affordances" (2014, p. 273). In other words, we experience only what we can, and hence we are not necessarily experiencing everything that is *there*. Furthermore, these "ontological filters" are not by-products of institutions, epistemological frameworks, or cultural patterns, but rather the "basic assumptions as to what the world contains and how the elements of this furniture are connected" that form those systems (2014, p. 273). The idea confronts us with the possibility that, as members of Western societies and thus its filters, we are unable to perceive environmental elements animists do, even though they may be right in front of us. Simultaneously, it implies that we bring with us basic assumptions of our own Being that some societies might find unthinkable,

232   *Devin Proctor*

such as an innate comparability between humans and machines—the foundation of cybernetic theory.

Cybernetics

The term "cybernetics" brings to mind the surplus of words appending the prefix "cyber" to denote something having to do with the internet—cyberspace, cyberterror, cybersex, cyberpunk, cyberbullying, Cyber Monday, *CSI Cyber*. Though contemporary use of cyber has narrowed the initial meaning into one of computer technoscience, Norbert Wiener's far more ambitious original vision was "the entire field of control and communication theory, whether in the machine or the animal" (1948, p. 11). The basic goal of cybernetics is to apprehend how systems (mechanic, biological, or social—including humans themselves) process and react to experience. The terminology itself has historic precursors. Specifically, it derives from the Greek *kybernetikos*, roughly translated as "good at steering" (Manovich 2002, p. 218). The ancient Greeks used it to refer to the "helmsman" of the State, the *kybernetes*. Wiener's concept of cybernetics as an agent of steering came from his experience working as a mathematician on missile guidance systems during World War II. He saw the workings of the system not as interconnected mechanical parts, but as a flow of information, constantly taking new data into account. These guidance systems were not the first artificial regulatory systems—Ctesibius built a self-feeding water clock in the third century, BCE. Nor was the guidance system the first machine with corrective self feedback—James Watt used a "governor" to regulate the speed of his steam engines in the eighteenth century. It was not even the first time someone had applied these concepts to humans—Wallace, in his co-authored address with Darwin to the Linnean Society, used Watt's centrifugal governor as a central metaphor to describe the process of natural selection (1858). What was new was the attempt to join all things, mechanic and organic, under a single behavioral model. Wiener's cybernetics of the 1940s–1960s portrayed this behavior working toward *homeostasis*—the idea that any system (and *everything* is a system) can preserve an internal state of balance by adapting to external conditions (feedback) from its environment. This pattern of homeostasis is not only the reason our bodies can keep themselves alive, but serves as "the touchstone of our personal identity" (Wiener 1950, p. 96). Every action or interaction of a system (person, machine, group) creates information (was it successful? why/ why not?), which returns to the system as "feedback loop." The system will then incorporate this new information in the next action. A simple concept described in overly technical language, it is best conveyed through an example: I say "hi" to a friend across a crowded room and get no response. Based on that information, I say "hi" again, but louder this time.

As cyberneticians, most notably Gregory Bateson, Margaret Mead, and Heinz von Foerster, worked with these theories, they came to realize that the feedback loops in social systems were doing more than simply reprocessing

Cybernetic animism 233

their own output. They began to argue that observers, often the cyberneticians themselves, were being affected by the feedback to the extent that they restructured the systems with every input, thus becoming a part of the system. Their incorporation into the process undermined the tidy concept of homeostasis and ushered in the much messier idea of *reflexivity*—the awareness that through their involvement, outside factors (and actors) remake the systems themselves. The framework blurs our comfortable borders between subject and object and between object and environment. Going back to my example from before: I say "hi" to a friend across a crowded room and get no response. People around me in the room make faces implying that my outburst goes against the decorum of the situation (we are in a museum). I try again, a little louder, but tentatively, so as not to upset the other actors now involved in the interaction.

The explosion of computer technologies in the 1980s led cybernetics into its current era, that of *virtuality*. The term "virtual" is commonly used to suggest something not quite "actual"—like 3D virtual environments—but in cybernetic use, virtuality is better understood as "the cultural perception that material objects are interpenetrated by informational patterns" (Hayles 1999, pp. 13–14). Virtuality reveals how information can create its own types of materiality, whether in an algorithmic code or a 3D rendering of a body, begging the question: can information itself *be* in the same way we believe living things can? On one hand, if concrete materiality is not necessary for information flows to exist, at what point is an information-based entity "alive"? On the other hand, could our bodies merely be prostheses for the information in our minds, forecasting the prospect of "uploading" our brains in the near future (Bostrom 2014)? These are central questions in Artificial Intelligence and Posthuman theories, respectively. In this virtual paradigm, when I see my friend in the crowded museum, I text her "hi" from my phone. When she receives the text, the words create a certain level of materiality. I was not "there" before the text, but now, in a sense, I am present in the museum with her as a flow of information.

Disrupting chronology, I would like to highlight a chapter in cybernetic history that gets less attention than reflexivity and has been largely obscured by the clamor of virtuality. In the 1970s, Maturana and Varela's work with autonomous biological systems led them to a more bounded vision of reflexivity: *autopoiesis*, wherein all systems are closed, like early cybernetics suggested, but they remake themselves based on information from outside the system. A useful example is the eukaryotic cell.[7] The cell is a bounded entity housing organized structures, like a nucleus, a cell membrane, and organelles. Molecules and energy from outside the cell trigger the cell to *produce* the elements needed for continuation from within the cell itself. In this sense, it does not merely reorganize itself, it remakes itself autopoietically (1980). When I say "hi" to my hypothetical friend in the museum, I do so with the experience of having been in a museum before and knowledge of contextual appropriate behavior. I consider the outside

234   *Devin Proctor*

information about place, social context, and noise volume before deciding how to best to get her attention.

To be clear, I am not asserting that autopoiesis (or cybernetics in general) accurately describes the fundamentals of human action. Rather, I believe that we, as members of Western societies, have come to understand ourselves this way. While cybernetic virtuality has an elegance that addresses internet inhabitation in a theoretical sense, actually experiencing one's own Being as a flow of information is a hard pill to swallow, as it works in opposition to our Cartesian filters. Autopoiesis, however, represents a prototypical Western Self: bounded individuals who make our own decisions based on internal processes and learn from past actions. The autopoietic framework has particular impact, because it draws from cellular and mechanic metaphors, both of which science often uses to translate murky concepts. On the surface, an autopoietic self may seem devoid of agency and invention, trapped in an echo chamber with no hope for transformation, but this is not so. We can be influenced by others; we can learn. We can experience epiphany and astonishment. All of these experiences, though, come from within our own minds, however strongly influenced by the outside. They are truly new thoughts, but they are our new thoughts. What we do *not* allow is the possibility of thinking another person's (or thing's) thoughts, or the insertion of a feeling/memory/desire into another person. In this way, our minds remain bounded and self-generative, building off of manifold intrinsic potentialities. Going back to the cellular metaphor, we recognize that a bounded stem cell in the human body can become—purely through autopoiesis—any one of our 220 different cell types. But when we view those cells as a collective, forming what we consider a *body*, made up of roughly 37 trillion cells—half of them non-human—we expose the contradiction in autopoietic thought. Donna Haraway reminds us that nothing is actually autopoietic, that "to be animal is to become-with bacteria" (2016, p. 65). Not only do we already accept that the body contains other organisms, but we also routinely inject ourselves with organisms (in the form of vaccines) to combat those that may someday enter into the body. This paradox makes sense only because of our Cartesian foundations: the body and the mind are separate entities and follow different rules. Therefore, logic can support a bounded mind filled with potential and a permeable body filled with bacteria.

Cybernetic animism

In the interests of synthesis, I will make some scaffolded assertions here. The body/mind split has become so ingrained in Western thought that it operates as an ontological filter; we experience Being in a way that presupposes this dualism. We comprehend this Being through autopoiesis—a bounded, yet utterly potential selfhood—acting as an epistemological filter of sorts. This double constraint orders how we experience things. According to Heidegger scholar Michael Zimmerman, "ontology is often so pervasive that people are

Cybernetic animism 235

unaware that they have a particular way of apprehending things. Usually, we think things really are the way they appear to us" (1986, p. 21). Or, as Maturana and Varela (the autopoiesis scholars) put it, "we do not see what we do not see, and what we do not see does not exist" (1987, p. 242). Now, obviously, in a material sense, what we do not see *does* exist. However, our perception does not include it, so it does not exist *to us*. They continue: "only when some interaction dislodges us . . . do we bring forth new constellations of relation" (242). So what then are these other "constellations of relation," hovering just beneath/beyond the ontic? The rest of this chapter will explore the dislodging interaction that can confuse our filters just enough to expose alternative constellations.

When we enter the digital space of the internet, we find ourselves (much like in any other environment) one type of thing among many other types of things. As discussed in the opening of this chapter, they (and we) are all *thing-ing* and Being in particular ways. How, though, are we to tell which things have personhood and which do not? In this setting, we are thrice constrained: ontologically by filters, epistemologically by autopoiesis, and technologically by affordance. Depending on the internet platform, affordances can limit interactions to "liking" or "following" or choosing from a number of pre-programmed quasi-emotional connections. And when we decide to "follow" another thing, or even have a conversation with it, how can we be sure that thing is endowed with personhood in the same way we feel ourselves to be? It could very well be a bot. "Guided by algorithmic behavior—*if this happens, do that; if that happens, do this* . . . bots are the first indigenous species of cyberspace, a class of creatures dazzling in its infinite variety" (Leonard 1997, pp. 7–8). Bots are programs that operate in ways that can mimic human-ity, but they also remember passwords and settings, organize data based on users' perceived preferences, and run complex multi-step operations that a human would find impossible. Due to our layered filters, we do not perceive any of this. We cannot "see" or "feel" the underlying code constantly hap-pening beneath and around us, weaving the fabric of the internet. "We do not see what we do not see." What we observe are icons, buttons, text and sound. We attribute meaning to these things and assign personhood when we believe another person lies behind their functioning. A member of the animist Runa, walking through the forest in Ecuador's Upper Amazon, faces a simi-lar situation. Being a "self" within "the forest's living ecology of selves," she must be aware of all the other possible persons in her surroundings (Kohn 2013, p. 208). Her survival requires recognizing and respecting the person-hood of the *Puma* (jaguar-predator) and avoiding any possible interaction with a *Runa Puma* (shape-shifting human-jaguar-predator). The Runa exist in a world of complex human, non-human, and human-mimicking person-hood similar to our experience of the internet. In these contexts, a ubiquitous assumption of possible personhood becomes the most rational approach.

The discussion above considers the conceptual basis of cybernetic animism—that Being-in-the-internet parallels animist experience in many

236   *Devin Proctor*

ways—but does not address its processual aspect. This I will approach through the earlier nagging question about the Otherkin: why so many, and why now? It is important to note most of the new Otherkin tend to be young people in their teens and twenties[8] who grew up with the internet as a facet of their childhood. Almost a century ago, the father of child behavioral psychology, Jean Piaget, postulated that all children are initially animists. Piaget's use of the term specifically means that children "will regard as living and conscious a large number of objects which are for us inert" (1929, p. 169). This experience of the world will slowly leave the child in the following four stages: up until four or five years old, children believe all things have life, thought and purpose (consciousness); at five to seven years, things that can move are conscious; at seven to nine years, things that move of their own accord are conscious; and by nine to twelve years, consciousness is restricted to animals (1929, pp. 171–186). Mead famously argued against this, stating the children she had studied showed no tendency toward animism, because it was not a facet of their culture (Mead 1932). While disputing "natural" animism inherent in children, this view also supports the possibility of "cultural" types in the West that I shall call (somewhat tentatively) Occidental Animisms.

As we teach children the difference between things, animals and people, we simultaneously expose them to an abundance of media that contradict our teachings, from *Aesop's Fables* to *Grimms' Fairy Tales* to *Teenage Mutant Ninja Turtles*. Throughout Western children's upbringings, they are confronted with non-human persons as the main characters of their stories. While it can be argued that these animals merely serve as anthropomorphic archetypes of personality traits—crows are cunning, lions are proud, sheep are gullible—that view underestimates the complexity of personhood and non-humanity these narratives communicate to children. Let us take one of the most beloved non-human persons in American culture as an example: Mickey Mouse. Mickey lives in a house and wears clothes and uses language. He is a mouse fully endowed with personhood, as is his good friend Goofy, a similarly clothed and communicative dog. But Goofy is not the only dog in Mickey's life. Pluto is Mickey's pet dog who sleeps on the floor, wears nothing but a collar, and has no verbal language. Pluto is simply an animal. From a very early age, children face this negotiation of dog-person and dog-non-person within the larger tacit recognition of non-human personhood as a matter of course, much like indigenous animists. These complex configurations of personhood are not only a facet of Mickey's world, either. As the father of young children myself, I can attest that most of the programming made for them involves animals that both do and do not have personhood. One very popular show features a cactus-person as a protagonist in a town dotted with inert cacti! Perhaps even more importantly, as these characters look through the screen and ask children for their help in solving problems or finding a lost toy, they recognize their personhood and invite them to take part in the animist environment.

Cybernetic animism 237

Many of us over the age of thirty remember the equally promising and terrifying accounts of how the internet would change us, but, as Mosco advises us, "the real power of new technologies does not appear during their mythic period . . . rather, their social impact is greatest when technologies become banal" (2005, p. 19). Internet technology is indeed banal and quotidian to today's young people. By age nine, and often even younger, children are now well-travelled internet citizens, at home and at school. Whereas the rest of us had a period of empiricist filtering-out of animism before diving into its cybernetic progeny, these young people transitioned seamlessly from one to the other. This is not to say that they are stuck in some phase of childhood— that would be a repetition of the condescension animists faced at the hands of Victorian anthropology. Instead, I am putting forward the idea that they have not yet been forced to un-know animism, to un-experience it before being confronted with its digital manifestation. And more than simply being invited into an animist environment, they begin to interact with other persons, both human and not.

Being in the internet requires *doing* through whatever affordance is present. One of the aspects of the internet as a medium that separates it from its precursors is that it demands the user's presence within the medium itself. Sundén describes this phenomenon as "actively having to type oneself into being" (2003, p. 3). The constant *doing* of oneself can be understood in Boellstorff's concept of the *cypherg*—a melding of Haraway's *cyborg* (1991), and Jaspers' *cypher* (1959)—"a figure of online corporeality, a figure whose recursively indexical being-in-world stands to fundamentally reconfigure what it means to be human" (Boellstorff 2011, p. 517). This type of recursive self-creation recalls the autopoietic structure: it exists with the goal of remaking and employs information around itself to that end. The need for continual active *doing* of oneself in the internet environment intensifies the process of recursive remaking. Further, the feedback information used in the remaking is gathered from interaction with various non-bodied elements that may or may not have personhood. Non-human persons sneak through the filters in the process of autopoietic regeneration. Could it be possible that continued experience within an animistic paradigm (the internet) has disclosed something that was already there, *opening* us to something that has been an option all along, lying just outside of our ontological filters? We inhabit bodies—that fact is inescapable—but perhaps they are not so bounded and programmatic as we have come to believe. With that, we arrive at a full definition: *cybernetic animism is the practice of interacting in digital spaces within an ecology of non-human and/or non-bodied elements and the process through which this interaction makes open-bodied identification available as a way of being-in-the-world.*

Artist Anselme Franke recently toured the world with a mixed media exhibition titled "animism," referring to the concept as a "ghost haunting modernity" (2012). The ascension of the modern era depended on the previous conquer-and-cover of alternate epistemologies (and ontologies) through the

238   *Devin Proctor*

dual projects of colonization and empiricist science. Philosopher Isabelle Stengers, who wrote the exhibition's accompanying text, observes that in the name of science, "a general conquest bent on translating everything that exists into objective, rational knowledge, . . . a judgment has been passed on the heads of other peoples, and this judgment has also devastated our relations to ourselves" (2012). These weakened self-relations may be gaining strength among many in the peripheries of the internet. Otherkin identity parallels a much larger number of younger internet users who view their bodies as plastic and negotiable rather than bounded, intractable vessels of predetermined sex, gender, psychological propensity, and personhood. Their bodies are *open*— to interpretation, to inhabitation, to negotiation, to change. Along with the growing number of trans and genderfluid identities, the internet hosts groups of posthumans, transhumans, healthy multiples, the neurodiverse, and many more who reject strict Cartesian views about the mind and body. I am not suggesting that the internet gave birth to the Otherkin, or any of these other groups. Many older Otherkin speak of having their "awakenings"—the gradual realization of their non-human internal selves—before being exposed to the internet. I am also not insinuating we will all soon identify as non-human or open-bodied. Rather, I am proposing that the cybernetic animist environment of the internet may be dislodging an increasing number of users from their ontological and autopoietic filters, exposing opportunities for alternate constellations of relation that have been there all along. Franke describes the ethos of "the modern" being built upon the rock of its own silence about universalized others, but that "the future grand narratives of modernity may well speak of this ghost from the perspective of its other, from its 'animist' side" (Franke 2012). As we keep ourselves occupied deciding what the current era is—postmodern, digital, post-industrial, late capitalist, Anthropocene—these narratives are already beginning to be spoken in the thick forest of the internet, teeming with personhood.

Notes

1 I am assuming you use the internet. In this chapter, I say *us* and *we* for convenience. Specifically, I am referring to people in Western, largely industrialized societies, with internet access. Further, the term *Western*, or *The West* is meant to specifically describe those nations in Western Europe and North America— sometimes referred to as "Occidental"—that arise from an historical trajectory including Greco-Roman philosophy, Judeo-Christianity, Enlightenment science, and the projects of empire and colonization.
2 In his own words: "If we let the thing be present in its thinging from out of the worlding world, then we are thinking of the thing as thing. Taking thought in this way, we let ourselves be concerned by the thing's worlding being" (Heidegger 1971, p. 174)
3 Affordances are the available ways an object can be acted upon, and the ways that object makes these actions known. Examples include curved door handles for pulling vs. flat plates for pushing, or icons on a computer screen that resemble buttons to be pushed.

4 There are a small number of Otherkin who believe that non-human elements can be passed through DNA or that their bodies are otherwise somehow biologically non-human, but the vast majority does not.
5 In Pagan traditions—which many Otherkin follow—the fae, along with other non-human entities and deities, exist on earth and can materialize in concrete form. For my purposes, and in the official definitions put forward by the Otherkin community, I am defining "on Earth" in purely scientific non-supernatural terms, limited to those presently observable or those with a fossil record.
6 Species dysphoria is a term used within the Otherkin community to describe a "persistent feeling of discomfort" about being "trapped in a human body" (Gerbasi et al. 2008). The term is meant to parallel gender dysphoria.
7 Eukaryotic cells make up all animals, plants, fungi, and protists, as opposed to prokaryotic cells, found in bacteria and archaea.
8 I base this on my own observations as well as the findings of an internal Otherkin community census. The census only had 291 respondents, but 113 were teenagers and 141 were in their twenties, so while the survey is not exhaustive, it certainly reflects a trend.

Bibliography

Bird-David, N., 1999. 'Animism' Revisited: Personhood, Environment, and Relational Epistemology. *Current Anthropology*, 40 (S1), S67–S91.

BloodyKitten, 2014. Being otherkin or therian isn't a choice. • /r/otherkin [online]. *Reddit*. Available at: www.reddit.com/r/otherkin/comments/1wbjnw/being_otherkin_or_therian_isnt_a_choice/ (accessed: 1 July 2018).

Boellstorff, T., 2011. Placing the Virtual Body: Avatar, Chora, Cypherg. *In*: F. E. Mascia-Lees, ed. *A Companion to the Anthropology of the Body and Embodiment*. Hoboken, NJ: John Wiley & Sons, 504–520.

Bostrom, N., 2014. *Superintelligence: Paths, Dangers, Strategies*. Oxford: Oxford University Press.

Cusack, C. M., 2016. Spirituality and Self-Realisation as 'Other-Than-Human': The Otherkin and Therianthropy Communities. *In*: P. Kosnáč, ed. *Fiction, Invention and Hyper-reality: From Popular Culture to Religion*. New York: Routledge, 40–57.

Darwin, C. and Wallace, A., 1858. On the Tendency of Species to Form Varieties; and on the Perpetuation of Varieties and Species by Natural Means of Selection. *Journal of the Proceedings of the Linnean Society of London: Zoology*, 3 (9), 45–62.

Davidsen, M. A., 2013. Fiction-Based Religion: Conceptualising a New Category Against History-Based Religion and Fandom. *Culture and Religion*, 14 (4), 378–395.

Davidsen, M. A., 2016. The Elven Path and the Silver Ship of the Valar: Two Spiritual Groups Based on J. R. R. Tolkien's Legendarium. *In*: C. M. Cusack and P. Kosnáč, eds. *Fiction, Invention and Hyper-Reality: From Popular Culture to Religion*. New York: Routledge, 15–30.

Descola, P., 2014. Modes of Being and Forms of Predication. *HAU: Journal of Ethnographic Theory*, 4 (1), 271–280.

Dreamsinger, J., 2012. Swanblood: Okay: I Know Some People Prefer . . . [online]. *Jarandhel's Tumblr*. Available at: http://jarandhel.tumblr.com/post/ 30096366885/swanblood-okay-i-know-some-people-prefer (accessed: 1 July 2018).

Durkheim, E., 1912. *The Elementary Forms of Religious Life*. New York: Free Press.

240 *Devin Proctor*

Evans-Pritchard, S. E. E., 1951. *Witchcraft, Oracles and Magic among the Azande.* Oxford: Oxford University Press.

Franke, A., 2012. Introduction: 'Animism.' *e-flux*, (36).

Gerbasi, K., Paolone, N., Privitera, A., Scaletta, L., Conway, S., Higner, J. and Bernstein, P., 2008. Furries from A to Z (Anthropomorphism to Zoomorphism). *Society & Animals*, 16, 197–222.

Grivell, T., Clegg, H. and Roxburgh, E. C., 2014. An Interpretative Phenomenological Analysis of Identity in the Therian Community. *Identity*, 14 (2), 113–135.

Hallowell, I., 1960. Ojibwa Ontology, Behavior, and World View. *In*: S. Diamond, ed. *Culture in History: Essays in Honor of Paul Radin*. New York: Columbia University Press, 19–52.

Haraway, D., 1991. A Cyborg Manifesto: Science, Technology, and Socialist-Feminism in the Late Twentieth Century. *In: Simians, Cyborgs, and Women: The Reinvention of Nature*. London, UK: Routledge, 149–181.

Haraway, D., 2016. *Staying with the Trouble: Making Kin in the Chthulucene*. Durham, NC: Duke University Press.

Harvey, G., 2006. *Animism: Respecting the Living World*. New York: Columbia University Press.

Hayles, N. K., 1999. *How We Became Posthuman: Virtual Bodies in Cybernetics, Literature, and Informatics*. Chicago, IL: University of Chicago Press.

Heidegger, M., 1971. *Poetry, Language, Thought*. New York: Harper Colophon.

Heidegger, M., 1996. *Being and Time*. Albany: State University of New York Press.

Hume, D., 1889. *The Natural History of Religion*. London, UK: A & H Bradlaugh Bonner.

Ingold, T., 1986. *The Appropriation of Nature: Essays on Human Ecology and Social Relations*. Manchester, UK: Manchester University Press.

Jaspers, K., 1959. *Truth and Symbol*. Albany, NY: College and University Press.

Johnston, J., 2013. On Having a Furry Soul: Transpecies Identity and Ontological Indeterminacy in Otherkin Subcultures. *In*: F. Probyn-Rapsey and J. Johnston, eds. *Animal Death*. Sydney, New South Wales: Sydney University Press, 293–306.

Kirby, D., 2008. Alternative Worlds: Metaphysical Questioning and Virtual Community Amongst the Otherkin. *In: Through a Glass Darkly: Reflections on the Sacred: Sydney Studies in Religion*. Sydney, New South Wales: Sydney University Press, 275–287.

Kirby, D., 2013. *Fantasy and Belief: Fiction and Media as Conjunct Locales for Metaphysical Questing and Spiritual Understanding*. Sheffield, UK: Equinox Publishing.

Kohn, E., 2013. *How Forests Think: Toward an Anthropology beyond the Human*. Berkeley: University of California Press.

Laycock, J., 2012. 'We Are Spirits of Another Sort': Ontological Rebellion and Religious Dimensions of the Otherkin Community. *Nova Religio: The Journal of Alternative and Emergent Religions*, 15, 65–90.

Leach, E., 1954. *Political Systems of Highland Burma: A Study of Kachin Social Structure*. London, UK: G. Bell and Sons Ltd.

Leonard, A., 1997. *Bots: The Origin of the New Species*. San Francisco, CA: Hardwired.

Lévi-Strauss, C., 1963. *Totemism*. Boston, MA: Beacon Press.

Lévy-Bruhl, L., 1926. *How Natives Think*. Oxford, UK: Allen & Unwin.

Lupa, 2007. *A Field Guide to Otherkin* (1st ed.). Stafford, UK: Megalithica Books.

Manovich, L., 2002. *The Language of New Media*. Cambridge, MA: MIT Press.

Cybernetic animism 241

Maturana, H. R. and Varela, F. J., 1980. *Autopoiesis and Cognition: The Realization of the Living*. Dordrecht, Holland and Boston, MA: Springer.

Maturana, H. R. and Varela, F. J., 1987. *Tree of Knowledge: The Biological Roots of Human Understanding*. Boston, MA: Shambhala.

Mead, M., 1932. An Investigation of the Thought of Primitive Children, with Special Reference to Animism. *The Journal of the Royal Anthropological Institute of Great Britain and Ireland*, 62, 173–190.

Mosco, V., 2005. *The Digital Sublime: Myth, Power, and Cyberspace*. Cambridge, MA: MIT Press.

O'Callaghan, S., 2015. Navigating the "Other" World: Cyberspace, Popular Culture and the Realm of the Otherkin. *Culture and Religion* 16 (3), 253–268.

Piaget, J., 1929. *The Child's Conception of the World*. Translated by Tomlinson, J. and Tomlinson, A. London, UK: Routledge & Kegan Paul.

Probyn-Rapsey, F., 2011. Furries and the Limits of Species Identity Disorder: A Response to Gerbasi et al. *Society & Animals*, 19, 294–301.

Robertson, V. L. D., 2012. The Law of the Jungle: Self and Community in the Online Therianthropy Movement. *Pomegranate: The International Journal of Pagan Studies*, 14 (2), 256–280.

Robertson, V. L. D., 2013. The Beast within: Anthrozoomorphic Identity and Alternative Spirituality in the Online Therianthropy Movement. *Nova Religio: The Journal of Alternative and Emergent Religions*, 16 (3), 7–30.

Shane, M., 2014. Some People Aren't People on the Inside. *In*: V. Venkatesh, ed. *Educational, Psychological, and Behavioral Considerations in Niche Online Communities*. Hershey, PA: Information Science Reference, 260–271.

Stahl, G. E., 1708. *Theoria Medica Vera*. Halle: Literis Orphanotrophei.

Stengers, I., 2012. Reclaiming Animism. *e-flux*, (36).

Sundén, J., 2003. *Material Virtualities: Approaching Online Textual Embodiment*. New York: Peter Lang International Academic Publishers.

Therian-Kin Corner, 2017. Definition. *Therian-Kin Corner* [online]. Available at: http://theriankincorner.boards.net/page/Definition (accessed: 1 July 2018).

Tylor, E. B., 1871. *Primitive Culture: Researches Into the Development of Mythology, Philosophy, Religion, Art, and Custom*. London, UK: John Murray.

Wiener, N., 1948. *Cybernetics: Control and Communication in the Animal and the Machine*. New York: Wiley.

Wiener, N., 1950. *The Human Use of Human Beings: Cybernetics and Society*. New York: Doubleday.

Willerslev, R., 2007. *Soul Hunters: Hunting, Animism, and Personhood among the Siberian Yukaghirs*. Oakland: University of California Press.

Zimmerman, M., 1986. Implications of Heidegger's Thought for Deep Ecology. *Modern Schoolman*, 64, 19–43.

12 Death in life and life in death
Forms and fates of the human

Connor Graham and Alfred Montoya

Introduction

This chapter traces the origins, meanings and characteristics of "the human" in recent time – its *forms*. The chapter contends that, instead of being immutable, "the human" has taken different forms, been ascribed different meanings, and exhibited different characteristics over time. Our approach to "the human" contributes to this volume on digital existence, which confronts existential questions centered on being and technology, with historical and anthropological awareness. We aim to show, through Foucault's (1971) insistence upon the *forms* of subjectivity as opposed to its substance, how understandings of "the human" are subject to change and transformation. Exploring these diverse understandings helps us to capture how human beings have related to each other and the world, and understood themselves at different points in time. This exploration also shows how human beings' relationships have developed in conjunction with new configurations of politics and technology.

To achieve our goal, this theoretical essay aims to carefully distinguish the concept of "human-as-is," the being, concrete, existing, mortal instance of a human being, from the concept of "human-as-category," the enframing, abstract, general, human being in discourse as an object. In embarking upon an exploratory project to map "the human," we hence define the "human-as-is" as referring to the real, living, thinking, walking creatures we are, whereas the "human-as-category" refers to conceptualizations of human beings (e.g., by anthropologists, politicians and philosophers). Thus, "human-as-is" persists despite the worlds of discourse and language that "human-as-category" depends on. "Human-as-is" is what "human-as-category" refers to and claims to know and thus our project here is to explore the exact relational nature of this reference and precisely how "human-as-category" describes and corresponds to "human-as-is." We wish to show, more generally, how the existential questions confronted in this volume are embedded in the worlds in which they are asked (and indeed enframed). We argue these worlds both assume and produce particular versions of "human-as-category" that exhibit family resemblance and have particular relations to "human-as-is."

Death in life and life in death   243

Through this exploration we will ultimately confront the question of the possible fates of "the human," its forms and the reality in which it is embedded, with regard to life and death, in a technology-shaped future. For example, Denisa Kera explores how new scientific understandings and technologies have exposed the human being as a "configurations of the 'network'," a barely-contained riot of diverse organic and inorganic elements seeking "to return to their inorganic past and future" (2014, pp. 185, 191). Under these conditions, death is simply the body losing control over its various components, a natural tendency toward entropy disintegrating the human being, understood as a temporary entanglement of elements. How might an examination of such a posthuman "human-as-category" inform and relate to the generalization of existential questions centered on "human-as-is"? More boldly, what might the limits of our existential preoccupations be in light of recent technological and scientific developments, and how might they be acknowledged and compensated for?

We argue, drawing on Foucault (1971), that a consideration of the "human-as-category" enlarges the scope of contextual elements enabling assertions about what the human being is or might become, placing these forms squarely within certain historical moments, and certain configurations of politics, economics and technology. Many reflections on individual existence, or propositions concerning the "human-as-is," such a "Man" and the "Human," are the products of particular times and places, providing windows through which to frame and view "human-as-is" in discourse. Some of these reflections and propositions concerning the "human-as-is," what we call its forms or the "human-as-category," appeared quite recently, the products of elite or expert discourses. And such *forms* will continue to appear for as long as we human beings exist and have the desire and power to reflexively consider ourselves, other human beings and the world in which we live. Though "the human" is colloquially deployed interchangeably with "people" and "persons," and typically conceptualized as a timeless given, often by elites, scholars have recently been pointing out the historical and contingent nature of this object. "The human" in human rights, for example, is of quite recent invention (Moyn 2010).

How then is "the human" enframed, defined, understood and given meaning in relation to digital technologies of the modern era and in the new debate about existential media? And exactly which human beings are involved in this enframing, understanding and meaning making? How effectively can they speak for all human beings? As John Durham Peters has argued, "The world and the human condition are pervaded recursively by human hand and crafting" (in Lagerkvist 2017, p. 100). That is, human beings fashion the world they inhabit, both conceptually and practically, generating the tools for, and ways of knowing about, that world and themselves. This may have happened in an everyday sense through history as human beings have lived their lives. But is the relationship between all human beings and technologies throughout time the same? How does the human-technology relationship

244   *Connor Graham and Alfred Montoya*

in-the-world correspond to different worlds of discourse and who has had a voice in these worlds?

In this chapter we use a broad definition of (digital) media as "vehicles that carry and communicate meaning" (Peters 2015, p. 2). We also conceive contemporary technology as "an existential and ambivalent terrain" (Lagerkvist 2017, p. 103). By drawing on prior work from outside existence philosophy, we aim to contribute further to the mapping of that "terrain," primarily by understanding the relationship between "human-as-category" and "human-as-is" in recent time. This mapping concentrates on how worlds of discourse account for *and*, more provocatively, in this act of 'accounting for,' might shape the very existence of human beings. This is a "terrain" and a moment that has been called the "epoch of equipment" (Dreyfus 1992, p. 175) because of the ubiquity of technologies of different kinds that frame human perception, action and existence. We believe it is important for the analysis of existential media to reflect upon how its discourse centered on digital media (re)conceives of "the human." In other words, inspired by the approach of Foucault, we interrogate the relationship and correspondence between the forms and reality of "the human," clarifying the grounds from which new forms of "the human" are emerging, and what these forms emphasize. We consider that these are necessary steps toward imagining new futures, relations and vulnerabilities for human beings, including considerations related to mortality. This approach carefully recognizes the distinction between the very real existence of "the human" and the different worlds of discourse, worlds that neither fully construct human beings nor are independent of them.

Our starting point for discussion is Amanda Lagerkvist's recently posited figure of the "exister" (Lagerkvist 2017, p. 101). This "exister" is grounded in and enframed by technology, insofar as humans and technology have always co-produced one another.

> The exister is mortal. She is a struggling, suffering and relational human being. Her intermediary position as a conscious (yet often clueless) embodied being provides for her the only known 'entry point' to navigate and craft the world into which she is thrown.
>
> (p. 101)

The exister moves through the world relying on her "tools of everyday existence", including digital media, to make sense of her "digital throwness," taking up the necessary task of making meaning under these new technological conditions (Lagerkvist 2017, pp. 99, 97). This provocative new figure is, in our terms, a conceptualization of a specific form of human being that is conceived from a particular historical moment and a specific configuration of technology, politics and ethics. It is a figure that has been elided in many studies of digital media due to a focus on a particular, modern imagination of progress. The "exister" is derived from concepts that emerged from

Death in life and life in death   245

a particularly productive and powerful mid and late nineteenth and early twentieth century thinking centred on human mortality, alienation, meaning and freedom. These concepts and concerns were impelled and nourished by widespread social and economic reorganizations in the wake of rapid European industrialization and urbanization, the imperial expansion that drove both, and the dislocations generated by the World War I and World War II.

The "exister" is also a particular, if expansive, proposal for "human-as-is," a figure rooted in earlier conceptions of human beings in existence philosophy such as _Dasein_ (p. 100) that precede the digital. It is pre-cultural, and beyond race, class or gender specificity, "stressing the hardship and struggle of any human life whether in scarcity or post-scarcity cultures" (p. 100). The "exister" designates the experiential or existential infrastructure shared by all human beings. Like its contemporary and cousin, the "Human" in "human rights," it emphasizes precarity, vulnerability and suffering, and claims for itself all human beings across time and space, and difference. The concept of the "exister" is a critical intervention that draws much-needed attention to embodied vulnerabilities. It is particularly useful for taking up all media as "existential media," producing new existential problems and offering new spaces for the consideration of old concerns (Lagerkvist and Andersson 2017, p. 2). It supports a diagnosis of the possibilities and challenges faced by those human groups for whom the ubiquity and penetration of digital media and ways of being have blurred the old categories of on- and off-line. Our analysis takes this figure, the "exister," up as addressing both "human-as-is" and "human-as-category."

This chapter presents its exploratory argument first by identifying and briefly contextualizing two treatments of "the human," those of Foucault and Virilio, identifying key transitions and examining the characteristics of each of these proposed forms. Both theorists reference human beings' vulnerabilities, including mortality. We draw on Foucault's observations on the origins of Enlightenment-era "Man," the living, laboring and speaking subject and object of knowledge, the more recent "Human" of human rights discourse, and Virilio's "terminal citizen," the connected, extended and disembodied victim of mediated urban life.

We then analyze more recent scholarship on human mortality and technology. We have selected works which seem to make a proposal for a "human-as-is," attempting to identify in these proposals the specific characteristics ascribed to the posited figures of "the human," or those characteristics assumed by their authors, with particular reference to "Man," "Human," and "terminal citizen." We have attempted to consider the relations with and correspondence to these three figures in these contemporary writings through particular attention to "classical existential themes": "Death: our finitude and the digital afterlife" and "Being there: presence and absence" (Lagerkvist 2017, pp. 103, 105). In this analysis, we identify the extent to which "Man," "Human," and "terminal citizen" retain coherence as figures with fixed sets of attributes. We also wish to consider the extent to

246   *Connor Graham and Alfred Montoya*

which they exert influence into the present and even potentially might shape our near future understandings of what it means to be "human." Through returning to the "exister," we end by considering how "human-as-category" might infect and inflect "human-as-is," the existence and living reality of human beings, both today and in time to come.

We take seriously Lagerkvist's assertion that "Questions concerning digital technologies are questions concerning human existence," and her analysis of the sets of new (digital) conditions not all of our own making, but not entirely deterministic either, into which we are "thrown" (2017, pp. 96, 97). Our machines, she writes, "have evolved into environmental and wearable tools of existence" as we have become "Reliant on devices that enable our lives" (2017, pp. 97, 98). We may agree with Peters who argues that "it is in the elusive and recalcitrant that we find the homeland of media, and thus the heart of what humans have wrought" and that "media, like human beings, are always in the middle between sea, earth and sky" (2015, p. 12). However, the recent reach, extent, agency and even intelligence of digital media and machines raise the possibilities of not only a reciprocal relationship between 'fleshy' and 'digital' existence, but of new forms of life (and death) that reach beyond a new instance of "human-as-category." As we hope to illustrate, in these prospective forms and fates of "the human," digital media is not only 'in between' or "a terrain" but integral to "human-as-is."

"Man" and "the Human"

We human beings are self-aware. We human beings have generated systematic religions and secular thought throughout the ages, seeking to make sense of ourselves, our condition and our vulnerabilities, driven by a profound knowledge of our own finitude. Existentialist thought, with its emphasis on being and its relationship to the world, is a modern attempt to grapple with such enduring sense-making. But can this discourse make general propositions about all of humankind? How do the largely privileged writings of European elites from the mid-nineteenth to the mid twentieth century connect with the experience and futures of the full range of urban human beings alive today? How might we theorize a global "human," past or future, and should such a figure exist?

The regimes of digitalization that permeate our contemporary world may seem to generate similar, if not identical dilemmas, for peoples across cultures and socioeconomic situations. Certainly, the concept of the "exister," and other propositions for "humans-as-is" aim to provide a lens or a framework for an exploration of these commonalities. However, internet penetration, for instance, is profoundly uneven across the planet. In 2017, the International Telecommunications Union, a UN body, estimated that while 84.4 percent of households in developed countries had internet access in some form, only 42.9 percent of households in developing countries, and only 14.7 percent of households in least developed countries did so (ITU

Death in life and life in death   247

2017). The report also indicates a gender gap of about 12 percent worldwide in terms of relative access to the internet between males and females (ITU 2017). Apart from these empirical issues, there are also problems of language: how does any concept speak for both the general human being and the subaltern?

In order to begin to take these questions seriously we draw a distinction between the "human-as-is" and "human-as-category." "Human-as-is," in line with existential writings, describes the being, concrete, existing, mortal instance of a human being in reality, the primal creature that lives, breathes and walks outside any conceptualization if itself in discourse. "Human-as-category," on the other hand, captures the enframing, abstract, general human that has been proposed in discourses of different kinds for different purposes (e.g., "Man," the "Human," etc). It draws our attention to the totalizing or globalizing "humanity projects" (Rees 2014) of various academic and political actors who have made proposals concerning the "human-as-is" over time and generalized it. Its aim is to provide a second order observation (Luhmann 1998) or analysis concerning human beings. Each of these human versions have different instances, and they can inform each other. So, for example, the existential acuteness of certain kinds of human beings' experience, such as suffering, illuminated through the "human-as-is" term, can be understood and responded to through a "human-as-category" instantiation, that of the "Human" in human rights.

In the *The Order of Things*, Michel Foucault traced the emergence of the Enlightenment figure of "Man," in our terms, a novel eighteenth-century proposition concerning the "human-as-is." In the Classical Age, according to Foucault, human beings did not consider themselves makers or artificers, but were simply agents of clarification and classification, through clear and certain ideas, of the world created by God. This relied on the assumption that the medium of representation, language, was reliable and transparent. The human being merely gave artificial description to an order that already existed through language and a conventional ordering of categories and resemblances (Foucault 1971; see also Dreyfus and Rabinow 1983). Human beings could not enter the Classical scheme as both ordering subject and posited object (Foucault 1971). "Man as that being who gets the whole picture as well as gets into the picture is unthinkable in the Classical episteme" (Dreyfus and Rabinow 1983, p. 27). For Foucault, it was not possible for human beings' existence to be called into question on its own account at this point in history, "since it contained the nexus of representation and being" (Foucault 1971, p. 311).

A new figure leaps into being at the end of the eighteenth century, a time of transition between craftsmanship and industrialization (Dreyfus 1992, p. 174). This figure, "Man," once merely one more creature amongst the others, albeit with a special role of clarifying God's creation, now finds itself a subject among objects, albeit one with a peculiar problem. Not content to understand only the objects of the world, "Man" turns the powers of reason

248   *Connor Graham and Alfred Montoya*

onto itself. "Man" becomes both subject and object of its understanding, an understanding now limited by a new conceptualization of language not as a timeless, transparent, God-given system, but as a web of meaning with its own history and mechanisms (Dreyfus and Rabinow 1983, p. 28). "Man appears in his ambiguous position as an object of knowledge and as a subject that knows: enslaved sovereign, observed spectator, he appears in the place belonging to the king" (Foucault 1971, p. 312). "Man," following Foucault's analysis, is in our terms, a "human-as-category," situated in discourse at a particular historical juncture. The "human-as-is" here is understood as corresponding to "human-as-category" which, in turn, brings "human-as-is" into being: relations are collapsed and the thinking, reasoning human being is celebrated. "Man," after all, is both subject and object, capable of reason and therefore responsible for conjuring up a representation of itself through specific ways of knowing and speaking about that self. "Man" is also an instance of "human-as-category," a set of relations and ways of knowing that are taken up by human beings and which shape human beings' experiences and expectations.

Having lost the ability to rely on a transcendental subject to guarantee the order of the cosmos and the transparency of the mode of representation of that order, "Man" is thrust back on its own limitations. "Man's finitude is heralded – and imperiously so – in the positivity of knowledge," writes Foucault (1971, p. 313). Human limitations are transformed by Enlightenment thinkers and scientists into the very basis of all positive empirical knowledge within what Foucault calls an analytic of finitude. Foucault famously predicted the end of "Man," as the fragmentation of language and the sudden opacity of representation that gave birth to "Man" at the end of the Classical Age was likewise losing out in a contemporary world. In this world "language is now emerging with greater and greater insistence in a unity that we ought to think but cannot as yet do so" (Foucault 1971, p. 386). "Man" was, he suspected, nearing its end. For our purposes, the "human-as-category" instance "Man" begins to seriously consider the very subjectivity and mortality, vulnerability and limitations of "human-as-is" as the means by which it produces knowledge about itself and the world. This gives rise to the empirical sciences and technological progress. Human vulnerability and limitations are no longer simply burdens, but are taken up as the very means of understanding and overcoming the vagaries of the world and human beings through specific linear, modern notions of progress. Such a system no longer needs be guaranteed by God.

However, the twentieth century, driven by tumultuous violence and scientific and technological developments, also proposed its own responses to the question of what human beings are today. In *The Origins of Totalitarianism*, Hannah Arendt identified a paradox concerning the figure of "Man" and its heir, the "human-as-category" instance we call the "Human." This "Human" is the object at the center of a global discourse and apparatus referred to as "humanitarian," or the figure we talk about when we talk about "human rights." "From the beginning," Arendt writes, "the paradox involved in the declaration of inalienable human rights was that it reckoned with an 'abstract' human being *who seemed to exist nowhere*" (1962, p. 291, italics added). This was an especially serious issue in the context of the refugee crisis driven by the rise of European fascism and the violence of World War II. For Arendt, the stateless refugee provoked an immediate and serious crisis for the domain of knowledge, discourse and practice then attempting to consolidate itself around this abstract "Human." This "human-as-category" had little practical correspondence to certain real human beings and their vulnerabilities. For instance, refugees, no longer part of a nation-state and who had recourse suddenly only to their status as human beings, found quickly that these lofty ideals provided little benefit or security:

> The world found nothing sacred in the abstract nakedness of being human. And in view of objective political conditions, it is hard to say how the concepts of man upon which human rights are based . . . could have helped to find a solution to the problem.
>
> (Arendt 1962, p. 299)

The "Human," through the latter half of the twentieth century, provided part of this solution. It emerged as a site of contestation, giving weight to itself primarily through elaboration of the rights said to be proper to it, and consequently, of the risks it acquired because of these rights. Thus this instance of "human-as-category" became populated and defined through an understanding of "human-as-is" as encompassing particular experiences and vulnerabilities and engagement with the world and other humans beyond self-knowledge. During the Cold War, the competing interests and ideological positions of the United States and the USSR, from the time of the UN commission that drafted the Universal Declaration of Human Rights (UDHR), contributed to shaping this figure. These interests provided it with rights emphasized by the Soviets (social and economic rights, concerned with access to economic resources and communal obligations/protections) and those stressed by the United States (civil and political rights, concerned with individual freedoms, free speech, etc.) (Johnson and Symonides 1998, p. 43). The new figure's ill-defined "abstraction," its status as a pure instance of "human-as-category," perfectly positioned it to accept these diverse new elements that took the form of rights and risks, giving it rhetorical power and allowing it to function as a cypher upon which a new universality could be projected. Far from being a handicap, the self-evidential but ambiguous nature of the "Human" became an essential aspect. The drafting committee of the UDHR, after its arduous deliberations, asserted, "we agree about the rights but on condition no one asks us why" (Hunt 2007, p. 20). Explanations and exactitude could in fact undermine the "Human's" force. As Hunt noted, "An assertion that requires argument is not self-evident" (2007, p. 20).

250   *Connor Graham and Alfred Montoya*

At the same time the twentieth century also produced new scientific theories through which human beings sought to gain some purchase on new instances of "human-as-category" relating to the kind of creature we were or were fast becoming, operating somewhere between "Man" and "Human." Freudian psychoanalysis, positing a developmental theory of the unconscious, circumvented if not undermined the prevailing theories explaining personality (race, heredity, etc). The truth of "human-as-is" could now be sought in the messy libidinal undercurrents that were said to underpin human experience. So provocative and compelling were these theories that, as well as entering popular discourse, and claiming exact correspondence with the essence of "human-as-is," great care was soon taken by its established authorities to further reify these insights as an instance by standardizing and policing the training of analysts in the psychoanalytic method. A sense of professionalism was also maintained through a close association with the medical field (Kerr 2004). Thus efforts were made not only to respond to the vulnerabilities that this account of the "human-as-is" provided, but also to establish and give credence to it. This movement is worth nothing here because, despite the antagonisms that may exist between psychoanalytical and existential thought (e.g., Sartre 1962), they both have a preoccupation with individual, reflexive and human-human interactions and human-world relations.

More recently new technologies have generated new notions of "where" human beings reside or how they may be defined, populating and extending the "Human" instance of "human-as-category." Some of these do so, once again, by acknowledging and emphasizing the experiences and vulnerabilities of the "human-as-is." According to Tobias Rees, bioscientists and health humanitarians are increasingly defining human beings biologically, in inclusive, global terms, beyond the confines of the social and the "national society-fostering logic" of the nation-state that defined twentieth-century humanitarian thinking (Rees, 2014, p. 470). For these actors, the nation-state is "a failed humanity project, precisely because the humanity that the nation-state secures is always an exclusive one, one focused on the nation – on the national society – only" (p. 270). In this radical perspective, and contra-Arendt, statelessness "appears in a different, (almost) positive light"; this "positivization of the stateless" representing a "major mutation of the 250-year-old space that has opened up the possibility of humanity" (p. 471).

Human and digital media

In the last section we have shown how, over time, "human-as-category" evolved both in terms of how it was defined and also in terms of its specific meanings. In this account we have illustrated how "human-as-is," specifically the human experience and vulnerability, helped to populate specific "human-as-category" instances. This section has also shown that, in the three examples we have considered, there are multiple, distinct accounts of "human-as-is"

Death in life and life in death 251

with different emphases, claims about completeness of correspondence and engagement with notions of being and existence. These examples have illustrated that readings of "human-as-is" may or may not obtain and claim "category" status such that they can perform widely in discourse: being both abstract enough to operate across distinctly different ideologies and publics and specific enough to be meaningful for these ideologies and publics. These same examples have also shown how understandings of "the human" have shifted towards emphasizing a relationship with and knowledge of the self as a human being, as well as relationships with other human beings.

Until now, we have tiptoed around the term "technology" and how exactly it might connect with human beings, the world and the relationship between human beings and the world. Consideration of technology is essential to our "experiment" because it has increasingly enframed and organized relationships with the world, as well as with other human beings. The instances of "human-as-category" we have presented in the last section are certainly characterized by technologies in the worlds of distinct times.

In this section, we move towards a more explicit treatment of contemporary technology, namely digital media, and its association with "human-as-category" and "human-as-is" through considering the writings of the French cultural theorist Paul Virilio. We also probe how "Man" and the "Human" have persisted, receded and/or morphed in the late twentieth-century and early twenty-first century, a time of changing forms of equipment (Dreyfus (1992, p. 175). In doing this, we also consider how such 'equipment' may be productive of certain vulnerabilities and even potentially transform mortality.

Virilio provides an alternative perspective to classical existential writings because of his largely overtly critical treatment of specifically modern technology, including digital media. His work does not assume particular "terrains" (Lagerkvist 2017), "groundedness" (Peters 2015), "equipment" (Dreyfus 1992), and "relations" (Ihde 1990) are neutral. Instead it questions their politics, how they came to be, how they transform the body, and what they are productive of in terms of life and living, including vulnerabilities. Although recent philosophical and existential approaches to technology may grapple well with its role in human beings' experience and contribution to human beings' existence (Rosenberger and Verbeek 2015, p. 26), a common preoccupation is with mediation, relations and their possibilities. Questioning the *forms* of "the human" new technologies might produce is less common. A brief treatment of Virilio's work provides insights into such forms, allowing for a critical retreat from the enframing force of technology that is itself characterized as a form of "cybernetic control" (Dreyfus 1992, p. 175). Like Foucault, Virilio's work allows us to further demonstrate how particular formulations of "the human," "human-as-category" in particular, have emerged at specific times and places, and under specific conditions. This work also shows how these formulations have been informed by conceptions of "human-as-is."

252   *Connor Graham and Alfred Montoya*

Virilio (1997) presents the end of the twentieth century as an epoch and "terrain" of collapsed, space and time, of light speed enabled through technology, advances in transportation and telecommunication such as air travel and videoconferencing. He also articulates a precise transformation in human experience, specifically sensing capabilities and therefore relations with the world and other humans, conditioned and organized by optical media operating at light speed, through the concomitant "tactility at a distance" (p. 10). As a result there is a profound change in the human's "*animal body*" (p. 11, italics author's own) and "muscular strength" (19). This change started during the industrial revolution in Europe and accelerated after World War II with the creation of infrastructures of which digital media form a part, "large, force-amplifying systems that connect people and institutions across large scales of space and time" (Edwards 2003, p. 221). Space and the *individual* body are transformed through "'transfer machines'" (Virilio 1997, p. 19) such as computer-aided design, networks and artificial intelligence, resulting in a "'terminal man'" (11), surfacing distinct from urban space and the home. This "terminal man" is a simulation, persistently visually present given "the celebrated retinal persistence" enabled by the light speed of media. These media are dominated by images and enabled by "statistical imagery" (Virilio 1994, p. 75, cited in Armitage 2013, p. 67) or "artificial images that can only appear through fast computation, deciphering and analysis of the pixels a computer graphics system can show on a screen" (Armitage 2013, pp. 67–78). These same images "create 'rational' visual allusions that damage people's comprehension and interpretation" (Armitage 2013, pp. 67–78).

The point of Armitage's treatment of the image here (and we can argue the "terrains" through which the "exister" roams) is that its production is not innocent. Its production and persistence are both approximal, algorithmic and simulated and reliant on a digital infrastructures and protocols over which the individual, experiencing human has little control. Thus, as urbanization (and technology) sprawl, the increasingly disabled, extra-sensory, persistent but complexly mediated body transforms in form through new human-world (or flesh-silicon, cell-bit) relations. Its individual, non-collective, diminished physicality and its relation to technology become key aspects and boundaries of its form and vulnerability. It is both situated in and beyond urban space (further informing what a "terrain" might be). Its technologically induced visual reach enables instant, pre-emptive mediated action as well as perception, rendering the importance and meaning of geography, place and even history, irrelevant. This describes what the enframing and organizing force of digital media might actually be today: deeply informing any conception of "human-as-is" with regard to the nature of experience.

But Virilio (1997, p. 20) goes beyond description: he suggests something tragic about this "'terminal man's'" shift towards velocity and the remote real-timeness, describing a loss of individual agency, physicality and will, a

Death in life and life in death 253

withdrawal into and "'cocooning'" in media and associated transportation technologies. He presents

> an individual who has lost the capacity for immediate intervention along with natural motricity and who abandons himself, for want of anything better, to the capacities of captors, sensors and other remote control scanners that turn him into a being controlled by the machine with which, they say, he talks.
>
> (p. 20)

Thus, the mediated nature of experience becomes a vulnerability, precisely because of the loss of control over senses and sensing, something crucial to "human-as-is." The final result is a "'terminal citizen' of a teletopical City that is going up faster and faster" (Virilio 1997, p. 21), a loss of "direct haptic experience . . . and with the grounds of human being, truly expressed" (Cubitt 2011, p. 72): "the world persists, but we are no longer in or of it" (p. 72). This is a critique of the distortion of mediation and its effect on human-world relations. A digitally mediated body and its senses, corrupts a real experience of the world. Thus, Virilio's critique is levelled against a persuasive imagination "the practice of the cosmopolis: a cosmopolis in which the material city of touch and contact is lost in the ephemeral, disappearing city of images and connections mediated by images" (Cubitt 2011, p. 71). Virilio's attacks the lack of critical engagement with information and the insidious production and assumption of a singular, static consumer. In the terms of Conley (2006, p. 77): "Viewers are glutted at teleports and listen to discourses aimed not at normalization but at the establishment of a unilateral and immobile consuming subject."

Virilio's "terminal citizen" depends on the human body being situated in the contemporary, networked city and having its senses augmented, mediated and extended through both analogue and digital, and particularly visual media. In this way, the "terminal citizen" materializes neither as knowing subject and known object, observed and observing nor as an abstract moral figure with retroactive rights. Instead it is a new "human-as-category" instance that is more influenced by human-world relations, specifically the role of technology in going beyond mediating towards organizing and enframing. This figure has an individuated body, even if that body, rather than being liberated, is continually weakened and rendered less authentic and self-aware and more placid through digitally-enabled cell-bit, flesh-silicon relations. This particular, real "human" form reads as doomed, less because of the ambiguity and opacity that "Man" suffers, than through its ignorant enslavement to economic mediation and circumscribed consumption brought about through visual relations. This is in contrast to the more abstract "Human" which, even if inherently vulnerable, is a protective (if retroactively protective), aspirational and self-aware figure (for how else would it self regulate?). "Terminal citizen" is both imbricated and brought

254   *Connor Graham and Alfred Montoya*

into being through digital media and thus only in a limited sense 'internally' free. Even its very presence as an instance of "human-as-is" is enframed by itself. The "Human," on the other hand, offers the tantalizing, if abstract possibility of liberty and autonomy and is therefore pliable as a figure for activism. "Terminal citizen," like "Man," is profoundly secular in its emphasis on individual experience: it does not seem to require an external authority (other than technology) for either meaning or existence. It is instead, like after-death communication, gripped by the ongoing experience of itself and the present (Lagerkvist, 2017, p. 104). We can observe how the "terminal citizen" is extended perceptually and sensorially, in ways that "Man" is not, and, because of these extended relations, is inescapably enmeshed in ways that the "Human" isn't either: the "Human's" very survival as an instance of a "category" has rested upon its mobility and concrete ambiguity. So we also begin to observe a very different, lurking and increasingly omnipresent mediating and mediated figure. This figure may itself be fallible and fragile and cannot easily be accounted for solely by "human-as-is" as we have discussed this with relation to other instances of "human-as-category," even with a generous acknowledgement of enframing technologies. It is only with the acknowledgement of temporal shift and worldly context of "human-as-category" that the range and extent of the digital, infrastructural force upon "human-as-is" is fully noticed and realized. It shows "human-as-is" is living and even being defined through digital technology. Virilio shows us that, as well as certain exclusions being necessitated in a contemporary context of near ubiquitous access and use of digital media among members of the global middle and upper socioeconomic classes in urban contexts that, certain inclusions create new, distinct vulnerabilities.

"Man," "Human," "terminal citizen" all espouse human beings' vulnerabilities differently, but all have a common sense of absence and mortality. They do not assume omnipresent digital thrownness quite to the extent of Lagerkvist's "exister." They instead suggest cell-bit, flesh-silicon boundaries and tensions. "Man's" vulnerability relates to the very sense of it not having any non-contingent meaning at all and thus being threatened with extinction. The vulnerability of the "Human" relates to its emptiness and dependence on death and suffering for meaning and power. In contrast, the "terminal citizen" exhibits an absence of any real, worldly engagement and will as well as a persistence and circulation that challenges even mortality. It is "terminal citizen," with its account of "human-as-is" through "human-as-category" that makes visible and critiques the historical, political and economic role of digital media. It is to digital media's affordance for creating human beings' vulnerabilities, particularly those of absence and mortality, that we turn in the next section.

Human now, life and death

What "human" inhabits relevant academic discourse on digital media and what kinds of vulnerabilities are articulated and elided? A simple starting

Death in life and life in death   255

point is a report produced through a meeting of Human-Computer Interaction researchers in 2007, which echoes some of the language of existential media studies and is ambitiously entitled "Being Human" (Harper et al. 2008). In this report "being human" is described variously as being transformation-oriented, as "a set of aspirations" (p. 9), and as necessarily influenced by current and future relationships with technology. The report argues for the importance of human values in the design of such technology: " 'being human' in our relationship with technology means that we need to bring to the fore and better understand human values and make them central to how we understand and design for a changing world" (p. 35).

The "human" in this excerpt reaches towards "as-category" status, while being less centered on the "as-is," human existence as lived through digital technologies. It has a profound relationship with technology, is even defined through these relations, and is also future-oriented. In this way it can be considered a hopeful advancement: none of the ambiguities and reflexive crises of "Man," vagueness and contestation of the "Human" or subjugation and distorted mediation of artificially extended subjectivities of "terminal citizen" are evident.

In this section we will begin to come to terms with key existential themes for digital media that also happen to be key, recently emerging themes in Human-Computer Interaction (HCI): mortality (Lagerkvist 2017, p. 103) and absence/presence (p. 105). While existential approaches to digital media may articulate these in terms of 'vulnerabilities,' HCI often understands them as value-laden, ongoing opportunities for design as the quotation from Harper et al. (2008) shows. So the question we now turn to is: What "human" is being proposed, brought forth and practiced in recent works that center on digital media, design and mortality? What are the defining features of the "terrain" that "the exister" is navigating? We reflect on this question through some key works from the last five years.

Graham et al. (2013) demonstrate, through analyses of current and emerging practices of grieving and memorializing online, that even after death "people's lives are extended, prolonged and ultimately changed in the present, future and in history through new circulations, repetitions, and recontextualizations" (p. 133). These authors conceptualize "human" in terms of some related but distinct articulations of "digital selves"; that is, the digital self as variously an "identity," "effigy" or "doppleganger" that enjoys multiple presences, both online and offline, and shapes how the human is "consumed, worked with and viewed after death," fundamentally altering our notion of bodily being (p. 134).

Virilio's "terminal citizen" appears relevant here through the focus on visual consumption, visual persistence, the augmented body and through the attention given to how the figures described are given shape or inflected by the publics within which they are enmeshed. These authors call our attention to "how publics are formed and connected with through different technologies as much as which publics are created and networked" providing the context for understanding the live(s) and death(s) of human beings (Graham

256   *Connor Graham and Alfred Montoya*

et al. 2013, p. 135). They call forth the potentially insidious and co-existent status of these digital formations and show how any understanding of mortality is deeply entangled with issues of absence and presence.

Christensen and Gotved demonstrate how online memorials alter the visibility of physical death, making death a part of our everyday lives, insofar as we are plugged into online social networks (2015). These authors, again reminiscent of "terminal citizen," conceptualize a figure caught up in "life," conceived as a dense web of significance, an individual node in a "meaningful structure" that is disrupted by the person's death, and that can be reconstituted by shared social/public rituals of mourning. But this figure is not entrapped in simulated life and commodified relationships. Instead, it is productive of sentiment and meaning: the public grieving associated with this figure, is "a quest to reestablish life as a meaningful structure without the deceased" and to bridge the gap their death has created (Christensen and Gotved 2015, p. 6). In this way the reflexiveness and meaning making of "Man" is apparent, and digital media is a key means through which this is achieved. Again we observe how mortality is profoundly altered by the new, inferred absences and prolonged presences enabled by digital media.

New internet technologies also generate anew an old problem for the deceased, as both remembering and forgetting are threatened by the mass production, circulation and consumption of images of the deceased by the living. What emerge are not just the age-old concerns about human beings being forgotten and obliterated, but concerns about being remembered "correctly," such that "even death is no longer a guarantee that one's story is over" (Graham and Montoya 2015, p. 10). The "human-as-is," in the present, may thus be characterized by a shift to a persistent representation decoupled from the body captured through "terminal citizen." But it also is constituted in the increasingly fragmentary and unregulated representations of the deceased made possible by the internet (Graham and Montoya 2015, p. 12). These potentially prolong one's engagement with the world beyond death. This is also precisely the kind of shift that Virilio describes through digital media with, for him, the negative consequence of detaching human beings from the real, as opposed to the experienced, world. Realizing the aspects of "terminal citizen," that relate to how human beings are connected to the world, allows us to anticipate the ongoing presence and changing mortality of the deceased in a world permeated by digital media. This realisation also shows the pathways to presence and absence the deceased afford.

Kern et al. (2013) provocatively assert that online memorials suspend the deceased indefinitely between life and oblivion through the actions of memory and speech permanently archived and publically displayed on social network sites. "If the dead are virtually memorialized, they never really die. The more in-depth the memorial and the greater its permanence, the more the deceased remain with the living" (Kern et al. 2013, p. 10). This attributes persistence to the dead, a consequence of the kind of visual, urban cultures that Virilio describes, making the real and unreal, the living and the dead

Death in life and life in death 257

indistinguishable and providing the dead with an enduring, if approximated visual presence (Virilio 1997). However, this assertion surely mistakes persistence for immortality. In this way, the "as-is" element of "the human" is neglected and shown to be crucial in understanding (and not mistaking) themes of presence and absence as they relate to mortality.

New problems also arise from the retention of digital materials related to the deceased, and the need to dispose of these symbolic materials to advance the grieving process (Sas et al. 2016; Lagerkvist 2017). The deceased enjoy a fragmentary and complex afterlife as oftentimes, the living do not always wish to retain painful reminders of the dead. The disorganization of people's digital collections make it "difficult to identify specific symbolic possessions to retain or to discard," meaning that grieving loved ones may accidentally encounter painful reminders unexpectedly, particularly online (Sas et al. 2016, p. 2). Thus the "as-is" properties of the human being and the visual persistence afforded by networks pose challenges for design. Those who try to dispose of digital materials find themselves instantly confronted by the "crude binary process" and "inflexibility" afforded by deletion (Sas et al. 2016, p. 2) with its own possible negative emotional and social outcomes. This lingering, fragmented persistence is somewhat reminiscent of the "Human" in how these various evocative fragments can be understood as having rights (e.g., to be retained) that are hard to act upon ahead of the tragedy of death. This work is also suggestive of the dual status of "Man," as both subject and object, as well as the multi-materiality and hybridity of the "terminal citizen" and its reliance on digital media for its circumscribed being and relations. Mortality may have changed, and in some sense the life of human beings has been extended, but the nature and subtlety of relations with human digital remains is defined through the mechanisms that generate, host and sort digital media.

Likewise, Staley has written about the etiquette of communicating around and with the deceased via social media platforms (2014). She notes that communication is directed toward the deceased themselves and rarely toward the community of mourners linked by the dead individual. This indicates that users imagined the deceased as a certain kind of entity; one aware of the activities of the living, and that was able to receive electronic communications from the living through digital messages (2014, p. 13) (cf. Lagerkvist, Chapter 9 this volume). "The implication is that, though the deceased's earthly body is lifeless, she retains some kind of body" that can see and hear these events and receive these messages (Staley 2014, pp. 14–15). Virilio's "terminal citizen" is evoked because of the deceased's visual persistence but so is the crisis of "Man". How might such a figure be considered both subject and object?

Nansen et al. (2014) claim that the dead can enjoy "new forms of social persistence" and are "animated": the dead are "no longer in repose, but socially active". They also claim they are *temporal*, subject to "worldly, secular and mundane engagements unmediated by church or sacrament" that are

258   Connor Graham and Alfred Montoya

temporary (2014, p. 113). This is an analysis echoed by Briggs and Thomas, who draw attention to the social life of one's digital footprint after death, thinking through the benefits and dangers posed by our "digital ghosts" (2014). This is in stark contrast to the kind of passive, living figures depicted by Virilio (1997) and the primacy of the visual that they depend on. These later analyses also begin to invoke not only a persistent presence by the dead but also their potential for social action through digital media and thereby a place in society for them, a presence despite an absence after death.

These scholars and others seem to argue that ICTs may afford a partial or depleted form of immortality in terms of what remains present online after death. By contrast, analyses, like those of Kera (2014), invert this familiar unidirectional orientation. Death becomes simply the body losing control over its various elements, because the body is not, in Virilio's (1997) terms, simply both depleted and sensorially extended through digital media. In fact, the body's very essence is a entanglement of flesh and silicon, cells and bits. The entropy-drive of those elements in their anarchic diversity is revealed to be a neutral state, rather than in any sense a "human" unity or identity. This treatment veers considerably from the "human-as-is" alluded to in other work we have considered here, towards a new posthuman means and category of being through digital media and particularly networks.

Other scholars argue that ICTs, and the rapidly evolved genealogy of older technologies that shaped their present form (photography, radio, telephonics, etc.) have provided the avenue, within the secular regime of knowledge of the late twentieth century, for the emergence of the "Human." This "abstraction" was from the beginning bifurcated between its physical/historical specificity, and its (after)life as a collective representation, curated symbol, or circulated cypher (Montoya 2015; see also Fukushima 2015). It also emerged just as these older technologies were obtaining ubiquity. Indeed, as we may move beyond an arithmetic and probabilistic media ordering regime (Cubitt 2011), it is perhaps the "Human" that is potentially the most persuasive category for its convenience, malleability and agency to act upon the living. While Virilio's "terminal citizen" may connect with distinct aspects of "human-as is" and "human-as-category" presented in recent literature on mortality and digital media, it is the "Human" that begins to evoke the necessary and felt social presence and post-mortem power of the distributed and increasingly non-optical remains of the dead.

Conclusion: we (late) moderns, under the open sky

In this chapter we have made key distinctions in order to gain some clarity regarding what particular human beings are talking about when they talk about "the human," creating a crude map of "the human" in recent discourse on digital media. To achieve this we have deployed, as a heuristic device, two versions of this "human" – "human-as-is" and "human-as-category" – in order to explore how "the human" has been conceived, proposed, responded

Death in life and life in death 259

to or acted upon in the recent past. We have maintained a special focus on the articulation of these figures with particular configurations of discourse and technology. We have traced some of the various instances of "human-as-category" through the recent past and considered its ongoing relationship to "human-as-is." It should be no surprise that we have found that conceptions of "human-as-category" are numerous and varied. We have discovered a tendency to simply conflate this "human-as-is" concept of a concrete, existing, mortal instance of a human being with an abstract proposal concerning a universal character or "nature" or form and to not question its possible transformation. It is possible that, as more of life is lived through digital media, "human-as-is" will be questioned more as "human-as-category" reaches in, informs and even shapes it to a greater and greater extent. It is notable that there are elements of both in the "terminal citizen," the most recent "human-as-category" we have treated, and in the way "the human" concept is discussed with regard to mortality, absence and presence. Indeed, the "exister," like "Man," seems to possess the ambition to emerge as a 'meta' "human-as-category" compressing the difference between "human-as-is" to nothingness regardless of time and context. Our meagre analysis of contemporary academic discourse, if connecting strongly with existential themes, shows that while it is possible to isolate and apply discrete instances of "human-as-category," there is no single, preferred instance across the scholarship we have considered nor even a consistent appeal to one, singular instance. "Man," "Human" and "terminal citizen" seem capable of coexistence.

It is tempting to consider recent new anthropology in the field of artificial intelligence (see Richardson 2015) as pointing to new locations where we might encounter and/or generate particularly new instances of "human-as-category" through explorations of "human-as-is." The quest to develop a truly human-like AI necessarily must involve some sense of what the "human-as-is" really is. Alan Turing's famous "Imitation Game" is often credited with proposing "an 'operational' or 'behaviorist' definition of 'thinking' or 'intelligence,' though he considered himself to have proposed merely a criterion rather than a definition of thinking" (Guo 2015, p. 4). As Turing later put it, his aim was to find out " 'how we think ourselves' by way of 'making a thinking machine' " (ibid), or, as we have seen with the "Human" and "terminal citizen," probing "human-as-is" through creating a new instance of "human-as-category". Turing considered this self-knowledge to be a particularly human characteristic. This observation both runs through "Man," the "Human" and "terminal citizen" and also necessarily expands our definition of "human-as-is." It is the point of connection between our two versions of "the human."

Yet this move to suggest another instance of "human-as-category" is perhaps the wrong one conceptually, underplaying how our exploration has allowed for another concept, on a par with "human-as-category" and "human-as-is," to emerge. Guo writes that "The digitization of social and

260   Connor Graham and Alfred Montoya

personal knowledge has created an abstract web of information in a digitized virtual reality, in which knowledge about ourselves has been reformulated digitally" by means of (simple, not true) AI technologies (Guo 2015, p. 6). Thus, the self-knowledge and knowledge of other human beings that are crucial to "human-as-is" have been externalized and disembedded, like the "Human" instance of "human-as-category," through and for an apparatus, in this case digital media. Guo quotes Julie Chu, who wrote that we are in the end all "encoding ourselves for the machine" (Chu 2001, p. 135, in Guo 2015) or, in the terms of McKelvey, Tiessen and Simcoe (2013) a "simulation machine," bringing forth extended and reshaped vulnerabilities as much as extended perception. These insights are in line with Lagerkvist's conflation of questions of existence with questions of technology (2017, p. 96) and argument that such technologies have become ways of being.

This perspective is suggestive not only of new exclusions, for human beings who are both absent and present, alive and dead for digital media, but also evokes a form of life that in its abstraction and ability to act upon the living is pervasive and persuasive enough to be beyond what any new "human-as-category" instance can describe. Digital media has enabled not merely extension through new forms of persistence, experience and circulation but has also become a force in the world. So we must "reengineer key concepts – such as attention, ownership, privacy and responsibility" to give us a framework within which "our onlife experience may be understood and improved" (Floridi 2015, p. 1). The ubiquity of digital media, for such scholars, may affect every aspect of "human-as-is," from our self-conception and sociality to our very conception of reality. However, the fate of "the human" cannot be considered through the perspective of human beings alone, as we have attempted here. We have made a world from the digital map we sought to use to describe it. We are now not only searching for the means to navigate the territory the map became, but are also exploring what we might mean to that territory.

By way of example, we suggest that the "Human," the object currently at the center of human rights and humanitarianism, is not only the product of a historical moment, a failed artefact or fabulous construct, but a new starting point for both critical perspectives and imaginative possibilities. This "human-as-category," as our analysis shows, points us toward specific issues of control and rights, and tells us something about today's historical, political, ethical and economic assumptions concerning the "human-as-is." It also, because of its impotence beyond a rights-focused apparatus and the limitations of its abstractness, forces a close examination of the precise nature of the time, politics and very materialities that make it possible, sustain and govern it. Its absences vividly bring forth distinct, if unpredictable, situated and fragile presences and less visible forces, including those that are non-human: the infrastructural, the algorithmic, the symbolic. It may be the result, over the past half century, of specific conglomerations of human beings or "existers" seeking to think, name and speak of themselves, to carve

Death in life and life in death 261

a space for themselves within, and navigate a world of rapidly evolving dangers driven by technological change.

In an essay on the status of storytelling under commercial and industrial conditions of production, Walter Benjamin reflected on time, technology and the experience of human beings, of what remained of the human being caught up in the inexorable, productive and destructive capacities of the modern world.

> A generation that had gone to school on a horse-drawn streetcar now stood under the open sky in a countryside in which nothing remained unchanged but the clouds, and beneath these clouds, in a field of force of destructive torrents and explosions, was the tiny, fragile, human body.
>
> (1968, p. 84)

We must be alert not only to 'who we are' or 'who we may be,' but also to 'who we have been,' as we imaginatively consider the possible fates of "the human" in times when digital media reach beyond the arithmetic and probabilistic and embrace the imaginative possibilities of a vectoral network that is "not self-identical, that plunges into accident and disappointment, and in which machines have as much to say as humans" (Cubitt 2011, pp. 87–88). What these new struggles and categories might be, is something only time will tell us, but we ignore or elide the trajectory of its becoming at our peril. In another vein, in that same essay, Benjamin (1968, p. 87) also reminded us that the erosion of long-held notions or meanings or forms, though troubling and disruptive, also makes it possible for us to recognize a new significance, a new beauty, in what is vanishing, under newly open skies.

Bibliography

Arendt, H., 1962. *The Origins of Totalitarianism.* Cleveland and New York: The World Publishing Company.

Armitage, J., 2013. Vision, Inertia, and the Mobile Telephone: On the Origins of Control Space and the Spread of Sociopolitical Cybernetics. *In*: J. M. Wise and H. Koskela, eds. *New Visualities, New Technologies: The New Ecstasy of Communication.* Surrey: Ashgate, 67–82.

Benjamin, W., 1968. *Illuminations.* New York: Schoken Books.

Briggs, P. and Thomas, L., 2014. The Social Value of Digital Ghosts. *In*: C. M. Moreman and A. D. Lewis, eds. *Digital Death: Mortality and beyond in the Digital Age.* Santa Barbara: Praeger, 125–142.

Christensen, D. R. and Gotved, S., 2015. Online Memorial Culture: An Introduction. *New Review of Hypermedia and Multimedia,* 21 (1–2), 1–9.

Chu, J., 2001. When Alan Turing Was a Computer: Notes on the Rise and Decline of Punch Card Technologies. *Connect: Art, Politics, Theory, Practice,* 1 (2), 133–139.

Conley, V. A., 2006. *Ecopolitics: The Environment in Poststructuralist Thought.* London and New York: Routledge.

Cubitt, S., 2011. Vector Politics and the Aesthetics of Disappearance. *In*: J. Armitage, ed. *Virilio Now: Current Perspectives in Virlio Studies.* Cambridge: Polity Press, 68–91.

262 Connor Graham and Alfred Montoya

Dreyfus, H. L., 1992. Heidegger's History of the Being of Equipment. *In*: H. L. Dreyfus and H. Hall, eds. *Heidegger: A Critical Reader*. Oxford: Blackwell, 173–185.

Dreyfus, H. L. and Rabinow, P., 1983. *Michel Foucault: Beyond Structuralism and Hermeneutics*. Chicago, IL: University of Chicago Press.

Edwards, N. P., 2003. Infrastructure and Modernity: Force, Time, and Social Organization in the History of Sociotechnical Systems. *In*: T. J. Misa, P. Brey and A. Feenberg, eds. *Modernity and Technology*. Cambridge, MA: MIT Press, 185–225.

Floridi, L. ed., 2015. *The Onlife Manifesto: Being Human in a Hyperconnected Era*. New York and London: Springer.

Foucault, M., 1971. *The Order of Things: An Archaeology of the Human Sciences*. New York: Random House.

Fukushima, M., 2015. Corpus Mysticum Digitale (Mystical Body Digital)?: On the Concept of Two Bodies in the Era of Digital Technology. *Mortality: Promoting the Interdisciplinary Study of Death and Dying*, 20 (4), 303–318.

Graham, C., Gibbs, M. and Aceti, L., 2013. Introduction to the Special issue on the Death, Afterlife and Immortality of Bodies and Data. *The Information Society*, 29 (3), 133–141.

Graham, C. and Montoya, A., 2015. Death, After-Death and the Human in the Internet Era: Remembering, Not Forgetting Professor Michael C. Kearl (1949–2015). *Mortality: Promoting the Interdisciplinary Study of Death and Dying*, 20 (4), 287–302.

Guo, T., 2015. Alan Turing: Artificial Intelligence and Human Self-Knowledge. *Anthropology Today*, 31 (6), 3–7.

Harper, R., Rodden, T., Rogers, Y. and Sellen, A. eds., 2008. *Being Human: Human-Computer Interaction in the Year 2020*. Cambridge: Microsoft Research Ltd.

Hunt, L., 2007. *Inventing Human Rights: A History*. New York and London: W. W. Norton & Company.

Ihde, D., 1990. *Technology and the Lifeworld*. Bloomington: Indiana University Press.

International Telecommunications Union, 2017. *ICT Facts and Figures, 2017*. ICT Data and Statistics Division. Geneva, Switzerland. Available at: www.itu.int/en/ITU-D/Statistics/Documents/facts/ICTFactsFigures2017.pdf (accessed: November 2017).

Johnson, M. G. and Symonides, J., 1998. *The Universal Declaration of Human Rights: A History of Its Creation and Implementation, 1948–1998*. Paris: UNESCO Publishing.

Kera, D., 2014. Necromedia-Reversed Ontogeny or Posthuman Evolution. *In*: C. M. Moreman and A. D. Lewis, eds. *Digital Death: Mortality and beyond in the Digital Age*. Santa Barbara: Praeger, 181–196.

Kern, R., 2013. Forman, A. E. and Gil-Egui, G. R.I.P.: Remain in Perpetuity. Facebook Memorial Pages. *Telematics and Informatics*, 30 (1), 2–10.

Kerr, J., 2004. 'The Goody-Goods Are No Good': Notes on Power and Authority in the Early History of Psychoanalysis, with Special Reference to Training. *Psychoanalytic Inquiry*, 24 (1), 7–30.

Lagerkvist, A., 2017. Existential Media: Toward a Theorization of Digital Throwness. *New Media & Society*, 19 (1), 96–110.

Lagerkvist, A. and Andersson, Y., 2017. The Grand Interruption: Death Online and Mediated Lifelines of Shared Vulnerability. *Feminist Media Studies*. Available at: https://doi.org/10.1080/14680777.2017.1326554 (accessed: 10 October 2017).

Luhmann, N., 1998. *Observations on Modernity*. Stanford, CA: Stanford University Press.

McKelvey, F., Tiessen, M. and Simcoe, L., 2013. *We Are What We Tweet: The Problem with a Big Data World When Everything You Say Is Data Mined* [online] 3 June. Available at: http://culturedigitally.org/2013/06/we-are-what-we-tweet-the-problem-with-a-big-data-world- when-everything-you-say-is-data-mined/ (accessed: 14 August 2017).

Montoya, A., 2015. Digital Relics of the Saints of Affliction: HIV/AIDS, Digital Images and the Neoliberalization of Health Humanitarianism in Contemporary Vietnam. *Mortality: Promoting the Interdisciplinary Study of Death and Dying*, 20 (4), 334–350.

Moyn, S., 2010. *The Last Utopia: Human Rights in History.* Cambridge, MA: Harvard University Press.

Nansen, B., Arnold, M., Gibbs, M. and Kohn, T., 2014. The Restless Dead in the Digital Cemetery. *In*: C. M. Moreman and A. D. Lewis, eds. *Digital Death: Mortality and beyond in the Digital Age.* Santa Barbara: Praeger, 111–124.

Peters, J. D., 2015. *The Marvelous Clouds: Towards a Philosophy of Elemental Media.* Chicago, IL and London: University of Chicago Press.

Rees, T., 2014. Humanity/Plan; or, on the "Stateless" Today (Also Being and Anthropology of Global Health). *Cultural Anthropology*, 29 (3), 457–478.

Richardson, K., 2015. *An Anthropology of Robots and AI: Annihilation Anxiety and Machines.* New York, NY and London: Routledge.

Rosenberger, R. and Verbeek, P.-P., 2015. *Postphenomenological Investigations: Essays on Human-Technology Relations.* Lanham: Lexington Books.

Sartre, J.-P., 1962. *Sketch for a Theory of the Emotions.* Trans. P. Mairet. London: Methuen & Co.

Sas, C., Whittaker, S. and Zimmerman, J., 2016. Design for Rituals of Letting Go: An Embodiment Perspective on Disposal Practices Informed by Grief Therapy. *ACM Transactions on Computer-Human Interaction*, 23 (4), Article 21.

Staley, E., 2014. Messaging the Dead: Social Network Sites and Theologies of Afterlife. *In*: C. M. Moreman and A. D. Lewis, eds. *Digital Death: Mortality and beyond in the Digital Age.* Santa Barbara: Praeger, 9–22.

Virilio, P., 1994. *The Vision Machine.* Translated by Julie Rose. Bloomington and Indianapolis: Indiana University Press.

Virilio, P., 1997. *Open Sky.* London: Verso.

Afterword

Charles M. Ess

Initial considerations

Existentialist thoughts and motifs – beginning with our *mortality* as the defining fact of human existence – can be found in the oldest and most foundational of human narratives. Examples begin with *The Epic of Gilgamesh* (ca. 1800 BCE) and extend through the "Garden of Eden" account in the book of Genesis and subsequent admonitions in the Wisdom books such as Job and Ecclesiastes. As Amanda Lagerkvist develops in more detail in her Introduction, specifically modern existentialism begins with Søren Kierkegaard, extends through Friedrich Nietzsche, and flourishes in the decades of and following World War II.

For manifold reasons, existentialism as at least a larger cultural phenomenon and force began to disappear in the 1970s. But despite modernist dreams of immortality via new technologies – including the "Digital Immortality" of transhumanism – mortality remains stubbornly with us. And the central imperatives of existentialism – acknowledge rather than deny your mortality, and so, begin to take responsibility for discerning and creating the meaning of your existence – thereby remain cogent for an authentic life (e.g., Lagerkvist and Andersson 2017, 5f.). At the same time, however, as Lagerkvist further makes clear, the emergence of digital technologies – including computational devices and networked communications – over the past five decades or so have radically transformed our human condition. *Contra* the assumption that technology is something external and independent of human beings, we are rather clear that human existence has been inextricably interwoven with technology since our earliest evolution. Especially distinctive about the contemporary era is that technologies of many sorts have *enveloped* our existence – so much so that, as Lagerkvist elaborates in the introduction, these technologies achieve a foundational *ontological* status: they become the ground of our being and the encompassing background of our existence. This means: as human existence is so fundamentally transformed by the technological developments of the past five decades or so – so existential thought and affect are correlatively transformed.

Lagerkvist argues that these developments are also entangled with our originary human precariousness. A central theme in the project of existential media studies, as it has been developing in the past four years in the context of the Existential Terrains program and the Digital Existence conferences, is precisely that of *vulnerability*. While vulnerability and mortality go hand in hand, the range of ways we are vulnerable and experience vulnerability in the contemporary digital era are in some ways distinctive – *prima facie* in negative or threatening ways. But vulnerability is also fruitful and positive. This irreducible ambiguity constitutes the knot of our digital existence.

In fact, the second Digital Existence conference foregrounded vulnerability in multiple ways, as its title "Precarious Media Life" suggests. In the following, I draw on the conference keynotes and many of the conference presentations to explore in further detail these large developments in existential approaches to life in a digital era. I begin with primary considerations about technology and vulnerability discussed in Mark Coeckleberg's keynote address as well as in his broader work (2013, 2017a, 2017b). Here I attend specifically to the themes of embodiment and natality. These initial considerations then point to a foundational shift accompanying the rise of digital and networked technologies – namely, the shift from more *individual* to more *relational* senses of the self. Our vulnerability – both as individuals but especially as relational selves, whose relationality deeply depends upon new technologies – then directly implicates the ethical. In particular, Coeckelbergh (2010), Verbeek (2011), and Vallor (2016) foreground *virtue ethics* as especially well-suited to our contemporary *existenz* as relational selves. I then take up Peter-Paul Verbeek's endnote at Precarious Media Life: the endnote offered both a summary of important highlights from the conference and their connections with his larger goal of "existentializing technology." I foreground especially the ontological and anthropological stakes in his philosophy of technology, along with the Kantian legacies at work here.

I then turn to digital religion (DR) and its multiple intersections with existential media studies (EMS). Drawing on Heidi Campbell and Mia Lövheim's (2011) taxonomy of four waves of DR, I first focus on the current fourth wave as explicitly attending to the existential (Campbell 2017b). Experiences of *transcendence* are the primary focus here – whether in connection with traditional or confessional religious beliefs, and/or in more "spiritual" fashion (i.e., as no longer constrained to specific dogma) or, indeed, secular experiences.

Second, these interweavings between EMS and DR bring to the fore what I take as one of the most pressing set of questions and issues confronting contemporary existentialists. On the one hand, both classic and contemporary existentialist approaches insist on the (relational-) *individual* as the one who is ultimately responsible for discerning and/or constructing the meaning of our existence. Very often, such meaning entails *resistance* to various forms of authority, including prevailing norms and practices. In the ancient Greeks, such resistance is exemplified in Antigone's decision to bury her brother Polyneices, in direct contradiction to Creon's order (Walker 2008). Similarly, Socrates refuses to follow the dictates of "the many," in the name of sustaining

266   *Charles M. Ess*

the integrity of his soul (*psyche*), if at the cost of his life. And on early readings of the Garden story in Genesis, the woman's *disobedience* – even to divine authority – is seen as the essential step in the primal couple's "growing up," i.e., their acquiring wisdom and autonomy (Ess 1995).

Resistance on both religious and rational grounds is likewise essential to the foundational existentialist maneuver of moving beyond prevailing beliefs and norms, as these often work against a felt recognition of mortality and thereby against our taking responsibility for meaning. But how is such resistance – what Mark Coeckelbergh denoted as "hacking our vulnerability" – conceivable or possible in the contemporary era? I close by reviewing what I see as especially helpful suggestions for how to do so by three contributors in the Precarious Existence conference, beginning with Margaret Schwartz and then keynoters Wendy Hui Kyong Chun and Beverley Skeggs. I conclude by noting how their concrete examples of how resistance is both possible and practicable in turn index a larger shift towards a post-digital era.

Philosophical approaches

The ambiguity of vulnerability – the centrality of embodiment

In his recent book, *New Romantic Cyborgs: Romanticism, Information Technology, and the End of the Machine* (2017a), Mark Coeckelbergh argues that our contemporary world is constituted by the deep interfolding of what we otherwise take as opposites in modernity – namely, rationalism and romanticism. On the contrary, most especially as facilitated by recent technologies and their development, the two increasingly blend into one another:

> As Enlightenment rationalists, we love machines. As romantics, we want life, love, humans, wonder and mystery. Now it seems that we can have both . . . Robots become friendlier, and cyborgs celebrate the union of humans and machine. Passion, relationships, beauty and the sublime are not to be found outside technology; smart technologies and media offer it all.
>
> (2017a, p. 15)

Coeckelbergh is nonetheless fully alive to the far more negative and threatening dimensions of this new enmeshment – specifically with regard to our central focus on *vulnerability*. In his keynote address, "Vulnerable Cyborgs Reloaded: From Narrative Technologies for Self-shaping to Vulnerability Transformations in Modernity and the Anthropocene," Coeckelbergh (2017b) reminded us of the trope of modern technology: in Descartes' terms, we are to use our new science, as a form of "mastery and possession of nature," with the specific aims of eliminating labor and disease – perhaps even death (cf. Ess 2017). In short, modern technologies – as manifested

Afterword 267

in, e.g., Google's project to "cure death" and the transhumanist goal of "digital immortality" (e.g., Popper 2013) – aim to eliminate the vulnerabilities inherent to us as embodied and thereby mortal human beings. But the irony or paradox is that the greater our engagement and entwinement with new technologies – beginning with our "always on" interconnectivity via social media and other internet-facilitated technologies (see Lagerkvist, chapter 9) – the ever more vulnerable we become in turn (Coeckelbergh 2013). Similarly attending to the existential vulnerabilities of the digital age, Coeckelbergh argued for taking ethical responsibility for our technological world, and for the vulnerabilities that we are also complicit in crafting.

The list of vulnerabilities here – first of all, in a negative or threatening sense – is staggering. They begin with threats to privacy from governmental and corporate surveillance; various forms of hacking, trolling, identity theft, harassment and bullying, and so on. At the same time, however, Coeckelbergh further observes the existential point, familiar from Jaspers (see Lagerkvist, Introduction) and others: our vulnerability has its positive or fecund dimensions as well. Paraphrasing Coeckelbergh slightly: we may have to die alone – but we are born in *relationship*; and so we can counterbalance *memento mori* with *memento nasci*. For Coeckelbergh, the newborn is a prime exemplar of the intrinsic and inescapable ambiguity of our vulnerability – i.e., its dual potentials for loss and creativity. The same can be said, I suggest, for new lovers (Ess 2011, 2016).

From the individual to the relational self – and (virtue) ethics

Moreover, this existential understanding of vulnerability foregrounds a foundational shift in our understanding of the self and personal identity accompanying the rise of new media technologies over the past five decades or so – namely, from a more *individual* towards a more *relational* sense of self. As the example of the newborn emphasizes, the relational self is all but completely defined by the various relationships that connect us with one another – beginning with the familial but extending throughout the social, as well as the natural and, for some, the transcendent. Whatever else they do, the contemporary technologies of networked communication – most especially social media – both facilitate and embody in turn our multiple relationships with one another. On the one hand, these manifold openings into hundreds and thousands of diverse "friendships," and any number of other kinds of relationships as mediated by these technologies, are unquestionably positive – including from existential perspectives. The field of Death Online Research (DOR), as discussed by Lagerkvist (Introduction), provides premier examples. As she and others have now well documented, the 24/7 availability of a compassionate ear in our moments of deepest and unshakable grief can make all the difference to our psychic and bodily survival (Chapter 9, this volume). Still more positively, in virtue ethics terms, these new forms of connectivity have opened up unparalleled venues and opportunities

268 *Charles M. Ess*

for our *flourishing*, for our unfolding our best capacities and abilities, both for ourselves and in concert with others.

But again, such interconnectivity simultaneously makes us deeply vulnerable in negative ways as well. Especially for young people, such connections – first and foremost via social media – are essential to an unfolding sense of self and identity. But as Annette Markham (2017) put it at the conference, more or less all of us, as entwined within new media technologies, use these as a kind of echo-location: like submarine SONAR systems, we send out a ping into the otherwise murky ether – hoping for an echo, a reply that thereby affirms our existence and tells us who we are. Dependency on such responses is in fact a primary marker of the relational self: at its extreme, there is no self apart from the relationships that make it up, and much of the work of such a self is to cultivate and sustain those relationships. Markham notes that especially for young people "vulnerability in this epoch is to be disconnected." This lack of connection is felt as a deeply existential threat: "When we have no response, and our self is identified through the flow of responses, we can feel bereft, vulnerable, non-existent" (2017).

In light of both the negative and positive possibilities of vulnerability, Coeckelbergh (2017b) asks the central question for us as "romantic cyborgs": Is there room to hack our vulnerability, or is resistance futile?

A primary way to hack our vulnerability, I suggest, is precisely by taking on the *ethical* implications of such relationality and vulnerability. In particular *virtue ethics* and an allied *ethics of care* are both consequences of the turn to relationality as well as a central approach to how we respond to and manage both the negative and positive sides of our existential vulnerability. This is the argument put forward by Ganaele Langlois (Chapter 7), Vincent Miller (Chapter 8), and also by Margaret Schwartz (Chapter 3) in this volume. This is in part, as I and others have illustrated elsewhere, as virtue ethics re-emerges over the past few decades, precisely in conjunction with the rise of the relational self. Most briefly, virtue ethics – whose keywords and aims include developing our best capacities (virtues) as requisite to our flourishing and enjoying what we experience, both individually and collectively as a good life – begins in world traditions such as Confucian and Buddhist thought, as well as Platonic and Aristotelian traditions, that presume the relational self (cf. Vallor 2016, pp. 35–49; Ess 2014). Coeckelburgh endorses a virtue ethics approach in his own work (e.g., 2010); and as we are about to see, Peter-Paul Verbeek makes especially important connections between virtue ethics and the central elements of his own analyses of technology and being human.

Ontology, anthropology and Kantian questions

In his endnote, "Existentializing Technology: Vulnerability in a Digital Age" (2017), Peter-Paul Verbeek draws on a number of sources in anthropology and philosophy of technology to first make clear that human beings

Afterword 269

have co-evolved with our technologies since developing our first tools. As Lagerkvist notes in her Introduction, the conception of "originary technicity" (Introduction; cf. Clemens and Nash, Chapter 1) is especially helpful here: affiliated specifically with Bernard Stiegler, for Verbeek this means that "something is missing in us: we need technologies to live our lives." This means in part that as we must live our lives through technology; technology not only defines our human condition but also is central to our ways of dealing with our human condition – i.e., our condition, we can note, as an *existenz*, or, in Lagerkvist's term, as *existers*.

Verbeek follows Coeckelbergh in foregrounding how this technologically-informed *existenz* is thereby one of a *self* that is at once individual and highly *relational*. Moreover, Verbeek's approach to existentialism is helpful on especially three points. First, he connects these views on human existence as technologically-mediated with the classic Kantian questions: What can I know? What ought I do? What can I hope? (A805/B833;[1] Kant 1965, p. 635). While in this volume, the initial Kantian epistemological question is subsumed under the first interest in ontology – the remaining two questions map directly into our shared focus on *ethics* and *transcendence*.

In the case of *ethics*: Verbeek conjoins the late Foucault with Kant and the Enlightenment in ways that return us directly to the primal existential imperatives of becoming conscious of ourselves and our possibilities. Specifically, in his last works on writing as a "technology of the self," (1988), Foucault argued for the central role of *literacy* (Ess 2014) in helping forge a sense of an especially more *individual* sense of selfhood. Foucault begins with the maxim of the Delphic oracle, as reported by Socrates, "know thyself" (*Phaedrus*, 229E; Connor Graham and Alfred Montoya, Chapter 12, this volume). As Ganaele Langlois explores here (Chapter 7), Foucault traces how, from (at least) the time of Socrates forward, such self-knowledge implicates the ancient *virtue* of *self-care (epimelēsthai sautou)*: such self-care, further, is facilitated and fostered in particular by the technology of *writing*. Most briefly, in writing we are able to set forth our selves – in diaries, letters, etc. – in ways that allow for subsequent reflection and, perhaps, self-critique: such critical *self*-dialogue can thereby inspire and issue in desires and efforts to become something different, a *better* self. In this light, writing emerges as a technology *par excellence* for fostering the virtue of self-care – and thereby, our own (re-) constructions of our selves (Ess 2014). As the connection with virtue and thereby virtue ethics implies, such technologically-mediated self-care and self-becoming are at once deeply ethical: specifically, as Verbeek puts it, such "ethics is what we will become."

Second, Verbeek interprets Kant's famous essay, "What Is the Enlightenment?" ([1784] 1991) through an existential lens. Specifically, Verbeek takes the points and challenges posed by Kant to push us to develop "a limit attitude" in which we recognize, to begin with, the fundamentally mediated character of our existence. Moreover, he highlights Kant's motto of the Enlightenment – *sapere aude* (have the courage to) think for yourself – as

270   *Charles M. Ess*

again a foundational starting point for a contemporary existential ethics of having the courage to acknowledge our mortality and vulnerability, and thereby move towards taking responsibility for our being and our becoming.

To invoke Kant in these ways, we should note, is thereby to invoke what for Kant was also a *virtue ethics*. Hence the connections here with Foucault and Kant thereby centrally connect virtue ethics with contemporary existential thought. Similarly, Shannon Vallor takes up the existential thought of José Ortega y Gasset as a primary driver in the development of her "technomoral virtues" (Vallor 2016, pp. 244–252).

Third, Verbeek notes that Kant's "What can I hope?" opens the door to religion (cf. Kant 1793). For his part, Verbeek highlights the connection here with our contemporary focus on how technologies organize and mediate experiences of *transcendence* – whether these take place in conjunction with more traditional religious frameworks and/or in varying degrees of independence from such frameworks. In both popular and, as we are about to see, the more precise parlance of digital religion, the latter sorts of experiences are often denoted in terms of "spirituality." Either way, this Kantian question thereby crystalizes a central connection between contemporary existentialism and digital religion.

Existential media studies and digital religion

As noted at the outset, existential insights and approaches to our human condition are rooted in and constantly overlap with what we might think of as religious frameworks and views, beginning with the admonitions of Siduri, the wine/wisdom goddess, who teaches Gilgamesh how to respond to his deep realization of mortality (Sandars 1972, p. 102). This instantiates the intrinsic – indeed, deeply historically rooted – interconnections between contemporary existentialism as taken up in existential media studies (EMS) and the field of digital religion (DR).

With beginnings in the earliest studies of what was then called computer-mediated communication (CMC), DR now stands as its own field within Media and Communication Studies. Heidi Campbell and Mia Lövheim (2011) are primary figures and authorities in the development of DR over the past two decades. As Campbell and Lövheim map out the first wave of DR in the early 1990s, analysis was shaped by prevailing binaries at the time – first, between utopian and dystopian approaches to all things internet, and second, between the online and the offline, and its corollaries such as "virtual" vs. "real," or, as William Gibson (1984) inspired many of us to think and say, between cyberspace and meatspace.

These dualisms, in fact, rest directly on Christian, specifically Augustinian foundations (Ess 2010). On multiple grounds, however, these dualisms grew increasingly suspect, if not simply irrelevant, by the mid- to late 1990s – thereby leading to DR's subsequent waves. For our purposes, the most important is the current fourth wave, first as it moves solidly beyond

Afterword 271

the virtual-real divide of the 1990s, emphasizing instead (as do many other empirically grounded findings) the effective blurring – if not erasure – of such a boundary in our uses of internet-facilitated communication in our everyday lives. The focus is thus on "religious actors' negotiations between their online and offline lives, and how this informs a broader understanding of the religious in the contemporary society" (Campbell 2017a, p. 17). More specifically, digital religion attends to how these negotiations transform our understandings of *religious tradition, authority, authenticity*, as well as *identity*.

Finally, a central trend in especially wave 4 research is how "religion in the broad sense is transformed as traditional notions of religious communities as tightly-bound institutions transition into more loosely-bound social relations that are highly *individualized*" (Campbell 2017b, p. 4; emphasis added, CME).[2] Campbell sees two large themes in these developments – namely, (1) (post) secularization of religion in a digital age, and (2) existential questions in digital religion (Campbell 2017b, p. 4).

The second large theme takes up "how living in a digital world is shaping both our attitudes and our practices relative to key existential questions," such as embodiment and authenticity (again), along with "beginning- and end-of-life issues" – i.e., natality and mortality (Campbell 2017b, 4f.). In particular, this existential turn includes attention to domains otherwise often overlooked in DR, including "how sexuality and gender are informed when the religious and digital contexts and outlooks intersect (i.e., Lövheim 2013)" (Campbell 2017b, p. 5; cf. Ess 2016). These clear linkages with EMS are especially explicit as Campbell directly takes up the work of Amanda Lagerkvist (e.g., 2016, in Campbell 2017b, p. 5).

In short, an important dialogue has already begun between existential media studies and digital religion: in this volume, the dialogue focuses especially on transcendence.

Transcendence

Existentialism and digital religion overlap perhaps most significantly in our shared explorations of transcendence, the theme of the third section of this volume. As Lagerkvist introduces the concept in terms of "existential strivings," the transcendent begins at but (seems to) extends beyond "the limits of the known" (p. 12). "Such strivings," she writes, "conjure what lies in the shadows, beyond our sense of control and, importantly, beyond words," as well as "beyond scientific methods and truth claims" (ibid).

In my experience, one striking example of such existential transcendence is the autobiographical account of a young woman who grew up under the aggressively anti-religious regime of the former East Germany (DDR – *Deutsche Demokratische Republik*). As reported by Manfred Pirner (2017), this young woman began to encounter (quasi-) transcendent experiences in specific videogames: eventually, she began to explore German Lutheran

272   *Charles M. Ess*

Christianity and ultimately chose to be baptized as an adult. Pirner sees here a strong example of the point made by Mia Lövheim: "what we are seeing is not necessarily the ruin of religious socialization, but rather the emergence of a different form" (Lövheim 2012, p. 155; cited by Pirner 2017). For Pirner, such experiences provide young people the freedom to address existential and religious questions in their own language – one that is, manifestly, strongly influenced by media experiences *per se*. This freedom means, moreover, young people use the media with religious elements for constructing existential meaning in their lives – but not necessarily religious meaning (Pirner 2018).

As experiences of *existential* transcendence thus emerge both within and beyond the boundaries of formal religion, they thus highlight a chief benefit of existential approaches in both multi-cultural and highly secular-rational societies: namely, they offer such experiences to those who otherwise might not deeply identify with a given religious tradition, and within a philosophical framework and language for coming to grips with these and other limit-experiences. As this example suggests, existential media studies and digital religion, as they approach both shared but sometimes importantly different experiences – beginning with transcendence – stand as two distinct but mutually complimentary frameworks. From my perspective, as this volume instantiates, exploring these shared foci of human existence promises to be extraordinarily fruitful. It is thereby a further concrete expression of the existential interactions with fourth wave digital religion.

Existential meaning and possibilities for resistance

Transcendence as extending across and between the more recognizably "religious" and the more secular existential is but one such interweaving in the history of these traditions. Again, existential thought in Western traditions begins within explicitly religious accounts such as *The Epic of Gilgamesh*, the second Genesis creation story, and the wisdom literatures. In turn, Antigone and Socrates are figures of both reason and religion – as are, arguably, most figures prior to the Enlightenment.[3] Even in the twentieth century, the otherwise secular right to conscientious objection is often rooted in such religious sources as the American Quakers and Mahatma Gandhi, who inspired the Baptist preacher of non-violent civil disobedience Martin Luther King, Jr. (who also invoked Socrates).

Existentialism makes clear that in order for us to move beyond a shared, *de facto* denial of our mortality and vulnerability, we – first of all, *individually* – must come to grips with ("feel on our bodies," *kjenner på kroppen* in Norwegian) the ultimate reality of these, and then move on to assuming the often daunting responsibilities for discerning and creating meaning in our *existenz*. This almost always means *resisting* prevailing beliefs, norms and practices. Such resistance may be dramatic and world-changing, as with Antigone's choosing to bury her brother Polyneices, directly contrary to Creon's orders

Afterword 273

and at the cost of her own life. As portrayed in Sophocles' *Antigone*, the debates in play arguably mark the beginning of Western foregrounding of the critical importance of *individual* responsibilities and choices vis-à-vis prevailing relational selfhood and duties to community authority – now portrayed as cruelly authoritarian (Walker 2008). Similar comments hold for Socrates' resisting Athenian communal authority: as he puts it in the *Apology* (and perhaps echoing Antigone), if the choice is between avoiding the death sentence called for in the face of his "impiety" and accusations of seducing the youth of Athens, but at cost of denying his own sense of allegiance to the gods and the health and well-being (virtue) of his "soul" (*psyche*) – then better to sustain the integrity of his (individual) soul rather than decline to communal authority (*The Apology*, 29d-30b/[1904] 109–11).

Whether on such grand or more modest scales, such resistance is essential to how we may "hack our vulnerability" – most especially in existential directions. Margaret Schwartz (2017), for example, showed in her presentation at the conference how the #sayhername movement works as a protest against racism and violence visited upon women of colour. Reinforcing the central importance of *embodiment* (see her Chapter 3 in this volume), Schwartz foregrounds how the protest depends on both online organization (as the hashtag signals) and offline manifestation of *bodies*. Indeed, a particular theme of (embodied) resistance is precisely the move away from "the digital" as an otherwise exclusive focus and seemingly all-encompassing environment of *existenz*.

At a broader level, Wendy Hui Kyong Chun likewise foregrounded a range of contemporary vulnerabilities in her keynote address, "Proxy Politics: From Global Climate Change to Racial Profiling." These include modelling and analysis techniques that seek to predict an individual's race, gender and personality based on minimal data – thereby rendering us all that much more exposed to manipulative and potentially unjust techniques, beginning with targeted advertising and extending to efforts at predictive policing. Chun's suggestions for hacking these vulnerabilities emphasized first of all our becoming more familiar with the technologies that so deeply interweave with our lives and actions – our *existenz*. We don't all need to be computer programmers or engineers, she observed: but all of us can develop a more informed understanding of how these technologies work "under the hood," so as to take greater responsibility for our uses of these technologies. As the increasing popularity of "maker spaces," hackathons, and so on suggest, it is certainly possible for the average user qua *exister* to become more familiar with how our technologies work. We thereby understand at a deeper level both the vulnerabilities they expose us to, as well as the possibilities for hacking these vulnerabilities. A first example of doing so would be to take up the many possible ways of better protecting privacy online, both for our own sake and that of those these technologies keep us inextricably interwoven with.

Coherent with this, in her keynote lecture, "What Are the Consequences of Tracking, Trading and Sub-priming the Subject Through Stealth?," Beverley

274   *Charles M. Ess*

Skeggs explored our vulnerabilities as online existers. Are we aware, she asked, that our personal data may be traded in milliseconds up to 70,000 times per day? To hack these otherwise tacit (and thereby all the more insidious) vulnerabilities, Skeggs first pointed to her research project, "A Sociology of Values and Value," which uses software to "track the trackers." Such counter-surveillance thus helps us to become more aware of and thereby take greater responsibility for our understanding of our selves and our personhood as our personal data are constantly scrutinized as sources of potential value.

Skeggs then highlighted various forms of *disconnection* as "cracks" in our digital existence that may help us recover a sense of agency and privacy that are otherwise deeply threatened (vulnerable) in a digital environment of total surveillance and our reduction to data objects for the sake of tracking, commodification and exchange. Skeggs offered the example of using cash to buy physical books, so as to thereby circumvent the tracking of our consumption behaviors online. Such disconnections, as Paul Frosh has observed, offer new forms of protest and exodus from the trap that identity has become under new conditions of digital existence (2017).[4]

Finally, especially Schwartz's emphases on embodiment and Skegg's call for disconnection are important examples and markers of what may be a larger shift towards a *post-digital era*, one marked *not* by the rejection of "the digital": especially given the ontological significance of the digital as an encompassing environment, such a rejection may not even be possible, much less at any sort of reasonable cost to contemporary *existenz*. Rather, a post-digital era is one marked by a renewed balance between the more digital and the more analogue (with the important caveat that this is not a binary distinction: cf. Floridi 2008). It is telling, for example, that analogue technologies, including film and vinyl records, as well as books, seem to be enjoying something of a resurgence. More broadly, media sociologist Simon Lindgren characterizes the post-digital as "an era where the digital is no longer new and exciting, but something that is commonplace and assumed" (2017, p. 298).

In this light, one of the primary benefits of further dialogue between existential media studies and digital religion would be to foreground our experiences and sources of such resistance and emancipation. Whether grounded in transcendence and/or more strictly secular-rational ethical sources such as virtue ethics, opening up these cracks seems essential to our emancipation and so to the existential project of becoming who we may be in a post-digital era.

Notes

1 "A" and "B" denote the standard reference to the first and second edition of *Die Kritik der reinen Vernunft*, 1781 and 1787, respectively.
2 Campbell specifically characterizes post-secularization and postmodern spiritual sensibilities as advocating "the peaceful coexistence between the spheres of faith

Afterword 275

and reason" (2017b, p. 4). Such peaceful coexistence thus echoes and reiterates the Kantian compatibilism noted earlier.

3 This is in part because the contemporary meaning of "religion" – i.e., precisely as something separate from, if not opposed to the rational and the secular – is first forged in Enlightenment definitions of the individual qua *rational* autonomy (so Kant) as free *from* religious authority.

4 This use of "crack" alludes in part to a well-known verse by Leonard Cohen: "There's a crack, a crack in everything. It's how the light gets in" (1992).

Paul Frosh has noted that this in turn refers to a conception in Jewish mysticism, *Shevirat HaKelim*, articulated by Isaac Luria, a sixteenth-century mystic and rabbi: "God created vessels into which he poured his holy light," but these were incapable of containing such a force. Shattering, the shards and "sparks of divine light" fell to earth: and so, "There is a crack in everything, it's how the light gets in" (Freedland 2016). Such a "crack," is thus a direct expression of *transcendence* – one that for Cohen is both religiously rooted but also existential.

Bibliography

Campbell, H., 2013. *Digital Religion: Understanding Religious Practice in New Media Worlds*. New York: Routledge.

Campbell, H., 2017a. Surveying Theoretical Approaches within Digital Religion Studies. *New Media & Society*, 19 (1), 15–24.

Campbell, H., 2017b. Religious Communication and Technology. *ICA Annals of Communication*, 41 (3–4), 228–234. doi:10.1080/23808985.2017.1374200

Campbell, H. and Lövheim, M., 2011. Studying the Online-Offline Connection in Religion Online. *Information, Communication & Society*, 14 (8), 1083–1096, doi: 10.1080/1369118X.2011.597416

Coeckelbergh, M., 2010. Robot Rights? Towards a Social-Relational Justification of Moral Consideration. *Ethics and Information Technology*, 12, 209–221. doi:10.1007/s10676-010-9235-5

Coeckelbergh, M., 2013. *Human Being @ Risk: Enhancement, Technology, and the Evaluation of Vulnerability Transformations*. Berlin: Springer.

Coeckelbergh, M., 2017a. *New Romantic Cyborgs: Romanticism, Information Technology, and the End of the Machine*. Cambridge, MA: MIT Press.

Coeckelbergh, M., 2017b. Vulnerable Cyborgs Reloaded: From Narrative Technologies for Self-Shaping to Vulnerability Transformations in Modernity and the Anthropocene. Keynote Address, 'Precarious Media Life.' Sigtuna, Sweden, October 30–November 1.

Cohen, L., 1992. Anthem. Sony Music.

Ess, C., 1995. Reading Adam and Eve: Re-Visions of the Myth of Woman's Subordination to Man. *In*: M. M. Fortune and C. J. Adams, eds. *Violence Against Women and Children: A Christian Theological Sourcebook*. New York: Continuum Press, 92–120.

Ess, C., 2010. The Embodied Self in a Digital Age: Possibilities, Risks, and Prospects for a Pluralistic (Democratic/Liberal) Future? *Nordicom Information*, 32 (2), June, 105–118.

Ess, C., 2011. Self, Community, and Ethics in Digital Mediatized Worlds. *In*: C. Ess and M. Thorseth, eds. *Trust and Virtual Worlds: Contemporary Perspectives*. Oxford: Peter Lang, 3–30.

Ess, C., 2014. Selfhood, Moral Agency, and the Good Life in Mediatized Worlds? Perspectives from Medium Theory and Philosophy. *In*: K. Lundby, ed. *Mediatization*

276   *Charles M. Ess*

of Communication: Handbook of Communication Science (Vol. 21). Berlin: De Gruyter Mouton, 617–640.

Ess, C., 2016. What's Love Got to Do with It? Robots, Sexuality, and the Arts of Being Human. *In*: M. Nørskov, ed. *Social Robots: Boundaries, Potential, Challenges*. Farnham, Surrey, England: Ashgate, 57–79.

Ess, C., 2017. God Out of the Machine?: The Politics and Economics of Technological Development. *In*: A. Beavers, ed. *Macmillan Interdisciplinary Handbooks: Philosophy*. Farmington Hills, MI: Macmillan Reference, 83–111.

Floridi, L., 2008. A Defence of Informational Structural Realism. *Synthese*, 161 (2), 219–253.

Foucault, M., 1988. Technologies of the Self. *In*: L. H. Martin, H. Gutman and P. Hutton, eds. *Technologies of the self: A seminar with Michel Foucault*. Amherst: University of Massachusetts Press, 16–49.

Freedland, J., 2016. Leonard Cohen, Judaism's Bard. *The Atlantic* November 19 2016. Available at: www.theatlantic.com/entertainment/archive/2016/11/leonard-cohen/508157/ (accessed: 10 February 2018).

Frosh, P., 2017. Response to Beverley Skeggs. 'Precarious Media Life.' Sigtuna, Sweden, October 30–November 1.

Gibson, W., 1984. *Neuromancer*. New York: Ace Books.

Kant, I., 1793. Die Religion innerhalb der Grenzen der bloßen Vernunft. *In*: *Kants Werke: Akademie Textausgabe*. Berlin: Walter de Gruyter, 1968, 1–202.

Kant, I., 1965. *Immanuel Kant's Critique of Pure Reason*. Trans. Norman Kemp Smith. New York: St. Martin's Press.

Kant, I., [1784] 1991. An Answer to the Question: "What Is Enlightenment?" Trans. H. B. Nisbet. *In*: H. Reiss, ed. *Kant. Political Writings*. Cambridge: Cambridge University Press, 54–61.

Lagerkvist, A., 2016. Existential Media: Toward a Theorization of Digital Thrownness. *New Media & Society*, 19 (1: 2017), 96–110. Online first June 13, 2016.

Lagerkvist, A. and Andersson, Y., 2017. The Grand Interruption: Death Online and Mediated Lifelines of Shared Vulnerability. *Feminist Media Studies*, 2017. https://doi.org/10.1080/14680777.2017.1326554

Lindgren, S., 2017. *Digital Media and Society*. London: Sage.

Lövheim, M., 2012. Religious Socialization in a Media Age. *Nordic Journal of Religion and Society*, 25 (2), 151–168.

Lövheim, M. (ed.), 2013. *Media, Religion and Gender: Key Issues and New Challenges*. New York: Routledge.

Markham, A., 2017. Echolocating the Self: A Granular Metaphor for Digital Technology as Tool, Place and Way of Being, Conference presentation 'Precarious Media Life.' Sigtuna, Sweden, October 30–November 1.

Pirner, M., 2017. Mediatized Religious and Worldview Socialization Processes among Young People. Workshop presentation, "Mediatisierung von Religion und Religiosität" [Mediatization of Religion and Religiosity]. Würzburg, Germany, 22–24 September.

Pirner, M., 2018. Experiencing Religion, Religious Experience and Media Experience: Explorations of an Intricate Relationship in the Context of Religious Education. *In*: U. Riegel, ed. *Religious Experience and Experiencing Religion*. Münster: Waxmann, 43–60.

Plato, 1914. *Plato in Twelve Volumes, I: Euthyphro, Apology, Crito, Phaedo, Phaedrus*. Trans. H. N. Fowler. London: Heinemann.

Popper, B., 2013. Understanding Calico: Larry Page, Google Ventures, and the Quest for Immortality. *The Verge* 19 September 2013. Available at: www.theverge.com/2013/9/19/4748594/understanding-calico-larry-page-google-ventures-and-the-quest-for (accessed: 1 July 2018).

Sandars, N. K., 1972. *The Epic of Gilgamesh*. New York: Penguin.

Schwartz, M., 2017. Say Her Name: Towards a Politics of Vulnerability, Conference presentation, 'Precarious Media Life.' Sigtuna, Sweden, October 30–November 1.

Skeggs, B., 2017. What Are the Consequences of Tracking, Trading and Sub-Priming the Subject through Stealth? Keynote Address, 'Precarious Media Life.' Sigtuna, Sweden, October 30–November 1.

Vallor, S., 2016. *Technology and the Virtues: A Philosophical Guide to a Future Worth Wanting*. Oxford: Oxford University Press.

Verbeek, P.-P., 2011. *Moralizing Technology: Understanding and Designing the Morality of Things*. Chicago: University of Chicago Press.

Verbeek, P.-P., 2017. Existentializing Technology: Vulnerability in a Digital Age. Closing Address, 'Precarious Media Life.' Sigtuna, Sweden, October 30–November 1.

Walker, K., 2008. Between Individual Principles and Communal Obligation: Ethical Duty in Sophocles's Antigone. *Mosaic: An Interdisciplinary Critical Journal*, 41 (3), 199–214. Available at: www.jstor.org/stable/44029648 (accessed: 1 July 2018).

Index

Note: Page numbers in *italics* denote references to figures.

abductive reasoning 68, 74, 75–76
abstraction 249
after-death communications 254
Agamben, G. 41
agential realism 57n2
Agre, P. 102
Al-Arian, A. 221
algorithmic closure 32
algorithmic gender 76
algorithmic interpolation 75–76
algorithms 17, 32, 53, 58n6, 160, 167
already-yet-only-now character 41, 51
alt-deletion 106
alternative social algorithms 167
alternative social media 166
Althusser, L. 121
always-thereness 199–201
analysis paralysis 139, 150n2
anamnesis/hypomnesis 46–47
angels 198, 199, 202, 206n5, 213
anima, definition of 229–230
animism: definition of 227, 230;
    Otherkin community as form of 228
anthropomorphizing media
    technology 195
anxiety 16, 41, 51, 91, 97–98n2,
    124–125, 137
aporia 53–54
Arendt, H. 87–88, 93, 248–249
Aristotle 57–58n4
Armitage, J. 252
artefacts: as interactive objects 66; as
    technical individuals 71
artificial intelligence 67, 252, 259
artificial regulatory systems 232
Ashley Madison hack 180–182, 183
Asplund, G. 189

assemblages: of embodied elements 81;
    feminism and 93, 96; human being
    as 177; individualized 68, 74; of
    original events 48; personhood and
    74; *see also* data assemblages
associated milieu 71; *see also* Umwelts
attention economy 2, 163–164
authenticity 9
autopoiesis 233–234
Avid Life Media 181
awakeness, as everywhereness 200–202

Badiou, A. 48–50, 55, 58n5
Barad, K. 57n2
Barley, N. 211, 223
Barthes, R. 124, 193
basanos 147, 151n11
becoming, transductive process of 52
behavioural correlation 72
Being: as data-encumbered 177–178;
    as embodied exposure 176–177; as
    existential exposure 173–176; as
    forgetting 40, 46; grounding in 7;
    history of 43; in the internet 237;
    by language 42; singular 184n1;
    technology and 8–9; *see also*
    vulnerable being
Being and Time (Heidegger) 40, 43, 174
being human 115–186; description of
    255; *see also* human/human beings
Being-in-the-internet 227–228, 235–236
being-in-the-world 17, 64, 212, 227, 231
being-singular-plural 175
being-toward-death 7, 12
being-with 173–174, 177
Benjamin, W. 261
Berardi, F. "Bifo" 163

Bielefeld Conspiracy: description of 100; as digital unworld 112; as false statement 110–111; reaction to 100
big data methods/methodologies 32, 69
biosemiotics 74
biosensory monitors 74
Bird-David, N. 231
Blas, Z. 168
body, as technology to be hacked 95
body/mind dualism 234–235
body-replication 124–125
body-schema 142
Boellstorff, T. 35, 214, 237
Bohm, D. 38
Boolean logic 49
bots 227, 235
Bourdieu, P. 120
Bowker, G. 102–103
Bratton, B. 106–107
Briggs, P. 258
Brookes, N. 179–180, 183
Brouwer, L. E. J. 55
Bucher, T. 161
Bush, V. 167
Butler, J. 7, 132n10, 173, 176, 177

Cambridge Analytica 69
Campbell, D. 200
Campbell, H. 270
Cantor, G. 48
capitalism 9, 51, 58n5, 96
capture model 102–103, 105
care: analysis of 42; practices of 87; as response to vulnerability 85
care of the self: mediation and 156–158; practices of 158; redesigning social media for 165–168; on social media 161–165
caring labour theory 87–88
causal theory 132n7
cellular automata 36–37
Chanter, T. 97n1
Charlie Hebdo attack 210–215
Charlie Hebdo magazine 219–221
Cheney-Lippold, J. 76
Christensen, D. R. 256
Chu, J. 260
Chun, W. H. K. 4, 7, 273
cisgender women 94, 96
Clark, T. 7
classical logic 30, 49, 55, 110
Cocozza, F. 179
Coeckelbergh, M. 266–267

co-individuation 44
commemoration 215–216
communications: after-death 254; computer-mediated communication (CMC) 270; with the dead 190–191, 194, 195–196, 257; lifeline communication 201, 203
computer-mediated communication (CMC) 270
connections, social media facilitating 159–160
connective awakeness 204
connective presence 16, 19, 201, 203, 204
connectivity: capitalism 9; culture of 4, 6, 10; ghost effects and 203; hyper-connectivity 16; informational 160; meaningful relations and 159; platform 119; sensations of 204–205; sharing vulnerability through 202; social 131–132n6; *see also* existential terrains of connectivity
constellations of relations 235
consumer subjectivation 163–165
contradictions 30, 54, 56, 72, 110
cooked data 108–109
Cook-Levin Theorem 58n7
corporate social media 163–164, 165
corporeal existence 172
Coté, M. 177–178
Coulibaly, A. 217
countability, leading to pointing function 85–86
counting functions 85–86
cracks in digital existence 274, 275n4
Cryptome secrecy archive 141
cybernetic animism 19–20, 227, 228, 234–238
cybernetics 61, 74, 232–234
cybernetic virtuality 234
cypherg 237

da Costa, N. 37–38, 55
Dancy, C. 150n7
Dasein (beings in/of the world) 41–42, 172, 174, 178
data: proliferation of 137–138; proliferation recession 138–142
data assemblages 103–105, 107, 110, 112; *see also* assemblages
data capture models 102–103
dataism 62, 68–70
dataveillance 73

280   Index

Dayan, D. 122
death/dead: as agency 190, 199,
    202; always-thereness 199–200;
    animating through film 193, 258;
    communications with 254; digital
    footprint of 258; electronic presence
    of 195–196; implied online presence
    197–200; media connection with
    192–193; one-way communications
    204; online memorials 194–195,
    197; ritualization of 211–212; social
    persistence and 257–258
death online 197–200
death rituals: in digital media 210,
    215–216; as life-crisis rituals 215; as
    a process 212
de Beauvoir, S. 3
deindividuation 157, 165
Deleuze, G. 93, 112, 165
Descola, P. 231
descriptive theory 132n7
dialetheism 45, 54, 55–56
differentiation 70, 71
digital, the: definition of 85; as process
    of counting and pointing 95
digital being 8, 18, 76, 172, 184;
    see also Being
digital conspiracy see Bielefeld
    Conspiracy
digital culture 106, 177
digital dead 19, 191–192, 202–204;
    see also death/dead
digital death and erasures 106
digital death rituals 215
digital erasure 102–105, 111
digitality, definition of 83
digital media: definition of 244; as
    elemental 3; existential approaches
    to 255; irreducible 9; ritual and 212;
    ritualization of death in 210–211;
    shaping lifeworld 3
digital media ethics 11
digital media technologies 159
digital mediatization 217
digital memorials 204–205
digital objects 107–108, 111, 133n19,
    166–167
digital ontology: as addendum to
    epistemology 38–39; Boellstorff's
    method 35; description of 29–31;
    quadrants of 35–36
Digital Philosophy (Fredkin) 37
digital physics 36
digital religion 5–6, 13–14, 265, 270–272

digital rituals 214; see also ritual
digital suicide 106, 107, 108
digital tagging see tagging
digital technologies, transcending role
    of 192
digital unworld 102, 112–113
digital urdoxa 177–182
disability rights 90
disconnection 274
disembodiment 195
disruption, as phase of mourning rituals
    216–217
Dreyfus, H. 42, 176, 183
Durkheim, E. 230

Edwards, E. 128
elemental media philosophy 3
embodied exposure 176–177
embodied vulnerability, experiences
    of 10
embodiment 81–99, 273
engagement, with mediated objects 156
epistemology 38–39, 40
epoch of equipment 244
erasures: data capture models 102–103;
    of digital objects 107–108; exclusions
    and 105; false data as 107–108;
    mechanisms of 108; public sphere
    and 104; relational 104–105; social
    unbundling and 104; ubiquitous
    forms of 105–107, 112
Ess, C. M. 11
essentialism 173
eukaryotic cells 233, 239n7
Evans-Pritchard, S. E. E. 231
exclusions, as erasures of the world 105
existence preceding religion 6
existential conditions 7–10
existential elucidation 12
existential experiences 10–12
existential exposure 173–176
existential media 1–4, 192, 201
existential media studies 4–6, 265,
    270–272
existential security 212, 215, 222–223
existential striving 12–14, 271
existential terrains of connectivity:
    conditions 7–10; definition of 6;
    experiences 10–12, 118; strivings
    for 12–14
existers 7, 10–11, 13, 244–245, 259,
    273–274
extended artefacts 66
extended self 127–128

Index 281

Facebook *see* social media
Facebook algorithm 160
face of another 175–176
face of the other 176
face-recognition technologies 119, 131n5, 133n18
Facial Weaponization Suite (Blas) 168
false data 107–111, 112–113
false thought 111
fecundity 10
feedback loops in social systems 61, 64–65, 75, 130, 232–233, 237
Feinstein, D. 139–140
feminist ontology 81, 96
feminist posthumanism 21n3
fictional data 110–111
film medium 193
finitude, focus on 12, 248
Floridi, L. 33–34, 36
folksonomy 119
forgotten repressions 48
formal logic 49, 55
Foucauldian machine of non-apparent power 104
Foucault, M. 146–147, 148, 151n11, 247, 248
'four causes' theory 57–58n4
Franke, A. 237–238
Franklin, B. 146
Frazer, J. 129
Fredkin, E. 36, 37
French, S. 103
Freud, S. 47–49
Frosh, P. 274, 275n4
functional relationships 72–73

Gabriel, M. 101, 109, 111, 112
Galison, P. 141
Gell, A. 62, 68
gender segregation in bathrooms 90
ghost effects 19, 192
Gibson, J. 150n4
Gibson, W. 270
Gitelman, L. 108
Google PageRank search algorithm 160
Gotved, S. 256
Graham, C. 194, 203, 255
Graham, S. 103–104
graves 189–190; *see also* tombs, as communication device
Greenwald, G. 150n4
grid of intelligibility 86
griefbot 192, 205
Grieve, G. P. 13

Guattari, F. 93
Guo, T. 259–260
GynePunk collective 16, 81–82, 93–96

hacking 94–95, 180–182, 266
Hallowell, I. 231
Han, B.-C. 11
Hand, M. 117, 128
Handelman, D. 214
handle 123, 132n12
Hansen, M. 73
Haraway, D. 83, 234
Harper, R. 255
Harrison, P. 173
hashtags 222, 224n2
Haunted Media: Electronic Presence From Telegraphy to Television (Sconce) 195
Hawkins, S. 37
Heidegger, M. 2, 39–44, 57–58n4, 173–174
Hekman, S. 82–83, 93
Held, A. 100
Hochman, N. 127
Holmes, O. W. 133n15
homeostasis 232–233
Hoover, S. 5
Hui, Y. 9, 51, 62, 107, 166
Human-Computer Interaction (HCI) 255
Human Condition, The (Arendt) 87
human consciousness, bypassing of 144
human energetics 71
human/human beings: being human 255; change in animal body 252; definition of 250; digital media and 250–254; forms of 251; as self-aware 246
humanitarianism 248–249
Hume, D. 230
Hunt, L. 249
hyper-connectivity 16
hyperindividualism 203
hyperobjectivity of the Anthropocene 137, 142

ICTs 258
Ihde, D. 2, 21n6
imaginary media 149
"Imitation Game" 259
Impact Team 181
in-between space 198
indexicality 123
indexical sign 123
individuation theory 45, 52, 63, 70–71

282   Index

indivisibilia 33
informational connectivity 160
informational objects 159
informational ontology 33–34, 36
information theory 62
Ingold, T. 231
institutional memory system 103
interface skepticism 109
International Telecommunications
    Union 246
internet: animist experience 227;
    awakeness of 200–202, 204; gender
    gap of 247; as literal lifeline 201; as
    transcendental force 196–197
internet penetration 246–247
interpassive movement 140
intuitionism 49, 55
invulnerability 18, 172–173, 178–182, 184
Irigaray, L. 86
irreducible media 9
isomorphy of structure 62
it from bit concept 36

Jaspers, K. 10, 12
Je suis Charlie ritual message
    218–221, *219*

Kant, I. 33, 40, 269–270
Kapferer, B. 212–213, 214, 221
Karp, R. 58n7
Karppi, T. 106
Kasket, E. 195
Kember, S. 86, 95
Kern, R. 256
Kierkegaard, S. 12
Kitchin, R. 102–103, 104, 108, 110
knowledge 31–33, 146–149
Krause, D. 37–38, 55
Kripke, S. 126

labour: bringing forth human life 87;
    toileting as 89–90; work vs. 87–88
Lacan, J. 48–49
Laches 147, 148, 151n10
Lagerkvist, A. 84, 106, 212, 221, 244,
    264–265
Lauriault, T. 103
law of contagion 129
law of excluded middle (LEM) 49, 55
law of non-contradiction (LNC) 49,
    55, 110
law of similarity 129
Leach, E. 231

Lefebvre, H. 101
Lemov, R. 150n9
Levin, L. 58n7
Levinas, E. 10, 83, 175–176
Lévi-Strauss, C. 231
Lévy-Bruhl, L. 120, 230
Lewerentz, S. 189
lifeline communication 201, 203
lifeworld: of archival subjects 178;
    components of 77n3; limitations of
    67; technologically enforced 11, 61;
    technology saturation in 1–3; *see also*
    Umwelts
liminality, as phase of mourning rituals
    216, 217–222
limit-situations in life 12
linguistic determinism 82
literacy, central role of 269
liveness, definition of 200
logic *see* Boolean logic; classical logic;
    formal logic
Lombardi, O. 38
Lövheim, M. 270, 272
Luria, I. 275n4

machines, as technical objects 45
"Man" 246–250, 256
Markham, A. 268
Marlow, C. 119
materialism 82; new 4, 7
mathematical logic 55
mathematics, as ontology 48
mattering 128–129, 133n19
Maturana, H. R. 233, 235
McKelvey, F. 260
McLuhanian vision of extension 143
Mead, M. 236
meaning and meaning making 10–11,
    87, 146, 256
meaningfulness: engaging with media
    and 156; existential communication
    and 201; hijacking capitalist
    imperatives 163; search for 157
media: definition of 86; film medium 193
media anthropology 211, 223–224
media artefacts 61, 66
media culture, religious institutions
    and 5–6
media death 210
media ontology, grounding us in being 7
media technology: anthropomorphizing
    195; networked radio 196; television
    196; wireless radio 196

Index 283

mediated objects, engagement with 156
Mediated Umwelt 65
mediation, care of the self and 156–158
mediatization, digital 217
Meinong, A. 110
memes, slogans and hashtags 218, 220, 221
Merabet, A. 217
Merkel, A. 100
Merleau-Ponty, M. 142, 144
meta meta-nihilism 101, 109, 112
metaphysical presencing 173
Metz, C. 124, 129
Miller, V. 11
Mills, S. 72
mimetic faculty 129
mind/body dualism 173
Mitchell, L. 178
Mitsein (beings with/of each other) 172, 173–175, 178
modern media 31
modern physics 43
modern set theory 48
Modern Spiritualist movement 195
modulation 51–53
'monstration' 122
mortality 264
Mosco, V. 237
Myerhoff, B. 211–212

Nafus, D. 74
name/naming: act of 120; as magical arts 130; sacredness of 120; stability of 132n10; subjectivation and 120; *see also* tagging
Nancy, J.-L. 105, 175, 176
Nansen, B. 257
narcissist behavior 164, 203
neoliberalism 11
networked images 127
networked radio 196
networks: distribution of power 92; as ritualistic totem 19
non-existence objects 110
non-human personhood 17–20, 65, 156, 227–229, 234–238
non-mediation 9, 13

Obama, B. 140
objective phenomenology 49
object oriented ontology 39
obscurantism 40
Occidental Animisms 236

Ohm, P. 183
one-way communication 202, 204
online memorials 194–195, 197, 204–205, 255
ontogenesis 70–71
ontological obsolescence 42
ontological realism 132n13
ontology: as centre of all thinking 40; digital ontology vs. 38–39; epistemology vs. 40; ethics before 83; feminist point of view 81, 96; metaphysics of being and 39; as pervasive 234–235
Order of Things, The (Foucault) 247
originary prostheticity 7
originary technicity 7
Origins of Totalitarianism, The (Arendt) 248–249
other, the 30, 50, 175, 176–177
Otherkin community 20, 228–229, 236
other-than-human persons 231

Paglen, T. 150n3
paraconsistent logics 38, 54–56
participatory media 159
personal data, control of 165–166
personal identity 232, 267
personhood: animism and 231, 235–238; complex configurations of 236; in digital assemblages 74; non-human 236; as partable 73; personal data and 274; of the *Puma* 235; tagging and 126
Peters, B. 85–86, 95
Peters, J. D. 3, 86, 126, 190, 193–194, 243, 246
phantasmagoric spaces 213–214
photographic dead 193
photographic incarnation 123–125
photography: connecting to death 193; as process of mattering 128–129; as spectral 128
photography theory 123–124
Piaget, J. 236
Pieper, J. 66–67
Pirner, M. 271–272
Plaskow, J. 90
Plato 147–148
plurality 87
poetry, Heidegger and 43–44
pointing functions 85–86
Pontormo, J. 146
post-convergent world 51

284 *Index*

posthumanism 21n3, 47
potentiality of being 72
power: as force 112; naming as
expression of 120
Priest, G. 55–56
primitive mentality 230
profundity, other-worldly experiences of
193, 212
progressive media theory 62
protention 162–163
protrusion 143–146, 149
psychoanalysis, importance of 47–49
publicness of life 87
P v NP problem 30, 53–54, 58n6
Pyyhtinen, O. 173–174

Quantified Self 142
quantisation 37
quantum field theory 57n2
quantum physics 37–38
quasi-Umwelt 66, 67

recession 138–142, 143, 149
reductionalist nature of data 74
Rees, T. 250
reflexivity 63, 64, 233, 256
regulative information 45
relationality of being 72
relational quantum mechanics
(RQM) 38
religious institutions 5–6
religious socialization 5, 272
reproduction 88
reputation economies 164, 165–166
resistance 265–266, 272–274
retention processes 162–163
Ricouer, P. 123
rites of passage 212–213
ritual: digital media and 212;
phenomenological approach to 214;
as transformative practice 213
ritual existence 12
ritualization of death/mourning
210–211, 216–223
Roncin, J. 217
Rotman, B. 177, 192
Rovelli, C. 38
Rubinstein, D. 126, 127
Runa Puma 235
Russell, B. 110

Sanctorius of Padua 146
Sauter, M. 69
Schütz, A. 64–65, 77n3

Schwartz, M. 190–191, 193–194, 273
Sconce, J. 195, 196, 203
Scott, L. 200
self, the: commercialization of 164–165;
socially mediated 164–165; tagging as
embodiments of 127–128; technology
of 269; transformation of 158
self-care 93, 269
selfies 125
self-knowledge 146–147, 149
self-mediation 158
self-representation 124, 125
self-tracking technologies 142, 146,
150n9
semiocapitalist enterprise 163
semiospheres 67, 72
semosis, as living process 67
Seneca, L. A. 148
sensemaking 145–146
set theory 48–50
shared vulnerability 11
Sheehan, T. 144–145
signals intelligence 75
Simcoe, L. 260
Simmel, G. 173–174
Simondon, G. 44–46, 62–63, 70–72
simulation machines 260
singular being 184n1
Skeggs, B. 273–274
Skene, Dr. 93
Slater, D. 132n13
sleep trackers 143
Smith, Z. 194
Snowden, E. 138–139
Snowden Files 139, 140–141, 150n4
social connectivity 131–132n6
social constructionism 82
social innovation 72–73
socially mediated self 164–165
social media: alternative 166;
attention economy of 2; awakeness
of 200–201; as central regulator
between self and others 159; digital
media technologies vs. 159; grief
networking 195; meaningful relations
and 159–161; participatory media
vs. 159; transforming informational
connectivity 160; YouTube videos
featuring deceased 215–216
social media algorithms 167
social media corporations 163–164
social media technologies 162–163
social network services (SNS) 119
social persistence 257–258

social tagging *see* tagging
social unbundling 104
Socrates 147–148, 265–266
software-generated infrastructures 102, 103
"software-sorted apartheid" 104
sovereign electronic world 195
spatial technologies 178
species dysphoria 229, 239n6
spiritual telegraphs 195, 204
Stahl, G. 229–230
Staley, E. 257
Star, S. L. 103
Stengers, I. 238
Stiegler, B. 46–48, 157, 162, 177
structuration 45
subjectivation 120, 162, 163–165, 168
subjective mortality 12
Sumiala, J. 12
Sundén, J. 237
surveillance 139–140, 142
surveillant profiling 63
symbolic dimensions in media life 211
sympathetic magic 129
systems modelling 34

tagging: as agent of replication 125; data streaming and 127; definition of 126; as deictic pointing 119–120; description of 16–17; digital tag 118; extended self and 127–128; on Facebook 118, 121, 131n5; with face-recognition technologies 131n5, 133n18; as incantation 122; as initial baptism 126; medical 117; military 117, 131n2; as operative sign 122; as power 123; promoting heterogeneity 126, 127–128, 130; singular embodied personhood and 126; on social network platforms 117–118; suppressing visual differences 127; utility of 119; Web-based tagging systems 119; *see also* name/naming
Tarde, G. 35, 71
Taussig, M. 129
technical being 45
technical reality 44
technicity 71–72
techno-existential closure 13
technologies, media: being and 8–9; conceptions of 21n6; countability of 85–86; double negativity of 48, 49; as forceful 2; as genetic proposition 44; mathematics and

49; pharmacological approach to 3; religious social shaping of 5; traditional vs. modern 9
technology of the self 269
television 196, 200
"terminal citizen" 253–254, 255–257, 259
"terminal man" 252–253
thinging 227–228, 235
thinking of equipment 41–42
thinking things 174, 178
Thomas, L. 258
Thrift, N. 103
thrownness: definition of 6; as embodied philosophy 84–87; existential experiences and 10; feminist ontology and 81; leading to vulnerability 84–85
Tiessen, M. 260
time, thought-experience of 40
toileting 89–90
tombs, as communication device 190; *see also* graves
totemism 230–231
trace-bodies 144, 150n9
trails of association 167
transcendence 12, 42, 199–200, 265, 271–272
transduction 70, 76
transductive ontogenetic model 56
transductive process of becoming 52
transfer machines 252
transformative practice 212–213
transgender rights 90
transindividuation 44–46, 52
transmission, institutions of 40
trolls/trolling 179–180, 229
true data 112–113
truth-telling techniques 146–147
Turing, A. 259
Turing machines 33, 58n6
Turkle, S. 3, 157
Turner, F. 65
Turner, V. 212
Tylor, E. B. 230

ubiquitous software 16, 102, 104, 107, 109, 111–113
Umgebung 65, 67
Umwelts: artefacts forming 66; definition of 65, 67; humans detaching from 66–67; individuation and 71; of personalized media environments 64–68; referring to sentient beings 65–66; semiospheres 67

286   Index

Umwelt theory, description of 15
unconscious, development theory of 250
undead media 193–194
Universal Declaration of Human Rights
  (UDHR) 249
unreflective familiarity 41
urban space 101, 103

van Gennep, A. 212
Varela, F. J. 233, 235
Verbeek, P.-P. 268–269
vernacular religiosity 13
verticality 107
virality, phenomenon of 11
Virilio, P. 251–253, 255–256, 258
virtuality of cyber technology 214, 233
virtual possessions 133n19
virtual-real divide 270–271
virtual reality 165
virtue ethics 265, 267–270
void-infinites 49
von Uexküll, J. 62, 64
vulnerability: ambiguity of 266–267;
  of bodily life 176; care as response
  to 85; definition of 177; embodied
  10, 83–84; examples of 18; feminism
  and 83–84; hacking 266, 268, 273;
  intense experiences of 178–182;
  lack of 172; mediated nature of
  experience as 253; as online existers
  274; online *Mitsein* and 180–182; as
  part of human condition 175–176,
177; as relational selves 265; shared
11; thrownness leading to 84–85;
types of 267; uneven distribution
of 177; urdoxic awareness of 179;
women and 183
vulnerable being 173–177; *see also* Being

Wallace, A. 232
Walter, T. 206n3, 206n5
Watt, J. 232
Web2.0 Suicide Machine 106
Web-based tagging systems 119
web memorials 194–195, 197, 204–205
what-has-been 193
Wheeler, J. 36
Whitehead, A. N. 110
Wiener, N. 232
Williams, J. 1–2
Willson, M. A. 175, 184n1
Winnicott, D. W. 158
wireless radio 196
Wittgenstein, L. 137–138
Wolfram, S. 36–37
Woodland Cemetery, Stockholm 189
worldliness 87
writing technology 49, 148

YouTube *see* social media

Zimmerman, M. 234–235
Zylinska, J. 86, 95